Mackenzie Walcott

The Cathedrals of the United Kingdom

Their History, Architecture, Monuments, and Traditions

Mackenzie Walcott

The Cathedrals of the United Kingdom
Their History, Architecture, Monuments, and Traditions

ISBN/EAN: 9783743400948

Manufactured in Europe, USA, Canada, Australia, Japa

Cover: Foto ©Lupo / pixelio.de

Manufactured and distributed by brebook publishing software (www.brebook.com)

Mackenzie Walcott

The Cathedrals of the United Kingdom

CATHEDRALS OF THE UNITED KINGDOM.

THE CATHEDRALS

OF

THE UNITED KINGDOM:

Their History, Architecture, Monuments, and Traditions.

WITH

SHORT NOTES OF THE CHIEF OBJECTS OF INTEREST
IN EACH CATHEDRAL CITY,

AND

A POPULAR INTRODUCTION TO CHURCH ARCHITECTURE.

BY

MACKENZIE WALCOTT, M.A.,
OF EXETER COLLEGE, OXFORD:
AUTHOR OF "THE MINSTERS AND ABBEY RUINS OF THE UNITED KINGDOM,"
"THE SOUTH COAST OF ENGLAND," ETC.

"The very majesty and holiness of the place where GOD is worshipped hath,
in regard of us, great virtue, force, and efficacy ; for that it serveth as a sensible
help to stir up devotion, and in that respect, no doubt, bettereth our holiest and
best actions in this kind."—HOOKER.

LONDON:
EDWARD STANFORD, 6, CHARING CROSS.
MDCCCLX.

TO MY FATHER AND MOTHER,

THIS VOLUME

IS INSCRIBED.

Knightsbridge,
  November, 1859.

NOTICE TO THE SECOND EDITION.

In deference to the kind and judicious suggestions of the friendly reviewers of the last Edition, some improvements and considerable additions have been made, a general introduction with a glossary of terms has been prefixed, and an uniform arrangement adopted in the present issue, which has been carefully revised in every page.

The present volume has been enlarged with a description of the Cathedrals of Ireland, Scotland, and the Isle of Man; an addition which, we hope, will prove acceptable to the reader, as it renders the book complete, and contains information hitherto not readily accessible.

Illustrations were intended to be given; but, on consideration, it appeared that the views would necessarily be so numerous that the cost of the book would utterly defeat the design of making it a volume within reach of ordinary purses.

Knightsbridge, 1859.

PREFACE.

"The land's antiquities are the most singular beauty in every nation."—*Weever*.

LOCAL Handbooks and Guides abound in minute details, are diffuse and prolix in description, and indulge in a natural and pardonable partiality for the great ornament of each particular city. To the inhabitant these qualities enhance their value, while they in no small degree detract from the convenience of the stranger, who requires merely the notice of salient peculiarities in the fabric, and that enlarged acquaintance with other churches, which insures a careful comparison of their similarities, and an accurate indication of the points of difference. Price and portability likewise enter into consideration: while it is difficult to make a choice, and discriminate between the frequently conflicting claims of the various works proffered to the visitors by the several publishers in each city. The attempt has now been made to produce a terse, clear, and faithful companion, based on the most trustworthy and recent authorities, which will point out those objects only which are most worthy of observation.

It has long been a subject of just reproach to English people, that, while foreigners seldom visit this country who have not first explored the galleries of art, studied the pictures and sculptures, and rendered themselves familiar with the architectural treasures of their native land, our wanderers along the ruin-clad shores of the Rhine, under the eye-blinding snow-capped Jura and St. Bernard, beneath the broad burning skies of Italy, among the churches and through the corridors of the richly-stored capitals of the Continent, the museums of Dresden, the frescoes of Munich, over the Sierras of Spain, and in the distant Syria and Egypt, display a most unpatriotic ignorance with regard to the noblest structures and fairest scenes at home.

Southey relates that he heard more than one American avow that it was worth while to cross the Atlantic to see one of our Cathedrals. Art, science, factory, and harbour, were common to the old and new world, but a church with memories was a novelty; it was worthy of a pilgrimage to tread the hallowed pavements of a structure built upon the resting-place of saints, and in which the sacrifices of religion had been offered from time immemorial, in a city purely religious in its interest, influence, aspect, and character. Those to whom these Cathedrals and solemn chants are familiar from childhood, cannot appreciate the anxiety with which a stranger takes his first glimpse of the building, lest the reality should fall short of his anticipation, or the glow of wonderment with which he is filled, while he gradually learns the munificence and marvels of the undertaking, the grandeur of conception, the difficulty of execution, and the durability of works so enormous.

Neither can it be forgotten, that under the shadow of these Houses of Prayer was set up the chair of the Master. They were for centuries the fortresses of religion—homes of the science and art of dark, rude ages; they garnered in their libraries, and multiplied with patient toil the MSS. which make the grand literature of our own times—the Chronicles, the Classics, the Fathers of Theology, and, above all, the sacred Word of God. They were schools of music, science, and art, the almonries of the poor, the seclusion of the penitent, the centres of dependent parish churches built on their granges, and served from their cells; their vineyards and farms were models of agriculture; they were the hostelries of the traveller, the barrier between the delays and assaults of feudal ignorance and the advance of civilization; the sanctuaries of the oppressed and fugitive in lawless ages. Their industrious tenants formed the road, built the bridge, reclaimed the fen, and supplanted' the forest with human dwellings. And now, while we reap the rich harvest of labours, sacrifice, and devotion, which animated the benevolence, and drew forth those alms of the faithful which render them autographs of the past and national heirlooms, these survive as visible, sterling, incorruptible witnesses; while all else has passed away—the lives, hopes, powers, discomfitures, dreams, sorrows, and endurance of the builders,—the indisputable evidence of their spirit of veneration, love, and desire to glorify the Eternal upon the earth, displayed in the obscurest corners, in the corbels of the darkest newel, and on the summit of the loftiest spire, where access is scarcely possible, which yet show as much care and finish as the noblest features open to the eyes of a multitude.

" Gothic architecture," says a great writer, " unites an exquisite delicacy and inconceivable skill in mechanical execution with the grand, the boundless, the infinite, concentrated in the idea of an entire fabric; a rare and truly beautiful combination of contrasting elements conceived by the power of human intellect, and aiming at faultless perfection in the minutest details, as well as in the lofty grandeur and comprehensiveness of the general design. A church is intended to symbolize in miniature the eternal structure of the spiritual church in Heaven."

It is an era of better taste than the miserable reign of the revived Classic style, when Sir Christopher Wren sneered at Gothic art, Fenelon compared a vicious style of rhetoric to its ornament, even old Bishop Tanner, antiquary as he was, qualified his acknowledgment of them as " noble buildings " by adding, "though not actually so grand and neat as Chelsea and Greenwich Hospitals." Gray, passing through York, merely mentions that walnuts were cheap; Horace Walpole quietly speaks of Bristol Cathedral as "very neat, and has pretty tombs ;" of Worcester, " it is very pretty, and has several tombs " (the diaper of one is commended because it served as the pattern of his staircase-paper at Strawberry Hill), " and clusters of light Derbyshire marble lately cleaned." Gloucester has no higher commendation than this : " The outside. of the Cathedral is beautifully light; the pillars in the nave outrageously plump and heavy. Kent designed the screen."

"To me," said Schlegel, "the sight of a splendid edifice is an ever-springing source of pleasure : I feel its grandeur more, and feel its beauty better the more frequently I behold it. The continual contemplation of a fine building unconsciously elevates a susceptible mind, and maintains it in a fit frame for appreciating the beauty of other works of art, while a taste for architecture seems, indeed, to form the basis of every other artistic taste."

Our readers will readily recall the well-known lines of Milton on surveying a Cathedral ; or the fine expression of Coleridge—" I am filled with devotion and with awe; I am lost to the actualities that surround me, and my whole being swells into the Infinite : earth and air, nature and art, all swell up into Eternity ; and the only sensible impression left is, I am nothing."

> May ne'er
> That true succession fail of English hearts,
> Who, with ancestral feeling, can perceive
> What in these holy structures ye possess
> Of ornamental interest, and the charm
> Of pious sentiment diffused afar,
> And human charity and social love.

CONTENTS.

CATHEDRALS—ENGLAND AND WALES.

IRELAND.

CATHEDRALS.

SCOTLAND.

CATHEDRALS.

CATHEDRALS OF THE UNITED KINGDOM.

INTRODUCTION.

The bright work stood still,
And might of its own beauty have been proud,
But it was fashioned, and to God was vowed,
By virtues that diffused in every part
Spirit Divine, through forms of human art.
Faith had her arch, her arch, when winds blew loud,
Into the consciousness of safety thrilled;
And Love her towers of dread foundation laid
Under the graves of things; Hope had her spire
Star high, and pointed still to something higher.

CHRISTIAN architecture is antagonistic to pagan art; it is spiritual rather than intellectual. The Italian style is a miserable compromise between the Gothic and Classic style, applied to ecclesiastical buildings. In place of a cold monotonous uniformity of plan, and stationary orders, Gothic art is progressive, and may yet be capable of further development on the noblest principles of construction; it is irregular, for every part is designed for use, and ornament is subservient to the highest purposes. Size is produced not only by magnitude but by the multiplication of parts. Vertical and aspiring, there are neither heavy horizontal lines, nor a confused combination of disjointed members independent of each other; every part grows out of that next to it, or is its continuation, typifying, from base to roof, Him, Who is at once the rock, the chief corner-stone, and a covert from the storm and a shadow from the heat, and the Temple of the Great City (Rev.

xxi. 22). For the external portico, devoted in its original design to idlers, and chilling in a northern climate, are found the superb internal arcades designed for worshippers : in place of a narrow, dark shrine, veiled and unapproachable, is spread a well-lighted, magnificent area, the delight of multitudes, in which to assemble them for service : in place of caryatides and memorials of human suffering, are sculptured saints and angels ; and for sacrificial garlands, skulls of beasts, masks and eggs, are seen the most magnificent associative sculpture, sacred symbols of Divine love, the mystic Triangle, the Cross, the Lamb, the Dove ; while the rich colours on pane and wall represent the bow of mercy set in the clouds.

A cathedral is "a mighty maze yet not without a plan ;" it is the embodied idea of the "spiritual house built of living stones" (1 St. Peter ii. 5); a scroll of the written Word of God, the Image of the Bride, and not the less expressive, because its mighty walls were reared, its arches rounded, its vaulting hung aloft by man aiding man ; and its exquisite delicacy, grace, and completeness, learned in communings with paradise and its blessed companies, in studies of all things beautiful in nature, that is, in the loftiest and purest aspirations of the human heart. It is the visible expression of abstract ideas : in every part the ingenious builders contrived to embody a suggestive symbolism, with a high devotional sentiment and great poetic beauty, even as the Temple of Jerusalem served as an example and shadow of heavenly things and a pattern of things in heaven. (Heb. viii. 5 ; ix. 1, 23.)

The prominent principle is that of triplicity ; thus a church contains in length—1, choir, 2, transept, 3, nave ; in breadth, 1, mid-alley, 2, north, 3, south aisles ; and in height, 1, base tier, 2, triforium, 3, clerestory.

> Three solemn parts together twine
> In harmony's mysterious line,
> Three solemn aisles approach the shrine,
> Yet all are one, together all
> In thoughts that awe but not appal,
> Teach the adoring heart to fall.

The church points to the east, as to the place of nativity, sacrifice, and second coming of the Redeemer; the first and last object in the mind and heart of a ransomed world. It was placed on an elevated site, or removed from common buildings, and open to the light emblematically of its destination, a place consecrated to the Most High for intercession between earth and heaven. The porch, nave, choir, and sanctuary, represented severally the Penitent, Christian, Saintly, and Heavenly life. The entrance-door, with its imagery of saints, signified Paradise; the stone screen before the choir, the portals of glory, through the power of the Cross which was elevated upon it; the crypt, the moral death of man; the cruciform shape, the Atonement. The apse indicated the place where the Redeemer's head was laid;, the great transept where His arms were spread; the choir transept the scroll of the cross; the radiating eastern chapels were the rays of the aureole about His head: hence we speak of the head, arms, and body of a church.

At Peterborough and Ely, the western transept forms the step of the cross, at Lincoln the figures of the Virgin and St. John might be drawn within the chapels at the foot of the cross, standing on the first step; the second step denoting the approach of other disciples.

By the cock upon the spire the beholder was reminded of St. Peter; how when apostles ceased to pray they fell. In the early mouldings may be recognized the touching memorials of the martyrs and their instruments of suffering—the cable, chain, sawtooth, hatchet, spike, rack-like chevron, lion-head, and faces and beaks of monsters; and the billet, which was another form of the faggot. It was only as the church had peace, that she exchanged these symbols for the flowers, the foliage, and palm-leaf of the succeeding styles. The foliage till late in the Early English style represented no particular leaf. In the Norman style the acanthus, the palm, the tree of knowledge, and of the forest, had but a slight difference.

The peculiar characteristics of the cathedrals are of considerable interest. There are three towers and spires at Lichfield; three towers at Canterbury, York, Lincoln, Durham, and Ripon. Salisbury, Norwich, Chichester, and Oxford have spires. There is no cloister at York, Winchester, Peterborough, Ripon, Rochester, Exeter, Ely, Lichfield, St. David's, Carlisle, Ripon, Manchester, or the Welsh cathedrals. Bangor, Manchester, and Ely have each a single western tower. Ely and Peterborough have central lanterns. Exeter has transeptal towers. Lincoln, Ely, and Peterborough have western transepts. There are aisleless transepts at Canterbury, Bristol, Norwich, St. Asaph, Bangor, Carlisle, Winchester, Worcester, and Gloucester. Llandaff and Manchester are not cruciform. Norwich and Peterborough end in apses. There are western screens at Salisbury, Lincoln, Peterborough, and Exeter. There is an eastern screen at Durham. York, Salisbury, Rochester, Hereford, Wells, and Worcester have a choir transept. Lincoln, Ely, and Durham have galilees. The cloister is on the north side at Lincoln, Canterbury, Chester, and Gloucester. Wells, Chester, and Chichester possess only three alleys; Hereford and Oxford two. Bangor, St. Asaph, and Carlisle have no Lady Chapel; at Rochester it is on the south side of the nave, on the north side of the choir at Ely and Canterbury; at the west end at Durham; at the east end at Peterborough. It is equal in height to the choir at Lichfield. At Bristol all the aisles are of the same height. Llandaff had only two western towers. Chichester and Manchester have additional aisles to the nave; Oxford to the choir. Chichester retains a detached bell-tower. At Wells, Gloucester, and York, the chapter-house is on the north side. Canterbury has a circular chapel at the east end. There are crypts at Canterbury, York, Winchester, Rochester, Worcester, Hereford, Gloucester, and Ripon.

The Ecclesiastical architecture of England has been divided into five styles: the dates are assigned with as much accuracy as is possible; but the transitions were gradual.

I. *Saxon.* Examples—the crypt of Ripon, and a part of that at York.

II. *Norman,* English Romanesque, or 12th century. Examples—the naves of Rochester, Durham, Oxford, Peterborough, and Ely.

III. *Early English,* Lancet, First Pointed, Early Plantagenet, or 13th century. Examples—Salisbury, nave and transepts of Westminster Abbey; transepts of York, naves of Wells and Lichfield.

IV. *Decorated,* Geometrical and Flowing, Middle Pointed, Edwardian, Later Plantagenet, Curvilineal, or 14th century. Examples—Choir and west front of.York, a great part of Exeter and Lichfield.

V. *Perpendicular,* Vertical, Horizontal, Late Pointed, Late Plantagenet, Lancastrian, or 15th century.— Example—the nave of Winchester.

The broad characteristics of each style are the following :
I. *Norman*—Will. I. to Rich I., 1066-1189.—The ceiling is flat; the ribs are flat bands crossing the vault at right angles, and are enriched with zigzags. The choir ends in a semicircle or apse. The doors are generally deeply recessed, with grotesque and various mouldings above the arch, which is invariably round; the windows have no divisions; the pillars are round or octagonal, sometimes channelled; the buttresses have but a slight projection, and are flat and broad ; arcades are common ; the roofs are steep, turrets are tall, the groining of the vault, which is often cylindrical or barrel, is plain, or at most has a zigzag moulding along the broad massive ribs; turrets terminate in conical spirelets ; mouldings consist of alternate rounds and hollows, with splays and few fillets, or are broken into zigzag lines, or form billets and beakheads. Transitional, 1189-1199.

II. *Early English*—Richard I. to Henry III.—1199-1272. The pointed arch contains the germ of the vertical principle; buttresses are enlarged to resist the lateral outward pressure from the roof downwards caused by its introduction; hence the pyramidal form of this style;

ribs are cross springers, crossing the vault at right angles, or even diagonally along the groins. The windows are long, narrow, and lancet-shaped, often combined in triplets or double; circles are often interposed between the lights and enclosing arch; the mouldings are more boldly cut; foliage or a dog-tooth ornament, *i. e.*, a square-edge, notched like a St. Andrew's cross, are used in the hollows. The arches are lancets (acute-angled), drop (obtuse-angled), foliated, or form equilateral triangles; the roofs have a high pitch; the ceiling is ribbed and groined, and usually stone-vaulted. Spires and the triforium are prominent features; flying buttresses are used; buttresses are divided into stages, with sharply sloping set-offs, and are usually pedimented; the angles are often chamfered. Capitals resemble inverted bells, and are wreathed with foliage. Crockets and knobs are set on the edges of pinnacles, usually circular, octagonal, or square, and sometimes shafted. Pillars are circular, octagonal, or shafted. The doors are deeply recessed, with small shafts in the jambs, are often flat, sometimes round-headed, the featherings are often trefoiled or cinquefoiled; when double they are divided by a single shaft, their chief ornaments consisting of iron scroll-work. Mouldings have outlines of rectangular recesses, or are alternate rounds and deeply-cut hollows : sometimes splays and small fillets are used. The vault has ribs along the apex, and additional ribs between the cross springers and diagonals. Piers frequently divide windows. Stone coffins of this and the preceding style are coped, ornamented with crosses, or bearing effigies of the dead, sometimes placed in low recesses, and occasionally simply canopied. Transitional, 1272-1307.

III. *Decorated*—Time of Edward I., 1307-1360—Edward II. to Edward III.; latter part of his reign, Transitional. —The tracery of windows is a distinguishing feature, which appears in the orbs, or ornamented spaces upon walls. The circles become pointed and flowing ovals; crockets and finials receive a more undulating outline; buttresses support angles obliquely; pinnacles are square or polygonal, with crockets and finials; the vaulting has the main ribs tied together by transverse, diagonal, and cross ribs; diaper-patterns cut in stone are profusely used; the triforium is a mere gallery; bosses are multiplied and the ribs entangled on the vaulting. The windows are of large dimensions, their tracery formed of geometrical figures, and, later in the style, flowing in wavy lines; while mullions divide the window below into many compartments: the doors resemble Early English doors, but are not so deeply recessed; the arches in large examples are pointed—in smaller, of ogee form; niched statues are introduced in the jambs, and windows and doors have often triangular or ogee canopies. The feather mouldings are seldom found wanting. Iron scroll-work is still employed on doors. Mouldings have usually large shallow hollows, ovolos, and ogees, the curve of contra-flexure; fillets and splays are often used; round mouldings have generally a sharp edge, or are convex in the middle and concave at the ends; enrichments are fanciful, leafage, heraldic, or masks; arches are drop, equilateral, or ogee. Stone-work is foliated, *i.e.*, cut into small hollows like spear-heads; buttresses are niched, and have triangular pediments, or pinnacles; pillars, in plan like a lozenge, have clustered shafts; walls are diapered, and hollows enriched with ball-flowers—a three-petal flower, enclosing a ball (the pomegranate of Castile, or the temple of Jerusalem), or a flattened blossom of four petals; arches are equilateral triangles; and the Lady Chapel is a prominent building. Tombs began to have canopied effigies introduced in the sides; slabs to be inlaid with brass, and sepulchral inscriptions introduced; and later, the sides were enriched with quatrefoiled panels.

IV. *Perpendicular.*—1377-1546—Richard II. to Edward VI.—The tracery from the window usurps walls and roofs, piers and arches are no longer in justly-balanced proportion; some members disappear, as the triforium,—others exaggerated, as the clerestory. Panelling is profusely employed; fan-tracery is much used; the pillars are clustered and of lozenge shape; pinnacles are usually square, the arches obtusely pointed, ogee, and four centred; window-tracery is vertical; transoms cross the mullions at right angles; the vaulted and depressed roof becomes very complicated; doors have a square moulding, forming a spandril, which is generally feathered or has tracery; large hollows are in the jambs on either side: the upper parts of capitals are often battlemented, or have the Tudor flower, a sort of angular fleur-de-lys; parapets are battlemented, gurgoyles universal. Its marked character is squareness: arches are ordinarily four-centred; doors are generally panelled; mouldings become flatter, rarely splayed, and have large shallow hollows, form ogees or undulate, or are concave in the centre and convex at the ends; splays are unfrequent; members are separated by quirks. Enrichments are very various, formed of foliage, grotesques, and heraldic devices; ceilings are flat, and usually divided into square compartments by ribs; and bosses and pendants are profusely employed. Large richly-canopied recesses are employed for tombs; and chantries and screen-work introduced about them.

In the provincial college of Canterbury, the Bishop of London is dean, the Bishop of Winchester sub-dean, the Bishop of Lincoln chancellor, the Bishop of Rochester provincial chaplain, the Bishop of Salisbury precentor. The Bishop of Worcester celebrated high mass before the Synod: the arms of the see are therefore ten Hosts. The Bishop of Winchester is prelate, the Bishop of Oxford chancellor, of the order of the Garter. The latter office was held by the Bishops of Salisbury from 1477 till the episcopate of Bishop Denison.

Officers of a Cathedral.

Dignitaries.

I. *Dean.*—The superintendant of the entire establishment.

II. *Precentor.*—The chanter, who regulated the musical services.

III. *Chancellor.*—The secretary of the chapter; librarian; the inspector of schools, and the reader of the lessons; and theological lecturer.

IV. *Treasurer*, or the *Sacrist.*—Had care of the plate, vestments, and furniture; provided necessaries of Divine service, and had oversight of the servants of the church, sacristans, etc.

V. *Sub-Dean.*—The vicegerent in the dean's absence.

VI. *Succentor*, or *Subchanter.*—Acted in the precentor's absence.

Canon.—A member of the cathedral having his name on its register or canon, a stall, and a vote in chapter.

Prebendary.—A stipendiary member of the cathedral, without a vote in chapter, but having a stipend (præbenda) and a stall.

Cursal.—A prebendary with rotatory not permanent duties. (St. David's, St. Asaph.)

Vicar Choral, Salisbury, St. Asaph, York—Same as Minor Canon. *Minor Canon*: at Christchurch called chaplain. *Priest-Vicar*—A minor canon at Lichfield, Hereford, Wells, and Exeter; so called as the representative of a particular dignitary. At St. Paul's minor canons bear the several offices of warden of the college (like that of custos, at Hereford); senior and junior cardinals, from the former custom of standing at either horn of the altar during high mass; and epistoler and gospeler, the duty of reading the Epistle and Gospel having anciently devolved upon them.

CLASSIFICATION OF CATHEDRALS.

I. Bangor, Bath, Chichester, Exeter, Hereford, Lichfield, Lincoln, Llandaff, St. Asaph, St. David's, St. Paul's, Salisbury, and York had chapters of secular canons, and formed cathedrals of the old foundation. II. The cathedrals once conventual churches, but instituted with deans and chapters by Henry VIII., were Canterbury, Carlisle, Durham, Ely, Norwich, Rochester, Winchester, and Worcester. III. The cathedrals of the new foundation were Bristol, Chester, Gloucester, Oxford, Peterborough, and Westminster; with the exception of Carlisle, Oxford, and Bristol, all were Benedictine abbeys. IV. The collegiate churches erected into cathedrals are Manchester, and Ripon. V. Man stood alone.

Popular Glossary.

Abacus, the uppermost part of a capital.

Aisle, the lateral passages on each side of the mid-alley.

Alley, the walk of a cloister.

Ambulatory, the aisle or procession-path behind the high altar; commonly, any passage, a cloister, etc.

Apsis (Greek), a bow, semicircular termination of a choir, etc.

Arcade, a series of arches.

Amice, a cloth worn round the neck.

Ashlar, squared or cut stone.

Aumbry, a locker or cupboard to hold sacred vessels.

Basso relievo, sculpture in low relief.

Bay, a severy; a compartment or division of an arcade or vaulting.

Bench table, a stone seat inside a church.

Boss, a projecting ornament at the intersection of the ribs or vaulting.

Bracket, a projecting support in a wall, to hold an image or lamp.

Broach, a spire rising from a tower without a gutter or parapet.

Campanile, a bell-tower.

Canopy, an ornamental arched projection over arches, doors, windows, etc.

Capital, the head of a pillar.

Carol, a study in a cloister.

Chancel, the choir, from Cancelli, the screen which parted it off from the nave.

Chantry, an endowed chapel in which masses were said for the founder of it.

Chasuble, the principal vestment of a priest, hanging in an oval form behind and in front, and embroidered with bands called orfreys.

Church-garth, the cemetery.

Choir, from chorus, the place where they sing.

Clerestory, the upper tier of windows, i. e. clear story.

Cope, a cloak-like vestment used ordinarily in processions.

Corbel table, a row of projecting stones to support parapets, a cornice on roof eaves.

Credence, a side altar to receive the sacred elements before consecration.

Crenellated, battlemented.

Crocket, projecting foliage on the sides of spires, arches, and pinnacles.

Cusp, a foliation in window tracery like a lance-point.

Dormer, a gabled window in a roof.

Dorsal, hangings at the back of an altar.

Diapering (diaspro, jasper-work), an ornament of flowers to decorate a plain surface.

Dripstone, the label or weather moulding, the outer moulding or projection above doors, arches, and windows, to throw off rain.

Encaustic tiles, tiles with devices burned in the furnace.

Feathering, arches and points in the ornaments of tracery.

Finial, foliated termination of the summit of a canopy, a pinnacle, etc.

Feretory, the shrine or depository of saints' relics.

Freestone, stone easily worked.

Groin, the vault formed by the intersection of two arched roofs.

Gurgoil, a water-spout.

High-pace, the raised floor below an altar.

Impost, a block capital.

Jamb, the side of a door.

Jesse tree, window, altar, etc., a representation of the Saviour's genealogy, in which the personages forming the descent are placed on scrolls of foliage to represent a tree.

Lantern, a turret with windows or apertures at the sides.

Lectern, a reading-desk to hold the Holy Bible, usually in the form of an eagle, symbolical of its passage through all countries.

Lich gate, a churchyard gate, with a shed above it, under which the coffin was rested.

Light, the opening in a mullioned window.

Louvre, a turret-chimney on roofs.

Maniple, a towel worn on the left wrist.

Mid-alley, the central walk between two aisles.

Minster, the church of a monastery, a collegiate church, etc.

Moulding, the outlines of angles of projections or cavities.

Mullion, upright stone bars which divide a window into lights,

Nave, the western portion of a church; from Navis, as the *ship* of Christ.

Newel, the central pillar of a circular staircase.

Niche, an arched recess in a wall for an image.

Ogee, a moulding with a double curve, one convex the other concave.

Orders, subdivisions of an arch, each having its own soffit.

Ovolo, a convex moulding.

Pane, the bay of a cloister.

Parclose, a screen.

Pediment, a triangular termination over porches or buttresses.

Pendant, a hanging ornament on roofs.

Parvise, a porch or room above it.

Piscina, a water-drain for rinsing the sacred vessels.

Poppy-head, the ornament on the tops of seats.

Presbytery, the retro-choir where the presbyters sat, the place of the high altar; sometimes the space between the reredos and eastern Lady Chapel.

Quatrefoil, cinquefoil, trefoil, a foliation or feathering of four, five or three cusps respectively, in an arch, making the hollow resemble four, five, or three leaves.

Quirk, a small acute recess in mouldings.

Quoin, the outer angle of any building, usually of ashlar.

Ragstone, stone from the quarry undressed.

Reredos, a screen behind an altar.

Respond, a half pillar attached to a wall corresponding with another pillar opposite.

Rib, a projecting band in vaulting.

Rood-loft, a screen supporting the cross or rood.

Rubble, fragments of stone of different sizes.

Sedilia, seats near the altar for the clergy.

Set-off, slopes of masonry dividing buttresses into stories.

Slyp, a passage between two walls; between the transept and chapter-house at Canterbury, Gloucester, Norwich, Peterborough, and Winchester.

Spandril, a triangular space on the flanks of arches, between the outer part of an arch and its square enclosing frame.

Spire-light, a window in a spire.

Splays, jambs of windows slanting inwardly. A champer is a flat slope, formed by cutting away on angle.

Stage, a storey.

Stall, a fixed seat enclosed.

Steeple, a tower or spire.

Stole, a narrow riband-like ornament, passing round the neck in front, and reaching below the knee.

String-course, a narrow moulding along the side of a building.

Tabernacle, a niche. Tabernacle-work is open ornamental work over stalls.

Triforium, Latin for thoroughfare; a passage or arcade between the lower arches and clerestory.

Transept (Latin), cross-wall, the projecting wing of a cruciform church.

Transom, a horizontal stone bar in the lights of windows.

Tympanum, the space between the opening of a doorway and the encircling arch above.

Vault, an arched roof.

GUIDE TO THE CATHEDRALS.

Bangor.

BANGOR is situated at the foot of a steep rock near the river Ogwen, in a vale half closed in with an amphitheatre of hills and open to the sea, with a fine view of the sparkling waters of the Menai Strait, and the water-front of Beaumaris, in the county of Caernarvon. The shore is famous for its different varieties and profusion of sea-weeds. Traces of a Norman castle are to be found on a rock opposite Friar's School, and, at the back, on the top of another hill is an ancient British camp, which commands views of Penmaen Mawr to the north, and Ddinas Dinorwig to the south. The Cathedral is dedicated to St. David; and, from the beauty of its situation, or the excellence of its music, gave name to the city—Ban Chor, the high or chief choir. The church was founded by St. Deiniol, 525, but was destroyed in 1071: the Synod of Westminster, 1102, empowered a collection of alms of the faithful to restore the buildings, which suffered again great damage in 1247, and were burned down in 1402, in revenge, by Owen Glendower, to punish the bishop, R. Yonge, who was a partisan of the English king.

The earliest portion of the present fabric, the CHOIR, was built by Henry Dene, bishop 1496-1500; the NAVE and TOWER were added by Pace de Skeffington, bishop 1509-1534. The roof was rebuilt by H. Rowlands, bishop 1598-1616, who likewise gave a peal of four bells, to which was added a fifth, by Humphrey Lloyd, bishop 1673-1689. Arthur Bulkeley sold the five bells of the church in the 16th century, and was so officious as to go down to the haven to see them shipped; but the bells sank with the bark before they cleared the straits, and the bishop soon after fell blind, and so continued to the day of his death. Considerable repairs were made during the episcopate of John Warren, bishop 1783-1800, who built the harbour and improved the palace. The plaster ceilings were set up by Bishop Cleaver, 1800-1807.

The Cathedral is cruciform: the tower battlement, with pinnacles and bold diagonal buttresses of six stages each, which bears the date A.D. 1532, stands at the west end and rises one story above the roof; the NAVE of six bays, which is used as a parish church, with a service in Welsh, has a clerestory of triplets under a pointed arch, as in the tower. According to the tradition all the windows of the nave were brought from the once adjoining church of St. Mary; those in the aisle are Decorated. There is a south door with a niche over it. Beneath the string course of the five-light Perpendicular window of the south transept, which is of one bay and aisleless, are remains of the church of the time of Edward I., to which date may also be referred the octangular turret at the north-east angle of the north transept. The greater part of the church is Perpendicular; the south aisle of the nave is Decorated. The font is octagonal and Perpendicular. Some buttresses in the south transept are of Early English character. A building on the north side of the choir serves for chapter-house, vestry, registry, and library. The lower story is of the same date as the choir. The organ, built by Green, was given by Dean Lloyd in 1779. There are no cloisters, no Lady Chapel, nor aisles to the choir and transept. The only remaining monu-

ments of interest are those of Bishops Vaughan and Rowlands, two alabaster busts, on the north side of the choir.
Prince Owen Gwynned, A.D. 1160, was buried here. The
five-light Perpendicular east window has good stained glass,
a memorial to Dean Cotton. The choir is aisleless and
has a battlemented parapet. On the south side it has
two pointed windows, and a five-light Perpendicular
window, 27 ft. by 13½ ft. Under the window of the south
transept is an ancient monument. At the altar Bishop
Robert of Shrewsbury, 1197-1213, was taken prisoner by
King John, and ransomed himself with a present of 300
hawks. In 1118, Archbishop Baldwin made Bishop Grey
take the cross in the cathedral, and declared that the
nightingale was wiser than a primate, for it never visited
a country so uncouth.

The Chapter consists of the dean, one prebendary, and a
treasurer; there are two minor canons, six lay vicars-
choral, and eight choristers. Eight stalls have been suppressed. There are two choral services on Sundays, and
one on Saturdays, eves, and festivals. The library contains 800 volumes, and the famous MS. Bangor Pontifi-
cal or Use, drawn up 1291. The Holy Communion is
administered monthly and on great festivals.

DIMENSIONS OF THE CATHEDRAL IN FEET.

	Length.	Breadth.	Height.
Nave . . .	141	60	34
Choir . .	53	28	34
Transept . . .	96	27	..
Tower . .	24	24	60
Total . . .	214		

The Episcopal Palace, built by Bishop Pace, is at
Bangor. The Friars' Grammar School was founded by
Dr. Glynne in the reign of Queen Elizabeth, 1557.

Among bishops of Bangor occur Anian, compiler of the
" Bangor Use," 1267-1307 ; Gilbert, Lord Treasurer, 1386 ;
Bayley, of whose "Popular Practice of Piety " D'Espagne
complained in 1689, from the pulpit in the Savoy church,
that " its readers were more than those of the Bible ;" the

heterodox Hoadly, the author of the Bangorian Controversy, and the orthodox Sherlock. Among its monks occur Pelagius the heretic and Nennius the chronicler; and among deans, Williams Bishop of Ossory. For one hundred years before 1541 there had been no resident bishop, and for two centuries previous to 1553, no prelate buried in the cathedral.

Arms: Arg., a bishop pontifically habited and holding a pastoral staff.

Bath.

But Avon marched in more stately path,
Proud of his adamants, with which he shines
And glisters wide, as also of wondrous Bath,
And Bristow fair which on his waves he builded.

BATH, the Aquæ Solis, the "Sun-Waters" of the Roman, was the "Hot Baths, or Sick Man's City" with the Saxon. It is beautifully situated within a semicircle of seven hills, upon the river Avon.

There is a hospital of St. John Baptist, founded 1180 by Bishop Reginald FitzJocelyn, adjoining Stall Street. One portion of the ancient walls, which were standing in 1778, remains in the Borough walls near the General Hospital; part of the east wall, of the date of 1500, is in Boatstall Lane. In the Institution, established 1824, are preserved a valuable collection of Roman remains found in the vicinity. Gildas and the ever-memorable John Hales were natives of the city. In the Grammar School were educated Prynne, Lysons the topographer, Archbishop Laurence, and Sir Sydney Smith. At St. Mary's Bathwick was buried John Mackinnon of Skye, who saved the life of Prince Charles Stuart after the battle of Culloden. Edgar was crowned at Bath 959. King Arthur fought a battle here in 520; and in a fight in the civil wars on Lansdown, Sir Bevil Granville was slain. Henry I. 1107, Henrietta Maria 1644, Queen Anne 1702-3, and Queen

Caroline in 1817, visited Bath. On Little Solsbury are many interesting remains; and on Hampton Down remains of the Belgic camp and Wansdyke.

The city well deserves its name of the English Genoa, and all circumstances natural and architectural are in its favour. The grey tower and pinnacles of the Cathedral are seen to rise boldly above the sombre masses of stone, for there is not a brick house in the city. The winding river flows between long wavy lines of buildings, and the landscape is closed in by mountain-like eminences of such size and grandeur, as would dwarf a minster of colossal proportions. It certainly forms a marked feature in a city where all other buildings being modern confer on it a greater aspect of antiquity; and where most associations are those of fashion and amusement, it is a standing commentary, a monitor, almost audible, of the passing interest of the present, the unchangeable character of the past, and the eternal issues of the future. These considerations conspire to give it a dignity, which it might not intrinsically, or in a different position, command. It was erected by an architect who braved the Italian taste of the day; and if there be an appearance of meagreness, it is the result only of narrow funds. The arches are elegant without being thin, and the roof of the choir is full of grace and lightness, as if suspended by invisible hands. There was here an ancient abbey of Benedictines when John de Villula translated the see from Wells to Bath. His successor, Godfrey, continued to reside here: but Robert the Norman in 1135 united the two sees. The present Church, dedicated to SS. Peter and Paul, was the last cathedral built in England. It had fallen into decay, when Oliver King, bishop 1495-1503, undertook its restoration. He had a dream like Jacob's ladder, and imagined that he heard a voice, saying, "Let an Oliver stablish the crown and a King build the church," words which he interpreted as a divine command to begin this good work. William Birde, prior 1409-1525, and William Holway, prior 1525-1534, continued the buildings; the arms of Adrian de Castello, bishop of the diocese, are plainly visible.

Although there were no eminent ecclesiastics in the convent, yet to the brotherhood Bath is indebted to their patronage of the loom in 1330. The shuttle was engraved on the Abbey House, and at one time adopted into their arms. At the dissolution in 1539 the royal commissioners offered the abbey to the inhabitants for 500 marks; but, owing to natural apprehensions on their part, they refused to entertain the thought: some merchants, however, with fewer scruples, purchased the glass, iron, lead, and bells, weighing in all several hundred tons, and valued at 4,800*l.* Nothing remained but naked walls: the cloisters, chapter-house, the priory-house, and the dormitory built by Bishop Beckington, which stood on the south side, together with the great abbey-gate, were destroyed. Humphrey Colles in 1542 became possessor of the ruined church; and on January 27, 1569, Edmund Colthurst gave the shell to the citizens, and sold the monastic buildings to Fulke Morley. In 1572 Peter Chapman began to restore the east end, and Thomas Bellot, (Steward of the Queen's Household and founder of Bellot's Hospital, Bath,) with Lord Burleigh and Thomas Earl of Sussex, completed the choir; while James Montague, bishop 1608-1616, gave 1000*l.* to roof the nave; and other eminent members of that noble house restored the west front. The abbey then became a parish church. In 1833 the houses which had been built against the north side were pulled down, and alterations, tasteless and unseemly, made in the interior, which is blocked up with galleries and pews. Pinnacles were at the same time added to the turrets.

The church is cruciform, consisting of a nave of five bays, a choir of four bays, and a transept of two bays without aisles. It is built of the oolite of the neighbourhood. On the east side of the south transept is a vestry containing some ancient MSS. The central TOWER is of two stories; the north and south faces are narrower than the east and west sides. Its composition is fine; the octagonal turrets are panelled, and the pierced battlement is rich. It contains ten bells and chimes.

> Forth from that hollow cage,
> Still, like a sweet melodious bird they sing
> Such varied notes, enchanting every ear.

The windows are a pair in each tier, included within a square case; the lowermost tier has a transom. They are of two lights on the north and south, of four lights on the east and west.

From the number of the windows (52), the church is so light as to be called the Lantern of England. The other characteristic points are the length of its choir, the narrowness of the transept, and the breadth of the nave aisles. The WEST FRONT is flanked with two turrets, square below, octagonal when clear of the aisles. On this is represented the dream of Bishop King. On either side of a ladder, with angels ascending and descending, are canopied figures of the apostles, and in a niche, passing through the battlement above it, the Holy Trinity; the whole surrounding space is filled in with angels standing on corbels. The paraphrase of Judges ix. 8 is also engraved in Latin and English.

> Trees going to choose their King
> Said be to us the Oliver King.

The magnificent west window is of seven lights with two transoms. The transept window of five lights with three transoms. The arms of King, Montague, and Bird are on the rich west door; on either side of which, in niches beautifully carved, are the statues of SS. Peter and Paul; in niches in the central mullions of the windows over the north door is King Edgar, and over the south King Osric, founder of the monastery in 679. The legend, 'Domus mea domus orationis'—My house is a house of prayer—appears in scrolls. The battlements on the entire front and about the great door are varied and very rich.

The ROOF of the NAVE is of wood richly panelled, but very flat; and that of the transepts and choir vaulted with the most intricate fan-tracery, like the tangled meshes of the sea-weed, the spoil of the coral meadows. It is observeable how the triforium, a prominent feature in earlier architecture, became a gallery in the Decorated period, and, as at Bath, in the Perpendicular period, disappears altogether. The broad-centred arches were employed to dazzle the eye with the clerestory of enormous dimensions, which they alone could support. A taller arch would have necessitated stunted pillars; in fact, the clerestory is the prominent feature of the church.

The flying buttresses are fine. The windows are mostly of five lights with good tracery. The modern screen by Manners, 1825, is set under the east arch, and blocking out the transepts fatally injures the effect of the interior. The organ is by Smith, and was built 1838.

On the south side of the CHOIR is the chantry of Prior Bird, A.D. 1515, now used as the episcopal throne. The exterior of the east window is 20 feet wide and 50 feet in height, within a square case which has circles in the spandrils; but within, it is of pointed form, with seven lights and three transoms. Underneath may be seen on the outside the bases of the former church built by Robert, Monk of Lewes, in 1137. The window of the east aisle is inserted in an arch which appears Norman. The Grange of the abbey, built by Prior Cantlow, 1449, is at St. Catherine's, Batheaston, and the Prior's Park still retains its name. It was once the seat of the generous Allen, (Fielding's Squire Allworthy,) where Warburton and Pope were frequent guests, and till recently a great Roman Catholic College. The palace of Bishop de Villula stood on the west side of the abbey. St. Mary Magdalen Chapel in Holloway was built by Prior Cantlow.

The chief monuments are those of—

Lord Byron's father; J. Bosanquet, with a sculpture of the Good Samaritan, by W. Carter; Sir William Draper, K.G., d. 1787; William Baker, bishop of Bangor 1723-32; Christopher Butson, bishop of Clonfert, d. 1836.

S. Aisle, Nave.—James Quin, the actor, epitaph by Garrick; Beau Nash, epitaph by Dr. Harrington; Bingham, by Flaxman; H. Kettencamp, by Bacon; Colonel Champion, by Nollekens.

N. Aisle, Nave.—Malthus, the political economist.

S. Transept.—Lady Jane Waller, wife of the Parliamentarian general; an effigy.

N. Transept.—Sir P. Frowde, 1674 ; Fletcher Partis, founder of the Widows' College, Bath ; Mary Frampton, epitaph by Dryden ; Sir R. H. Bickerton, by Chantrey ; Dr. Sibthorp, the Botanist, by Flaxman.

Choir.—Hoare, the artist, by Chantrey ; Lady Miller, the muse of the famous " Batheaston Urn," by Bacon, sen.

Nave.—Altar-Tomb and Effigy, Bishop Montague, 1618.

The walls are encrusted with tablets of every size and ugliness, as a wit wrote :—

> Each niche, well filled with monument and bust,
> Shows how Bath waters serve to lay the dust.

An entry in Pepys' Diary, A.D. 1668, disproves the legend that King James II. drew his sword and mutilated Sir W. Waller's nose on his effigy : but Warner relates that Father Huddlestone set out, in that king's presence, the altar in the Roman manner, when Ken mounted the pulpit, which then stood in the nave, and inveighed vehemently against the act.

During the demolition of the Priory-house a sacristy was found hung with alb, cope, and chasuble, quite perfect, but as the air entered they dissolved in dust. Two chests were discovered which the workmen averred were empty, but one shortly after retired from business.

DIMENSIONS OF THE CATHEDRAL IN FEET.

	Length.	Breadth.	Height.
Nave	136	72	78
Choir	74	20	..
Transept	126	..	..
Tower	{ E. and W. 36 } { N. and S. 25 }		162
Bird's Chantry	16	8	..
Total	210		

There are no choral services. There is a daily service at 11 A.M. Arms : Gules, two keys addorsed in bend sinister ; the upper arg., the lower or, enfiled with a sword in bend dexter.

Bristol.

BRISTOL, the Bric-Stowe ("Place of the Chasm") of the Saxon, in allusion to the gorge through which at Clifton the river flows, and in mediæval times called the Queen's Chamber, as London was the King's, stands on the Avon, down whose stream in 1497, sailing in the Matthew, Sebastian Cabot waved his farewell when in search of the new world. From it, May 2, 1838, the first steamer, the Great Western, crossed the Atlantic.

William of Worcester, Hannah More, Sir T. Lawrence, Bird the artist, Baily the sculptor (his " Eve at the Fountain" is in the Philosophical Institution, and his "Justice" in the Council House), Southey, and Coleridge were natives of the city, and Cottle, whom Byron apostrophises with " Phœbus ! what a name," Sebastian Cabot, the learned Grocyn, and Chatterton. William Cann, the mayor, 1648, was the first civic authority who proclaimed there was no king in England. Blankets and brass are said to have first been made here ; the first by a citizen T. Blanket, the latter by Dutch workmen in 1705. The following sovereigns have been at Bristol : Stephen, a prisoner, 1141 ; Eleanor, the damsel of Brittany, was a captive in the castle, 1201-1241 ; King John, 1209 ; Henry III., keeping Christmas, 1216 ; Edward I. for the same purpose, and holding a parliament, 1286 ; and again 1288, Henry VI. 1446 ; Edward IV., 1461 ; Henry VII., 1487 ; Elizabeth, Aug. 15, 1574 ; Queen Anne, 1613 ; Charles II. and his queen, 1663. In the Guildhall are Henry VII.'s sword, 1487, and a pearl scabbard of 1431.

Bristol boasts of St. John's, built 1397, with a crypt and an effigy of its founder, Walter Frampton, of the 14th century, and altar tomb of T. Rowley, died 1478 ; Allhallows, with a recumbent statue of E. Colston by Rysbrack ; the Temple Church, with its leaning tower, 3 ft. 9 in. out of the perpendicular, built 1118, completed 1460 ; SS. Philip and Jacob, has an Early English tower and

Norman font. In St. Peter's churchyard, Savage the poet (died 1743) is buried; in the church is a brass of R. Lord, 1461. The Priory Church of St. James, built 1130, the tower 1374, has some fine Norman portions; in the south aisle is the effigy of the famed Robert Earl of Gloucester, died 1147. St. Werburgh's, built 1190, tower 1385; St. Stephen's, Perpendicular, with a tower 130 ft. in height, built 1472, with a recessed canopied tomb and two fine effigies of John Shipward and his wife; and St. Mark's, or the Chapel of the Gaunts, founded in the 13th century, an architectural gem—the tower built 1487. The reredos is Perpendicular, the rest of the building Early English or Decorated. It contains some good sedilia, and the monuments of (north side) Miles Salley, Bishop of Llandaff, died 1516; in the mid alley, of Sir Maurice de Gaunt and Sir Robert de Goumant, effigies as crusaders; south aisle, Sir Henry de Gaunt and Sir Maurice and Catherine Berkeley (the dame died in 1361), effigies of the 14th century; and Flemish cinque-cento glass, dated 1543, purchased from Fonthill; north aisle, John Carr, altar-tomb, and a bust of Sir J. B. Haberfield. In the Poyntz Chapel, Perpendicular with fan-tracery roof, are some Spanish encaustic enamelled tiles (azuleios), of the age of Charles V., like those in the Alcazar at Seville. The High Cross of Nailsworth stone was restored, after the original cross now at Stourhead, in 1851, by Thomas of Lambeth, at the entrance of College Green, at a cost of 300*l*. The following buildings are of interest :—Two gatehouses, and part of the walls of the 17th century; St. Peter's Hospital, erected 1400; a crypt of St. Andrew's Church under Nos. 22 and 32 High Street; Back Hall, built in the 15th century; Canynge's House in Redcliffe Street, with a Perpendicular hall and louvre; and the Perpendicular hall, with a fine timber roof, in Colston's House in Small Street, where Charles I. was entertained; Bartholomew's Gateway, Christian Street, Early English; Gate to Spicer's Hall; Perpendicular door of the Guard-House; the Dormitory, 86 ft. by 23 ft., with a roof of the 14th century; and the Lesser Hall, 49. ft. by 24 ft. 3 in., of

the Dominican Friary, Marshal Street; the crypt of St.
Nicholas, 1503, with a stone coffin of the date 1311. In
Queen Square is a statue of William of Orange, by Rys-
brack.

" That pryde of Bristowe and the western londe,"

the church of St. Mary Redcliffe, is cruciform, with aisles
to nave, transept, and choir, with a south porch, priest's
house, and Lady Chapel. The first stage of the tower and
inner north porch are Early English, and were built
1294-1301, by Simon de Burton ; the upper portion of the
tower is Decorated: a great portion of the spire, of the
period of Edward I., was destroyed by a storm in 1445.
The Decorated transept was built by William Cannynge
I., about 1369. The nave and aisles were built, 1445, by
William Cannynge II. The choir is surrounded by an open
stone screen, and formerly possessed three large paintings,
by Hogarth, of the Entombment, Resurrection, and Ascension. The east window, by Wailes, 1853, was the gift of
Sir J. K. Haberfield and Robert Phippen. The Lady
Chapel is Late Perpendicular. The vaulting of the church
is extremely rich. The clerestory in the transept has a
curious screen of quatrefoils on either side of the lights.
The outer north porch, once St. Mary's Chapel, is a hexagon
of Decorated work: it has a penitential cell, or relique
chamber. In the treasury above was a coffer in which
Chatterton averred he had found the poems of Rowley.
Over the inner porch (Early English) is the treasury or
Sacristan's chamber. In the south transept is a monument of Cannyng, with effigies erected 1646; an effigy of
Dean W. Cannyng, formerly a merchant royal, died 1468,
brought hither from Westbury, 1647; (from the inscription on this monument is gained the first mention of ships
of large tonnage in England); and the armour of Admiral
Sir William Penn, father of the founder of Pennsylvania :
and there are two canopied monuments, and the brass of a
knight, to the brothers Mede of the 15th century, east end
north aisle. There are altar-tombs (north transept) of
Lord Robert of Berkeley, a purse-bearer, and Sir John

Ivyns, died 1439, justice of Common Pleas; an incised slab
to Cannynge's cook; and an effigy in slight relief of John
Lamington, who died in 1398, and two stone coffins in the
south porch. In the chancel are the effigies of John Jay,
died 1480, and his wife. Great repairs have taken place,
and some good wood-work erected, under the able conduct
of Mr. Godwin. The iron gates were set up by William
Edney, in 1710, at a cost of 110*l.*

DIMENSIONS OF THE CHURCH IN FEET.

	Length.	Breadth.	Height.
Nave	128	52	54
Choir	60	52	53
Transept	117·6	47	..
Tower	..	..	200
Lady Chapel	38	23	..
Total length	239	..	..
Spire	26·4 diam.	..	36

The resemblance of the grand doorway to one in Batalha
may be accounted for by the fact that the latter was the
work of David Hacket, an Irishman, in 1400, bishop of
Ossory.

On the south side of the College Green stands the mutilated Cathedral of the Holy Trinity, formerly the Abbey
Church of the Augustine Canons, and founded A.D. 1142
by Robert Fitzharding, mayor of the town. At the dissolution, June 4, 1542, King Henry VIII. converted it into
a Cathedral Church. The materials employed in its construction are red sandstone and yellow limestone magnesian. It is of a late and rich Decorated style, passing
into Perpendicular, and consists of a choir of four bays
with aisles and a transept all of uniform height, built by
E. Knowle, abbot 1306-32, and John Snow, 1332-41; an
east ambulatory or procession path, and a Lady Chapel of
two bays, both of which are now thrown into the choir;
and a large central tower low and massive. The NAVE was
destroyed in the 16th century before its creation into a
cathedral, which saved the remainder of the building.
Although wanting in external effect from this serious
loss, the whole building is fine, and so very rich in excel-

lent detail within, as to compensate by its chapels, monuments, and roof for its curtailed size. The finest effect is obtained when the shadows deepen, and the daylight falls tenderly, then pales as it ebbs, dimmed and dying along the aisles. The interior is then impressive, with day sufficient to display the beauties, and enough of night to throw a solemnity over the defects—like the light with which we see in dreams. The "mural flora," as M. de Caumont prettily terms it, composed of ivy, oak, vine, trefoil, herb bennet, rose, and lilies, attests the artist's passionate love and careful study of nature, as their tendrils wind and flow, and blossom interwoven over capital and boss, while the building shadows the Divine immensity, and the prominent sign is the symbol of His infinite pitying love. Nor can there be a more clear and touching display of the calm and safety of His providence, than when the silent aisles wake with the song of the red-breast warbling unharmed on their sculptured foliage. On one of the pinnacles of the organ about 1773, one of these birds (according to the mediæval legend its bosom was stained with the blood of the cross, while it strove to tear out a thorn from the brow of the Crucified) took up its station during the hour of prayer, and was fed with crumbs by the sexton till its death in the winter of 1787. This incident furnished the subject of some pretty lines by Rev. E. Lowe, preserved in Hannah More's poems. The figure of a ram playing on the violin on one of the piers, goes to prove that the bow was, as it is said, intreduced about the 14th century, probably by a musician in a Nuncio's train. Bristol and Ripon have no super-altars.

On the north-west side of the choir is the elder LADY CHAPEL of four bays, the most ancient portion of the building and of the 13th century, probably the design of Abbot David, who died 1234. On the east side of the south transept is the Newton Chapel, and to the south of the south aisle of the choir are the vestry and sacristy, formerly the Berkeley Chapel, with its antechamber, built by Thomas, Lord Berkeley, about 1281, with a peculiar roof, the principle of carpentry having been applied to stone.

Of the CHOIR two bays westward constitute an ante-choir,
an arrangement of the space which has involved the loss
of the ancient procession-path at the back of the altar.
A very great improvement, however, in the distribution of
the seats is now promised by the chapter. The NORTH TRAN-
SEPT was built by Abbot Newland, 1481-1515. The west
window was rebuilt 1629. The chapter-house was built in
1250.

The TOWER is square, flanked with pinnacled buttresses ;
it is arcaded with five traceried arches, of two stories,
and pierced with pointed two-light windows on each of
the four faces ; the parapet is embattled ; there is a north-
east stair-turret. It was commenced by Walter New-
bury, abbot 1428-63, and completed by William Hunt,
1463-81. There is a peal of five bells ; the largest
was cast 1570. Abbot Hunt added the upper part of the
south transept, the embattled parapet, and pinnacles round
the church, which he roofed anew. In the aisles the side
walls are strengthened by lateral beams of stone supported
by pointed arches, which are met in the centre by the ribs
of the stone vaulting. The stall-work was added by Robert
Eliot, abbot in 1515, and the episcopal throne by Paul
Bush, bishop 1543-53. The brass eagle is in one of the
parish churches. The reredos is partly of the time of
Edward I.; the upper part was added by William Burton,
abbot 1533-37. The glazing in the east windows of the
south and north aisles was the gift of Dean Glenham.
The elaborately traceried east Jesse window of nine lights,
and the other four choir windows are of the date 1320.
In the west and south transept is some Perpendicular
glazing; and in the Elder Lady Chapel is glass of the
reign of Edward I. The organ-screen was erected about
1541. When Bishop Thornborough, 1603-16, was diocesan,
the mayor built up a gallery near the pulpit, but the
bishop had it pulled down, saying he would not have " the
temple of God made like a playhouse." The civic authorities were so affronted that they with a petty conceit
seceded to St. Mary's Redcliffe. Felton his successor
tried to win congregations by an imitation of Andrews'

popular, though somewhat grotesque style; until he "nearly spoiled his natural amble by following his artificial trot." Westfield never entered the pulpit without a shudder, yet was so pathetic as to be known as "the weeping prophet." The organ was built by Renatus Harris, 1685.

The iconoclasts of the Great Rebellion inflicted much damage; and the bishop's palace, with the library, was burned in the riots, 31st October, 1831: the books were destroyed by fire or thrown into the Avon, though 1100 volumes were recovered from marine-store dealers. In Bishop Howell's time the rebels ransacked the palace, dragged him out savagely, and left his dying wife to perish in the unroofed room. Furnaces were erected on the site of the altar. He died within a fortnight, and the good citizens took charge of his orphan children. The erection of a white marble cross over the chapel altar was wickedly distorted into a charge against Bishop Butler of unfaithfulness to the Church of England.

Of the CLOISTERS, of Perpendicular work, only the north and part of the east walk remain. The oblong CHAPTER-HOUSE, that marked and indispensable feature of English, in distinction to continental, arrangement, to hold the diocesan parliament, has a vestibule of three round arches! it is a most interesting specimen of Late Norman, built by Abbot Richard, 1148-86. The arcaded walls, the intersecting arcades, and the variety of the mouldings render it most imposing. The Transitional Norman gateway, a most elaborate specimen of the style, with a superstructure of the date 1480-1502, is on the south-west of the church. The excellence of the oolite has preserved sharp and fresh the minute details of carving. The vaulting, A.D. 1160, assumes a slightly pointed form, although the other arches are semicircular.

In the Lower Green is the Norman gate of the bishop's palace. Grey and William, bishops of Bangor, had been priors of St. Augustine's.

Bristol numbers among her bishops Lake and Trelawny, two of the seven bishops, the latter commemorated in

the famous Cornish ballad; Guy Carleton, the hunting
bishop; the munificent Boulter, Primate of Ireland; Butler,
the author of the Analogy of Religion; Robinson, the last
prelate who held an office of state, or went as an ambassador; Newton, the commentator on Prophecy and
patron of Garrick; the scholar Monk; and learned Kaye.
Hakluyt, the collector of voyages, and S. Lee, the orientalist, were two of its canons. So poor was the see in the
reign of Elizabeth, that Doctor Holdsworth refused it,
saying he " would have no Bristol stone."

The principal monuments are those of—

Mrs. Mason, epitaph by her husband, and Mrs. Elizabeth Draper,
Sterne's " Eliza," by Bacon;· W. Powell, the tragedian, epitaph by
Coleman; Mrs. Middleton and Robert Southey, by Baily; Elizabeth
Stanhope, by Westmacott; Maria Elwyn, by Chantrey; Dr. Foster,
editor of the Hebrew Bible without points; and the gravestone of
Edward Bird, the artist, in the Cloister; Rev. S. Love, epitaph by
Hannah More; Bishop Butler, epitaph by Southey.

The stellated canopies of many of the ancient tombs
resemble the Spanish architécture at Seville. The more
interesting memorials and effigies are of—

In the Choir, N. Side.—Edmund Knowle, Abbot, rich tomb and
effigy under a recessed arch, d. 1332; Morgan Gwillym, the last
abbot, d. 1553.
S. Side.—John Newland, abbot, effigy, d. 1515; Sir John Young, d.
1603, effigy.
N. Aisle—Bishop Bush, 1558, cadaver; Sir C. Vaughan, d. 1630,
effigy.
S. Aisle.—Maurice Lord Berkeley, d. 1281, effigy; Thomas Lord
Berkeley, d. 1243, his effigy as a Templar; Thomas Lord Berkeley
d. 1321, altar-tomb.
Lady Chapel.—Maurice Lord Berkeley, d. 1368, of wounds received
at Poictiers, and Lady Elizabeth, effigies; a slab with a cross fleury;
Abbot David, 1234, effigy.
Newton Chapel.—Sir Henry Newton and his dame, effigies, d. 1599;
Sir John Newton, effigy, d. 1666; Sir R. Codrington, d. 1618,
painted effigy with his dame and seventeen children; grey altar-
tomb, Sir R. N. Cradock, judge.
Wall of Muniment Room.—Coffin slab with a carving of the Descent

into Hell. Outside the choir, under the seats, a fragment of the slab of Robert Fitzhardinge, lord of Berkeley—the founder.

There are two daily choral services, at 11 and 3, and the Holy Communion is celebrated monthly, and on festivals. The Chapter consists of a dean and four canons. There are three minor canons, six lay vicars, and six choristers. Two stalls have been suspended. The bishop's palace is at Rodborough Manor, Stroud. The deanery was built 1234.

Arms: Sable, three crowns in pale, or; the coat of King Edmund the Elder, buried at Puckle, near Bristol.

DIMENSIONS OF THE CATHEDRAL IN FEET.

	Length.	Breadth.	Height.
Nave	was [118]	[70]	43
Choir	175	73	
Transept	128	..	..
Tower	..	..	133
Chapter-house	43	25	26
Cloisters	were 103	103	

Canterbury.

CANTERBURY, the Saxon Cantwarabyric, " City of the Men of Kent," was by the Britons called Durwhem "the swift river," in allusion to the Stour, on which it is situated. No city can show a greater number of churches, monuments, and sites of interest; and no city has done less to preserve them : till within a hundred years, town-walls, gates, towers, and old buildings stood as in centuries since. Happily, a better feeling is now prevalent, and the good work of restoration and repair has been begun, and nowhere more honourably and with such long and consistent devotion as by this munificent Chapter.

The Danes burned Canterbury in 849 and 852; in 918 Elfleda drove them out; in 1011 they again took it, but King Canute came as a pilgrim and hung his crown in the nave, and restored the body of the martyred Elphege. In 1519 Henry VIII., the Emperor Charles V., and the Queen of France visited the Primate. Charles II. was here in 1660. Canterbury was the native place of Linacre, Marlowe, Richard the great Earl of Cork, Aphra Behn, and Lord Tenterden.

The West gate, flanked by two lofty round towers with the bridge adjoining, was built by Archbishop Sudbury in the reign of Richard II. In St. Peter's Street the Dominican Friary now serves as a wool-house; the Refectory is a Socinian meeting-house—in it Defoe preached; near it is the house of the Knights' Templars, afterwards used by the priests of the Black Prince's Chantry. On the south side of King's Bridge, in the High Street, is the Hospital of St. Thomas Eastbridge, founded by Archbishop à Becket; in the same street is the gateway of the Augustine Friary. In Lamb Lane is the Hospital founded by Archdeacon Langton in the 13th century. Palace Street derives its name from the archiepiscopal palace (the scene of the death of the Black Prince), very small portions of which now remain. In the former Great Hall here, were kept the bridal feast of King Edward I. and Margaret in Sept., 1299; the banquet given to Henry VIII. and Charles V. by Warham; and the entertainment offered to Queen Elizabeth on Sept. 7, 1573. The brick gateway was built by Archbishop Parker. In Northgate suburb are the remains of the Priory of St. Gregory, founded by Lanfranc for Austin Canons; and his other foundation, the Hospital of St. John, with a thatched wooden gateway. The Lazar-house of St. Nicholas Harbledown has a gatehouse and a chapel of the eleventh century. In St. George's suburb is the gateway of St. Sepulchre's Priory, a Benedictine nunnery, founded 1100: the famous Maid of Kent and great impostor, Elizabeth Barton, was a professed member of the house. At the corner of Mercery Lane and High Street is the presumed "Chequers" hostelry of Chaucer, built by Chillenden, prior 1390-1411, now let out in tenements. It contains "the dormitory of a hundred beds," a room upheld by wooden pillars, and possessing a high pitched roof. The Dane John is the mound on which stood the dungeon of the castle ; the keep, 88 by 80 ft., is a gas factory; adjoining it is the Martyrs' Field, the scene of Marian persecution. Considerable Norman remains are observable in the parish churches of SS. George, Mary Bredin, Mary Magdalene, and Dunstan. In the latter is preserved Sir Thomas More's head : adjoining is the picturesque gateway of the Roper mansion, his daughter's home. In the ancient church of St. Martin, which is built for the greater part of Roman brick, was Queen Bertha's oratory ; and it formed the first cathedral of St. Augustine.   In the font it is said King Ethelbert was baptized. With its lich-gate the church has been restored by Hon. D. Finch. Roman bricks are seen also in St. Mildred's church. Queen Bertha's postern leads from the Cathedral to the Abbey. Of the magnifi- cent abbey of St. Augustine only two gateways remain ; the cemetery, or St. Ethelbert's gate, built by Thomas Ickham, Sacrist in the reign of Richard II., and a superb great gateway built in 1287, flanked by two turrets and embattled. At the north-east angle of the cemetery is the ruined chapel of St. Pancras, 31 feet long, 21 feet wide, rebuilt 1387.   In 1844 Mr. Beresford-Hope recovered the site from occupation by a publican, restored the gateway, and built a chapel, 60 by 18 feet, partly the original Guest Chapel. The Guest Hall is the present refectory. Mr. Butterfield was the architect of the Missionary College, which was incorporated June 28, 1848. The new buildings are of flint and Caen stone dressings, and Kentish ragstone. In 1389, King Richard and his queen were guests here for a week; in 1573, Queen Elizabeth kept her court in the abbey ; and King Charles and Henrietta visited it June 12, 1625, as did their son, Charles II., on his way to Lon- don in 1660.

The entrance to the Cathedral is by the Christchurch Gate, built by Prior Goldstone in 1517. On the right hand is the old schoolhouse of the Priory. The Cathedral consists of a SOUTH PORCH, a CENTRAL and two WESTERN TOWERS ; a NAVE of nine bays with aisles ; a CHOIR of six bays, with aisles; a CHOIR TRANSEPT forming an additional bay, with two APSIDAL CHAPELS in each wing, those on the south dedicated to SS. Stephen and Martin; a PRESBYTERY of two bays with aisles; an EASTERN AMBULATORY with aisles; ST. THOMAS' CHAPEL of four bays, apsidal, with a magnificent procession-path and aisles; and to the east the circular À BECKET'S CROWN; on the north of the Chapel of St. Thomas is KING HENRY IVTH'S CHANTRY; on the south of the PRESBYTERY is the apsidal ST. ANSELM'S CHAPEL, on the north is a similar CHAPEL OF ST. ANDREW, opening into the treasury, and the external auditory; to the east of the north wing of the great transept is the LADY CHAPEL, to the east of the south wing ST. MICHAEL'S CHAPEL. From the CHOIR TRANSEPT is a passage to the BAPTISTERY, north of which is the LIBRARY. Parallel with the north side of the north-west transept and Lady Chapel is the CHAPTER-HOUSE, and on the north side of the nave is the CLOISTER; the space southward of the choir formed the Cemetery, or God's acre, sown with the seed of the resurrection; "the Oaks" was the convent garden, the Norman doorway is in the precinct gate eastward of the choir. The ancient stone house on the left side turning round the Becket's Crown formed the Honours, the Guest Hall (a nave and aisles 150 ft. by 40 ft.), for the reception of visitors. Considerable remains of the Infirmary are observable; the Chapel and Common Hall, of flint, with three tall pointed windows, built in 1342. Near it was St. Thomas's well. At this point occurs "the Dark Entry," a Norman cloister built by Prior Wibert about 1167, with a curious bell-shaped tower, which served as the monks' conduit; above it is now the Baptistery. On one side is the gate of the great cloisters. The arch and ruins towards the Green Court are those of La Gloriette, the Prior's rooms built by Prior Hathbrand, 1379. Passing the chapter, once the Prior's chapel library, the Prior's, or Court Gate, leads into the Green Court; on the east side is the Deanery, built by Dean Godwin, 1570, after a fire on the site of the Prior's lodgings. In it Hooper welcomed Queen Mary. At the north-east corner a large gateway opens into the follings, or foreigns, the space beyond the conventual jurisdiction. On the north side, were the ancient Dean's great hall, waterhouse, granary, refectory, frater-house, brew-house, bake-house, and domestic buildings, among which great part of the dormitory remains, with a gateway and steps. At the north-west angle is the Norman precinct gate of the priory, which stood on the south side of the court; the back entrance to it, or Larder Gate, still remains. At the south-west angle is the arched door which led to the palace. The Stranger's Hall was on the west side. In the north-west angle is likewise the Norman staircase, with an open arcade which led into the north hall, 150 ft. by 40 ft., allotted to the stewards of the priory court; the arches on which it was supported alone remain; above them the King's School has been built by Mr. Austen, 1855. They form a passage into the Mint yard. It is the only staircase of the period known to be in existence. In the King's School were educated Harvey, the physician, Lord Thurlow, and Lord Tenterden, who often said, he envied as a boy the lay-clerk's gown, the summit of his ambition! Within the ancient Almonry, on the north-west of the Green Court, stood the chantry of St. Thomas à Becket, which Henry VIII. converted into a mint, and Cardinal Pole made the King's school. In the high wall, probably a portion of Lanfranc's building, leading to the north-west entrance of the Cathedral, are the remains of the covered way to the cloisters, by which the primates entered, but their ordinary approach was through a large gateway with a square tower of flint and ashlar.

No Cathedral presents a more solemn and imposing exterior: the two western towers, full of grandeur and beauty, and the central steeple, one of the most graceful examples of pointed architecture, give dignity to the vast and picturesque pile, grander even now than when it burst upon the view of the motley train of pilgrims to à Becket's shrine, who halted on the neighbouring hill to kneel in devotion, and then to rise and shout for joy at the sight of its beauty.

> A dim and mighty minster of old time,
> A temple shadowy with remembrances
> Of the majestic past.

Within reigns a chastened but sovereign magnificence, every way worthy of the metropolis of the Church of England, and the flights of stairs required, owing to the height of the crypt beneath, add an air of vastness and sublimity to the whole effect. Complete and impressive, the lofty arches, the many-coloured clerestory, the noble simplicity, and grand proportions render it a magnificent spectacle to the eye, darkling in the soft calm twilight till it grows accustomed to gaze. Gostling says he has seen the eyes of the negroes, whom American colonists brought with them, sparkle with admiration at the view. No church in England has gathered about it greater historical recollections, or possesses more numerous accessories of ancient state. The church, first built on this site by St. Augustine, suffered great injury from the Danes in 938, and still more by a fire in 1067. Lanfranc, archbishop 1070-86, completed a new building, on the same plan and with the same dimensions as the church at Caen where he had been prior, of which Anselm, archbishop 1093-1109, with Ernulph and Conrad the priors, enlarged the choir and built the CHOIR TRANSEPT, western portion of the CRYPT or undercroft, the largest, finest, and most interesting in England, measuring 163 by 83 ft. 6 in., and chapels of SS. Anselm, Andrew, and the Holy Trinity. William Corboyl, 1123-36, restored the church after a fire in 1130; once more a fire destroyed the choir, September 5, 1174, which was rebuilt by William of Sens 1175-8, who, owing to a fall from a scaffold, was compelled to return to France; the TRINITY CHAPEL, eastern part of the CRYPT and BECKET's CROWN were rebuilt by William the Englishman, 1179-84. The latter was possibly erected on the site of the ancient circular Baptistery and Tomb-house of the Saxon primates, and occasionally used as a Chapter-room. It bears some similarity to the east end of the Marien Kirche, at Lubeck. The stone enclosure of the CHOIR, 14 ft. high, was built by Henry de Estria, prior

1304-5; and in 1363, the Chantry of the Black Prince in the crypt. Simon Sudbury, 1376-82, commenced the rebuilding of the NAVE and MAIN TRANSEPT, with St. Michael's Chapel, (the architect was Chillinden, prior 1376-1410,) and built the west gate. The NAVE was continued by William Courtenay, 1382-97; Thomas Arundel, 1397-1414, gave a peal of five bells to the north-west BELL TOWER or Arundel steeple, which was rebuilt in 1840; the NAVE was completed in 1400; the CLOISTERS and CHAPTER-HOUSE were in progress, and the chantry of Henry IV. erected in 1412. The vaulting of the CHAPTER-HOUSE was set up between 1391 and 1411. Prior Goldstone, 1449-68, built the LADY CHAPEL, and completed the south-west Chichele or Oxford, formerly St. Dunstan's, tower. Selling, prior in 1472, completed the central Angel or BELL HARRY TOWER, as it has been variously called, from the bell or a gilded angel standing on one of the pinnacles now lost. It is the glory of all towers, of two stages with two two-light windows, transomed in each face, the lower tier being canopied, combined in one superb and harmonious structure, surrounded by octagonal turrets at each angle. Prior Goldstone II., about 1495, added the two buttressing arches, and ornamental braces beneath it. The great Dunstan bell, recast by Mears, weighs three tons ten hundredweight.

The WESTERN FRONT is flanked by two towers: in that upon the south, the Chichele steeple, over the porch is a central niche, in which was represented St. Thomas à Becket's martyrdom, on a panel of the 15th century; it is now the Bell Tower: from the northern or Arundel steeple (which was rebuilt in 1840 by Mr. G. Austin at a cost of 25,000l.), a leaden spire, 100 feet in height, was removed in August 1705. The WESTERN WINDOW is of seven lights, with three transoms; the WEST TOWERS are each of six stages, with two two-light canopied windows in each of the two upper tiers on the front, but three on the sides, and a large four-light window below ranging with those of the aisle; the base tier like the buttresses has rich panelling. The parapet is battlemented. There are four large double

pinnacles at the angles. In the gable is a peculiarly-shaped
window filled with intricate tracery, over a deeply recessed
and niched porch. Above the aisle windows are quatrefoiled
squares, the clerestory consists of three-light windows.
The MAIN TRANSEPT has a Perpendicular 8-light window with
panelling in the gable, and a pinnacled octagonal west
turret; the front of the choir transept is Norman, with
arcades, a large round window, and three lights in the
gable. The west turret is arcaded and crowned with a
short spire. The clerestory, as in the choir and à Becket's
Crown, consists of lancets. The south side of the Cathedral is by far the most picturesque and perfect, as seen from
the Green Court. The NAVE of eight bays has no triforium. Each bay consists of a huge arch resting on
filleted pillars, this is subdivided into the pier arch with
the clerestory, and panelling reaching to the string-course
above. It is paved with Portland stone. The roof under
the lantern was painted in fresco by Mrs. Austin. The
vaulting and vaulting shafts are the prominent features of
the nave, and the pier arches are quite subordinate; these
shafts are banded, as at Bath, like Early English. The
MAIN TRANSEPT has no aisles. The north wing bears the
name of the Martyrdom, the site of the murder of St.
Thomas à Becket, near St. Benedict's apsidal chapel, (now
built over by the Dean's chapel,) Dec. 29, 1177, while
vespers were being sung. The west door at the cloisters
by which he entered, and the Caen pavement by the wall
on which he fell, remain. The Primate was mounting the
stairs to the north aisle, now removed, to seat himself in
his patriarchal chair, when the knights seized him; he then
clung to the pillar awhile, but fell on the spot, now noted
by a square stone, under the blows of their swords. The
handkerchief stained with his blood is in the church of
St. Maria Maggiore at Rome. In 1299 at its altar Edward 1.
was married to Queen Margaret. The soft and silvery
glazing of the north window was given by Edward IV.:
to the eastward is the LADY CHAPEL, parted off by a
beautiful canopied screen. The stone roof is exquisitely
carved. The south window of the MAIN TRANSEPT is filled

up with portions of old French glass. A chapel on the east of the south wing is that of St. Michael; above it is a parvise built in the 15th century. The CHOIR of five bays offers the earliest instance of the pointed arch in England, as well as of groining on a large scale, owing to a French influence at the moment when the native architects were working out a complete round-arched style, like that of Germany. It is approached by noble flights of stairs: the screen, of the 15th century, has been recently restored with its niched imagery of founders and saints. The clerestory of the choir is filled with stained glass, representing our Saviour's genealogy. The carvings on the stalls were wrought by Grinling Gibbons. The triforium has shafts of Petworth marble; the disuse of this material and Purbeck and Bethersden in the succeeding styles is attributed to their liability to flaw, when set in a perpendicular position. The crimson velvet on the altar was the gift of Queen Mary II.; a chalice was presented by an Earl of Arundel in 1636. The reredos was set up by Mr. G. Austen, in the decanate of Hon. H. Percy, late Bishop of Carlisle. Some of the tapestry-hangings, given by Prior Goldstone (1494-1517) for the choir, are now used on festivals in the cathedral of Aix in Provence. In 1643 a Puritan, nicknamed Blue Dick, one Richard Culmer, with a body of fanatics, demolished much of the stained glass; the brasses were destroyed, and the monuments injured, while the nave was the barrack of the ribald soldiers of the Commonwealth, who committed great excesses. In 1641, at Epiphany tide, the Puritans wreaked their profanity and sacrilege on the choir and monuments. In 1660, 12,000*l*., were required to fit the church for the decent celebration of divine service. The throne, a gift of Archbishop Howley, cost 1200*l*: it was carved by Flemish workmen from the designs of Mr. Austen. The stone pulpit, by Butterfield of London, was put up in 1846. The eagle is dated 1663: it is used as a litany desk, while the lessons, as at Wells and Westminster, are read from the stalls. The organ was rebuilt by Samuel Green, and used at the Handel Festival in Westminster Abbey in 1784; removed from the screen to the south triforium in 1827, and enlarged by Hill, 1842. In this cathedral Archbishop Theodore first introduced the ecclesiastical chant. In the choir are pointed arches: the triforium consists of two round arches in each bay, each subdivided into two pointed arches. In the Trinity Chapel the lower pillars are round, and the triforium is an arcade of lancets, the clerestory in both is an arcade of threefold arrangement in each bay, a broad window between two narrow lancets. In the CHOIR TRANSEPT the triforium has round windows in an arcade of lancets over a similar range. On the wall of the north choir transept is a fragment of a fresco of the conversion of St. Hubert.

In the apse, approached by broad flights of stairs, is St. Thomas' (formerly the TRINITY CHAPEL), surrounded by a double arcade of columns, with arches pointed where the span is narrow, more rounded where it is wider. There is a curious mosaic pavement in it, with the signs of the zodiac, in white marble, serpentine, and porphyry, brought from St. Augustine's Abbey. It resembles those French labyrinthine pavements which were supposed to represent the temple of Jerusalem, and were marked with stations to supply the place of a pilgrimage to the Holy Land. It contained the sumptuous shrine of St. Thomas à Becket, whose wealth of jewels and blaze of gorgeous splendour dazzled the eyes of Erasmus, before which he says Midas and Crœsus would have seemed beggars. The primate's body was translated hither with considerable pomp, July 7, 1220, in the presence of the king. A crescent of some foreign wood on the roof, in allusion to his mother's Saracenic birth, stands over the site of his shrine. To this tomb great numbers of pilgrims came, especially at the times of jubilee: seven such festivals were held, the latest in 1520. In 1177, at his former grave, was held the meeting of Philip, Count of Flanders, with Henry III., who again on his return from Normandy in 1178 and 1180 visited the Cathedral, and in 1180 received Louis VII. of France, who made splendid offerings to the church. In 1184, with the Archbishop of Cologne and Count Philip, he knelt once more before the grave of the archbishop. King Richard I. coming afoot from Sandwich, offered his thanksgivings here on his release from his Austrian dungeon 1194. Henry V. came on his return from Agincourt ; Emmanuel, emperor of the east, in 1400; Sigismund, the emperor of the west, in 1417 ; and Henry VIII. with Charles V. at Pentecost 1520. In April, 1538, Henry VIII. for thirty days directed a summons to à Becket to appear to answer for high treason. The miserable farce ended in the despot wearing the regal jewel of the shrine as a thumb-ring. Edward I. in 1299, offered here the crown of Scotland. The steps are worn into hollows by the knees of the pilgrims. At the shrine was always offered one of the state canopies borne by the barons of the Cinque ports at a coronation.

The eastern extremity, of circular form, is the Crown of à Becket. Some decayed frescoes are on the walls. It contained the patriarchal or metropolitan choir, of grey marble, once the throne of the pagan kings of Kent, in which the archbishops are enthroned, recently removed to the south-east transept : the primates anciently sat here during the communion service, until after the consecration of the sacred elements, when they removed into the choir,—a tradition drawn from their place in the old Byzantine churches, where the altar stood in front of the clergy in the chord of the apse. The triforium has two pointed arches with lozengy mouldings, and a broad pointed window in the clerestory of each bay : the piers have lozengy and chevron mouldings. The stained glass of the east window is of the 13th century. In the south aisle of the choir, divided off by the screen of Archbishop Meopham's monument, is the chapel (anciently that of SS. Peter and Paul) and tower of St. Anselm, with a window built by Prior Oxendon, 1336; above is a cell with a grated window commanding a view of the high altar ; it is believed to have been used as a place of imprisonment for the monks, and as a watching chamber of the shrine. King John of France is, traditionally, said to have been immured in it. During fires, ban-dogs were employed as guards of the shrine. In the choir, according to the romance of King Arthur, the brave knight Sir Gawain, who fell at the landing upon Dover shore, was buried. Westward of this chapel is the CHOIR TRANSEPT, the two apses were the chapels of SS. Stephen and Martin. The south apsidal chapels were those of SS. John and Gregory, and in them were once the tombs of four Saxon primates. In the north aisle of the apse is King Henry IV.'s chantry, with rich fan tracery in the vault. In the north aisle of the choir, corresponding to St. Anselm's, is St. Andrew's Chapel: a flight of stairs leads to the audit-room in St. Andrew's Tower, which again opens into the Treasury or Great Armoury, formerly the sacristy, and now the place in which the charters and muniments are kept; above these rooms are the chambers once used for signing and sealing deeds. Two beautiful stained-glass windows are in the north aisle.

From the NORTH-EASTERN TRANSEPT the former monks' passage to the priory leads into a circular chamber now used as a baptistery, in which stands a font the gift of Bishop Warner of Rochester, 1787; it was called Bell Jesus, because formed on the model of a bell lost at sea on its passage from Rome. To the right is the library, and to the left the entry of the cloisters of eight bays on every side. On the north side is a range of stone seats, divided by shafts of stone and covered with canopied niches. The panes are mullioned, and the stone roof groined with seven hundred shields on the bosses. On the east side is a rich doorway leading to the dormitory, and at the west end of the south alley is the entrance to the Primate's palace. A door on the west opened into the cellarer's apartments. The library was erected on the site of the prior's chapel, with the original ambulatory beneath, which led into the circular Norman baptistery, seventeen feet in diameter. The CHAPTER-HOUSE is approached from the east walk, and has a trefoiled arcade canopied on the east, a large seven-light window, and a roof of Irish oak. It was built in 1264, repaired in 1304, and the upper part rebuilt in the

15th century. From the Martyrdom a flight of steps
conducts into the UNDER-CROFT, of which the south aisle
under St. Anselm's Tower has been the meeting-house of
Walloon and French Huguenots since 1568, when their
looms were set up in the crypt, in consideration of the
introduction of silk weaving, first practised by Walloons
here. It was the scene of the severe penance and flagel-
lation of Henry II. after the murder of à Becket ! he
received five strokes from each prelate and abbot, and
three from every one of the eighty monks. Ten archbishops are buried in this crypt, dark and obscure like
sepulchral recesses. Under the choir transept is the
Chantry of the Black Prince, founded by him, 1366, on his
marriage. The central chapel of St. Mary Under-croft has
Perpendicular stone parcloses. St. John's Chapel is to the
east of the Black Prince's chapel, with an inner chamber
to secrete the sacred vessels and relics in times of alarm.

Stained glass has been profusely introduced. On the
north side of the choir is a memorial window to Archbishop Howley by Willement. The triplet in the south
choir aisle is by Wailes : in the aisle of the Presbytery,
south side, two windows were contributed by Dean Lyell.
In the east chapel of the north CHOIR TRANSEPT is a
memorial to Canon Spry, and in the west window of the
tower, in the south aisle of the nave, a similar tribute
to Sir Robert Inglis. The Messrs. Austen have given
windows in the north-west tower, in the clerestory of the
nave, the subject being angels ; and commenced a series
of English kings on the north side of the nave, and kings,
queens, and prophets, in the south aisle.

> What awful perspective ! while from our sight
>   With gradual stealth the lateral windows hide
>   Their portraitures : the stone-work glimmers, dyed
> In the soft chequerings of a sleepy night.

The iron-work of the windows is very observable for
their elegance and variety of pattern. Gondomar, the
Spanish ambassador, offered for one of the three 13th
century windows, in the aisle of the Trinity chapel, its

weight in gold, or as many golden broad pieces as would completely cover its surface. The subjects are miracles of à Becket. The general use of stained glass, which, like frescoes, formed the books of the unlearned, was one cause of the introduction of decorated tracery for its more effective setting.

The principal monuments are the following :—

Nave.—Bishop Broughton, of Sidney; effigy by Lough, in a cope.

Undercroft, Lady Chapel.—Archbishop Morton, d. 1500, effigy; Joan Lady Mohun of Dunster, d. 1395, effigy; Isabel, Countess of Athol, d. 1292, effigy; Archbishop à-Becket, stone screen of his early shrine.

Nave, N. Aisle.—Hadrian Saravia, the friend of Hooker; Orlando Gibbons the musician; Sir John Boys, d. 1612, effigy; Admiral Sir G. Rooke, the conqueror of Gibraltar.

N. W. Transept.—Archbishop Peckham, d. 1292, altar-tomb with imagery in niches, effigy of Irish oak under a rich pedimented canopy; Archbishop Warham, d. 1534, effigy under a chantry-like canopy. In this wing were buried Archbishops Stafford and Dean.

S. W. Transept.—W. Shuckford, author of " The Connection," etc., a slab.

Lady Chapel.—James Wedderburn, bishop of Dunblane, flat stone. In it two long plain stones overlie the graves of archbishops Islip and Arundel.

St. Michael's Chapel.—Archbishop Langton, d. 1230,—slab with a floriated cross, only the head appears through the wall; the altar stood over it. Margaret Holland, d. 1449, and her two husbands, John Marquess of Dorset, d. 1409, and Thomas Duke of Clarence, d. 1421, of a wound received at Beaugy,—effigies.

St. Thomas's, or Trinity Chapel.—King Henry IV., d. 1413, and Queen Joan of Navarre, effigies; Edward the Black Prince d. 1376, effigy under a flat testoon, his gauntlet, surcoat, and scabbard above it; the iron railing with various devices is the original closure; Cromwell stole the sword. Archbishop Courtenay, d. 1397, effigy and altar-tomb; Archbishop Theobald, d. 1160, a shrine; Dean Wotton, effigy by Banim; Odo Coligny the Huguenot; Cardinal Chastilion, d. 1571, from eating a poisoned apple, coped tomb.

Becket's Crown.—Cardinal Pole, d. 1558, plain tomb.

Choir, S. Side.—Archbishop Sudbury, beheaded 1381, noble canopied monument; Archbishop Stratford, d. 1341, canopy, altar-tomb, and effigy; Archbishop Kempe, d. 1454, altar-tomb and an elaborate wooden tester. The diaper on the south side, from its similarity to the tracery in the window of St. Anselm's Chapel, probably of the date 1330, still marks the site of St. Dunstan's shrine. That of St. Alphege was on the north side.

Before St. Anselm's Chapel.—Archbishop Meopham, d. 1333, coped tomb, with an open and very beautiful screen with sculptures. In the chapel St. Anselm was buried, 1109.

Under S. Window.—Archbishop Bradwardine, d. 1349, raised tomb.

Choir, N. Side.—Archbishop Bourchier, d. 1486, raised tomb of Bethersden marble under an arch; Archbishop Chichele, founder of All Souls' College, Oxford, d. 1444, raised tomb, screen with imagery and effigy and cadaver, restored in polychrome, 1846; Archbishop Howley, effigy in a cope by Westmacott.

South Choir Aisle.—Archbishop Hubert Walter, d. 1215, effigy and altar-tomb, Archbishop Walter Reynold, d. 1327, effigy, both of alabaster.

N. E Angle, S. E. Aisle.—Archbishop Winchilsea, d. 1313; the site marked by broken shafts.

The bodies of St. Blaze, St. Wilfred, and St. Audoen of Rouen were buried in different chantries.

On Feb. 11, 1850, their old colours were set up in the south aisle over a memorial to H.M. 31st regiment, by Richardson. In the north aisle are suspended the colours of the 3rd Buffs, and some Affghan flags captured by H.M. 50th regiment,—a beautiful tribute to Him who is Lord of Hosts as well as Prince of Peace. Inglethorpe, Bishop of Rochester, was buried here.

DIMENSIONS OF THE CATHEDRAL IN FEET.

	Length.	Breadth.	Height.
Nave	178	71	80
Choir	180	40	71
Great Transept	124	..	..
Choir Transept	154	..	..
Central Tower	35 square	..	235
Chichele Tower	..	..	130
Arundel Tower	..	..	130
Cloisters	144 by 144		..
Chapter-house	87	35	52
Total length	514	..	..

The Chapter consists of a dean and six canons, six stalls

having been suspended; there are six minor canons, six preachers, twelve lay-clerks, and ten choristers. The library contains 6000 volumes. There are two daily choral services, at 10 and 3. The Holy Communion is administered weekly. The total income of the Chapter in 1852 was 25,211*l.* Their expenditure in repairs within 14 years amounted to 31,960*l.*; and since 1823 to 100,000*l.* wholly from capitular revenues. The archiepiscopal palaces are at Lambeth and Addington.

Among the eminent metropolitans are found the Saints Augustine and Dunstan, famous in art ; the accomplished Theodore, Lanfranc, Anselm, who first enforced the celibacy of the clergy ; Pascal II., saluted as the pope of the other world ; the martyred à Becket, princely Langton, learned Bradwardine, exiled Langham ; Chichele, founder of All Souls' College, Oxford ; gentle Warham, unhappy Cranmer, gentle-hearted Cardinal Pole ; and Parker, Whitgift, Laud, and Sancroft—one a martyr, the other deprived for his principles ; Wake, Tillotson, Tenison, and Secker : a glorious gallery of historic portraits. Then among monks or dignitaries appear the names of two popes, Adrian V. and Gregory XI., three Cardinals, Feringes Archbishop of Dublin, Tenison and virulent Bale of Ossory, Osbern the "English Jubal ;" Eadmar, Gervase, Thorn, and R. D'Avesbury, historians ; Dean Stanhope, Hadrian Saravia, J. Casaubon, J. G. Vossius, S. Shuckford, C. Elstob the Anglo-Saxonist, and Earl Nelson.

Arms : Az. on a cross, arg., the letter X surmounted by the letter I sable.

,Carlisle.

CARLISLE, a contraction of Caer-llu-gwell, ("The City of the Army by the Wall,") stands finely situated on a considerable eminence, at the confluence of three rivers—the Eden, Caldew, and Petrel. "Merry Carlisle" is poetical from its associations with King Arthur's Court, Albert Græme's lady love, Adam Bell, Clym of the Clough, William of Cloudeslee, and King Arthur in the Bridal of Trierman; and romantic in its history as a border town, for siege and inroad, march and countermarch, foray on the Scottish border, and sharp spurring in reprisal to sweep off the cattle grazing beneath its moated wall; the object of attack by William the Lion of Scotland, in Leslie's rebellion, by Scot, and Roundhead, and Cavalier, and the last of the Stuarts proclaimed King by the corporation in their robes. The hills beyond Inglewood forest, Skiddaw, Helvellyn, and Crossfell, form the background to a luxuriant plain, laced by the three rivers silver white; and from the castle keep can be seen Solway Frith, Burgh-on-the-Sands, where Edward I. died in his harness, and Way Church and Brunswick Hill in Scotland. The keep of the castle was built by Rufus, augmented by David I. of Scotland, 1135, and is famous for the rescue of Kinmont Willie by Scott of Buccleuch: under its gate rested one night the heroic Sir William Wallace. Only a small staircase remains of the royal palace in Carlisle Castle, the hall having been destroyed in 1827, and the chapel in 1835 desecrated into barracks. From the gate-house Waverley watched Fergus Mac Ivor go out to execution. The tower in which he stood was the prison of Mary queen of Scots, 1568, and bore her name. The following kings have visited Carlisle: Rufus, 1094; Henry I., 1122; Edward I., 1298 (in Parliament), and 1306, and again in parliament 1307; Edward II. in 1307; and Edward III. in 1335. King David of Scotland died here 1153.

The Cathedral is dedicated to the Holy Trinity. It was the abbey of a monastery of Austin Canons. It is rich and delicate in display of detail; and of whatever disappointment the unfinished exterior is the cause, yet within, the greater the attention, the closer the examination which is bestowed upon it, the more admiration will this church call forth; fresh beauties will ever be unfolding themselves, and the foot will be the more loth to quit the choir the longer the visitor with eye unsated lingers at the threshold. In 1639 it appeared to great disadvantage, "like a great wild country church, outwardly, so was it inwardly neither beautified nor adorned one whit. The organ and voices did well agree, the one being like a shrill bagpipe, the other like the Scottish tune ; the sermon in the like accent. The communion was received in a wild and irreverent manner." The visitor now will grieve over the loss of the nave, which has marred a superb and admirable structure, and recall the fine lines as he looks on the remnant that survives :—

> Oh ! for the help of angels to complete
> This temple angels governed by a plan;
> How gloriously pursued by darling man,
> Studious that HE might not disdain the seat
> Who dwells in Heaven ! 'twere an office meet
> For you on these unfinished shafts to try
> The midnight virtues of your harmony :
> This vast design might tempt you to repeat
> Strains that call forth upon empyreal ground
> Immortal fabrics, rising to the sound
> Of penetrating harps and voices sweet.

The TRANSEPT and NAVE are of the simplest and most massive Norman type, and built of coarse red freestone, quarried probably at Rickerby, by Walter, governor of Carlisle, in the reign of Henry I., 1092-1101. The CHOIR (like the tower built of red sandstone) was commenced in the episcopate of Sylvester de Everdon, 1247-54 ; and continued by Bishops Welton, 1352-62, and Thomas of Appleby, 1363-96, after a disastrous fire in 1292. The upper part of the central tower was erected by William Strickland, bishop 1400-19. The door on the south side of the choir and tabernacle-work were built by Prior Haithwaite, 1382-1433, and the opposite door by Prior Senhouse in 1507, whose motto it bears :—

> " Vulnera V Dei
> Sint medicina mihi."

The projecting canopy over the entrance of the choir was added about 1250. The organ-screen is of the time of

Bishop Percy, 1452-62; the stalls are of the period of Edward III. The cinque-cento screen, north of the choir, was built by Leonard Salkeld, prior, in 1542-47: in it portions of Gondiber's screen are inserted. The Scots, under General Leslie, destroyed the greater portion of the nave, dormitory, chapter-house, and cloisters, to erect guardhouses and batteries in June 1645.

The TOWER is not in the centre of the transept; it contains a peal of six bells (one the gift of Bishop Strickland), and is divided into two stories; the first has two windows, each of two lights; the second has one of three lights Decorated on each face; at the north-east angle is an engaged turret.

The east front of the CHOIR contains a Decorated window of nine lights, 48 ft. high by 30 ft. in breadth, with rich tracery in the top, the most superb in England; the arch probably the work of Bishop Welton. The lower part is of the time of Edward II.; the stained glass, representing the general resurrection, is of the time of Richard II. Artistic, easy in design, admirably adapted to its constructive position, and harmoniously balanced, it takes the highest rank as a master-piece for dexterity of handling and perfection in execution. Above it is a triangular window with foliated tracery. The gable is surmounted with a cross. Gigantic buttresses, with statues, SS. Mary, Peter and Paul, James and John, in niches, and lofty crocketed pinnacles, flank it. The aisles are lighted by triplets; but some of the windows are large, and have tracery Decorated or Perpendicular. The parapet is plain. The buttresses are shallow. The clerestory has none. The windows are in combination of threes, and filled with Decorated tracery.

The Norman NAVE, of which two out of eight bays remain, since 1813 has been used as the parish church of St. Mary. The arches of the nave, built c. 1100, are cylindrical, 14 ft. 2 in. high, but 17 ft. 6 in. in circumference. The windows are round-headed in the nave. The clerestory and triforium were built 1140-50.

The TRANSEPT is of two bays; the north wing had an

apse. The south wing has an eastern chapel. The north
wing was rebuilt, after a fire, by Bishop Strickland, in
1401. It is narrow, small, and plain. The ceiling is of
wood, in square compartments once richly paiuted. The
north window of the transept is of six lights, Perpendicular. Two wells are in the transepts—one in the wall of
the south transept is 25 ft. deep, the other near the north-
east tower-pier is oval, 3 ft. 7 in. by 3 ft. 2 in., built of
ashlar, and 45 ft. deep.. They were made to drain a
spring which runs through the transept, and had caused
a settlement of the Norman work. The south transept
was built c. 1100 ; the clerestory added 1140-50. Fragments of the square Norman font are built into the walls.
There is no crypt.

The CHOIR, Early English, composed of eight bays, divided by clustered columns, with sculptured capitals of
leaves and flowers, and ball-flowers in the mouldings, has
a triforium of three pointed arches, trefoiled and of two
lights in each bay with a string-course above and below.
Over the triforium rises a lofty clerestory, likewise of three
pointed arches, and beneath the windows is a gallery,
pierced with quatrefoils : both are of the latter part of
the 14th century. The easternmost bay is of the period
of Edward II. The curious fact that old arches rest upon
later pillars is accounted for by the re-use of old materials
in the reconstruction of the latter in the 14th century.
They were enriched with red roses and gold monograms
by Prior Gondiber. The vaulting of the aisles and arcades
is of the 13th century.

Great restorations were commenced by Mr. Christian,
under the decanate of Dr. Tait, now Bishop of London,
at a cost of 15,000*l.* He discovered in 1855 a cross of the
7th century built into the south transept in 1300, and a
curious fresco on the north-east pier of the tower. The
unique hammer-beam roof completed by Bishop Appleby,
which had been plastered over in 1764, when the ancient
bishop's throne was destroyed, was opened and coloured
by T. Pyffers, under the direction of Owen Jones ; the
transept roof was raised, and in the north wing a Deco-

rated window inserted. Repairs are being conducted by Mr. Purday.

The organ, by Avery of London, was set up in 1806. Water power was in 1858 applied to the bellows. The engine is under the immediate control of the organist by suitable gearing which leads to the valves of the cistern. The font is hexagonal.

From the south aisle a chapel projects ; St. Katherine's Chapel (now the choristers' vestry) has a screen with the initials of T. Gondiber, prior, c. 1484, and adjoins the east wall of the south transept. In this chapel are preserved three almeries, a helmet of the 14th century, two ancient copes, and the well-known ivory horn given by Henry I. to the priory. The destruction of vestments at the Reformation is very remarkable ; St. Paul's had 128, Lincoln 250, and York 320 suits, of which not one remains. Such was the beauty of English embroidery-work, that in the reign of Henry III., Pope Innocent IV. sent bulls to the bishops to send a considerable quantity to Rome. In the choir aisles are curious legendary paintings of SS. Cuthbert, Anthony, and Augustine, of the time of Prior Gondiber. On the tower-piers legendary stories were painted.

Prince Charles Edward, in 1745, during his occupation of the city, installed Thomas Coppock, a clergyman of Lancashire, openly in the cathedral, which subsequently was made the prison of the garrison by the butcher Duke of Cumberland.

The principal monuments are—

Bishop Law.
Choir.—Richard Bell, bishop, d. 1496, a superb brass ; Henry Robinson, d. 1616, brass.
N. Aisle.—Archdeacon Paley ; Bishops Sylvester de Everdon, d. 1254, effigy ; Appleby, d. 1365, stone coffin ; Halton, d. 1324, effigy.
S. Aisle.—Sir T. Skelton, temp. Henry V., arched recess.
St. Catharine's Chapel.—Bishop Welton, d. 1362, tomb and effigy.
N. Transept.—Altar-tomb of Prior Senhouse, on which certain rents were paid ; Chancellor Fletcher, memorial window.

DIMENSIONS OF THE CATHEDRAL IN FEET.

	Length.	Breadth.	Height.
Nave	{ 43 former- ly 135 }	..	..
Choir	140 ft.	72	72
Transept	113 f. 2in.	21 ft. 2 in	..
Tower	..	..	127
Total length	219		

The Chapter consists of a dean and four canons. There are two minor canons, eight lay vicars, and eight choristers. Choral service is sung twice daily, at 10 and 3, and the Holy Communion is administered monthly. The capitular income is 6698*l.* a-year. The library contains 3174 volumes. The repairs have cost 15,000*l.*

Arms: Arg. on a cross sable, a mitre of the field.

Carlisle, Oxford, and Bristol, were the only chapters of Austin Canons whose churches became cathedrals. Carlisle numbers among its bishops Sylvester de Everdon, Lord Chancellor; the brave John de Kirkby, the soldier-bishop, who routed stout Earl Douglas in battle; Thomas Merks, whose fidelity to his fallen master, Richard II., is familiar to readers of Shakspeare; Oglethorpe, who in Bonner's borrowed mitre and robes had the courage to crown Queen Elizabeth; the learned Usher, who with his failing eyes followed the sunshine from room to room; and Nicholson. Among its dignitaries appear Dean Smalridge, who "carried a bucket here to quench the flames which Atterbury had kindled;" the Erastian Paley; and Percy, Bishop of Dromore, who here caught his love for reliques of Border-minstrelsy.

The Abbey gateway was built by Christopher Slee, 1528. The tower of the deanery was restored, and the magnificent roof in it erected by Simon Senhouse, prior, 1507. It has a curious square-headed oriel of the 15th century. The refectory, which is 100 ft. long by 32 ft. broad, was built by Thomas Gondibour, prior 1484-1501; it is used as a library, chapter-house, and school. At the end is an ancient stone confessional. Beneath is a crypt. The entrance from the cloister into the church still exists.

The episcopal palace is at Rose Castle.

Chester.

Queer, quaint old Chester,
Grotesque and honest art thou sure,
And so behind this very changeful day,
So fond of antique fashions, it would seem
Thou must have slept an age or two away.
Thy very streets are galleries. . . .
Old Rome was once thy guest, beyond a doubt,
And thou dost hoard her gifts with pride and care,
As erst the Grecian dame displayed her jewels rare.

CHESTER (Ceaster, "the Camp"), built, according to the enthusiastic Sir Thomas Eliot, by a great-grandson of Noah, was a Roman station of Agricola's XXth Legion, and is situated on the Dee. The ground-plan preserves the form of the camp—a parallelogram with four gates, the four streets crossing in the centre. It was the border-fortress of Edward I., the loyal stronghold of Charles I. ; and contains —a circumstance unique in an English city except London, and only paralleled in Dublin and Rome—two cathedrals, St. John's having at one time served as the church of the see of Lichfield.

The walls of Chester are complete, three-quarters of a mile in circuit, and of mouldering sandstone, Roman at the base: the towers were built 1307. At the north-east angle, on the old circular wall, built in the reign of Edward I., is built the Phœnix-tower, so called from the crest of a city company. The room above was built in 1618 : from it Charles I. watched the battle of Rowton Moor, Sept. 24, 1645. On the north-west, approached by Bonwaldesthorne Turret, is the Water-tower, built 1322 by John Helpstone. It is now fitted up as a Museum. At a remote period ships came up the Dee, at high-tide, and lay moored under this tower. A house, the only one spared in the plague, bears the inscription,—"God's providence is mine inheritance." The Castle has Roman vaulting, Norman walls, and an Early English, or Late Norman, gatehouse and chapel. The Stanley House, or old Palace, is dated 1591. Bishop Lloyd's house, 1615, has sculptures of Scriptural subjects. The prospect from the walls of the quaint houses—gnarled, wrinkled, honeycombed, fancifully carved gables and galleried rows built back over the cellars ; and the Dee Bridge, built 1280, with the vale of the Dee, curved like a silver belt, and historic Caernarvon beyond, and the blue hazy line of the Welsh mountains in the distance,—is very striking. The site of the town is an irregular bed of sandstone ; the vaults half underground may have been built to fill up the hollows. The substructures are chiefly of the 13th century ; the houses are not earlier than the reign of Elizabeth. The Roodeye meadow below was the place of tournaments, and derived its name of Cross Island from a rood that was visible on it only at flood-tide. A crypt of the 13th century still remains in Bridge Street. On one of the neighbouring hills prayed the monks of Bangor, in the battle between the Welsh and Ethelfrith, slain to a man by the pagan Northumbrians from superstitious fears.

Bishop Wilson was educated at Chester. Randle Holmes and Sir John Vanbrugh were natives. Royal visits have been paid to Chester by Henry VII., in 1156 ; John, 1212 ; Henry III., gathering his nobles against Llewellyn, 1260 ; Edward I., marching to the conquest of Wales, 1274-1276, 1294 ; Queen Eleanor, 1284 ; Edward II., 1312 ; the Black Prince, 1353 ; Richard II., 1394 ; Margaret of Anjou, to rouse her Lancastrians, 1455 ; Henry VI., 1470; Henry VII., 1495 ; Prince Arthur, 1499 ; James I., 1617 ; Charles I., retreating from Benton Heath ; James II., 1687. Richard II. was led a prisoner through its streets, 1399. The Welsh, 1300, did homage here to Prince Edward of Caernarvon.

The Collegiate Church of St. John Baptist, founded by King Ethelred in the 7th century, was in 960 part of the monastery, to which, from his own palace, King Edgar compelled the eight tributary Scotch and Welsh princes sullenly to row his royal barge upon the Dee,—Kinerd of the Scots, Malcolm the Cambrian, Macchus the pirate, and the Welsh Dufual Griffith, Howel Jacob, and Indethal. The present church was commenced by Peter, Bishop of Lichfield, as his cathedral, in 1075 ; in it he was buried 1086. The Early Norman part, the massive piers, and semicircular arches of the nave, were built 1067-95 ; the triforium and clerestory above them belong to the end of the 12th century. The fall of the great tower crushed the choir ; the northern tower fell and destroyed the west end of the nave : the south, originally Norman, was cased, and the upper part built in the time of Henry VII. The porch is Early English.

It was a tradition related by Giraldus that King Harold escaped from the battle of Hastings, and died here as a recluse. Earl Randle, being surrounded by the Welch at Ruddlan Castle, was relieved by his constable Roger de Lacy at the head of an army of harpers, gleemen, and minstrels, hastily collected during St. Werburgh's fair. Until 1756, on St. John Baptist's Day, the anniversary of the earl's release, all the musicians of the county, under some gay young Dutton, went in procession to St. John's church. In February fair-time, a glove is hung out on St. Peter's tower, as the symbol of the staple trade, one fortnight before and during the fair, as a sign that persons not freemen may carry on their trade and sell their wares without let or hindrance.

The Benedictine Abbey of St. Werburgh, irregular and heavy, built of the crumbling, ragged, red sandstone of the country, was founded in 1053 for Benedictine monks by Hugh Lupus, Earl of Chester. In 1211 the choir and central tower, and a great portion of the church, were completed after repairs which occupied ten years ; the inroads of the Welsh had so impoverished the monastery.

In 1263, William de la Zouch, Justiciary, occupied the Abbey with soldiers! the monks and nobles were constantly at feud ; but in 1284 the king's court of Westminster ruled in favour of Abbot Simon de Whitchurch ; and Edward I. directed Reginald de Grey to supply venison from the forest of Wirall and Delamere, to feed the monks while they were rebuilding their church.

The Cathedral consists of a central and south-west tower, a NAVE of seven bays, with aisles ; a south porch ; a CHOIR of five bays, with aisles ; a LADY CHAPEL of three bays, with aisles of two bays ; a SOUTH TRANSEPT of five bays, with aisles ; a NORTH TRANSEPT of one bay, with a SACRISTY on the east ; on the north side is a VESTIBULE, opening eastward into a CHAPTER-HOUSE of three bays. On the north of the nave is the CLOISTER, with the REFEC-TORY on the north side.

The West front consists of an eight-light and canopied Perpendicular window, with a band of elaborate tracery succeeded by ordinary tracery of the period in the head, set between two banded octagonal turrets, which are bat-tlemented. The west door is peculiar : it consists of an arch under a square head, with foliated spandrils and a range of angels in the mouldings, deeply recessed under a larger arch with another square head. On each side are four crocketed niches, with pedestals denuded of their statues. To the west is a four-light canopied window, under a panelled band, and flanked by a rich but empty niche on either side. The door of the south porch is Tudor, with two two-light square-headed windows, and a canopied niche, and an intervening rich band. The win-dows of the aisle and clerestory of the nave are Perpendi-cular ; the parapet is shallow. The south transept, as long as the choir and as broad as the nave, has a Perpendicular clerestory and south windows, the former of four-lights and with two transoms. The windows of the aisles are Late Decorated, and of four lights, separated by buttresses. This description applies to the south side of the choir, but the aisles are extended within one bay of the east end of the Lady Chapel, which has Perpendicular windows ; the great east window is of the same date. Traces of Early English architecture appear in the north side of the choir and chapter-house. The north window of the transept and windows of the nave are Perpendicular. The south walk of the cloister is gone. The CENTRAL TOWER rises one story above the roofs ; the parapet is embattled, and on each angle is an octagonal turret ; in every face are two canopied windows, each of two trefoiled lights, with a quatrefoil in the head.

The west front, south porch, cloisters, clerestory, and roof of the nave and transept and central tower were the joint work of Ripley, and John Birkenshaw, abbot 1493-1537. The SOUTH-WEST TOWER was commenced in 1508; the portion of it then completed is used as the bishop's court; the base of a corresponding tower forms the entrance to the palace.

Of the early Norman period still remain the lower portion of the north-west tower, now part of the palace, the same part of the north wall of the nave, the whole of the north transept, the four great piers of the central tower, cased with work of the fifteenth century, and the two great eastern piers of the choir, cased with work of the 13th century.

In the NAVE the capitals on the north side bear the initials of S(imon) R(ipley), abbot 1485-92. They were added at the same time as the vaulting shafts. The two eastern arches of the nave belong to the tower, and are earlier than the rest; the square piers, probably Norman, were altered in the 14th century. The arches and pillars are of the 15th century, with vaulting shafts attached to the face of each pillar, and reaching through the capital to the springing of the vault, on which the tracery was begun but never completed. The west front has a large eight-light window, Perpendicular, filled by O'Connor with stained glass to the memory of Rev. P. W. Hamilton of Hoole. It is flanked by two turrets. There were five apses in the Norman church : the springers for fan-traceriod roofs and incipient flying buttresses are still discernible to tantalize the visitor. The exterior north wall of the nave contains six recesses for tombs of the early abbots.

The SOUTH TRANSEPT, the parish church of St. Oswald, rebuilt in the 14th century, is out of all proportion to the rest of the church, and is of the same character as the nave. An aisle remains, but was much altered in the 15th century.

The vestry in the NORTH TRANSEPT (which is of the Norman style, and has a good oak roof) has a vault of the end of the 12th century ; the entrance-door is of the 14th century ; it contains a chest of beautiful iron-work of the 13th century. The north transept contains some fine tapestry, representing Elymas the Sorcerer struck blind ; brought from a French nunnery, and long used as a dorsal for the High Altar.

The Early English work extends only to the two eastern bays of the choir, the jambs of windows of the choir aisles, with the vaulting shafts and springers of the vault both of the choir and aisles. The western part of the CHOIR and vaulting of the Lady Chapel were begun about 1281, and are Transitional Decorated. The roof is plaster. The exterior of the whole Cathedral was cased with stone, and Perpendicular tracery intruded into the windows, in the reigns of Henry VII. and VIII. On either side of the Lady Chapel is a chapel, (St. Mary Magdalen's and St. Nicholas',) of the time of Henry VIII. In the south wall of the choir aisle are two fine recesses for tombs, and in one is a stone coffin with a floriated cross of the 13th century.

The stone organ-screen, Decorated, is of the 14th century ; the organ was built by Gray and Davison, 1844. The bishop's throne was originally St. Werburgh's shrine, of the date of the reign of Edward III., pure Decorated, and has been restored by Canon Slade : here Edward I., in 1278, made his offerings on the complete subjugation of Wales. It was removed at the Reformation from the eastern chapel. There are two fine aumbries, Decorated ; the forty-eight stalls, with their tabernacle work and canopies, are of the latter part of the 15th century. The new reredos is by Hussey ; the lectern was given by the chancellor ; the glazing of the east windows of the choir and Lady Chapel is by Wailes. The pulpit is modern.

The stained glass of the Cathedral was almost wholly destroyed by a mob in 1683 during the stay of the Duke of Monmouth in Chester : the buildings suffered greatly during the Civil Wars.

The LADY CHAPEL, restored by Hussey, is fine Early English, with good vaulting, ribs and bosses of the time of Edward I., sedilia and piscina.

A good Norman doorway leads into the CLOISTERS, which are of the 15th century, and are on the north side of the nave ; the south walk is destroyed ; on the west side is the Norman substructure of the dormitory, long called the Guest Hall erroneously, built about 1100 ; it was divided into domestic offices. Under one of the prebendal houses is a fine Norman crypt, which once supported the Great Hall. The school, 98 by 34 ft. (once the REFECTORY, built about 1220 by Ranulph, Earl of Chester), on the north has a fine pulpit ; its oaken roof was re-·moved in 1804.

The abbot's lodge was rebuilt as the palace by Bishop Keene, 1753. The deanery was formed out of St. Thomas's Chapel. The walls and gatehouse of the Close were built about 1380. This gateway consists of a lofty arch and side postern. Before it were ranged the booths of the merchants at the abbot's fair, thatched with reeds from Stanlow marsh ; and the five and twenty guilds played Adam and Eve in the Abbey.

The CHAPTER-HOUSE, built 1142-48, with the porch and vestibule built about 1220, is an oblong room with good vaulting and lancet lights, running parallel with the north side of the choir. It contains the flags of H.M. 22nd (Cheshire) regiment. The vaulted passage on the north of the vestibule led to the infirmary, now destroyed ; the straight stone staircase to the Guest Hall. Beneath are chambers of the 13th century.

The principal monuments are the following :—

Choir, S. Aisle.—An altar-tomb, and three slabs with floriated crosses to Abbots Berchelsey 1324, Bebington 1349, and Mershton 1385 ; Dr. Samuel Peploe, by Nollekens ; Dean Smith, by Banks ; Bishop Bridgeman of Sodor and Man, 1682, was buried here.

N. Aisle, Nave.—Captain John Napier, epitaph by Sir Charles Napier.

S. Side, Nave.—Memorial window of Mrs. Richards, 1852. There are similar memorials of H. R. Hughes, and members of the Humberton and Anson families.

DIMENSIONS OF THE CATHEDRAL IN FEET.

	Length.	Breadth.	Height.
Nave	160	} 74 ft. 6 in.	78
Choir	125		
Lady Chapel	65	..	33
Transept	180	{ S. Wing 80 } { N. Wing 40 }	..
Tower	..	..	127
Cloisters	110 square	..	..
Chapter-house	50	26	36
Vestibule	33 f. 4 in.	27 f. 4 in.	12 f. 9 in.
Total length	365	..	..

The Chapter consists of a dean and four canons: there are four minor canons, six lay vicars, and eight choristers; choral service is sung twice daily, at 10 and 3, and the Holy Communion is celebrated monthly. The library contains 1100 volumes. In nine years previous to 1852, 10,000*l.* were spent upon the fabric. The income of the Chapter is 5522*l.* Upwards of 8000*l.* were spent on repairs between the years 1823-35.

Arms : Azure, three mitres argent. The Cathedral was constituted Aug. 4, 1541.

Chester has among its bishops the names of Brian Walton, the editor of the " Hexapla ;" Wilkins, one of the founders of the Royal Society, and prophet of steam ; the learned Pearson, whose very dross was gold ; and energetic Porteous : and in its list of dignitaries, Chillingworth and Dean Smith, translator of many of the classics. Higden was a monk of the abbey.

Chichester.

CHICHESTER—probably the Regnum of the Romans—is the contraction of Cissa (an Anglo-Saxon prince, who flourished 814), and ceaster, castrum, a camp. The streets follow the lines of a Roman camp. The walls are planted with trees, and serve as walks. In the year 681, Archbishop Wilfred, having been driven from York, built a monastery, and founded the see at Selsey (the Isle of Seals). On the creation of Roger de Montgomery as Earl of Chichester, by his influence the see in 1085 was translated to Chichester, situated on the Lavant, at the termination of a creek of the British channel, and at the foot of the South Downs. The learned Bradwardine and Archbishop Juxon, Hayley and the poet Collins, were natives of Chichester: Selden was educated here. Queen Elizabeth visited the city, August 25, 1551. The remarkable points of interest are a portion of the ancient walls; St. Mary's Hospital, with a Perpendicular gateway; a chapel 47 ft. 6 in. long, with fine traceried windows, sacristy, oak stalls, sedilia, and piscina, divided by a rich Decorated oak screen from a refectory 83 ft. long, of the 14th century; near South Street is the Vicar's Hall, with an ancient lavatory and reader's pulpit, of the 14th century; the market cross, built by Edward Storey, bishop 1477-1503, and the Early English Guildhall, formerly the chapel of the Grey Friars. In St. Olave's Church, rebuilt 1310, was found in 1852 a Saxon arch constructed out of Roman tiles. St. Andrew's is built over a tesselated pavement; it is the burial-place of Collins.

The site of Chichester endows it with a peculiar character: it is the only Cathedral which can be seen at sea; its spire was a landmark alike to the pilgrim to its shrine, and to the mariner entering the historic waters of the naval stronghold of England.

The Cathedral, which is dedicated to St. Peter, was begun by Bishop Ralph after the year 1114. It had two Norman towers at the west end; a nave with a single aisle on either side; a transept with an apsidal chapel on the east of each wing; and a choir with a semicircular ambulatory opening into three radiating chapels as at Gloucester. The nave with its adjoining aisles, with the triforium built by Bishop Ralph, who died 1123, remains. The whole was roofed with wood, and rebuilt after a fire, on Oct. 19, 1187, by Bishop Seffrid, who added the uppermost stories of the south-west tower, and the clerestory of the nave. The columns were refaced, the clerestory rebuilt, the choir elongated and squared at the end, the roof vaulted, the eastern aisles and the walls of the nave aisles pierced with arches for lateral chapels. The feast of the dedication was kept in 1199. Bishop Simon FitzRobert, 1204-10, brought marble from Purbeck and Petworth for the shafts. The beauty of the dark-veined costly material, highly polished, is now lost, as we have not the contrast it was designed to offer to the brilliant colours on arch and pier and roof: the introduction of stained glass, which destroyed the effect, coupled with the brittleness and wasting decay of the marble, led to its disuse. Bishop Neville, 1222-44, commenced the spire, and built the CHAPTER-HOUSE upon the east side of the south transept. De S. Leopold, bishop 1288-1304, added the LADY CHAPEL, now the library. John de Langton, bishop 1305-36, completed the PRESBYTERY, SACRISTY, the SOUTH TRANSEPT and its beautiful window (47 ft. high by 27 ft. wide), and the BELL TOWER. The stall-work and reredos were given by Bishop Sherborne. The church consists of a NAVE of eight bays and four aisles; a NORTH TRANSEPT with an eastern chapel, or, possibly, a chapter-house, and a SOUTH TRANSEPT, each of one bay with chambers instead of aisles; CHOIR of three bays (the tower is thrown into it and forms another bay), and PRESBYTERY, or east ambulatory of two bays, with aisles, a vestibule parted by solid walls from the ambulatory aisles which formed chapels, and a LADY CHAPEL of four bays. The WEST FRONT is composed of a gable and wall of three stories, a SOUTH-WEST TOWER, the "old Belfry," its two upper stages good Early English, of Isle of Wight stone, without pinnacle or parapet, and a deep plain porch. In the quatrefoil above it was the Saviour sitting in Doom. Over the porch is a triplet; in the gable two Pointed windows, with a large Pointed window below them. On the north-west is a very fine detached campanile or bell-tower, Perpendicular, massive and square below, of four stages, surmounted by an octagonal lantern, battlemented, connected by small flying buttresses, with octagonal turrets, that spring from the angles above the battlement. The north wall of the nave has some curious buttresses, resembling that on the great tower at Ely. In place of a north-west tower, destroyed by Waller, is a sloping embattled wall. In the SOUTH TRANSEPT is a richly-traceried window, Decorated, of seven lights, and above it a beautiful rose window. The parapet in the transept and choir has a trefoiled string-course. The east end is composed of three lancet windows, with a rose window of seven foliated circles of the choir, in the gable; it is flanked by arcaded pinnacles with small spires.

The CENTRAL TOWER, which is battlemented, with octagonal turrets at the angles, also battlemented, has in its principal or second story two couplets in each face, with a quatrefoil in the head, each under a Pointed arch. The spire is of beautiful design, octagonal; in each face is a window of two lights, flanked by pinnacled turrets, crocketed and canopied. Two broad bands of great elegance surround the spire. It is a popular saying, that the master-mason built Salisbury spire and his man Chichester spire. Murray the aeronaut was killed when descending from it in a parachute. The angle at the summit is about 13°, at Salisbury and Norwich only 10°; at Lichfield it varies from 12° to 13°. But if the church has neither grandeur of dimension or beauty of detail, the colour of its material is faultless; the pyramidal grouping of parts perfect, the harmony and outline of the building beyond praise. The visible axis and centre of the church is formed by the spire, and a line let fall to the ground.

The NAVE of eight bays is well proportioned, with massive piers, round arches, a double triforium, the upper forming the clerestory. The lower triforium is composed of two round arches divided by a pillar, under a round arch, the clerestory of triplets in each bay. The base story consists of massive piers with round arches. In the choir the clerestory consists of lancets; the triforium in the ambulatory has pointed-arches. The vaulting is of stone. The range of side chapels, corresponding with the divisions of the aisles, gives a variety of character and expression to the nave, by the eye penetrating in every direction and discovering new views in every alteration of position, but the effect is not equal to the direct threefold avenue, to which, in other English Cathedrals, the sight is limited. In this nave, severe, almost cold in its simplicity, is offered a signal disproof of the fanciful theory which derived the origin of Pointed architecture from the forest avenue and the interlacing of its boughs. The Norman is grisly, massive, monstrous, huge blocks, heaved up with iron hands and sturdy patience, like a rock set against the storm of battle; and the pillar beyond only became more slender, and the roof more light and tracery star-like, when the walls might be perforated with security, as the times grew more peaceful and war more unfrequent. The roof of the LADY CHAPEL still retains portions of the colour and design with which Bishop Sherborne adorned the vaulting of the church throughout. There are eight bells in Langton's tower.

The more observable features of the Cathedral are its detached bell-tower (Langton's, built 1304-36) on the north-west, built with the stones of Ryman's tower at Wittering; the additional north and south aisles in the NAVE for the reception of chantries were built in the reign of Henry III. On the south side is an ancient altar-slab built into the wall. Elgin and Manchester Cathedrals, St. Michael's and Holy Trinity Coventry, Abingdon, St. Martin's Leicester, St. Mary's Taunton, and Kendal, are other instances of such an arrangement. It is quite a foreign feature, found at Notre Dame, Milan, Seville, Cluny, Amiens, Beauvais, and Cologne. Antwerp has seven aisles. It is on the whole a felicitous compensation for the shortness of the nave, the broadest in England except York; a substitution of transverse for longitudinal perspective; and if the piers were more slender, its indefinite multiplication of views would produce a rich and complex effect. A chapel of St. Faith, founded in the 12th century, adjoins the east entrance to the cloister.

The side walls of the SOUTH TRANSEPT were decorated by Bishop Sherborne's orders, 1508-36, by Theodore Bernardi, with two large paintings (each 12 ft. long by 8 ft. wide) of the foundation of the see, and the confirmation of the Cathedral charters, with a series of portraits of English kings and his predecessors down to his time. On the opposite wall are pictures of bishops from Wilfrid to George Day, who died 1556.

Over the reredos in 1508 was constructed a minstrels' gallery, probably the cause of the platform behind the altar; which was not the site of St. Richard's shrine : it was an unseemly arrangement, and there is no reason for regret at its destruction. In the vestry, on the west side of the SOUTH TRANSEPT, is a Saxon chest of oak, 8 ft. by 20 ft., with five locks, brought from Selsey; above is the old chapter-room. In the CONSISTORY COURT, of the date of Henry VI., in the story above, over the south porch, Early English, is a sliding panel, which leads to the treasury and evidence chamber, though popularly described as a dungeon where the Lollards were imprisoned. The NORTH TRANSEPT, formerly the sub-deanery parish church of St. Peter, was thrown into the Cathedral by the late dean in 1841. The restorations have been made under the charge of Mr. Carpenter and Mr. Butler, architects. Bishop Mawson gave the throne in 1749. The stalls were painted and gilded in 1731, when the marble was laid down. The organ-screen, built in 1447, was the oratory of Bishop Arundel. It is of three arches with quatrefoils in the lateral spandrils, with an arcade of niches above. The wrought-iron doors of the CHOIR are simple and effective. The organ, by Renatus Harris, 1678, was improved by Byfield in 1725, Gray and Davison in 1844, and Hill, 1851. The pulpit was erected in 1830.

The principal monuments are the following :—

Presbytery.—Norman coped stones ; Bishop Ralph, d. 1125. *North Side.*—Bishops Seffrid, d. 1171, and Hilary, d. 1161. *South Side.*— Ducal family of Richmond, a simple stone with inscription as simple —" Domus ultima," 1750.

S. Aisle Choir.—Canopy recessed tomb, and effigy of Caen stone ; Bishop Sherborne, d. 1536 ; Maud, a Purbeck slab, two hands lifting a heart.

N. Aisle Choir.—Bishop Rickingale, d. 1426, alabaster effigy in a recess.

South Transept, under S. Window.—Bishop Langton, d. 1340, effigy and recessed tomb. *South Side.*—Bishop Godfrey, d. 1088, stone coffin.

South Transept, St. Mary Magdalen Chapel, North Side.—A table tomb, a screen of three compartments and effigy, restored 1847 by Richardson. Bishop St. Richard, the last canonized Englishman ; the oak screen of the shrine is preserved in the Chapter-room. King Edward I. attended the translation of St. Richard in 1276, and in 1297, when he gave a royal guerdon to Lovel the minstrel who was harping at the shrine, where the king found him. Some of the relations of the Earl of Arundel having infringed on his manorial rights at Houghton, Bishop De S. Leofardo compelled the young nobleman, the most gallant of knights and courtiers, to do penance for three days, and come on a pilgrimage to the shrine.

N. Aisle Nave, Arundel Chantry.—Richard, 13th Earl, (died 1376,) and Countess of Arundel, (died 1372,) of Caen stone, late in the 14th century, restored by Richardson 1843. *St. John Baptist's Chantry.*—Table-tomb and effigy, Caen stone, of the so-called Lady Abbess, 1270, probably Maud, Countess of Arundel, the patroness of Bishop St. Richard, brought with that of Earl Richard from Lewes Priory church after the dissolution. (Flaxman preferred it to any in England.) Collins the poet, medallion by Flaxman (there are eight other monuments by this sculptor): he is represented as he was found reading by Johnson at Islington.—" I have but one book and it is the best." Epitaph by Hayley and Sargent. Rt. Hon. W. Huskisson, (Carew,) statue.

In the North Aisle, to the east, is the first memorial window set up in England by Wailes, 1842, the gift of Dean Chandler; a memorial window of Lady L. M. Lennox, set up in 1852 by Wailes ; one of Sir Thomas Reynell, is by O'Connor, 1848 ; and another of F. E. Freeland, by Willement, 1844 ; Bishop Otter, bust by Towne.

S. Aisle.—Memorial window of Bishop Shuttleworth, 1847.

These monuments present a complete series of English monumental sculpture ; from the rude smooth sarcophagus, with its low-gabled lid graven with the emblems of the cross, succeeded by the recess, endeared by the canopied and recumbent effigy, to the pillowed stage of the figure in a posture, or shrunk to a pedestal for a statue, shutting out all memory of death.

The west windows, and that over the cloister door, representing St. Stephen's martyrdom, are by Wailes. The east window was set up in 1844. There are fifty sockets of brasses still remaining.

In the LADY CHAPEL are preserved chalices and the heads of pastoral staffs, which have from time to time been found during repairs ; a leaden cross, with an absolution inscribed upon it, was found in Bishop Godfrey's tomb. A good oak armed-chair, of mediæval simplicity, and a ring with a stone called Basilidian, an amulet-gem, found in 1829, are also shown. The library contains the service-book of Archbishop Herman of Cologne, and Eustathius on Homer, with the notes of Salmasius. In the SOUTH CHOIR AISLE two Norman panels, bassi relievi, are inserted, representing the Raising of Lazarus, and Martha and Mary before Christ, which were probably brought from the old Cathedral at Selsey : they were removed from the piers of the central tower in 1829. The Cathedral was used as a barrack by the soldiers of Sir William Waller, who committed horrible devastation, and demolished the north-west tower on December 29, 1643. Stained glass, organ, carved work, and ancient monuments were ruthlessly destroyed, and what was left was some years after completely demolished by the troopers of Sir Arthur Hazelrigge, in 1648.

DIMENSIONS OF THE CATHEDRAL IN FEET.

	Length.	Breadth.	Height.
Nave	156	91 f. 9 in	62 f. 3 in.
Choir	105	59	60
Presbytery	56 f. 2 in	..	..
Lady Chapel	62 f. 9 in.	20 f. 7 in.	22
Steeple { Vaulting, 67 f; diameter of Tower, 42 ; Spire, 32 ;) }			271
S.W. Tower	..	..	95
Transept	131	34 f. 3 in.	..
Campanile	..	..	120
Total length	380	..	..

The Chapter is composed of a dean and four canons, there are five minor canons, seven lay vicars, and ten choristers. There are four Wykehamical prebends.

There are two daily choral services at 10 and 4: the

Holy Communion is administered weekly. The income of the Chapter in 1852 was 5095*l.* ; their expenditure in repairs during fourteen years was 2178*l.*, and since 1846, aided by subscriptions, 4090*l.*

Arms: Azure, the Saviour seated on an eastern tomb, mitred as the High Priest and nimbed, a mound in His left hand, His right hand raised in benediction, a sword issuing from His mouth (Rev. i. 16).

Among the bishops, who were formerly the queen's confessors, we find St. Wilfrid, who taught the Sussex fishermen the use of the net; Seffrid, who was deposed; Hilary, who would not sign the Constitutions of Clarendon without the clause "saving our Order;" Ralph de Neville, Lord Chancellor; Sir Richard Chandos de la Wyche; John de Langton and Ralph de Stratford, Lord Chancellors; Adam Moleyns, Lord Privy Seal; Reginald Pecock, the Arian; munificent Sherborne; Andrewes and Montague; Gunning and Patrick; Henry King, the poet; Manningham, who refused to whistle the prayers through a keyhole, when Queen Anne desired him to read to her from an adjoining room; and Hare, the opponent of Hoadly. Among the dignitaries may be mentioned loyal Dean Ryves, the author of Mercurius Rusticus, the learned Hammond, and Dallaway the topographer.

In the Bishop's Palace, is an Early English chapel with sexpartite ceiling, a niche, with an exquisite fresco of the Blessed Virgin in a quatrefoil, a square kitchen with a grand timber roof, and a hall remarkable for a timber ceiling with heraldic badges, built by Bishop Sherborne; adjoining are the Bishop's and the Canon's Gate, the latter also his work.

Durham.

Fair on the half-seen stream the sunbeams dance,
Betraying it beneath the woodland bank—
Grey towers of Durham ; begirt by winding Wear,
Well yet I love thy mixed and massive pile,
Half church of God, half castle 'gainst the Scot :
How fair between the gothic turrets glance
Broad lights, and shadows fall on front and flank,
Where tower and buttress rise in martial rank,
And girdle in the massive donjon keep,
And from their circuit peals o'er bush and bank
The matin bell with summons long and deep,
And echo answers still with long resounding sweep.

DURHAM, through the Norman Duresme, is a corruption of Dun Holme, " the hill with the girdle of water." William Rufus was twice here, King John in 1213, Henry III. in 1244, Edward I. twice, Edward III. thrice, Edward IV. once : Edward II. in 1322, and Henry VI. in September 1448, offered at St. Cuthbert's shrine. David II. was here 1333, and James II. of Scotland 1424, King James I. was here April 13, 1603. Charles I. passed three times through the city. It was the birth-place of the humane Granville Sharp.

The most interesting objects are the gateway of Kepyer Hospital, the ruins of St. Mary's Hospital, St. Oswald's Church, Late Decorated, so shaken by coal mines as to be dangerous, the ruins of Neville's Cross, and the noble old bridge at Framwell gate, built by Bishop Flambard—two arches with the ribs are perfect. The Castle, on Palace Green, now occupied by the University, founded June 1, 1837, is principally Norman, but with additions from that period to the present time. The Keep is an irregular octagon, its widest diameter being 63 ft. 6 in., its least 61 ft. ; and has been restored to form College rooms. Elvet bridge, rebuilt 1225-8, altered 1806. Bishop Hatfield built the Bishop's and Constable's Hall, the octagonal tower, and great hall, 132 ft. by 36 ft., and 54 ft.

high, afterwards curtailed by Bishops Fox and Neile: the
former erected the minstrel-niches and the kitchen, 1499;
and Tunstal the gallery chapel, the gatehouse, and staircase tower; and Langley the great north gateway. There
is a fine Norman Chapel. In the Castle, Fox entertained
Princess Margaret, 23rd July, 1502. The University contains University College, Hatfield's Hall, and Cosin's Hall.
The Castle, rebuilt by the King in 1072, received its
north front from Bishop Pusar, 1174, who added the city
'wall from the gaol gate to the water gate. The principal churches are St. Mary's Bailey, which has a
sculpture of the Saviour, c. 1200, and a coped tomb of a
Prior; St. Oswald's Elvet, which has a good roof and
stall-work in the chancel; St. Giles, c. 1112, with a tower
built 1414; and St. Mary Magdaleue chapel, built 1439.
Flambard, in 1112, built the gate of Kepyer's hospital.

Sir Walter Scott records the translation of St. Cuthbert
to Durham—

> When, after many wanderings past,
> He chose his lordly seat at last,
> Where his Cathedral, huge and vast,
> Looks down upon the Wear.

It is said that the exact resting-place of St. Cuthbert
was a secret revealed only to three Benedictine monks at
one time, and on the demise of one of them, transmitted
to a successor. The dedication to St. Cuthbert was
changed at the Reformation to that of Christ and St.
Mary. The offerings at the shrine from 1378-1513 have
been calculated at 66,000l. sterling.

The first stone of the Cathedral was laid August 11, 1093,
in the presence of Malcolm, King of Scots, by Bishop
William of Calais. During the vacancy of the see, 1095-9,
the monks completed the CHOIR, aisles, and TRANSEPT. Ralph
Flambard, bishop 1099-1128, finished the NAVE to the
vaulting, and the whole of the aisles, which were vaulted
by Algar, prior 1109-37. Geoffrey Rufus, bishop 1133-43,
built the CHAPTER-HOUSE. Hugh Pusar, bishop 1153-95,
built the GALILEE. Richard Poore, bishop 1228-41, built the
NINE ALTARS and CENTRAL TOWER to the first story, which

was finished in the 14th century. Melsonby, prior 1232-44, made the groining, Early English, of the nave and south transept. Between 1388-1437, the CLOISTERS were completed, and in 1380, Lord Neville erected the beautiful ALTAR-SCREEN, Early Perpendicular, of Caen stone, carved in London at a cost of 533*l.* Thomas Hatfield, bishop 1343-82, built the pulpit, the great west window and that in the north transept. Anthony Bec built the vestry and vaulted the choir, while Hunton was prior, 1290-1381. The apsidal CHAPTER-HOUSE, built 1133-43 by Bishop Rufus, 34 ft. 5½ in. wide and 45 ft. high, was, till Wyatt in 1799 cut it in two, 77 ft. in length. No longer as once to the eye of Harold the Dauntless—

> O'erhead with many a scutcheon grand,
> And quaint devices interlaced,
> A labyrinth of crossing rows,
> The roof in lessening arches shows.

Wyatt, who deserved the fate of Sisyphus, pared the exterior, and added compo pinnacles to the west towers and compo crockets and canopy to the north porch. Forty altars once stood in this church, and in the north aisle of the choir lived an anchorite.

No Cathedral appears to greater advantage. It has a magnificent position on the steep river-bank, 40 ft. in height, and almost insulated by the broad and rapid Wear, and seen through the openings of the wooded slopes, and hanging gardens of noble forest-trees, ash, and sycamore, crowns walls and castle and tower, and rises in the boldness of its beauty above the whole tier of lesser and secular buildings, their supreme and noblest ornament. The history of the see is at once poetical and romantic, and the fabric was singularly preserved during the stormy time of the Reformation and Civil wars. It has, from its situation and memorials, familiar in legend, ballad, song, story, been emphatically called the English Zion.

The Cathedral consists of a CENTRAL and two WEST towers, a west chapel, and GALILEE of five alleys and three bays; a NAVE of eight bays with aisles; a TRANSEPT with each wing of three bays, and having six chantries forming an eastern aisle; a CHOIR of five bays with aisles; and a CHAPEL OF THE

Nine Altars of seven bays, forming a broad transeptal east front.   There is a north-east porch, which forms the principal entrance to the nave ; and on the south side of the nave is a cloister ; on the east side of the cloister are, next the transept, the parlour, the chapter-house, and cells for offenders, and the deanery-hall to the south east of which is the Prior's Chapel with a crypt.   On the south side are the refectory and kitchen ; and on the west, the dormitory. The stone used in the construction of the church is the red stone of the neighbourhood.

This superb and stupendous Cathedral, was happily characterised by Dr. Johnson as one remarkable "for rocky solidity and indeterminate duration.

Bishop Aldhune consecrated the first cathedral Sept. 4, 999 ; it was completed by Bishop Edmund 1021-41.   On Aug. 12, 1093, Bishop William of Calais, in the presence of Malcolm king of Scots, laid the foundation of a new choir, which, like its aisles, terminated in an apse: a screen parted off the central chevet for the tomb of St. Cuthbert.   Bishop Flambard, 1099-1128, finished the nave and transept, except the roof of the former, which was added with stone groining by J. Melsonby, prior 1233-44: the north-east cloister door and a west door formed the entrances.   The west window, with a representation of a Jesse tree, was added by W. Forcer, prior 1341-74.   The perpendicular window in the south transept with glazing illustrating the Te Deum, was built in 1450 ; that in the north transept with glass portraying the Four Doctors by Prior Forcer, and restored by Prior Castell 1494-1519.   Prior Hotoun in 1289 vaulted the choir. In the south choir aisle the windows were built by Prior Forcer : in it was built the famous Black Rood of Scotland, captured from King David Bruce at the battle of Neville's Cross.   The Perpendicular tracery in the other windows of the church was inserted by Prior Wessington 1416-1446. Geoffrey Rufus built the chapter-house 1133-40; Bishop Pusar erected the galilee in 1154, having begun an eastern chapel for the reception of a congregation of women, but a storm that followed was attributed to the anger of St. Cuthbert, and he recommenced his design and completed it at the west end. The two large north and south doors of the nave are of this date. The Chapel of the NINE ALTARS was commenced by Bishop Poore and Prior Melsonby in 1245, and occupied forty years before it was finished. In the marygold are fragments of glass of the 15th century : in the north window are relics of glazing with the acts of Joseph. The central tower was commenced by Bishop Farnham in 1247. The west door of the nave was closed up by Bishop Langley 1406-38, windows inserted and side doors made into the nave. The CLOISTER was commenced 1368, and completed by Bishop Skirlaw 1388-1406. The DORMITORY over the song school and treasury on the south-west of the Cathedral was built 1598-1401 ; the COLLEGE gate, with St. Helena's Chapel over it, by Prior Castel; the EXCHEQUER in Palace Green, by Bishop Neville 1437-57. The upper parts of the WESTERN TOWERS were added by Prior Darlington 1241-1257 ; and the LANTERN TOWER was built by Prior Bell 1464-1478. The spires were removed from the western towers in 1657 : a peal of eight bells by Hodgson, 1693, was placed in the north-east or Galilee tower, under which was St. Saviour's chapel. The DEANERY was built by Prior Wessington 1416-46 : the octagonal KITCHEN, the diameter of which is 36 ft. 8 in., with its singular and unique groining, by Prior Forcer. The three-light windows of the cloister were restored about eighty years ago. The roof is panelled and enriched with bosses. Bishop Cornwallis, then canon, saved the Galilee from destruction. The REFECTORY on the south of the cloisters was converted into a library by Dean Sudbury in 1680.

The GALILEE, at the west end of the church, consists of five compartments. In the base tier are two arcades of round-headed arches under a band of reticulated work ; above this the three central windows and battlement are of the date of Bishop Langley : the outer aisle windows are Early English. Each of the WESTERN TOWERS have four transitional arcades, alternately of pointed and round-headed arches. The battlement is modern. Over the

great seven-light Decorated WEST WINDOW is an arcade of
seven round-headed lancets with reticulated mouldings;
in the gable are five similar but narrower lights. On the
north side of the NAVE and CHOIR the clerestory is of three-
light windows; in the NAVE, triforium, and aisles they are
two-light; on the south side they are all of two lights, and
have Perpendicular tracery. On the south side of the CHOIR
the clerestory consists of single round-headed windows,
and the triforium of two very small lights under a semicircular arch truncated. In the choir-aisles there are
four-light windows Decorated. The buttresses throughout are shallow; the parapet insignificant; that of the
clerestory rests on a corbel table. The north porch has a
fine Norman arch. The central tower is of two stories;
in the lower are two lofty transomed windows, each transomed, canopied, and of two lights, divided by canopied
shallow buttresses; the upper windows, divided from the
lower tier by a rich band, are smaller, of two lights and
canopied. The parapet is battlemented. At the angles
are double buttresses, with crocketed pediments and
niched statuary. The NORTH TRANSEPT has a superb Decorated six-light window; in the spandrils of the front
are circles with statues of a prior, and Bishop Pusar;
above these is an intersecting arcade; in the gable are
three niches, the central being canopied. On the east
side is a square arcaded turret; and on the west a much
larger turret, square below, but octagonal and arcaded
above. The SOUTH TRANSEPT has an arcade of round arches
above a Perpendicular window, and reticulated mouldings
in the gable, which is flanked by two arcaded turrets
which are incomplete. In the Chapel of the NINE ALTARS
the east front somewhat resembles that of Glasgow Cathedral: it consists of a double tier of three lancets in the
north and south compartments; in the centre over three
lancets is a magnificent marygold of 24 trefoiled lights,
above which is a triplet between two pinnacled turrets,
octagonal and arcaded. Similar turrets flank the north
front, which contains a beautiful six-light Decorated window, above which is an arcade of five trefoiled arches

and three trefoiled niches in the gable. On the north-west turret is a sculpture representing the traditional determination of the resting-place of the body of St. Cuthbert by the monks who bore it following a cow. The south front has two tiers of lancets in couplets, the bays being divided as on the east side by buttresses; they are filled with Perpendicular tracery, and have quatrefoils in the spandrils above. Similar tracery was removed from the other windows in 1795. In the gable are five lancets, the central triplet being pierced; two triple-arcaded turrets with tall spires flank it. Along the face of the Norman portions of the north side of the Cathedral is a round-headed arcade; but the turrets of the transept, the porch, and north front of the east chapel have been unhappily modernized.

The GALILEE, which occupies the same position as St. Joseph's Chapel at Glastonbury, consists of five aisles, and the effect is similar to that of the mosque of Cordova on a small scale. The name of Galilee was given to the place of reception of women penitents, and the hearse of the dead, who were supposed to stand to the religious as the Galileans to the Hebrew of Hebrews. So strictly was St. Cuthbert's repugnance to women regarded, that Queen Philippa, having been received without the knowledge of the monks within the precincts, was required by them, on the discovery of her presence, at once, and that at midnight, to leave the prior's lodgings. A blue line of stone on the floor of the nave marks the limit which women entering the minster were bound to observe; a monk at noon daily preached in the galilee from an iron pulpit to a congregation of women. In this chapel the wooden roof is plain and the arches have chevron mouldings. In front of the original west door of the nave is Bishop Langley's chantry, with remains of colour and the altar-slab in the floor; to the south was St. Mary's altar, to the north that of Our Lady of Pity, with painted drapery, rich bands of ornaments, and figures of Pusar and Cœur de Lion; the chapel of Ven. Bede faced his tomb.

The NAVE consists of five principal compartments divided by four huge piers, 23 ft. in circumference; to the east three have pillars alternately round and shafted; of the former, two are channelled with chevrons; two with network mouldings in bold relief, and two are fluted. The two westernmost bays are each of a single arch; the others each include two arches; the two easternmost alone have plain mouldings, the bases and capitals are without ornament. The triforium, and clerestory, and roof, are almost the same throughout the church; the former consists of two round-headed arches, resting on columns and included beneath a large arch in each bay: the clerestory consists of triplets of round-headed arches, the central being of larger span than those on the side: in the choir the windows are single. The ribs of the vaultings have chevron mouldings. In the aisles there is an arcade of intersecting arches. Bishop Maltby gave the two windows at the west end—one of Ven. Bede, by Wailes, the other of St. Cuthbert by Willement. The FONT in the south aisle was given, in 1621, by Dean Hunt; it has a sculpture of the Baptism in Jordan, and stands below a superb octagonal spire-like cover of red oak, 30 ft. high. The TRANSEPT contained in its east aisle the following chantries, reckoning from north to south: SS. Nicholas and Giles; St. Gregory; St. Benedict; Our Lady of Houghal (now the Vestry); St. Mary of Bolton; and SS. Faith and Thomas. The aisle is parted off by one clustered and two circular pillars, one of which has chevron, the other spiral channels. The LANTERN TOWER pours down a stream of light, as the vaulting stands over the upper story; the sides have beautiful panelling, foliated and canopied, with a gallery-walk pierced with quatrefoils and resting on a bold corbel table at the base of the lower tier of windows.

The screen and stalls were given by Bishop Cosin, 1660-74, and are of Debased Gothic, the work of James Clement, who died 1690. The wainscot was designed by Lord Castlereagh. The clock in the south transept erected 1621, and the glass, were preserved in the Civil Wars; unhappily, the Chapter never thought of the stalls, and

with many ancient tombs they were destroyed by the
4500 Scottish prisoners who were confined here after
the battle of Dunbar, in 1650. On either side of the CHOIR
are four pillars, two clustered and two circular, with spiral
channels. The key-holes for lifting materials remain in
the roof. The bosses are enriched with sculpture. In
the single bay which forms the PRESBYTERY, the triforium
consists of three pointed arches, with toothed mouldings
under a pointed arch, with quatrefoils filled with foliage
in the spandrils, and the clerestory has two richly ornamented and shafted lancets. The THRONE is formed of
Bishop Hatfield's magnificent tomb. The pulpit is hexagonal, of Italian design etched with figures of Apostles.
The organ, built by Schmidt, 1684, was improved by
English, 1823, and Bishop, 1844-7. The unrivalled REREE-
DOS, given by John Lord Neville, is of Caen stone, and
wrought in London, at a cost of 800 marks. It occupied
one year, 1380, in erection. It consists of ten detached
piers, between which on either side are four tiers of
canopied niches. In the basement are two doors to the
shrine. Five lofty, airy pinnacles, with niched open work,
and four lesser in the intervals, wrought with the most
elaborate care, complete this unrivalled screen. Nine
cressets, ever burning before the marygold beyond, threw
out the statuary in the niches into strong relief.

In the FERETORY, or shrine of St. Cuthbert, are collected
statues from the exterior niches of the church, caryatides
which once supported the roof of the Chapter-house
and bosses. A descent of eight steps leads down to
the Chapel of the NINE ALTARS, those reckoning from
north to south of St. Michael: SS. Aidan and Helen;
Peter and Paul; Martin and Edmund; Cuthbert and
Bede; Oswald and Laurence; Thomas of Canterbury
and Catherine; John and Margaret; Andrew and Mary
Magdalene. The walls are arcaded with trefoiled arches
having quatrefoils in the spandrils. An inner arcade
adds depth to the windows; each alternate column is
of black marble. On the south side is a curious double-
ribbed window, united by through-stones to the mullions

of the outer window. A transeptal chapel at the east
end occurs also at Fountains Abbey and at Peterborough.

In the CLOISTERS in the east aisle remain the stone stalls
where the daily almsmen sat, and on the south side is
the Maundy door. The roof is flat, but panelled, and of
Irish oak ; the windows have intersecting tracery. There
are eleven panes on each side. In the centre is the base of a
conduit. There is an Early English crypt under the deanery
chapel ; and a Norman crypt beneath the refectory—

The principal monuments are the following :

Galilee.—Venerable Bede.   The title is said to have originated thus:
the monk who was composing the epitaph fell asleep when he had
written

Hâc sunt in fossâ Bedæ......ossa,

when a brother coming in, added the convenient word " Venerabilis."

Nave.—Bishop Langley, chantry and tomb. *South Side.*—Ralph
Lord Neville, who led the English van at Neville's Cross, d.
1368, and his wife Lady Alice, mutilated effigies; John his son, d.
1389, and Lady Matilda Percy, daughter of Hotspur, mutilated
effigies; Bishop Neville, d. 1457, blue slab, brass gone : a slab
without a brass ; Prior Burnaby, d. 1464 ; Dr. J. Britton, an effigy.

Choir.—Bishop Hatfield, d. 1382, effigy and magnificent tomb ;
Bishop Skirlaw, mutilated tomb, d. 1388.

S. Aisle.—Memorial to H.M 68th regiment, by Gaffin.

South Transept.—Bishop Barrington, by Chantrey.

Nine Altars, South Side.—Bishop Van Mildert.

DIMENSIONS OF THE CATHEDRAL IN FEET.

	Length.	Breadth.	Height.
Towers . .	34	33	216f. 8in.
West Towers	..	..	143
Nave . .	235f. 6in.	81f. 1in.	69f. 6in.
Choir to east end	179f. 4in.	77f. 2in.	76
Nine Altars .	129f. 5in.	34f. 2in.	..
Transept .	171f. 9in.	..	..
Galilee . .	80 N. to S.	50 E. to W.	
Total exclusive of Galilee .	{ 413f. 10in.	..	..
Chapter-house	[77]	34f. 5in.	45
Cloisters .	146	144	..
Dormitory .	193f. 7in.	38f. 1in.	..
Refectory. .	49f. 2in.	30f. 2in.	..

In 1635 the altar, which cost 200*l.*, and was the gift of Dean Hunt, was of black branched marble, supported upon six columns of touchstone, and ornamented with two double gilt candlesticks; the organ recently erected cost 1000*l.* There were divers fair copes of several rich works of crimson satin embroidered, with embossed work of silver, beset all over with cherubim curiously wrought to life; a black cope wrought with gold, with divers images in colours; and four other rich copes and vestments; the most beautiful had been given to the king in his progress. One was the gift of Queen Philippa after the battle of Neville's Cross in 1346; another presented by king Charles, bore the ominous symbol, the head of Goliath in the hand of David; three of the 14th century are preserved. The cope was disused in divine service at Durham, in July, 1760, in the time of the irritable War-burton, who found the collar chafe his cauliflower wig. Dr. Waagen dwells with delight on the stores of illumin-ated MSS. in the library : the most interesting are a Bible, the gift of Bishop Pusar; a treatise on the Psalter, with a miniature of its donor, Walter de Calais ; and an old Bede roll. The ivory comb and stole cross, portions of the vest-ments of St. Cuthbert and other ecclesiastics, with needle-work by King Alfred's sister, are preserved.

The Chapter consists of a dean and eight canons, four stalls being suspended. There are six minor canons, ten lay vicars, and as many choristers. The income of the Chapter is 57,801*l.*, a year; and within fourteen years previous to 1852, 27,000*l.* were spent on the fabric. The library contains 11,000 volumes. There are two daily choral services at 10 and 4.

'*Arms.*—Az. a cross, or, between four lions rampant, arg., the letter D sable on the cross.

Among the bishops, long princes palatine, occur the names of St. Aidan, St. Cuthbert, who introduced the practice of burial in churches, and St. John of Beverley; Edmund, who obtained the mitre when the chapter was divided, by saying, " Why not elect me ?" Flambard and Poore, the architect; Godfrey Rufus, Lord Chancellor ;

Hugh Pusar, who purchased the earldom of Northumberland, and had Richard's sneer to bear, "I am a crafty
workman—out of a veteran prelate I make a stripling
earl;" Anthony Bek, who led the second line at Falkirk
with thirty-nine banners at his back, patriarch of Jerusalem and king of Man, and the subject of the popular
legend of the bishop who met the weird Henry le Gros
Veneur in the glades of Middleham forest; the learned
Bury, the friend of Petrarch, and founder of the University
library at Oxford; Hatfield, who fought at the head of
his archers before Calais; Fordham, Lord Privy Seal;
Skirlawe, the Lord Keeper, who came with 2000 horse one
day too late to Otterburne to stay the hunting in Chevy
Chase; Cardinal Langley, Lord Chancellor; Cardinals
Baynbridge and Wolsey; Fox, the founder of Corpus
Christi College; Ruthal, who died of grief when Privy
Seal, having given in an inventory of his own fortune in-
stead of a survey of the crown estates to the king; sour
Pilkington, who refused to wear a college cap because "his
head was not four-cornered;" ambitious Neale; venerable
Morton; learned Cosin; Lord Crewe, whom the king
promised to befriend because "a gentleman had entered
the church," and two kings keenly detested; Talbot, whose
martial habit was satirised by Wharton; the saint-like
Butler; Barrington, who sacrificed two cathedrals to
James Wyatt; and the munificent Van Mildert. Among
the dignitaries are found the names of three Cardinals;
Turgot, Archbishop of St. Andrews; Simon the historian;
Prior Hotoun, founder of Durham College; Archdeacon
William, founder of University Hall, Oxford; primitive
Bernard Gilpin; gloomy Foxe; Brevint; Dean Comber;
and Francis, Earl of Bridgewater.

Ely.

On one of the larger islands formed by the river Ouse, in the fen district, which, before the marshes were drained, was entirely compassed with waters fringed with willows, the monastery of St. Etheldreda of Ely, or Elige, the Willow Island, was founded. In the fair of St. Audrey (such was the corruption of her name) showy but ordinary laces were sold to the poor folks, hence the opprobrious epithet of " Tawdry." Such secluded and inaccessible retreats were commonly chosen by the Saxons for security, when the open parts of the country were overrun with armies. The " hardy outlaw," Hereward, the last of the Saxons who held out against William of Normandy, retreated upon the fastness of Ely : and a party of the barons, after the loss of the battle of Evesham, here made their last resistance to Edward.

The parish church of St. Mary has a good spire and tower, an Early English chancel and chapel, and round columns in the nave.

The ground-plan of the Cathedral is cruciform, consisting of a GALILEE, WEST TOWER and WESTERN TRANSEPT, a CENTRAL OCTAGON, a NAVE of twelve bays, CHOIR of three bays, PRESBYTERY of six bays, and TRANSEPT of three bays, with aisles to each; and a LADY CHAPEL parallel to the north wall of the choir.

The Norman portion of the church was commenced in 1081 by Abbot Symeon, the brother of Walkelyn, Bishop of Winchester, and was finished 1130-1174 ; it was unceiled, but closed with a timber roof covered with lead. The MAIN TRANSEPT was finished about 1083, the NAVE in 1150, the WEST TRANSEPT 1170. The original circular apse was demolished by Bishop Northwold, 1229-54, in order to construct a presbytery and shrine of the patron St. Etheldreda, which stood immediately under a boss in the choir that bears her image. This bishop likewise built the palace ; the PRESBYTERY was finished after seventeen years, in 1352, at a cost of 500l. The church was dedicated in the presence of King

Henry III. in honour of SS. Mary, Peter, and Etheldreda, Oct. 20, 1252. The WEST TOWER was built by Bishop Ridel in 1184-90; the lantern and angular turrets were added in 1382, and necessitated the strengthening of the tower in 1405 and 1454. Eustace, bishop 1197-1220, about 1215 erected the GALILEE PORCH. The CENTRAL TOWER fell Feb. 20, 1321. Bishop Hotham, 1316-1337, then rebuilt the CHOIR from the octagon to Northwold's presbytery, at a cost of 2034*l*. On March 25, 1321, the LADY CHAPEL was commenced by John of Wisbeach, and finished in 1349; the OCTAGON, begun 1322, was finished in 1342; the upper story in 1380. In 1338 the stall-work, by Richard de Saxmundham, was erected in the choir. John Barnet, bishop 1366-1374, inserted three windows in the presbytery to the south and two to the north. The windows in the north aisle were added by Bishop Gray 1440. The chapel of Bishop Alcock was built in 1488, that of Bishop West in 1534.

From the roof of King's College Chapel, at Cambridge, the distinctive west tower, central lantern, and majestic bulk of the present Cathedral, like a mountain in a plain, give a far-off promise of a place worthy the traveller's halt; and when the wind is fair, many a mile is heard the music of the chiming bells, tantalizing as he continues his journey along the dull melancholy fen-road, which appears as interminable as it is straight. From Stuntney Hill is the best view. They occupy a site rendered famous by the old ballad of King Canute—

> Merrily sung the monks within Ely
> When Canu*e the king rowed thereby:
> " Row me, knights, the shore along,
> And listen we to these monks' song."

A very striking peculiarity is this single WESTERN TOWER. No English cathedral except Bangor and Manchester has such a termination. The other feature of rare occurrence—found, however, also at Lincoln and Peterborough—is the WESTERN TRANSEPT, which forms a magnificent vestibule to the church. Unhappily the northern portion has either fallen or been demolished: it was perfect until the Reformation. The original design was that of a screen covered with arcades, its northern and southern fronts flanked by two tall turrets at either end, and its centre formed by a lofty tower, which contains some of the earliest instances of the Pointed arch in England, and was once crowned with a spire by Northwold, 1229-55 : the grand portal, worthy of a church such as this, is of the first magnitude and importance. It bears some resemblance to the front of Kelso. The foreign appearance induces a belief that it may have been intended to enter it from a court partially covered in, or from an open square like that in front of a Basilica. Barnack stone is used throughout the Cathedral. Now the north wing is in ruins : an octagon and turrets set on the top of the tower has destroyed its proportions, and endangers its stability ; while from below a Galilee porch projects, which, however intrinsically beautiful, is here a blot and disfigurement. It is Early English, and in two stories, the lower composed of an arch subdivided by a single shaft into two trefoiled arches, and having in the spandril foliated tracery. The upper has three lancets; and the whole front has four arcades of trefoiled arches, with a stilted battlement and flanking pinnacles. The clerestory is in each bay of the nave composed of three round-headed arches, the middlemost containing a window. The aisles are of two stories, embattled, each bay being divided by buttresses, in place of plain flat pilasters, as in the clerestory. The windows are Decorated or Perpendicular, except in the case of three original windows on the south side.

An observable peculiarity at Ely is, that the building of the transepts preceded that of the nave. The northern gable is superior to that on the south; it is flanked by turrets crowned with spires; and in place of the southern window of seven lights has two Perpendicular windows side by side, above the old Norman structure below, each story of which has three round-headed windows. As in the nave, a corbel table forms a line above the clerestory and the triforium. In 1321 the central tower fell, and Alan de Walsingham, sacrist, then constructed an OCTAGONAL TOWER ; a unique design, of which there are but three other instances—Peterborough, Batalha, and Evreux. He

thus divided the weight upon eight piers, and set upon it
a wooden roof in order to provide against the recurrence
of such a calamity. It was an original, bold idea, carried
out with consummate skill and a master hand. The
OCTAGON is of one story; the north, south, east, and west
faces being the broader, have an arcade of six arches trefoiled and canopied, while the other four faces being
narrower contain only three, but beneath each of them is
a pointed window of four lights with flowing tracery in the
spandril. Where the angles would meet, hexagonal turrets
are inserted; an open parapet surrounds the whole. From
the centre rises an octagon, or upper lantern of wood
cased with lead, 30 ft. in diameter, and of two stories, with
lights of simple tracery below, and canopied panels of two
arches above, beneath a rich parapet, and flanked with pinnacles. From it Wren designed the lantern of St. Paul's.

The appearance of the south side of the choir is rendered
truly grand by the succession of broadly-spreading buttresses below, which are met by flying buttresses from the
clerestory: each stage is panelled and traceried, with niches
and statues, and a range of crocketed pinnacles, giving an
exquisite lightness to these indispensable supports, but
here additional ornaments, of the fabric. The east end
is of three stories, the upper and lowermost each of three,
the middlemost containing five lancets, flanked by square
turrets, with trefoiled panels: the eastern ends of the
aisles are plain; on the north is a Norman arch with an
insertion of Decorated tracery: on the south, a Perpendicular window; the former is in Bishop West's, the latter
in Bishop Alcock's chantry. Parallel with the north side
of the choir, with its western front on a line with the east
aisle of the transept, is the LADY CHAPEL, of unusual size,
and occupying an extraordinary position, owing to a public road on the east side passing over the ground which
otherwise would have been made its site. The east and
west fronts have an arcade of niches both above and below their great windows, which are flanked with pinnacled
double buttresses: a pierced parapet surrounds the building, which is lighted by five windows on either side.

The entrance is through the GALILEE, the sides adorned each with two arcades of trefoiled arches below, and cinquefoiled in the upper tier. The shafts are of Purbeck marble. An exquisite double doorway, divided by a pier of clustered shafts, admits to the space under the western tower, and discloses the magnificent perspective of a

> Pile, large and massy, for duration built;
> With pillars crowded, and the roof upheld
> By naked rafters, intricately crossed,
> Like leafless underboughs, 'mid some thick grove,
> All withered by the depth of shade above.

Mr. H. L'Estrange, who recently painted the roof of the west tower in fresco, is now engaged in depicting on the nave-roof a tree of Jesse. The elaborate ornament of this part of the church has been attributed to the fact that a covered gallery communicated with the palace, and by it the bishops always entered the Cathedral. The enormous arches which bear up the TOWER were added in 1405, in order to support the weight of the octagon on its summit; although they have been attributed to the reign of Henry VI., and said to have been added with the intention of lengthening the nave and affording strength to the tower when its foundations were found to have been seriously weakened. A melancholy interest attaches to the south-west transept, now the Baptistery, as the place of Mr. Basevi's death, 1845: while visiting the church his foot caught in a nail, and, falling, he was killed on the stone floor. The APSIDAL CHAPEL OF ST. CATHARINE projects eastward from the south-west transept.

The Norman NAVE of thirteen bays has a lofty and unusually light triforium, of an arch in each bay beneath a larger arch, and clerestory of three arches in each bay. The roof is of wood, while the aisles retain their original stone vaulting: the south aisle only has three of the original windows; all the rest are late insertions. In the north aisle are the traces of a door which formerly led into the church of St. Cross: at the extremity is a relic of the latter part of the 7th century, part of the sepulchral cross

of Ovin, steward to Queen Etheldreda, brought from
Haddenham. While the aspect of the nave is sombre
and plain, its vast dimensions and loftiness give it an impressive effect; and its very gloom enhances the impression
of wonder and delight produced by the flood of light,
which is poured down on the magnificent space under the
OCTAGON, which is to be restored as a memorial to Dean
Peacock. When the stained glazing is completed—

> The storied windows richly dight,
> Casting a dim religious light—

no interior will more forcibly inspire those feelings of reve-
rential awe which ought always to be raised in a building
devoted to the Creator's glory and service. Four lofty
arches display the four arms of the Cross, on the ground-
plan. Four subordinate arches in the intervals open
obliquely into the aisles; over each is an arcade of three
canopied trefoiled niches, beneath an exquisite Decorated
window of four lights. In the spandril of each bay is a
niche with a crocketed canopy, resting on short columns,
once gorgeous with gold, azure, and vermilion; the corbels
not, as in the large shafts, wreathed with flowers and
foliage, but sculptured with subjects taken from the legend
of St. Etheldreda :—first and second marriage of Etheldreda; taking the veil; her staff budding; water springing
up to save her from Egfred; rescue of a malefactor;
institution as abbess; death and translation. In the
centre of the vaulting of wood, with a span of 30 feet, is
the lantern, lighted by a pointed window in each face.

The TRANSEPT has east and west aisles, but in the south
wing the western aisle is parted off into a library and two
vestries. The vestry door was brought from Bishop
Alcock's palace at Downham. The Perpendicular hammer-beam roof is painted with devices. It is indeed a
place for angels' worship, the ante-chambers of the Divine
presence—

As if upon my throbbing heart the breath of GOD its influence shed,
So entered I that minster high with timorous joy and faltering tread; .
Words cannot paint what there within awoke my spirit's ecstacies,
The darkly brilliant windows glowed with martyrs' pious effigies;

Into a new and living world rich imaged forth I gazed abroad,
A world of holy women and of warriors of the host of GOD.
Down at the altar low I knelt, thrilling with awe and holy love,
Heaven and its glorious mysteries were pictured on the vault above;
But when again I looked up, arch, roof, and pictured vault were gone,
Full opened was the door of heaven, and every veil had been with-
    drawn.

In each Cathedral certain portions and effects adhere to the memory—fretted shrine, chantry, or ornamental subordinate detail. At Ely the CHOIR and OCTAGON can never be forgotten. In them we see the most exquisite copy of nature—the bossy vaulting like the starry deep-blue sky, the shafted pillar like the moulded stem, the pointed arch like the petals of summer flowers. The observer is at a loss to which to accord the preference—the elaborate enrichment, the infinity of ornament, the variety and intricacy which address the imagination in the choir, or the simpler elegance and grace, and vast triforium, of the faultless presbytery.

The liberality of the present Chapter and the noblemen graduates, and other members of the neighbouring university, here emulates the piety of elder days. The work of restoration, under Mr. G. G. Scott, has been alike munificent, artistic, and judicious. The Early English CHOIR is of three bays; the Decorated PRESBYTERY of six bays. The organ was built by Hill in 1851. The organ-case was blazoned by Castell of London. Three deeply-recessed lancets of equal height, with a range of five unequal lancets above, form the termination of the CHOIR, for grouping the most magnificent composition in England, the details most exquisite, the gradual diminution of its stages giving it a wonderfully aspiring effect. Through a bequest of 1500l. by Bishop Sparke, these east windows are filled with glass by Wailes. The old altar-piece, the release of St. Peter by the Angel, the work of José de Ribeira, was a gift of Bishop Yorke, 1801. The reredos of stone, with five sculptures, by John Phillips of London, of our Lord's ministry, was the gift of Mr. John Dunn Gardner: the figures are twenty inches high. Above the groined canopy of the central bay is the Transfiguration. The other subjects are—The Entry into Jerusalem, Washing the Apostles' feet, The Last Supper, the Agony, and Bearing the Cross. The twisted shafts are surmounted by angels, and inlaid with coloured stones. The orfrey of the frontal of the altar was the work of Miss Agnes Blencowe. The stall-work of Alan de Walsingham, which fills three bays of the choir, has been augmented by canopied seats and an open rood-screen of noble design and excellent workmanship, carved by Rattee and Philip of Cambridge, after G. G. Scott's designs. The superb brass gates are by Potter, of London, and the iron metal-work by Hardman, of Birmingham. By a local tradition the bishop has no throne, but sits in the abbot's place, and the dean in the prior's seat, in the angles of the screen. The sermon from time immemorial has been preached in the nave, and the congregations from the parish churches come in the morning to hear it.

In the north transept are four windows by Wailes and Moore ; in the south transept the windows are by Gerente and Howes. In Bishop West's chapel the windows are by Evans.

S. Aisle, Nave.—A series of eleven windows by Gerente, Warrington, N. J. Cottingham, Hardman, Gibbs, Howes, Wailes, and Moore.

Chapel of St. Katherine.—The Baptism of our Lord, Wilmhurst. the other windows are by Wailes.

N. E. Window of the Octagon (which has been rebuilt), the gift of Cambridge undergraduates, 1849. Wailes. The *South East* window was the gift of the Rev. E. Sparke.

Choristers' Window, by F. Oliphant and W. Dyce, R.A., the gift of T. Ingram.

The Puritans destroyed the ancient stained glass of the choir clerestory. Cromwell, in January 1644, then residing at Ely, swept out the congregation at the head of his troops. At the east end of the north aisle is Bishop Alcock's chantry ; and in the south aisle the chapel of Bishop West, with very good gates. THE LADY CHAPEL, now the parish church of the Holy Trinity, is of the date of Edward III. : the traces of its windows, its arcades,

and canopied niches, are superb; and it contains a
curious series of sculptures in relief, with subjects taken
from the life of the Virgin.

The principal monuments in the church are the following :—

Choir.—Bishop Alcock, d. 1500, chantry

N. Aisle.—Bishop West, d. 1533, chantry; the original iron gates
remain in the recesses.

Choir, N. Side.—Bishop Gray, d. 1478, slab.

Fourth Bay.—Bishop Redmayne, d. 1506, effigy with a Jesse candlestick, four kings and four dragons, and a sculpture of the Fall.
His arms in black paper, 1478, are on an adjoining pillar.

S. Aisle, Choir.—Brass of Bishop Goodrich, 1554, effigy in vestments,
mitred and with a pastoral staff; Dean Tyndall, 1614, brass.

Choir, S. Aisle Arch.—Bishop Hotham, d. 1337, restored by Richardson.

Presbytery, N. Side, 5th Bay.—Bishop Kilkenny, d. 1256, effigy.

Presbytery, S. Side 2nd Arch.—Bishop Barnet, d. 1374.

Fourth Bay.—Bishop Heton, d. 1609, effigy in a cope.

Near the Steps of the Altar.—Bishop Northwold, d. 1254, restored
by Richardson, effigy, monument with sculptures of St. Edmund.

Presbytery, 3 Arches.—Bishop De Louth, d. 1298, restored in polychrome; the accomplished John Tiptoft, Earl of Worcester, Chancellor and Lieutenant of Ireland, beheaded 1470; Cardinal Luxem-
burgh, d. 1443, restored.

Ambulatory of Choir.—A coffin-lid of black marble, of the 12th
century, brought from St. Mary's Chapel.

Osmund, a Swedish bishop; Ednorth, of Lincoln;
Alfwyn, Elfgar, and Athelstan, of Elmham; Brethroth,
Duke of Northumberland; and Archbishop Wolstau, of
York, 1002, were buried here.

THE DIMENSIONS OF THE CATHEDRAL IN FEET

	Length.	Breadth.	Height
Nave	250	78	76
Choir	64	78	70
Presbytery	95	..	..
Transept	179 f. 6in.	74 f. 6in.	..
Lady Chapel	95	46	60
Galilee	44 f. 9in.	..	..
Octagon	..	65	..
West Tower	48	..	266
Extreme length	517		

The Chapter consists of a dean and eight canons; there are five minor canons, eight lay vicars, and 12 choristers. There are two choral services daily, at 10 and 3·30; the Holy Communion is administered monthly and on great festivals. The income of the Chapter in 1852 was 16,214*l.* Their expenditure on the fabric in the previous fourteen years was 28,000*l.*, including 4800*l.* public subscriptions, and in special gifts 4000*l.* The library contains 4000 volumes. Among the bishops occur Godfrey Ridel, who was called by à Becket an arch-devil and limb of antichrist, and when summoned to Rome to pay for his mitre, replied, " I have a Gospel dispensation, and have married a wife, and therefore I cannot come; the Viceroy Longchamp, affecting kingly state, yet the first to discover Cœur de Lion in his dungeon; Eustace, Lord Chancellor; W.de Kilkenny and John de Kirkby, Lord Keepers; Hugh de Balsham, founder of Peter House, Cambridge; John Hotham, Lord Chancellor, equally prepared to take part in war or delicate affairs of state; Philip Morgan, Lord Keeper; Cardinals Langham, Bourchier, Morton, and Luxembourg, who held out the Bastile for three days as governor of Paris; Alcock, founder of Jesus College, Cambridge; Redman, who when he entered a town had the church-bells rung that he might collect the poor, to each of whom he gave sixpence in alms; Nicholas West, who set fire to the Provost's lodge at King's College, because he was disappointed of the Proctorship; Goodrich, Lord Chancellor; Cox, whom Elizabeth swore she would unfrock when he protested against the ornaments of her chapel; Andrews, Wren, Gunning, and Patrick. Among the dignitaries were three cardinals, and Wedderburn, Bishop of Dunblane. The bishop's palace is at Ely: he retains the town house, Ely House, Dover Street.

Arms: Gules, three keys erect, or.

Crossing the deanery garden, is the infirmary chapel, of a date a little earlier than the west front of the Cathedral. The restored priory chapel in the deanery, which appears to advantage from the chestnut walk, was built by John de Craudon, prior 1321-1341: it has a very curious pave-

ment, representing the fall of Adam, in the high pace.
The north-east angle of the cloisters, which were destroyed
in 1650, remains : the Norman doorways are remarkably
fine ; that on the north-east was the monks' entrance,
that on the north-west, four bays from the west in the
south aisle, was the prior's. The chapter-house has been
destroyed. Some copes—one of green velvet, of the
15th century, with the Annunciation represented on
the hood, and on the orfrey figures of SS. Andrew,
James, Katharine, &c.,—are preserved in the vestry. It
was built by Bishop Eustace, 1200-15. The deanery,
built in the 13th century, was the refectory. The sacristy
was built by Alan de Walsingham. The stables were the
abbey-grange. The kitchen, store-house, and hall of the
Guest-house, and vaults of the almonry, form part of the
prebendal houses. The western gate of brick, with battlemented and low towers, was built by Prior Buckton, 1440.
The bishop's palace, altered by Bishop Keene, was built
by Bishops Alcock and Goodrich; the former was the
architect of the Great Gallery, 100 feet in length: in it
is the Tabula Eliensis, a picture of the time of Henry VII.,
representing the 40 knights whom William I. quartered on
the abbey. There is also a curious picture of Bishop Cox's
funeral.

Exeter.

EXETER was the British Caer Isc, "The City of the river
Exe," and the Iscan-Ceaster of the Saxon. It is situated
on a hill, and for an old city, retains very few remains of
antiquity. It was taken by King Stephen in 1136, and
besieged by William I. It has been visited by Henry
III.: Edward I., who kept Christmas 1285, was with his
queen here 1286, and alone 1297; Edward, the Black
Prince, with the captive King John of France, 1357, and
alone 1371; Henry VI., 1451; Richard III., Sept. 8,
1483; Charles II., 1680; and William III., 1688. It re-

sisted a siege by Perkin Warbeck, 1498. George III. and
Queen Charlotte, Aug. 1789, were for two days the guests
of the dean. Among the natives of Exeter may be mentioned Sir Thomas Bodley, Simon Ockley, Eustace Budgell,
Tom D'Urfey, Lord Giffard, Sir Vicary Gibbs, Peter Lord
King, Sir W. Petre, Cardinal Langton, Princess Henrietta,
Maria, Duchess of Orleans, and the "Judicious Hooker,"
born at Heavitree. It was called Monk Town, from the
number of its monasteries. It was taken by Prince
Maurice, 1643; by Fairfax, April 1646. The principal
churches are All Hallows in the Walls, St. Paul's, and St.
James, with stained glass in the windows: St. Laurence's
and St. Mary's Major have oak screens; St. James' has a
pulpit of carved Spanish work; and St. Paul's a font of
black marble. The gateway, three bastions, and part of
the walls of Rougemont Castle, where Richard III. forecast
his impending death. The Guildhall has remains at the
back of the 15th century, with an upper story added a
hundred years later. The College Hall is of the 14th
century; St. John's Hospital is of much interest. St.
Wynard's Hospital Chapel in Magdalen Street; it is of
the 15th century. The massive Norman crypt of St.
Nicholas' Priory (Mint Lane) is now used as a kitchen.
There are some good Elizabethan timber houses; at the
corner of North Street there is a house of the 15th century.

The Cathedral takes a high rank among those of
the second class; but the unusual position of the towers,
and want of height, render the exterior ineffective.
The church is composed of a NAVE and CHOIR, with aisles,
Lady Chapel, and a TRANSEPT formed out of the TOWERS,
as at Ottery St. Mary, Narborne and Chalons-sur-Marne
in France; Blois has no transept; Angouleme has towers at
the ends of the transepts. It is believed that these towers
were at the west end of the old cathedral, of which St
Andrew's and St. James' chapels were the transepts. The
roof is crowned with a fleur-de-lys ridge ornament of lead,
the only example of that decoration which remains on
an English cathedral.

Bishop William Warelwast, 1107-1136, began to build a Cathedral 1112, of which the TRANSEPT TOWERS alone remain ; it was not completed till the episcopate of Henry Marshall, 1194-1206. The present Cathedral was commenced by Peter Quivil in 1288 ; the first four eastern arches of the choir were completed in 1310, by Bishop Stapleton. John Grandison, bishop 1327-70, completed the CHOIR, vaulted the NAVE, built by Bishop Bytton, 1293-1307, and it is said, built the WEST FRONT in 1360, and organ-screen. Bishop Bruere, 1224-1244, built the LADY CHAPEL, completed by Bishop Quivil, 1281-91 ; Walter Bronescombe, bishop 1257-80, the chapels of St. Mary Magdalene and Gabriel. Thomas Brentingham, bishop 1370-95, made some minor additions to the west front, and added the cloisters and east window of the choir in 1392. Edmund Lacy, bishop 1420-58, built, and Bishop Booth in 1478 completed, the upper part of the CHAPTER-HOUSE, the lower portion being of the date of Henry III. John Booth, bishop 1465-78, erected the episcopal throne. Bishop Stapleton erected the sedilia. The reredos is by John Kendall, 1818 ; the pulpit dates from 1560. The havoc made by the rebels is only too apparent in the injured effigies. The stone font, a copy of that at Beverley Minster by Rowe, was set up in 1842. The ancient wooden lectern is now in St. Thomas' church.

The stone of which the church, for the most part, was built, came from Bere, near Colyton, that for the vaulting, from Silverton ; the pavement of the choir is Caen stone. The disuse of encaustic tiles on floors after the period of the Reformation, was caused by the introduction of marble by John of Padua, and other Italian artists employed in England. The old painted glass was bought at Rouen in Normandy, 1303, 1317-1323. The west window bears date 1766, and is by Peckett. The WEST FRONT, restored by Kendall in 1817, is composed of three stories : the first is an elaborate screen, with a central doorway, and covered with canopied imagery work ; in the second is the great west window of the nave, 32 feet by 27 feet, glazed by Peckett 1766, of nine lights, trefoiled, with a superb rose of 12 quatrefoiled lights, and an inner foliated marygold of 10 lights foliated. The upper story is formed by the gable. One very striking feature of the Cathedral is the rich Decorated tracery of the windows, set between bold flying buttresses. The buttresses of the nave and aisle have the " Devonshire pinnacle " rising out of small battlements. Within, the splendid stone vaulting of nave and choir is the most beautiful in the kingdom, and the whole building is remarkable for grace and minute finish ; the uniformity of the choir and nave render it very imposing. The chapels and screens are numerous, and contain details of the utmost delicacy and beauty. We feel the intense unusual silence, and the echo of the measured tiptoe tread runs down the vault like a voice enjoining silence in a whisper.

On the frame

At such transition from the fervid air.
A grateful coolness falls, that seems to strike
The heart, in concert with that temperate awe
And natural reverence which the place inspires.

Every student of our mediæval treasures must have observed the poetic and picturesque aspect of these structures, the creation of a varied outline by means of projections, breaks in the building, unequal and irregular, all tempered and modulated by a refinement of taste, which makes the whole diversified building pleasing to the eye, breadth being added to the base, and the height of the main fabric increased by the contrast. This perfection was the result of the honesty of purpose in the builders, and it was attained by a progressive combination of contrivances and of ornaments separately devised. The pointed arch, the clustered column, mullioned light, and deep portal, were not simultaneously produced. Successive enrichments were independent inventions, and only by their gradual accumulation was the gorgeous cathedral completed to command the admiration of generations. To the devoted energy and enthusiasm of the Freemasons, then a religious corporation, must the rapid progress and grand results be referred ; to the constant intercourse and correspondence among fraternities spread over Europe, the active intelligence of those architects errant, ever seeking excellence and unknown perfection, whose secret died with them—a body which numbered amongst its Grand Masters, Chichele of Canterbury, Giffard and Wolsey of York, St. Swithin, William of Wykeham, De Roche and Waynflete of Winchester, Gundulph of Rochester, Beauchamp of Sarum, and Stapledon of this see.

On the south-west angle is ST. EDMUND'S CHAPEL, now the consistory court; and into the five bays of the nave the north porch forms an entrance: above it is an elaborate MINSTRELS' GALLERY, with twelve quatrefoiled niches, with imagery of angels sounding on instruments of music —it is of the reign of Edward III. The cithern, bagpipe, harp, organ, pipe, tambourine, trumpet, and shawm appear. On the east side of the NORTH TRANSEPT is St. Paul's, and to the east of the SOUTH TRANSEPT, St. John Baptist's chapel. Beyond, the CHAPEL OF ST. ANDREW on the north, and the CHAPEL OF ST. JAMES on the south, form a sort of eastern transept. The aisles of the choir terminate in the CHAPEL OF ST. MARY MAGDALENE, with an adjoining CHAPEL OF ST. GEORGE on the north, and in the CHAPEL OF ST. GABRIEL, with an adjoining CHAPEL OF ST. SAVIOUR, on the south. The triforium throughout the church is light, consisting of arcades of four trifoliated arches in each bay, with a gallery of open stone-work, of double rows of quatrefoils, behind which rises the clerestory. The ORGAN-SCREEN of three arches, with its modern panelled additions, made in 1819, is very fine : its panels are painted with examples of early art—Scripture subjects from the Creation to Pentecost, forming thirteen oil paintings in the style of the date of Edward III. There were two altars under this screen, dedicated to St. Mary and St. Nicholas. The stalls are of good design, the bishop's throne, of black oak, is unrivalled, and forms a pyramid fifty-two feet in height, reaching almost to the roof. The three sedilia, with rich open-work canopies, are exquisite. The stained glass of the east window is the original glazing, 1396. The Early English CHAPTER-HOUSE was built 1224-1244; the upper part, Perpendicular, was added in 1427; into it, in 1822, the library was removed from the Lady Chapel: it is an oblong with a richly panelled and pointed roof, on the south side of the south transept tower. It has Early English arcading of couplets, and four-light Perpendicular side-windows, and a seven-light east window. The cloisters were destroyed by the fanatical Puritans, when the Cathedral was parted by a traverse into two meeting-houses, one for the Presbyterians and the other for the Independents: this wall Bishop Ward pulled down, and spent 25,000l. on the restorations.

The westernmost arch of the CHOIR is very acute, not more than a fifth of the others in width, in order to accommodate it to the towers. The TOWERS are of eight stages, battlemented. The south has four arcades of round-headed, intersecting, chevroned, pointed and trefoiled arches, with square arcaded buttress turrets. The north and south windows are rich Decorated; the east window is of nine lights trefoiled, in three compartments; Early Perpendicular, under a rose window of nine quatrefoiled lights. In the SOUTH TOWER are eleven bells; the tenor, weighing 7552 pounds, was given by Bishop Grandison, and having been cracked in ringing a peal for the discovery of the Gunpowder Plot, was recast by Perdue, in 1676, who also recast the famous Tom of Exeter, which weighs 12,500 pounds. This bell was brought from Llandaff Cathedral in 1484, by Bishop Courtenay, who built an octagon and a spire on the north tower; they were removed April 25th, 1752. The spire on the south tower was removed before 1618. There is an ancient astronomical clock of the date of Edward III. in the north transept, given by Bishop Courtenay. The upper dial was added 1760. The only CRYPT is under St. James' Chapel, in the south transept. The NORTH TRANSEPT is St. Paul's; the SOUTH WING St. John's tower.

The organ, built by Loosemore, 1664, at a cost of 2,000l., and the gift of Bishop Ward, was rebuilt by H. Lincoln in 1819, and improved by Byfield and Gray. The musical service was celebrated in no other church of England with

such great solemnity and excellence. Cosmo de Medici
mentions it in 1669 as the best; in the kingdom ; and Defoe, in his tour, says " The solemnity, decency, and affecting harmony of the service, and the numerous congregation who attend, summer and winter, 6 A.M. prayers, and
their grave and pious behaviour, render the Cathedral a
glory to the diocese, the envy of other choirs, and the admiration of strangers."   Viols and other instruments,
besides the organ, were used at Exeter until the civil
wars, as at Lincoln.   Here, as at Lichfield, the Litany is
sung by a priest-vicar and a lay-vicar.   The faldstool is
found .here, at Canterbury, York, Lincoln, Lichfield, and
Oxford.

DIMENSIONS OF THE CATHEDRAL IN FEET.

	Length.	Breadth.	Height
Nave . .	180	60	68
Choir . .	132	54	68
Transept .	140	32	68
Lady Chapel .	65	35	40
Chapter-house .	55	28	50
Towers .	28	28	145
Total length .	387	..	..

The Chapter is composed of a dean and six canons, two
stalls are suspended.   There are four priest-vicars and
eight lay vicars-choral, (who form a college founded by
Henry IV.,) and ten choristers.   There are two daily
choral services at ¼-past 10 and 3.   The Holy Communion is celebrated weekly.   The income of the Chapter in 1852 was 11,431*l*, and their expenditure on the
fabric in the preceding fourteen years, 16,113*l*.   The
library contains 5000 volumes, and includes the valuable
MS. Domesday of Cornwall, Devon, and Somerset. Bishop
Hall, alluding to the poverty of the see, said " it made him
a baron, but a bare one."

Among the bishops occur Warelwast, the blind bishop,
who resigned, having " small joy of the world ;" who ex-
amined St. Anselm's mails at Dover, and when he found no
money in them suffered him to quit the kingdom ; Robert
Chichester, the pilgrim and indefatigable collector of re-

liques; Eske, "the light of the English Church;" Brewer,
the crusader who fought under the walls of Acre; Walter
de Stapledon, founder of Exeter College, Oxford—beheaded
by a London mob at Cheapside Cross; Grandison, who
constituted himself or his cathedral heir general of the
property of his clergy, and barred the gates against the
visitation of the primate; Stafford, Lord Chancellor; Fox
and Oldham, who predicted the fall of the monasteries
when his friend founded Corpus Christi College, Oxford;
Coverdale, translator of the Holy Bible; the tolerant
Turberville; Wolton, who when expiring said "a Bishop
should die standing," and rose to his feet; Colton, of whom
from his hesitation in speech, so that he could say no more
than Amen, his enemies avowed that he lived like a bishop
and died like a clerk; pious learned Hall, who was buried
in a churchyard, for, said he, "God's house is no meet
repository for the body of the greatest of saints;" Brown-
rigg, who never saw his diocese; Seth Ward, who would
not marry because he could not afford a poor wife and
would not be dependent on a rich one; Gauden, the reputed author of Eikon Basilike; the learned Sparrow;
Trelawny, for whom the miners sang,

> And shall Trelawny die?
> There are thirty thousand underground shall know the reason why;

Blackburne, the converted buccaneer; and quaint Blackall.
Among the dignitaries, occur the names of William of
Exeter, Adam Murimuth, Jonathan Toup, Anthony Hor-
neck, and Deans Milles and Lyttelton.

The Bishop's Palace, on the south, was let to a sugar
refiner during the rebellion. The chapel is Early English.
There is a fine chimney-piece set up by Bishop Courtenay.
In the Close at midnight Peter de Lechlade the precentor
was murdered as he returned from saying his office: the
King was at Exeter, and summarily ordered the mayor and
citizens to be hung, and the close to be forthwith walled
and rendered secure with gates. A house on the north
side has a bay window of the time of Henry VII., and a
fine wooden ceiling.

Arms : Az. a stag's head caboshed arg.: between the attires across pattée fitchée of the last.

The principal monuments are those of—

St. Gabriel's Chapel.—General Simcoe, 1806, Flaxman ; Northcote (statue), Flaxman ; Sir J. Gilbert and Dame, effigies, date of James 1.

N. Transept.—William Sylke, d. 1508, curious fresco of the Resurrection above the chantry, built 1485 ; contemporaneous, discovered 1853, the almost defaced painting adjoining Is of the 14th century.

S. Transept, N. E. Angle.—Bishop Leofric, d. 1072, canopy of the date of Henry V., with imagery.

S. Transept, S. E. Angle.—Bishop John the Chanter, d. 1194.

N. Choir Aisle.—Sir Richard Stapledon, knt., effigy ; brother of the bishop.

St. George's Chapel.—Sir John Speke, knt., d. 1518, chantry-screen, effigy ; outside is a Roman pavement, discovered 1843.

St. Saviour's Chapel.—Bishop Oldham, chantry-screen, effigy, d. 1519.

Lady Chapel.—Bishop Peter Quivil (floriated cross), d. 1292.

N. Wall.—Bishop Bartholomew, d. 1148, effigy ; Bishop Simon de Apulia, d. 1223, effigy of Purbeck marble.

W. Front.—Bishop Grandison, chantry, d. 1370, St. Rhadegund's Chapel.

S. Aisle, Choir.—Bishop Cotton, d. 1621, effigy with canonical cap.

N. Aisle.—Bishop Carey, in parliamentary robes, d. 1627.

N. Aisle, N. Side of Choir.—Bishop Stapledon, d. 1326, founder of Exeter College, Oxford, effigy under a canopy.

Nave.—Hugh Courtenay, Earl of Devon, d. 1377, and Countess Margaret, d. 1391, effigies ; brass of Sir Peter Courtenay, d. 1409.

S. Aisle, Choir.—H. de Bohun, Earl of Hereford, slain at Boroughbridge, d. 1322, effigy.

St. Mary Magdalene's Chapel.—Sir Peter Carew, slain in Flanders in the time of Queen Elizabeth, effigy ; Judge Doddridge, d. 1628, effigy ; Wm. Parkhouse, d. 1540, a cadaver.

N. Side of Choir.—Bishop Marshall, d. 1206, effigy, Purbeck tomb with imagery.

S. Aisle, Choir.—Bishop Chichester, d. 1155, slab of Purbeck marble, brass removed ; Sir Arthur Chichester, his brother, effigy.

S. Side of Choir.—Bishop John Wolton, d. 1595 altar-tomb.

St. Mary Magdalene's.—Bishop Stafford, d. 1419, screen, altar-tomb, canopied effigy.

St. Gabriel's.—Bishop Bronscombe, d. 1280, screen and canopy of 15th century ; superb tomb, effigy, contemporaneous.

Gloucester.

GLOUCESTER, the British Caer Glow, "The Fair City," and
Saxon Gloweceaster, is situated on the Severn, in a vale
remarkable for beauty even amongst the wonderful series
of southern valleys of England. J. Taylor, the Water-
poet, was a native of Gloucester. The royal visits have
been the following: Edward Confessor 1053 and 1063;
William I. 1072; Rufus and Malcolm III. 1093; William
II. 1099; Henry I. 1123; Henry II. 1175; Henry III.
1234; Edward II. 1319; Richard II. 1378; Richard III.
1483; Henry IV. 1420; Henry VII. 1485; Henry VIII.
1535; James II. 1685 and 1687; Prince of Wales 1807.
Parliaments sat here 1084, 1234, 1279, 1320, 1403, and
1407. On Alney Isle was fought the duel for a crown
between Edmund Ironside and Canute, in the front of
both armies. The city suffered greatly from fire and the
ravages of the Danes; in 1087 during the contest of Rufus
and Count Robert; in 1263 in the battles of Henry III.
and the barons. In 1461-2 the Parliamentarians held
out against the king, and after the Restoration the walls
were destroyed as a disgrace. So full was Gloucester
once of churches, that the proverb ran "As sure as God's
faith is in Gloucester."

Within a century gates and walls have been destroyed,
the High Cross destroyed, and the ancient conduit removed
to a private garden. There still remain the cruciform
barn, a 15th century stable, and part of the gatehouse,
which George Selwyn begged to set on the top of his
mountain of Llanthony Priory of Austin Canons; the
choir of the Grey Friars church of the 15th century;
the interesting church of St. Mary de Lode, Early
English, lately restored; St. Mary le Crypt, Late Perpendicular; St. Nicholas, with its once beautiful spire
truncated; the Booth Hall of wood, formerly the Shire
Hall; the Norman Chapel of St. Mary Magdalen Hospital,
of the date of King Stephen; the west gate, of the

Tudor period, near a bridge of five arches built in the reign of Henry II.; and the New Inn, built of chestnut wood by Turning, a monk of the 15th century, with two tiers of galleries leading to dormitories, still fit to receive an audience of Chaucer's pilgrims, or display the mummeries of a band of Shakspeare's carriers. It served for the accommodation of visitors to King Edward's tomb. The crypt Grammar School is Late Perpendicular; at the end of Northcote Street is a 15th century timber house, with a rich corner post; not far from it is a magnificent oak gateway.

The Cathedral of St. Peter, approached through the west gate, the ancient entrance of the precinct, was formerly the minster of a mitred abbey of Benedictines. Its dedication was changed to that of the Holy Trinity on the creation of the see, September 3rd, 1541. It stands in a secluded enclosure, and an air of solemnity breathes round it in keeping with its sacred associations. Of whatever prejudice or partisanship history may be suspected, this cathedral is at least an incorruptible witness of what our forefathers could achieve: even externally it continues the great design of its construction; it ennobles the taste and appeals to the sympathy of the lowliest; it is impressive to the ignorant, it arouses the imagination and uplifts the mind of the educated passer-by, as powerfully as the recesses of the Carthusian forest affected the mind of Gray with the perception of a more present Deity. Its open portals invite the mourner to consolation, the stranger to a home, the anxious to an oracle that cannot err, for he who turns aside to pray loses no step upon his journey. Within, all is peace, serene and unbroken; no common light subdued and tranquil plays through the panes dyed by time, or glass tinged with every rainbow hue, or with only the more glorious golden network of the restless sunbeam flowing along the floor: every distant form, that walks dimly in the far-off aisles, seems shrunken to a lesser span; the building appears to dilate in the uncertain light which scarcely discloses the depths that add increased mystery to its intricate formation.

The Cathedral consists of a CENTRAL TOWER, a SOUTH PORCH, a NAVE of eight bays with aisles, a TRANSEPT of one bay with an apsidal chapel in each wing, a CHOIR of five very unequal bays with aisles, and eastern ambulatory, with an apsidal chapel on either side ; and a cruciform LADY CHAPEL.

Robert, Bishop of Hereford, laid the first stone in 1089 ; and the NAVE, CRYPT, and chapels, completed by Abbot Serlo, who was also the architect of the CHAPTER-HOUSE, were consecrated by the Bishops of Worcester, Bangor, and Rochester, in 1100. Abbot Morwent, 1420-37, built the WEST FRONT, the SOUTH PORCH, and two west bays of the NAVE. The vaulting of the nave and the misereres of the choir were completed between 1228-43, in the abbacy of Foliot, by the monks' own hands. The SOUTH TRANSEPT was erected 1310-30. The Abbeys of Bristol, Keynsham, and Malmesbury refused to receive the dead King Edward, when Abbot Thokey bore him reverently, beneath a gorgeous pall, (drawn by stags, as the legend went,) from Berkeley to Gloucester. Edward III. and thousands of pilgrims with gifts and offerings at the tomb enabled the abbot to commence great buildings. He built the SOUTH AISLE of the nave 1307-29 ; Abbot Wigmore, 1329-37, built the NORTH TRANSEPT, St. Andrew's aisle. The LADY CHAPEL, begun by Henley, abbot 1457-72, was completed by Abbot Farley before 1498 ; the remainder of the CHOIR by William Parker in 1514. The CENTRAL TOWER was the work of Abbot Sebroke, 1455-7, and finished by Robert Tully, afterwards Bishop of St. David's. The choir vaulting, 1337-51, with the stalls on the Prior's side, was added by Adam Staunton. The CLOISTERS, commenced in 1375 by Abbot Horton, were finished by Abbot Frocester, 1381-1412 ; . the former finished the PRESBYTERY and stalls on the abbot's side. The vaulting of the choir, Abbot Borgfield saw finished before 1381.

The WEST END contains under a pierced parapet and pa- nelling, a large nine-light window, filled with stained glass, to the memory of Bishop Monk, by Rev. T. M. Murray, 1858, and is flanked by pinnacled turrets, without gable or towers. There is a four-light window transomed on either side. A SOUTH PORCH forms the chief approach. It is of two stages, with six canopied niches above the doorway, angular turrets, and a pierced battlement, of the richest workmanship. The panelled parapet of the clerestory is battlemented, the buttresses of the base tier are pinnacles with gable niches and imagery. The aisles have three light Decorated windows, with rich geometrical tracery ; the clerestory windows are of simpler design.

The TRANSEPT has an eight-light Decorated window, and is flanked by square turrets crowned with spires, and arcaded where even with the gable, which has eight round-headed chevroned lancets. But the glory of the church, its apparent strength undiminished by the elaborate carving of quatrefoil bands, and canopied arcades of trefoiled arches, is its sumptuous CENTRAL TOWER of two stories, massive and stately, of commanding majesty, soaring royally above the fabric, and yet, from its lavish ornament and admirable proportions, light and elegant ; not so graceful, but with far more dignity than a spire. In each face of the two stories are two canopied two-light windows, above which is a pierced and embattled parapet, with square turrets of open work, crowned with perforated spires, but wrought almost beyond the natural capacity of stone. The Cathedral is built of fine-grained and ill-cemented oolite, shelly oolite and red sandstone (north side) intermixed. The tower is of shelly oolite ; the latter contains eight bells, the largest weighs 6,500 pounds.

The seven NAVE arches are semicircular, with plain massive piers below, and a Norman triforium ; the clerestory is Perpendicular, as are the west front, the two western arches, and the rich bossed tracery in the groining above them : the rest is plain. The NAVE floor was found by Mr. Waller to have been raised above its original level : the piers support arches, as at Oxford, out of all proportion to the incumbent structure, the first unequal struggle of the builders to gain an impossible height in Norman work.

The chapel in the NORTH TRANSEPT is Early English. Between the stalls of the choir and the NORTH WING is a chapel. In either choir-aisle, on the north-east and south-east, is a similar chapel. In the SOUTH TRANSEPT is a curious stone confessional, rich and elaborate, Perpendicular, with colossal angels stooping over it.

No contrast can be more abrupt and striking than the transition from the solid simplicity and massive grandeur of the Norman NAVE, with its ponderous circular columns and arches enriched with fillet and double cone mouldings, into a transept, choir, and Lady Chapel elaborately traceried, and displaying on every side fancy and grace.

The dignity and breadth of the CHOIR are lost in the loftiness of the vaulting, and the rich design and expanse of the east window, bowed from standing on the foundations of the original apse, of eight orders and fourteen lights, 78 feet long by 35 feet in width, glowing with stained glass; at a near approach like a paved work of sapphire stones and gems of every hue, but from the western door, the ruby and topaz, the emerald and opal, all are toned down by distance and melt into a lustrous grey. It contains 2798 square feet of glass of tints multitudinous as the tissue of tapestry, of the time of Edward III., when the material was produced at one shilling the square foot, so that the original cost was 139*l*. 18*s*. The choir is spacious, grand, and imposing, and yields to none in symmetry and effect. So ingenious is the transformation, that the eye can scarcely realize the fact that, here over the solid parts, at a distance from their surface to soften and enrich, has been dropped a network of mullions, arches, and tracery, like a veil of lacework drawn over some stately figure, or gossamer tangled in bushes that tuft themselves in solid rock. At Gloucester the Pointed style is added to the Norman, at Winchester they are amalgamated. Here the original multangular east end is rendered nearly square by these additions. The panelled walls, the thirty-one tabernacled stalls, with grotesques under the misereres, the airy lightness and lavish ornament, complete a whole, magnificent

and marvellous in conception; while over all, the roof
rests on the side walls as softly as the snow-flake on a
flower. To use the words of an accomplished poet, it is

> An immense
> And glorious work of fine intelligence!
> Give all thou canst; high Heaven rejects the lore
> Of nicely calculated less or more.
> So deemed the man who fashioned for the sense
> These lofty pillars; spread that branching roof,
> Self-poised and scooped into ten thousand cells,
> Where light and shade repose, where music dwells
> Lingering and wandering on as loth to die:
> Like thoughts, whose very sweetness yieldeth proof
> That they were born for immortality.

The CHOIR extends by one bay into the nave. The organ-
screen, by Smirke, was erected in 1823. The organ, built
by Harris, 1670, was improved by Willis, 1847. Screens
fill the base story and the round arches of the triforium;
the clerestory is of four-light windows. In the triforium
is an ancient diptych, 10 ft. by 7 ft., of the 15th century, and
Italian workmanship; it represents a Doom and the New
Jerusalem. In some of the windows are very interesting
remains of Early Perpendicular and Decorated glass.
The tiles bear the arms of Plantagenets, Clares, and
Despencers. The LADY CHAPEL is partially seen through
the screen-work at the back of the modern reredos, which
becomes in its upper stage the east window of the choir.
The triforium chapels look down through their screens
into the church; and owing, to the superior elevation of
the choir, a flat window in the nave arch admits light
with a marvellous effect.

Horace Walpole narrates a curious anecdote: he found
in the choir, next the altar, a huge pew furnished with
green damask curtains and two bird-troughs full of canary
and rape seed. Its poor crazed occupant, a Mrs. Cotton,
bribed the Chapter with contributions towards white-
washing the walls, to give her this aviary, as she believed
her daughter had transmigrated into a robin-redbreast.

A curious whispering gallery, 75 feet long, 3 feet wide

and 8 feet high, is in the triforium, between the choir
and Lady Chapel, and is mentioned as a curiosity by Lord
Bacon. On the wall are written these lines—

> Doubt not but GOD who sits on high
> Thy secret prayer can hear,
> When a dead wall thus cunningly
> Conveys soft whispers to the ear.

The LADY CHAPEL, rich and elaborate Perpendicular, is
peculiar, being cruciform; the rich reredos and high pace
remain. The glazing of the east window, of nine lights
and four orders, is of the latter half of the 15th century.

The CLOISTERS, a paradise of architecture, yet used as
stables by the rebel troopers, for extent and tracery
unsurpassed, are on the north side; in the south alley
is the lavatory; and the " carols," or recesses, where the
monks wrote and illuminated missal and chronicle, remain
perfect as when they were first erected, with the sculpture
sharp and fresh. The door at the north-east angle leads
to a groined Early English passage, which opens into a
SMALL CLOISTER. To the east of it is part of the INFIR-
MARY CHAPEL, Late Perpendicular. During the session of
Parliament, 1378, the monastery was like a fair, says the
chronicler, and the garth was so trampled by wrestlers
and ball-players that not a blade of grass was to be
seen.

In the east walk is the entrance to the CHAPTER-HOUSE,
built 1088-95, with an east end and vaulting added by Foliot in 1242: it is an oblong, and was fitted up as a library
in 1826-7. Roger Earl of Hereford and Walter de Lacy,
a Norman knight, and Richard Strongbow of the 11th
century, were buried in the chapter-house which has been
restored: while the library, first established for the Parliamentarian soldiers, has been removed to the building
long known as the College School, and formerly the
Convent Library.

A CRYPT, restored by Waller, divided by two rows
of · small pillars, extends beneath the transept, choir,
and Lady Chapel: with the chapels in the triforium

and choir aisles it forms three chapels one above the other; an arrangement unique in this country, but resembling the triple church of Assisi. The principal features of the Basilica are very observable: the *apsidal chapels*, in it places of secret prayer, study of God's word, and affectionate commemoration of the holy and dear departed; the *triforia*, in it the galleries for women-worshippers, above the *aisles*; the *apse*, the shell or cupola of the catacomb over the recess, in which great saints were laid; the *crypt*, retained on the theory that the primitive churches were built over catacombs, for the sake of the association which recalled the times when the persecuted Christians met in caves of the earth, before Constantine translated them to the Basilicas, so significant as being the palace of the King and sovereign judgment-hall, and also as symbolical of the moral death from which the Saviour redeemed His church. In the *crypts* are found the earliest instances of the pointed arch, as circular arches were found to gather damp. They were often termed confessionaries, as serving for the burial of the holy departed; and were used as places for retired devotion. The pointed arch passed from the crypt into the arches of construction, such as pier arches, in the Transitional period, while the arches of decoration, such as those of windows and doors, were semicircular.

The principal monuments are those of—

S. Side of Organ Screen.—Abbot Sebroke, d. 1457, chantry and effigy.

N. Side of Choir from West to East.—Abbot Parker, chantry and effigy, early part of 16th century; King Edward II., d. 1334, elaborate canopy, chantry, and effigy, the finest specimen of Decorated tabernacle-work extant; the Viceroy Osric, effigy older than the tomb which is of the date of Henry VIII.

S. Side of Choir.—Abbot Serlo, d. 1104, bracket and effigy.

N. E. Chapel of the Holy Apostles.—Duke Robert of Normandy, d. 1134, effigy of oak ; he was buried in the chapter-house.

S. Aisle Nave.—A Knight and Lady, said to be of an Earl and Countess of Hereford, effigies brought from Llanthony Abbey. Mrs. Ellis, of Minsterworth, a memorial window, 1859, by Clayton and Bell.

W. End Nave.—Dr. Jenner, originator of Vaccination, statue—

R. W. Siever, sculptor; Robert Raikes, founder of Sunday Schools, d. 1823—Rickman, sculptor.

Lady Chapel.—Judge Powell, d. 1713, statue.

N. Wall Nave.—Mrs. S. Morley, d. 1784—Flaxman, sculptor.

E. Wall, S. Transept.—A bracket in the form of a mason's square, with two figures of masons as corbels; the monument of Gower and his apprentice, who completed the choir.

DIMENSIONS OF THE CATHEDRAL IN FEET.

	Length.	Breadth.	Height.
Nave	174	83f. 10in.	67 f. 6 in.
Choir	140	34f. 6in.	86
Lady Chapel	92	24f. 4in.	46 f. 6 in.
Transept	128	43f. 6in.	S. 86f. N. 78
Tower	41 f. 14 in.	40f. 4 in.	225
Cloisters	146 by 145	19	18 f. 6 in.
Chapter-house	68	35	
Total length	423 outer, 400 inner.		

Henry III. was crowned in the abbey church with great pomp, October 28, 1216. A small portion of the priory is observable on the north-west side of the Cathedral, and part of the refectory and Norman arches in a wall near the little cloister. Close to the Minster gate, Early English, Bishop Hooper suffered at the stake, Feb. 9, 1555. Gloucester Hall, now Worcester College, was founded 1283 in Oxford, for the education of the monks. The Deanery was the abbot's house.

The Chapter is composed of a dean and four canons— two stalls were suspended. There are two daily choral services at 11 and 3. There are three minor canons, six lay clerks, and eight choristers. The income of the Chapter in 1852 was 7963*l.* Their expenditure on the fabric in 1839, 3701*l.* The library contains 2650 volumes.

Arms: Or, three chevronels, gules, between ten torteaux.

Gloucester numbers among its bishops—Wakeman, Ravis, and Miles Smith, translators of the Holy Bible; stiff-necked Hooper, who atoned for his inconsistencies with his blood; Goodman, the only prelate beside Parker of Oxford who seceded to the Church of Rome; Frampton, who believed in ghosts and fairies; learned Huntingford and scholar-like Monk; and Warburton, whose works are more known

than read, and his name more familiar than his works.
Robert of Gloucester, the metrical chronicler, was a monk;
and the learned Hyde, Hadrian Saravia, and Dean Field,
author " Of the Church," were dignitaries.　There were
suffragans of Gloucester in very early times : the names of
Eldad and Theonus occur in old chronicles.

Hereford.

HEREFORD, the ancient Hên Fford, " The Old Road," is
situated on the banks of the broad cheerful Wye, in the
midst of a fertile, beautiful, and well-cultivated valley,
famous for pleasant orchards, delicious gardens, and
extensive pasture-lands.　The principal events connected
with the city, are its pillage by the Welsh, 1055 ; its cap-
ture by King Stephen, 1141 ; its surrender to Sir W. Waller,
1643 ; and its siege by Lord Leven and the Scots.　Owen
Tudor was beheaded here, 1461 ; Despencer in 1322 ; and
Edward II. dethroned 1326.　In St. Peter's church, rebuilt
1390, are seven ancient stalls.　All Saints has a lofty spire
and ten stalls with canopies and misereres.　In Widemarsh
suburb is a stone hexagonal pulpit cross of the 15th century, near the south side of the lodgings of the Prior of a
Dominican friary.　In Eigne suburb is the mutilated
White Cross, built in 1347 by Bishop Charlton. The Wye
bridge is of the 15th century. Salmon were so numerous
that indentures contained a clause that apprentices should
not eat of them more than twice a week.　One side of the
city prison is a portion of the Bye-street gate.　John
Gwillim the herald, and unhappy Nell Gwyn, and Garrick,
were natives of Hereford.　Phillips the poet died here.
In the Grey Friars, Owen Tudor was buried.　The theatre
was the nursery of Clive, Siddons, and Kemble.　A parliament sat at Hereford in 1326.　The shire hall is Jacobæan,
84 ft. by 34 ft., and of carved timber, resting on an open
arcade.

It is only on a close approach that the great tower appears creeping over the trees, and breasting solemnly their dark-green depths, as if nature had given both beauty and retirement to this fine old pile. The best view is at the sudden turn by the bridge over the Wye, to see the time-honoured steeple for the first time at early morning, when the winged gleams of light sever ridge and roof into one glowing mass, apart from the common buildings beyond and the darker foliage beneath, and project their shadows upon the gleaming river, like dark-hued jewelry flung idly on a mirror; or under the parting glances of a westering sun, when the windows glisten and blaze, every pane flashing like flaming gems.

The church is composed of a NAVE of seven instead of the original nine bays with aisles, a CHOIR of four bays with aisles, and LADY CHAPEL of three bays, a MAIN and a CHOIR TRANSEPT, and a NORTH PORCH of two bays. The south wing of the west transept is of one bay, has no clerestory but a Chapter-house, sacristy, and vestibule in place of an east aisle. The north wing of two bays has an eastern aisle. The lofty and well-proportioned choir extends across the transept. Attached to the north aisle is the lateral CHANTRY-CHAPEL of Bishop Stanbury. The EASTERN TRANSEPT is laterally divided into two aisles. From the south wing a door leads into the single alley, 100 feet long, of the "Lady Arbour" cloister to the Vicar's College, a quadrangle about 100 feet square: the term "Lady Arbour" is but another form of expression for "The Paradise" of other churches. On the north side of the LADY CHAPEL is the descent to the crypt, which is 50 feet long by 40 feet in breadth, and of two aisles, here called Golgotha; and on the south side is the octagonal chapel of Bishop Audley, built 1492. The CLOISTERS, good Perpendicular, are on the south side of the nave. Only the east alley of eight panes and the south walk of nine panes remain. The windows are of four lights with Perpendicular tracery. On the west side is the music-room, 80 feet by 40 feet in height and breadth, built 1760. The west alley was destroyed to give place to a grammar-school of Edward VI.

The principal entrance to the Cathedral is in the third north-east bay of the nave, under a double PORCH of remarkable size, the outer portion built by Bishop Booth. The chapter-house was destroyed by Cromwell's soldiers.

Upon the foundations of a church dedicated to King Ethelbert the martyr in 1012, and burned by the Welsh and Prince Griffith in 1055, Bishop Robert Lothingar in 1079 commenced the present Cathedral, on the plan of that of Aix-la-Chapelle, which was completed by Bishop Raynelm 1107-15. The RETRO-CHOIR was the work of De Vere, bishop 1186-99 ; the LADY CHAPEL and CRYPT were erected about 1200. De Braose, bishop 1200-15, built the lower portion of the CENTRAL TOWER, the upper part is a century earlier. Bishop Cantilupe built the NORTH TRAN-SEPT, 1275-82 ; the earlier part of the NORTH PORCH, (Bishop Booth, 1516-35, built the later portion) choir, clerestory, and south-east cloister door. The CHAPTER-HOUSE, the main CLOISTERS, the aisles of the nave and choir, and the CHOIR TRANSEPT, were built before the end of the episcopate of Stanbury, 1452-74 ; Edmond Spofford, bishop 1426-49, being a considerable benefactor.

The injury which has befallen other cathedrals was mostly wreaked by the soldiers of the Commonwealth. At Hereford, it was reserved for one man in modern times to destroy what had escaped fire and sword—Mr. James Wyatt in 1788. The ancient west front, 80 feet broad, consisted of a steeple, as at Wimborne, 130 feet high, and very similar to the central tower ; it was built by Bishop Braose. In the reign of Henry VI. in place of the three round-headed windows over the noble Norman doorway, built by Bishop Lozinga, a large Perpendicular window was inserted, which weakened the walls. No attention was paid to the necessary repairs of the structure ; and on Easter Monday 1786, the tower, 130 feet high by 80 feet in breadth, fell and destroyed four bays of the nave. The same year was marked still further by a sale of all the brasses in the church to the weight of two tons. Seventy similar memorials were sold, in 1645, by the Parliamentary soldiers. The present miserable front cost 18,000l. ; the vaulting, clerestory, and west front are Wyatt's addition in the nave, which has lost 15 feet of its former length : by the removal of the old groining the pitch of the roof has been altered. Cottingham, 1841-1851, pulled down, rebuilt, and coloured the roof of the nave. The restoration is happily now in the hands of Mr. G. G. Scott.

The north side of the NAVE is plain but impressive. The parapet is plain with a corbel table, and the buttresses are gabled and shallow. The clerestory windows are of three lights foliated, the aisle windows of four lights, with geometrical tracery. On the south they are later in style. Bishop Booth's PORCH of two stories, consists of three broad, open, arches, with windows above them to light the parvise. The spandrils are highly enriched, and octagonal staircase turrets, terminating in lanterns, flank the sides ; the roof is groined, as at Salisbury and Durham : it is on the north side where the population was most numerous, because in it certain portions of the ritual of Baptism, Matrimony, and Benedictions, were said. At Sarum, the porch was also a Galilee. The NORTH WING of the MAIN TRANSEPT, rich Early English, now used as the parish church of St. John Baptist, is remarkable for its western untransomed windows rising nearly the whole height of the wall ; the triforium has semicircular arched mouldings enclosing a triplet, and the aisle has shafted triplets with circles in the head ; the north window is of six lancets, subdivided by a central pier, with plain geometrical tracery in the head, below a foliated arch ; in the gable is a three-light window ; the lateral buttresses are gabled.

Internally, in the NAVE the pillars are circular and massive, with simple capitals, and arches adorned with the chevron moulding : the triforium consists, in each bay, of two round arches, each including two similar arches enriched with the chevron. The clerestory has a wall gallery, and very lofty round-headed arches, divided by the vaulting shafts of the roof. The FONT is Norman, circular, with twisted columns resting on lions, and images of the Apostles in an arcade. The east wall of the SOUTH WING of the MAIN TRANSEPT has five arcades of round-headed arches, two being occupied by the triforium and clerestory. In the NORTH WING the triforium is of three trefoiled lights, under three quatrefoiled circles within a triangular-headed arch, Early Decorated, which like the peculiarly straight arches of the base tier, has a four-leaved flower ornament in the mouldings. The clerestory consists of foliated circles, with a deep splay to a chevroned string-course, above which the wall is richly diapered. An arched doorway led to the shrine of St. Thomas Cantelupe, and a turret near the choir to the watchers' chamber. The parapet in the exterior is trefoiled.

The sides of the LADY CHAPEL have two lancets under pointed arches in each bay, with circles intervening, under an arcade and machicolated parapet. The east end is a beautiful example of Early English architecture; five lancet windows, now filled with stained glass as a memorial of Dean Merewether, beneath oval and lozenge-shaped panels, internally with quatrefoils in circles, within five mouldings, over which is an arcade of trefoiled arches resting on slender shafts; elaborate ornaments of four-leaved flowers, and foliated capitals, and clustered shafts, add to the superb effect. Bold double angular buttresses flank it, crowned with tall spiral pinnacles. The east end of the CHOIR has a Perpendicular window of five lights flanked with pinnacled buttresses. The clerestory has Early English windows of two lights each, with quatrefoils in the heads; and a double arcade, the undermost of long lancet arches, the upper of small arches trefoiled.

The great feature of the church is its grand CENTRAL TOWER of two stories and battlemented, divided by a broad band of quatrefoil tracery. On each face of the belfry are four canopied two-light windows, trefoiled, with a quatrefoil in the head, set between buttresses, which, like the buttresses at the angles, are covered with a bead or bulb ornament : it had a broach spire 92 ft. high until 1792. The pinnacles were added in 1858.

The fifty canopied stalls of oak in the CHOIR are of the

age of Edward II., and were restored under the care of Dr. Meyrick of Goodrich Court. The roof is vaulted throughout the church. The lower arches and triforium are semicircular: the former has a chevron moulding, the latter consists of two round arches under a similar arch, all elaborately enriched with the chevron; the clerestory is Early English; a pointed arch in each bay is subdivided into lancets, with a trefoiled arch on either side. Here, in 1141, King Stephen took his seat crowned. To the east of the high altar stood the shrine of St. Thomas de Cantelupe. The enamelled shrine of St. Ethelbert, 7 inches long by 8½ high, and 3½ in breadth, was in the possession of Canon Russell in 1804. It is of oak, covered with enamelled copper, which is engraved with figures. It was the work of Greek artists, who, in the time of Henry III., migrated from Constantinople to Rome. The Norman arch at the east end is magnificent. The reredos is a memorial of Joseph Bailey, M.P., designed by Cottingham and executed by W. Boulton of Lambeth in 1853. It has five deeply-recessed panels, with alti rilievi of our Lord's passion, in Caen stone, and above the cresting are six angels bearing the instruments of suffering. The organ was built by Father Schmidt, 1686, the gift of King Charles II., and has been improved by Byfield, Green, Avery, and Bishop. The custom for the lay vicars to take part in the Litany, in some choirs, is by tradition from the time when they were in orders. In 1634 the twelve singing men here were all ordained, and most of them M.A.'s, living together as at the University. The altar-piece, by Leeming, a copy of that of Magdalen College, was given in 1816. The east window of the choir, 40 ft. by 20, was painted by Buckler from West's picture of The Last Supper. The men sit in the choir on the north side, while women are seated on the south. In the CHOIR TRANSEPT, which is of two aisles equal in height and width, divided north and south by three columns and two piers; the windows of four lights have Early Geometrical tracery. It was probably parted off for four altars. The Perpendicular Stanbury Chapel has a rich groined vault, or

Carnary, as it was the depository of disinterred fragments of the bodies of the departed, and used for special services for their repose.

In the present chapter-house, adjoining the south-west transept, is one of the oldest maps extant, a Saxon Mappi Mundi with Jerusalem in the centre, with inscriptions of the date of Henry III. The vicars-choral occupy a college built by Bishop Stanbury in the 15th centrry. The triennial meetings of the choirs at Gloucester, Worcester, and Hereford, for charitable purposes, in rotation, established by Dr. Bisse in 1724, took their foundation in a weekly musical assembly in the hall of this College, and their subsequent annual meetings previous to that date. Part of the wall of the old decagonal chapter-house, rich Decorated, on the east of the great cloister, remains. In 1634 the windows were filled with rich glazing, and its walls adorned with forty-six ancient frescoes. The Lady Arbour, or BISHOP'S CLOISTERS, are of later date than the main cloister.

DIMENSIONS OF THE CATHEDRAL IN FEET.

	Length.	Breadth.	Height.
Nave	130	74	70
Choir	96	76	64
Main Transept	150	..	64
Choir Transept	106	..	..
Presbytery	24	..	..
Lady Chapel	75	..	..
Cloisters, square	100	18	..
Tower	..	..	140
Total length	325	..	..

Arms : Gules, three chevronels, or.

The principal monuments are the following—

E. Aisle, N. Main Transept, St. Catharine's Aisle.—Freestone shrine of Bishop Cantilupe, d. 1282, with knights treading on lions and dragons.

Transept, N. Wing.—Bishop Aqua Bella, d. 1269, effigy, triple arcade, and canopy; Bishop L. Charlton, d. 1369, effigy under a rich pedimented canopy; Bishop Westphaling, effigy. Phillips the poet is buried here.

S. Main Transept.—Bishop Trevenant, d. 1403; Alexander Denton, d. 1576, and his wife, effigies.

Choir Transept, N. Side.—Bishop Richard Swinfield, d. 1317, tomb; Bishop Godwin, tomb.

S. Aisle, Choir, N. Wall.—Bishop Mayo, d. 1516, the canopy of unusual design and altar-tomb with images, effigy; Bishop Raynelm, d. 1115, effigy under a triangular-headed arch, and an open arcade above. *S. Wall.*—Bishops De Vere, d. 1199, Foliot, d. 1186, Betun, d. 1145, and Melun. d. 1167, effigies in triangular recesses. There is a brass of Dean Frocester, d. 1529, on the floor.

Nave, N. Aisle.—Bishop Boothe, d. 1535, effigy. *S. Aisle.*—Sir Richard Pembridge, K.G., d. 1375, effigy; Bishop W. De Lorraine, d. 1079, effigy, tomb in an arched recess; effigy of Bishop G. de Bruse, d. 1200.

Lady Chapel, N. Wall.—Humphrey de Bohun, effigy, time of Richard II; effigy of a lady, with frescoes under the recessed arch; several black incised slabs of the earlier part of the 15th century, the hands and face inlaid with white marble; a fragment of St. Etbelbert's image. Bishops Lothingar, d. 1095, Clyve, d. 1119, and Mapenore, d. 1219, effigies. *S. Wall.*—John Berew, dean, effigy under an arch.

N. Choir Aisle, S Wall.—A bishop, effigy, alabaster tomb with images.

Chapel of Bishop Stanbury.—Effigy of the founder, d. 1464.

Undercroft.—Incised slabs, with elaborate decoration, to A. and E. Jones, c. 1500.

The Chapter consists of a dean and four canons. There are six minor canons, six lay vicars, and eight choristers, There are two daily choral services, at 11 and 3, and the Holy Communion is administered monthly and on great festivals. The expenditure (1852) on the fabric within fourteen years was 4141*l.*, and from subscriptions, 23,257*l.*; within fifteen years, 34,000*l.* in all have been spent. The library contains 2000 volumes. The total income of the Chapter in 1852 was 6594*l.* The palace adjoins the Cathedral. It was originally of the 12th century. Part of the modern house stands within the Norman timber hall.

Among the bishops of Hereford occur Leofgar, who wore his knapsack as a priest, and when bishop gave up chrism and rood and took to his sword and spear, to die at Glasbury in battle with Prince Griffith; Robert of Lorraine, the star-gazer, who would not journey to the consecration of Lincoln, because the planets were un-propitious ; De Clive, whose brief tenure caused the pro-verb no Bishop of Hereford lives long ; Foliot, à Becket's enemy ; D'Aqua Blanca, the crusader, whom Robin Hood robbed in the glades of merry Barnsdale at Allen-a-Dale's wedding ; St. Thomas de Cantelupe, the last canonized English bishop ; the traitor Orlton ; Charlton, Lord Treasurer ; Cardinal Castello ; Westphaling, who never smiled, and in his oration to Queen Elizabeth refused to stop when she desired to speak, lest he should mar the rest by loss of memory ; Bennet, the enthusiastic ten-nis-player ; Godwin, the historian of his order ; Herbert Croft, who boldly denounced rebellion and sacrilege in his pulpit here, though the Roundheads levelled their muskets at his heart ; Bisse, who rose by the distaff, and Hoadly by heresy ; and the scholar Huntingford.　Among the dignitaries appear Simon de Frene the poet ; Adam de Murimuth and Polydore Vergil, chroniclers ; two Car-dinals, and Baron Saye and Sele.　Baxter refused the see.

Lichfield.

Lo, with what depth of blackness thrown
Against the clouds far up the skies,
The walls of the Cathedral rise,
Like a mysterious grove of stone,
With fitful lights and shadows blending ;
As from behind, the moon ascending
Lights its dim aisles and paths unknown.
Only the cloudy rack behind,
Drifting onward wild and ragged,
Gives to each spire and buttress jagged
A seeming motion undefined.

FROM Borowcop Hill is obtained the best and most strik-ing view of Lichfield ; the cathedral and its trees close the landscape in front, the deep-toned bells swelling like

angels' music across the fields ; on the one hand is a plain
stretching to the swells of Needwood Forest—on the other,
rises over a flat valley, with a brooklet wandering through
it, the huge black wall of smoke miles to the west and
never dispersed above the coal districts, which at night—
with their flaming mouths and hoarse-sounding pyramids
of fire soaring up—present a terrific spectacle.

Lichfield has been variously derived—from lych, a marsh,
from its situation ; or lych, the dead, from a tradition of a
famous battle of three kings who slew each other on the
field. Poor Major André, writing to Miss Seward, says,
"Lichfield ! ah, of what magic letters is that little word
conceived—let nobody talk to me of its original meaning :
the field of dead bodies. Oh, no such thing ; it is the field
of joy—the beautiful city." It has long been associated
as a city with the names of Ashmole, Darwin, Johnson,
Garrick, Henry Salt, Seward, Smalridge, and Newton.
In the church of St. Michael, on its sloping hill, is an effigy
of William de Walton, of the date of Edward III. It has
a fine spire, a good font, and a noble avenue of elm trees
traversing the parish cemetery, which covers seven acres
of ground.

St. Chad's Church, Stowe, has a south door, fine Early
English. On Ascension Day the children visit the neighbouring well, which is wreathed with sculptured roses,
and on the arch bears the initials of the Saint, and adorn
it with living garlands. St. John's Hospital, built in the
reign of Henry VI. for a master and thirteen almsmen,
is remarkable for its many chimneys and pretty chapel.
The Grammar School is an ancient structure of brick.
At Whitsuntide an annual procession takes place to Borowcop hill, the site of the battle, which is commemorated
on the City Seal ; although tradition says the Cathedral
stands on ground hallowed by the blood of martyrs slain
in the Diocletian persecution, 286. Johnson wrote Irene
here. Richard II. kept Christmas here 1397, and two
years after was a prisoner in the Castle ; Queen Elizabeth,
1575, and the Princess Victoria, 1832, visited Lichfield ;
three times in 1643 King Charles I. lodged in the Close.

'At Maples Hayes, two miles distant, is the famous Botanical Garden of Dr. Darwin's poem.

Situated on an eminence, if the unsightly buildings on the south of the Close were swept away, and a lawn laid down to the lake-like water in the dell, unruffled, save by the breeze or the glidings of its many swans, this exquisite Cathedral would appear to full advantage over the trees which fringe the banks, and in point of situation be inferior to no other church. Though, comparatively with the greater minsters, of small proportions, yet with its three beautiful spires, its richness of ornament, and grace and loveliness, it presents even now an effect almost magical, while it stands solitary and alone without cloister or precinct wall, gate or ancient monastic building. It is the most complete to the eye. Of a pale rose colour, it looks as if hewn out of some soft mellow sunset—

> The fading tints of western skies.

The church of St. Chad consists of a NAVE of eight bays, with aisles of exquisite beauty—in loveliness nothing can surpass it—and CHOIR of eight bays with aisles, a TRANSEPT with each wing of two bays having an eastern aisle, and a LADY CHAPEL. There is no cloister. The orientation of the choir, a north-easterly deflexion out of the line of the nave, to typify the drooping head of the Crucified, is observable, but is not so great as to injure the perspective. The choir of Canterbury has a southerly bend. The character of the NAVE and TRANSEPT is curious,—Early English, neither simple as Salisbury nor rich as Lincoln, yet more akin than either to Decorated. The CHOIR is Decorated; the east end is hexagonal. On the south side of the choir are two sacristies; on the north side are a vestibule and chapter-house.

Roger de Clinton, bishop 1129-49, commenced the building of the TRANSEPT, CHOIR, AISLES, and CHAPTER-HOUSE; the latter was completed 1224-38: the works were continued by Nonant, 1188-98, and Stavenby, 1224-40. The completion of the CHOIR and NAVE may be assigned to the time of Hugh de Pateshull, 1240; William de Langton

and Roger de Northburgh, 1296-1360, completed the
TOWERS and LADY CHAPEL and walled the Close. Bishop
Heyworth, 1420-47, was the last great benefactor. Between 1788-95 very extensive repairs were carried on, the
roofs of the aisles being raised and two of the spires
partly rebuilt. The glass in the LADY CHAPEL, dated
1530-40, bought by Sir Brooke Boothby when the abbey
of Herckenrode, near Liege, was destroyed by the French,
was set up in 1805. It came over in 340 pieces, each
measuring about 22 inches square, and was arranged by
the ingenious Rev. W. G. Rowland, of Shrewsbury, who
received a prebend for his labours. The other windows
are comparatively modern; the west window was restored
by King James II., and glazed with glass by Brookes,
by Dean Addenbrooke, 1776. The former window had
mixed flowing and geometrical tracery. The organ was
built by Green in 1789.

This Cathedral possesses a romantic history. In 1643
the Royalists, under the Earl of Chesterfield, fortified the
Close, then surrounded by a wall built by Bishop Langton.
They were attacked by the rebels, under Lord Brooke,
who expressed the impious wish to behold the day when
no cathedral should be left standing, and demanded a
sign from heaven. He was shot in the eye by "dumb
Dyott," from the middle tower, on March 2, (St. Chad's
Day,) while giving orders, in a place in Dam Street now
marked by an inscription :—

> 'Twas levelled when fanatic Brooke
> The fair Cathedral stormed and took ;
> But, thanks to Heaven and good St. Chad,
> A guerdon meet the spoiler had!

The garrison surrendered to Sir John Gell. Among other
orgies of the republicans, they hunted a cat with hounds
through the aisles, and mimicked the christening of a calf
at the font. On April 24, Colonel Rousewell in his turn
capitulated to Prince Rupert, and the Close was occupied
by Colonel Bagot and the Cavaliers, until July 10, 1646.
Upwards of 2000 shot and 1500 grenades were fired

against the sacred building, the lead was cast into bullets, and the central spire laid low. It was found necessary, in the episcopate of Bishop Hacket, to restore the fabric at an enormous expense, and it was re-consecrated December 24, 1669. The morning after his arrival he set his eight carriage horses to clear away the rubbish: after eight years the bells were hung in the steeple; then old and infirm he went into an adjoining chamber to hear them chime their first peal: "It is my knell," he said, and in a few hours he had passed to his rest. The choir is in course of restoration by that able architect, G. G. Scott.

If the west fronts of Wells and Peterborough may claim the preference, Lichfield may fairly challenge the third rank. Built when architecture was in its prime, of matchless beauty, it combines chasteness with richness of ornament, admirable proportions, and symmetrical arrangement. Two TOWERS flank a gable with trefoiled panels intricately arranged over a large and beautiful Decorated window of six lights, with a rose and quatrefoiled circles in the head; the whole face is covered by four trefoiled and canopied arcades, once containing statues, the range over the great door alone remains: in the upper story of each tower is a window of two lights, with a quatrefoil in the head. They are flanked by hexagonal stair-turrets, and end in parapets of open stonework, of quatrefoils in diamonds, and crocketed pinnacles at the angles. The hexagonal spires soar up into the sky, marvels of elegance, delicately banded at intervals, and with four successive tiers of canopied spire lights. Over the gable (in the centre of which is a statue of King Charles II., the work of Sir W. Wilson, once a stonecutter at Sutton Coldfield,) is seen the grand central spire. There are three doorways: the CENTRAL PORTAL is parted by a shaft with a tall niched figure of the Virgin, and on either side in the deeply-recessed splays of two orders are canopied statues of the Evangelists. The outer and inner arches are foliated, and the mouldings filled with exquisitely wrought foliage. The iron scrolls on the doors are a fine specimen of metal-work : in the arcade above are twenty-five statues of the kings of England, from Penda to Richard II., restored by Joseph Harris of Bath in 1820-1. Only inferior to this portal are the doors to the TRANSEPT, especially that on the south wing, with statues of the Saviour and the Baptist, adjoining which is an external altar-tomb with a rich canopy and effigy of an ecclesiastic of the 14th century : the local folk-lore relates that it is the effigy of one of two brothers, rivals in rearing the spires ; the one who was worsted clasped a huge stone, and threw himself from the pinnacle, and is here represented as he fell. The NORTH DOOR has five arches filled with ovals—two of foliage and flowers, two of patriarchs and saints, and one of angels. The CENTRAL TOWER rises only one story above the roof, and has on each face canopied windows, each of two-lights trefoiled with a quatrefoil in the head, under a simple battlement, aud with pinnacled turrets at the angles. The SPIRE is six-sided, similar in detail to those at the west, but is crocketed along the sides : the sky being seen through the windows gives it an indescribable appearance of lightness. Sir Christopher Wren designed onē similar for the central tower of Westminster, which really requires an open wooden spire like that of Amiens. The polygonal CHAPTER-HOUSE is on the east side of the north transept, which has Perpendicular windows in the clerestory and triforium ; the library is above, and both have two-light windows under a pointed arch ; the north and south sides are equal ; the east and west ends are three-sided apses ; its central pier is a single column, unclustered ; the upper building is a plainer copy of the richly ornamented structure beneath. The parapet of the choir and Lady Chapel has a rich band below the battlements. The clerestory of the choir is composed of four-light Perpendicular windows ; those of the aisle are of three-lights and late Decorated. The LADY CHAPEL, with its lofty trefoiled three-light windows, rich tracery, and graceful flowering canopies and semihexagonal apse, gives a beautiful termination to the Cathedral.

Each bay of the NAVE is composed of clustered columns, with capitals of wrought foliage and flowers, every feature of the largest cathedral found in admirable proportion to the lesser size ; the spandrils above are filled with quatrefoils ; the triforium is of two arches, each similarly subdivided with a quatrefoil in the head : the clerestory is of three trefoiled lights, arranged in a triangular curved framework. The groining of the vaulting is in harmony with its carvings of leaves on the central bosses, and network of diverging ribs. Behind the temporary altar stands a seven-branched candelabrum, like a Jesse candlestick. The four massive piers which support the CENTRAL TOWER are of clustered shafts, bound with three fillets. The TRANSEPTS are wholly unequal to the rest of the church. The arcaded vestibule of the CHAPTER-HOUSE, a long octagon with the corners cut off, and that room with its rich central shaft, and beautifully groined, are, however, very fine. The aisles of the CHOIR and NAVE have a beautiful arcade ; a similar series of trefoiled arches supplies the place of a triforium ; the windows of the clerestory are Perpendicular, but set in a frame of quatrefoils like the transept of St. Mary Redcliffe, Bristol. Over the door of the Consistory Court in the south choir aisle is a MINSTRELS' GALLERY ; adjoining is an ancient vestry with hooks in the vault for lamps. In 1634 three rich ancient copes were preserved in the vestry ; at 6 a.m. prayers were said in the Lady Chapel, which had eight stained windows ; one hundred statues covered the west front ; three gates led to the walled Close ; and the castellated palace possessed a hall 100 ft. by 56 ft., nobly roofed with Irish oak, and painted by Bishop Langton with the history of the wars of Edward I.

The gem of the Cathedral is its exquisite LADY CHAPEL, which has no rival : a range of stalls extends beneath the windows, nine in number, and seven of them glowing with stained glass, while between each pair are niches and canopies and brackets, emptied of their images, but still, though denuded, with every characteristic of richness and delicacy of taste and finish.

> There is more
> In such a survey than the sating gaze
> Of wonder pleased, or awe which would adore
> The worship of the place, or the mere praise
> Of art and its great masters, who could raise
> What former time, nor skill, nor thought could plan.

The evil genius of English Cathedrals, James Wyatt the Destructive, incited the monstrous removal of the exquisite screen of Bishop Langton, which divided this chapel from the choir, to make a reredos and organ-screen.

The chief monuments are the following :—

S. Aisle Choir.—Bishop Langton, d. 1321, effigy; Bishop Pateshull, d. 1241, effigy with stigmata; Bishop Hacket, d. 1671, mitred effigy, his pastoral staff in the left hand; Captain Sir Humphrey Stanley, of Pipe, time of Henry VIII., effigy—the scroll of confession in the hand, and the unclad body, are the marks of penance which were imposed upon him as the condition of burial in holy ground, he having been excommunicated but reconciled before death; Dean Heywood, d. 1492, cadaver.

S. Transept.—Dr. Johnson, bust; David Garrick.

N. Transept.—Miss Seward's parents—Bacon, jun., sculptor; Sir Walter Scott wrote an epitaph for it.

N. W. Tower.—Lady Mary Wortley Montague—Westmacott, sculptor.

S. Transept.—Andrew Newton, d. 1806, founder of the College for Widows of Clergymen, Lichfield; Memorial to the 80th Regiment, rendered interesting by three flags captured at Sobraon, suspended over it in 1850; Lieut.-Col. P. J. Petit, H.M. 50th Regiment, a brass by Waller, 1854.

S. Choir Aisle, E. Wall.—The famous Sleeping Children, by Chantrey —the two daughters of the Rev. Wm. Robinson, celebrated by Mrs. Hemans' beautiful lines; Archdeacon Hodson, an exquisite altar-tomb, with bassi-relievi by Street.

The superb monuments of Lord Basset and two Lords Paget of Beaudesert were destroyed by the rebels.

DIMENSIONS OF THE CATHEDRAL IN FEET.

	Length.	Breadth.	Height.
Nave	177	66	60
Choir	}195	{37	..
Lady Chapel		{27	..
Transept	152	45	..
Central Steeple	..	..	258

	Length.	Breadth.	Height.
Western Steeple .	..	..	183
Chapter-house	45	28	23
Total length .	379	..	..

The Chapter consists of a dean and four canons; there are five minor canons, six vicars-choral and twelve choristers. There are two choral services daily at 10 and 4. The Holy Communion is celebrated weekly. The expenditure on the fabric during fourteen preceding years amounted to 9000*l.*, while the income of the chapter in 1852 was 2941*l.* The library contains 3000 volumes, and the following MSS.—Textus S. Ceaddæ, A.D. 720, a MS. formerly belonging to Llandaff Cathedral; Chaucer's Canterbury Tales; the Valor Ecclesiasticus of Nicolas IV.; a Koran taken at Buda; and Dives and Pauper, first printed by Pynson in 1483.

The palace is Eccleshall Castle, Stafford, and there is an episcopal house in the Close, rebuilt by Bishop Wood 1690. Some of the prebendal houses on the south-west contain specimens of ancient brick-work.

Arms: Per pale arg. and gules, a cross potent and quadrate in the centre, between four crosses, all counterchanged; the cross charged with the letter D sa.

In 681-691, 703-737, there were bishops of Lichfield. From 786 to 803, Lichfield was an archbishopric, with the suffragan sees of Hereford, Worcester, Leicester, Sidnachester, Elmham and Dunwich, while the province of Canterbury was limited to London, Winchester, Rochester, and Salisbury. The see numbers among its prelates: St. Chad; Roger de Clinton, who bought the mitre for 3000 marks, and died as a Crusader at Antioch; Gerard la Pucelle the canonist; Hugh de Nonant, who vowed that if he had his will there should be no cowl left in England; Pateshull and Langton, Lord Treasurers; De Meyland, who could not speak English; Northbury, Lord Keeper; Close, one of the architects of King's College Chapel; Smith, founder of Brasennose College; accommodating Lee, who married the Tudor Blue Beard and Anna Boleyn; ambitious Neale; learned Overall; Abbot, who shot the keeper in deer-stalking; aged

Morton ; brave Hacket, who preached at Holborn in defiance of the Roundhead's musket; Lloyd, "old Mysterio," who perplexed himself with study of the Revelation; stout-hearted Hough, who resisted King James at Magdalen ; Hurd, whose pen set the mitre on his head ; the Earl Cornwallis, and classic Butler. Among the dignitaries are found five cardinals, and Archbishops Segrave and Fitzralph of Armagh, Hervey of Dublin, John of Marseilles, and Robert Nares, the glossarist. Calamy refused the see.

Lincoln.

Lincoln is the British Lincoil, " The Place of Fens." Its present name is formed of the syllable Lin, and coln, the abbreviation of the Roman colonia.

Lincoln has received the following royal visits : King Stephen, 1147, who kept Christmas ; Henry II. 1158 ; King John, to meet William of Scotland 1200, 1204 ; Edward I. 1280, 1305, who confirmed Magna Charta ; Richard II. 1386 ; Henry VI. 1446 ; Henry VII. 1485 ; Henry VIIL 1541, that fatal visit to Catharine Howard. Parliaments were held here 1301, 1302, 1316, 1317, 1327. John of Gaunt's stables formed the St. Mary's or Merchants' Guild Hall, the most extensive range of building of the 12th century now remaining.

Near the PALACE GATEWAY is the chantry-house of Lord Cantilupe, c. 1366, with a bay window. The ruins of the Norman CASTLE, with its Lucy tower or keep, founded by William I. are deserving of remark, as is the Roman Newport Gate, built of ferruginous oolite, the entrance to the Ermin Way. GUILDHALL is the ancient Stone-bow, of the 15th century, in High Street, a large gateway flanked by circular turrets, battlemented ; in niches upon the south fronts are statues of St. Mary and Gabriel the archangel. At the west end of the church of St. Mary le Wigford is an ancient chantry, of the early part of the 14th

century, now called St. Mary's Conduit.   Near it is a good
15th century timber house.   An oriel (c. 1390) in the
castle-yard once lit the mansion of John of Gaunt; and
on Steep Hill is the Late Norman house of Beleset de
Wallingford, hanged for clipping money in the reign of
Edward I.   St. Anne's chapel and Bede Houses, the Mint
wall, a Roman building, the Grey Friars, now the Mecha-
nics' Institute, and the churches of St. Michael, St. Mary's
Guildhall of the 12th century, and St. Peter-at-Gowts,
(with a Norman tower), are all interesting.

Accustomed as we are to the sight of our magnificent
minsters, it requires some stretch of the imagination to
appreciate the difficulties of their first architects :—

> A temple framing of dimensions vast,
> And yet not too enormous for the sound
> Of human anthems—choral song, or burst
> Sublime, of instrumental harmony,
> To glorify the Eternal.

Each greater cathedral has supplanted humbler edifices ;
the rude piles were gradually developed into the churches
which now appeal so vividly to our feelings of devotion,
only in proportion to the growing wealth of the builders,
and their slow but certain advances in science and taste.
The Cathedral of Lincoln contains within its compass
every variety of style, from the massive, simple Norman, to the last stage of Pointed art.   We see it now
changed from its former magnificence ; for in 1540, 2621
ounces of gold, 4285 of silver, besides countless pearls of
immense value, diamonds, sapphires, rubies, carbuncles,
and other gems, were pillaged from its treasury, and in
later times its towers have been shorn of their spires ; and
yet even now it admits of a great doubt to decide whether
this church has any rival, although a small superiority in
some respects has been claimed for the metropolitan
church of York.   Lord Burlington, the English Palladio,
decided in favour of Lincoln.

Seen from six counties, far across the immense extent
of level marshes, now drained and fertile ; and even from

the distant hills of Buxton in Derbyshire, prominently over the wide plain, may be seen the far-famed towers of Lincoln—"stately and air-braving," dyed with the hues of the depth of heaven and clothed with the calm of eternity. Rising from the open valley of the Witham, high over the trees, gardens, and houses of the city, and the ivy-covered castle-keep, the grandeur of the Cathedral is unsurpassed; founded on a rock, it stands out in bold relief against the sky, in colossal but exquisite proportions. No site approaches this in point of command, except Armagh, Cashel, or Durham—the perfect symbol of the spiritual church, the city set on a hill that cannot be hid. The dreary fen country makes the contrast all the more forcible here. Nothing finer can be conceived.

The church consists of a CENTRAL and two WESTERN TOWERS; a WEST TRANSEPT, each wing having an EASTERN CHAPEL; a NAVE of seven bays with aisles; a GREAT TRANSEPT, each wing of three bays, and with three eastern chantries; a GALILEE PORCH on the south-west angle; a CHOIR of seven bays with aisles; and a south chapel called Bishop Longland's Chantry. A CHOIR TRANSEPT of two bays, with two apsidal chapels in each wing; to the north wing is attached on the south St. Hugh's Chapel. To the south wing on the south, a lavatory and three sacristies; a PRESBYTERY of three bays with aisles, rendered cruciform by Bishop Fleming's Chapel on the north, and Bishop Russel's on the south; a CLOISTER north of the choir, with a vestibule opening into a CHAPTER-HOUSE.

The Cathedral was commenced by Bishop Remigius, on the plan of Rouen, 1075-92: in the latter year Robert Bloet completed and consecrated it. After a disastrous fire, Alexander, 1123-47, repaired and vaulted it with stone. St. Hugh, 1186-1203, built the EAST TRANSEPT and CHAPELS, the CHOIR and CHAPTER-HOUSE, the east front of the WESTERN TRANSEPT, and made additions to the original WEST FRONT of Remigius; his architect was Godfrey de Noiers. The GALILEE PORCH and west side of the MAIN TRANSEPT were finished shortly after his death. The CLOISTERS, Late Geometrical Decorated, and rood-screen, were commenced in the reign of Edward I. Hugh of Wells, 1206-35, completed the NAVE. One of the canons in 1237 was preaching on the state of feud existing between the chapter and the bishop, and as he exclaimed, " Were we silent, the very stones would cry out," the ill-built central tower fell with a frightful crash, shaking the whole church to the foundations. The bishop (Grosteste, 1237-54) then rebuilt the CENTRAL TOWER as far as the first story above the roof, which he completed with vaulting: rebuilding also the central gable, the tower at the east, and the central pediment at the west of the great screen. The upper portion was begun and finished with a spire by D'Alderby, 1300-19 : the incomparable angel choir, commenced by Lexington in 1256, was completed by Oliver Sutton, 1282. The statues and windows in the west front, the choir stalls, and the upper part of the south front of the great transept are referred to John Welbourne, treasurer and clerk of the works, 1351-81. William Alnwick, 1436-50, built the great west window, in place of a triplet (as he did at Norwich), and upper story of the WEST TOWERS. The spires on them were removed in 1807. Henry Burgh-ersh, 1320-42, built the BURGHERSH CHAPEL ; Richard Fleming, 1420-31, that of the Holy Trinity ; John Russell, 1480-95, that of St. Blaise, and John Longland, 1521-47, that of St. Katharine. The church is built of the oolitic and calcareous stone of the vicinity, Haydor near Grantham.

The WEST FRONT consists of a broad Early English screen on a Norman base covered with arcades, and flanked by octagonal towers crowned with pinnacles. The lateral arches and jambs of the centre arch, the bases of the towers, and adjacent gable are remnants of the original Norman front, On the south is the statue of St. Hugh, on the north Bishop Bloet, " the Swineherd of Stow." Beneath a gable, like the parapet highly enriched, is a lofty pointed arch, with a Perpendicular window with a cinquefoil above it : under an arcade of canopied statues of kings, from William I. to Edward III., set up 1370, is a Norman door, deeply recessed. On either side is a tall stilted Norman arch, with a door beneath. A series of sculptures, rude and quaint, but of high interest, represent the Expulsion from Paradise, the Building of the Ark, Noah landing on Ararat, Daniel in the Lions' Den, the Assumption of the Blessed Virgin, and the Doom; round the south angle is the Deluge. The formation of a western screen here, as at Peterborough, Ely, Salisbury, and Exeter, was a foreign innovation. But the signal defect in all is the extent of space and masonary unrelieved by glass, on which the play of light and reflection of the sky-tints add so much animation to a building, and is to it what the motion of wavy smoke, or the countless smiles of gleaming water, are to the view in a landscape. Above this front appear the TWO WESTERN TOWERS, each worthy to be the central steeple of the noblest cathedral. From a base of three tiers of arcade, on either face, rise two windows, each of two lights of enormous dimensions, with superb canopies and parapet; at the angles are turrets panelled at the top and crowned with pinnacles. When each alone is so beautiful and highly decorated, the effect is iuconceivable which is produced by them in combination, with the CENTRAL Rood, or BROAD TOWER, of similar design but far more richly decorated, so full of state, and dignity, and majestic grandeur, that no church in England, or on the Continent, can be cited in the same description. It was the utmost daring, or rather an inspiration of genius, whioh emboldened the architect to erect such a structure on four arches. It is so perforated for lightness, with galleries and passages, as almost to have two walls, an outer and inner shell. The wooden spire of the Rood Tower was blown down in 1547. In the north-west tower was hung the famous Great Tom (possibly a corruption of Grand Ton), cast at Lincoln in 1610. Having been cracked in December, 1827, it was recast by Thomas Mears of Whitechapel in November, 1834, and added to the central tower in April in the following year. In the vaults of Lincoln, Richard de Bardney says the fragments are concealed of Grosteste's magic talking head of bronze, the familiar whioh revealed secrets to him. At the burial of St. Hugh—

> A' the bells o' merrie Lincoln
>   Without men's hands were rung;
> And a' the books o' merrie Lincoln
>   Were read without man's tongue;
> And ne'er was such a burial
>   Sin' Adam's days begun.

So ran the legend at Canterbury that at à Becket's death the bells rang of their own accord; and at Cœur de Lion's coronation the bells of Westminster were rung in first peal at Compline by unseen hands.

As nature builds her porphyry pillars, her winding rocks, her glacier-floors, her soaring peaks and mountain-ridges, a temple to the Creator, religion, by a marvellous creation, unlike any former architecture, devised one made with hands to His honour. Size in Egypt, beauty in Greece, strength in Rome, have attained perfection: this new invention of a vigorous and unenervated race, full of fervent devotion and sacred enthusiasm, and capable of lofty conception, consisted not only in the symmetry of masses combined in clear definite forms, but in the uninterrupted continuation of vertical lines as the symbol of cloud-piercing thought. At Lincoln an instantaneous devotional effect is eminently produced, an overwhelming and surprising sense of awe, as we enter through the porch, dark like earth, into the nave, with a solemn silence reigning throughout the vast extent, broken but by the echoes of a footfall, hastening away fainter and fainter till it is lost in the far distance; all is mysterious, dim, and holy also, and then through the windows, like transparent walls set with the imagery of heaven, pours in a light which swallows up the gloom, as death is lost in the immortal life— the earthy sinks, the eternal has arisen.

On the north side of the nave-aisles is the MORNING SERVICE CHAPEL, containing the Norman font of Remigius, a square bowl with four supports and a round central pillar; that on the south is the CHAPEL OF ST. HUGH. Between the towers is the great architectual curiosity, the *catenarian beam*, formed of twenty-three stones, eleven inches in depth, but of unequal sizes, twenty-nine and a quarter feet long, twenty-one inches broad, twenty-one inches in diameter at each end, and only twelve inches in the centre; cemented solely by lateral presure, which was designed to gauge the settlement of the towers. The windows in the aisles, under a rich parapet, are Pointed lights set in an arcade, between gabled flying buttresses and smaller buttresses alternately. The parapet of the clerestory is remarkable for its flowing tracery, and for a series of canopied niches, which break the uniform regularity of the high pitched roof of the nave, of nicest workmanship, that once had held

> The sculptured image of some patron saint,
> Or of the Blessed Virgin, looking down
> On all who entered those religious doors.

An unique appendage is attached to the south-west side of the transept, which has no aisle upon that side— a GALILEE PORCH. The front of the SOUTH TRANSEPT is a gable double crocketed, set between two tall pinnacles, below a Decorated window of five lights, traceried in the head, with a band of quatrefoils; under it is a rose window of flowing tracery, or wheel-of-fortune, as such windows were called, from sculptures showing the course of human life; rare in this conntry: beueath it are pointed windows. In this transept stood D'Alderby's silver shrine. The CHOIR TRANSEPT is of four stories, three with windows of one light each, the upper an arcade of five arches, in a gable, which is flanked by octangular turrets, pinnacled. Three small sacristies and a lavatory form a kind of western aisle; on the east are two apsidal chapels. The PRESBYTERY now appears, its windows filled with geometrical tracery, its buttresses with crocketed finials and pediments, shafts clustered at the angles, and canopied niches in their faces. A superb SOUTH PORCH, with a deeply-recessed portal, gabled and flanked with pinnacles, retains statues of the Evangelists. The image of the Virgin, which adorned the column which divides the two foliated arches of entrance, is lost. Above, is a sculpture of the Doom. Against the south-east pier are Queen

Eleanor, and King Edward treading on his enemies. In
the next pier is Queen Margaret of France, restored 1858
by Earp of London. On the east side is the CHAPEL OF
BISHOP BLAISE ; on the west the CHAPEL OF ST. CATHA-
RINE. On the north side of the presbytery is a portal,
not so highly ornamental, with a single CHAPEL OF THE
HOLY TRINITY on the east side.

The east end of the PRESBYTERY consists of three gables,
with crosses, the central the loftiest, separated by double
buttresses, enriched with panels of shafts, canopies, and
brackets, and terminating in octagonal pinnacles and spires
crocketed. The central window is of eight lights, with
geometrical tracery in the head ; above it, divided by a
string-course, is a window of five lights with tracery of
the same character. There is a similar disposition of the
windows that light the aisles, only the tiers are divided by
an arcade ; another, trefoiled, traverses the whole breadth
of this exquisite front, which seems a blossoming of stone
with leafage and flower, petrified on the instant.

In the NORTH FRONT of the MAIN TRANSEPT is a porch,
beneath a pedimented canopy. In the gable, flanked with
turret pinnacles, are seven lancets accommodated to the
slope of the roof; under these is a circular window with
plate tracery, and above an arcade of seven lancets. The
range of triplets in the clerestory throughout the church
on this side is very grand. The nave aisles have pedimented buttresses, alternately large and small, with lancets
intervening. In the clerestory there is a continuous
arcade. The parapet is plain in the whole north side,
except in the choir, where it is of quatrefoils. The north
front of the choir transept is of four stages : in the two
lowermost are two single lights, above this is an arcade,
and in the gable a triplet, flanked by shafted turret pinnacles, and double buttresses. From the north end of the
CHOIR TRANSEPT a VESTIBULE leading into the CLOISTERS (Late
Geometrical Decorated, about 1296), which here occupy
an unusual position, situated, indeed, on the north side,
as at Canterbury and Gloucester, when the early foreign
architects transferred the custom of their sunny native

land, which required cool shade, to this country; but
here on the side of the CHOIR, whereas they, in all other
instances, adjoin the nave. The north alley is a monstrous
piece of Doric absurdity, built by Sir Christopher Wren,
and supports the library. The other walks are composed
of bays, in each of which is a pane under a quatrefoil of
four lights. The vaulting is of wood. In the south-west
angle is a portion of a Roman tesselated pavement, discovered in 1793. On the east side of the cloister is the
decagonal CHAPTER-HOUSE, with a vaulting of stone supported internally by a central pier of Purbeck marble with
ten engaged columns, and externally by flying buttresses.
The windows, of one light each, are set in pairs. It was
probably the first erected in this form in England, as the
earlier examples at Bristol, Gloucester, Peterborough, and
Durham, were oblong. The west front consists of three
pedimented arcaded compartments, with a triplet in the
central gable, above a large round window.

> . . . O! that I amid thy sumptuous aisles
> May kneel, or thread your intricate defiles,
> Adown the nave to pace in motion slow,
> Watching with pleasure ere the tall tower grow
> And mount at every step, with loving wiles
> Instinct, to rouse the heart or lead the will
> By a bright ladder to the world above ;
> Open thy gates, great monument of love
> Divine, thou Lincoln on thy sovereign hill.

The NAVE is divided by piers, with eight columns without
fillets. The triforium is in each bay, of two arcades alternately of two and three arches with quatrefoils in the head ;
the clerestory being uniformly of three pointed lights in
each compartment. The open CENTRAL LANTERN with
stone vaulting, 127 feet from the pavement, and a double
arcade, the uppermost only a clerestory, and set on piers,
each of twenty-four clustered columns 48 feet high, alternately of stone and Purbeck marble, is enhanced by the
soft glow of the rose windows, each 24 feet in diameter,
filled with stained glass of the 13th century: the subject
of the glazing, intensely brilliant, in the north wing is the

Church militant and triumphant. A similar story to those related of the pillar in Roslyn Chapel, and the marygolds of Rouen, is attached to these windows, that one was the work of the master, the other of the apprentice, who was murdered for his display of superior skill. In France, rose-windows bore names according to their position; on the north, rose of the winds; on the west, rose of the sea; on the south, rose of heaven. It is the most perfect and valuable in England. The ROOD-SCREEN has some exquisite workmanship; the organ-screen above covers the tabernacle-work. The organ, built by W. Allen in 1821, was enlarged by his son in 1851. Parcloses of admirable Perpendicular-work shut off the CHANTRIES, three in each of the eastern aisles of the TRANSEPT. Reckoning from north to south there are (St. Nicholas') Thomas Fitzwilliam's, (St. Denys') Canons Richard Sutton and William Wolvey's, (St. James's) Bishop Buckingham's, (St. Edward Martyr's) Henry, Duke of Lancaster's, (St. Andrew's) Bishop Lexington's, (St. Giles') Canon Tailboys' chantries. Mr. Pugin considered the oak STALLS, sixty-two in number, with their intricate canopies, misereres, sculptured with subjects grave, and gay, and ludicrous, and carvings of kings and angel minstrels, the finest in England : they are of the 14th century. The reredos was set up by Mr. Essex, and in the centre is a picture of the Annunciation, by the Rev. William Peters.

In the east aisles of the CHOIR TRANSEPT are four apsidal chapels; the CHANTRIES, numbering them from north to south, of Canon Burton, Canon Thornaco, Joan Lady Cantilupe, and Bishop de Wells; in the south-west is the chapel of St. Hugh; at the north-west are sacristies and a lavatory. The PRESBYTERY has been aptly called the ANGEL CHOIR, from the thirty images of the heavenly host playing on the shawm, harp, zebec, cittern, tabor, and pipes of various kinds. Bending forward from the walls, their forms appear animate in the doubtful light, heightening the devotional sentiment which the surrounding architecture inspires, and connecting religious feeling with each soaring line, like a stone arrow shot upward,

which the eye traces till they they are lost apparently t ⁖
meet in another region.

These ingenious sculptures, probably ordered by Grosteste, and the work of English artists, form a series of thirty
scriptural subjects. Angels represent, by their attitudes
or accessories—(1.) The Patriarchs; (2.) David; (3.) as
the Psalmist; (4.) as King; (5.) Solomon's greatness;
(6.) Abijah's sentence; (7.) Division of Israel and Judah;
(8.) The sins of the former; (9.) Daniel xii. 7 ;ʳ(10.) Isaiah,
2 Kings xix. 3; (11.) Ezekiel, chap. xviii.; (12.) Jeremiah,
Lamentations; (13.) Minor Prophets; (14.) A Soul in
Prayer; (15.) The Virgin Blessed by all generations;
(16, 17, 18.) The Fall in Paradise; the Passion-crown and
Veronica; and Sacrifice of Christ; (19, 20, 21.) Resurrection and Judgment; a Soul offered before the riven side of
Blessed Jesus; the Soul weighed in the Balance; Propi-
tiation with incense, Rev. viii. 3; (22, 23, 24.) Reward and
Martyrdom; the Crown and Palm of Life; Names searched
for vainly in the Book of Life; Rev. xx. 11. 15; (25, 26.)
Praise; (27.) Proclamation of the Everlasting Gospel, Rev.
xiv. 6; (28.) Celestial Harpers, Rev. xiv. 1; (29.) The
Sun of Righteousness, and the Church as the Moon shining
by His reflected Light, Rev. xii. 1; (30.) Christ, Alpha and
Omega, Rev. xxii. 10.

The glazing of the east window, was put up, in 1855, by
Ward and Hughes; underneath was St. John Baptist's altar,
once the chantry of Queen Eleanor. The details of this
presbytery are beyond all praise, the proportions faultless.
The style is seen here in its utmost perfection. On Oct.
6, 1280, St. Hugh was translated hither in the presence of
the king, the queen, archbishop, seven prelates, and six
abbots, to his shrine, and before it was consecrated Beck as
bishop of St. David's. The watching-chamber of oak still
remains. The clerestory is of triplets; the triforium of
two arches in each bay, subdivided into two pairs of
shafted couplets under a quatrefoil.

King Stephen sat crowned in the minster in 1147, and
in it John of Gaunt, "time-honoured Lancaster," was married 1396.

During the Civil Wars the church was occupied as a barrack by the Parliamentary soldiers, who committed great devastation and wanton and disgraceful mutilations at the storming by the Earl of Manchester, May 5, 1644. Before that period eighty-seven tombs were in the nave alone.

The Cathedral covers 2 acres, 2 roods, and 6 perches of land.

DIMENSIONS OF THE CATHEDRAL IN FEET.

	Length.	Breadth.	Height.
Nave . .	255	80	80
Choir . .	158	80	74
Main Transept .	222	66	74
Choir Transept .	170 with chantries 44		72
West Front .	174	..	..
Lady Chapel (Angel Choir) .	116	82	72
Cloisters N. and S.	118 E. and W. 90		..
Chapter-house .	62	62	42
Central Tower	53	53	268 f. 4 in.
Western Towers	35	35	206
West Front .	173	..	83
The Spires were	..	..	101
Total length .	486	..	..

The principal monuments are those of—

Lady Chapel, or Angel Choir.—Sir Bartholomew, Baron Burghersh, d. 1356, effigy beneath a canopy with three tabernacles.

N. Aisle.—Bishop Henry Burghersh, d. 1340, effigy—the head supported by evangelistic symbols; Robert de Burghersh, father of the bishop.

S. Aisle.—Nicholas, Lord Cantilupe, d. 1355, chantry, effigy; Prior Wymbish of Nooton, effigy.

S. Transept.—Remains of the shrine of D'Alderby.

Trinity Chapel.—Bishop Fleming, d. 1430, effigy and cadaver.

St. Blaise's Chapel.—Bishop Russell, altar-tomb and screen, d. 1495.

St. Katherine's Chapel.—Bishop Lougland, altar-tomb, chantry, and screen, d. 1547.

Choir, N. Side.—Bishop Bloet, d. 1123, an Easter tomb with three knights, armed, watching; in the recess the crucifix was kept during Good Friday and Easter Eve. Bishop Remigius, d. 1093.

Choir, S. Side.—Catherine Swinford, d. 1403, and her daughter Joan, canopy ; Countess of Westmoreland, d. 1440.

Nave.—Window, gift of C. T. D'Eyncourt, by Eaton and Butler, 1858.

In the *South Aisle* the modern glazing is by Preedy, that of the *North* by Ward.

S. Choir Transept.—Bishop Kaye, recumbent figure by Westmacott, with stained glass as an additional memorial in the windows.

St. Paul's Chapel.—A window by A. and H. Sutton, 1858 ; cinque-foil in west front, by Crace, 1858, the gift of the Right Hon. C. T. D'Eyncourt.

Cantilupe Chantry.—A window glazed.

South Aisle.—Fragment of the monument of Sir Hugh, a child crucified by the Jews in 1225, the subject of many a popular ballad, and Chaucer's—

> The bonny boys of merrie England
> Were playing at the ba',
> And wi' them stood the sweet Sir Hugh,
> The sweetest of them a'.

A similar story is related of a Sir William at Norwich.

Cloister.—Norman coffin-lid of Remigius, split by the fall of the roof in the fire. There is an incised slab representing a rose-tree.

The Chapter of the Cathedral consists of a dean and four canons. There are four minor canons, eight lay vicars, and ten choristers. The Litany is sung by two lay vicars; an extraordinary and irregular arrangement. There are two daily choral services at 10 ; three in summer, four in winter; the Holy Communion is celebrated monthly and on festivals. The expenditure on the fabric in fourteen years was 21,756*l.* ; the income of the Chapter, in 1852, amounted to 8800*l.* The library contains 4500 volumes ; among them an invaluable collection of old English romances, by Archdeacon Thornton, 1430-40. The early books of Caxton were sold by the Chapter to Dr. Dibdin, and others, to purchase more available literature ! The palace is at Riseholme near Lincoln.

Arms : Gules two leopards or : on a chief azure, enthroned and sceptred, the Blessed Virgin and Holy Child Jesus, both nimbed : in dexter chief, the letter D sable.

Lincoln can boast of an illustrious line of bishops. SS.

Birinus and Hedda; Robert Bloet, Lord Chancellor; De
Blois, Chief Justice and founder of four abbeys; Walter de
Constance, the Crusader; St. Hugh de Grenoble; the
learned Grosteste, who Bale says appeared to Pope Inno-
cent at Naples, and of whose speaking "head of bronze"
Gower tells tales as marvellous; Henry Burghersh, Lord
Chancellor, whom the folks averred walked as the Green
Verderer in Tinghurst Common, till the canons made res-
titution and laid the unquiet spirit; Buckingham, Lord
Keeper, who resigned rather than accept translation to
Lichfield, and so "preferred no bread to half a loaf;"
Fleming, founder of Lincoln College, Oxford, who threw
Wycliffe's ashes into the Swift; Russell, Lord Chancellor;
Cardinal Wolsey; Smith, founder of Brasenose College,
Oxford; Longland, who urged on Queen Katharine's di-
vorce; Chaderton who astonished Cambridge by his sermon on marriage, comparing the discovery of a good wife
to a search for an eel in a barrel of snakes; Barlow, "the
barley loaf" of the Puritans; aspiring Neile; learned
Sanderson, the last bishop who wore a moustache; Barlow the second, nicknamed bishop of Buckden, as he never
once visited his cathedral; Wake and Gibson; facetious
Thomas, who, like Hoadly and Gooch, married five wives;
and learned Kaye. Among its dignitaries occur twenty-
nine cardinals; Archbishops Peter of Lyons, and John of
Bordeaux; Walter Mapes, the Anacreon of the 11th
century; Henry of Huntingdon; Polydore Vergil; H.
Thorndike, W. Outram, L. Echard, S. Pegge, W. Paley,
and George Herbert, "the sweet singer of the Temple."

The wall of the CLOSE was built by Bishop Sutton; the
EXCHEQUER GATE was built in the time of Edward I.
There are remains of the deanery of the 13th century.
In the Close are portions of houses of the 14th and
15th centuries. The GATEWAY of the VICAR'S CLOSE,
which once formed a quadrangle, is of the date of
Edward I. Bishop Alnwick erected the buildings now
used as stables, 1450. The BISHOP'S PALACE, picturesquely described by old Leland as "hanging on the slope
of the hill," was begun by Bishop Chesney. The GREAT

HALL, 75 ft. in length by 55ft. in breadth, consisted of a nave and aisles, now in ruins, erected by St. Hugh de Grenoble. The TOWER ENTRANCE was the work of Bishop Alnwick. On March 31, 1617, King James I. was here royally entertained by Bishop Neile, as Longland had received Henry VIII. and Queen Catherine Howard.

Llandaff.

EMINENT as the Principality is for natural scenery, the rocky chines and rugged mountains of North Wales, and the soft beauty of the wooded pastures and noble hills of the southern counties, it can lay but slight claim to architectural pretensions. St. David's and St. Asaph have indeed the cruciform plan and central tower of a cathedral, but Bangor (though cruciform), and Llandaff, possess only the features of a common parochial church; and the tower of Wrexham and the priory church of Brecon are not approached in external dignity by any of the four. In the civil wars the Cathedral was converted by one Milles into an ale-house; the choir became a calf-pen, the font a hog-trough; one transept was used as a stable, and the other wing as a post-office.

> The reverend pile lay wild and waste,
> Profaned, dishonoured, and defaced;
> The civil fury of the time
> Made sport of sacrilegious crime,
> For dark fanaticism rent
> Altar and screen and monument,
> And peasant hands the tombs o'erthrew.

A more deplorable state than that of Llandaff (Llan-ar-daf, the " Church on the Taffy "), till the late dean commenced the restoration, is inconceivable. A steep descent leading to the west front forms a striking and singular approach.

The Cathedral is dedicated to SS. Peter, Paul, Dubricius,

Teleiau, and 'Odoceus. At the east end flows the river Taff, often turbulent, but usually flowing softly by the low-lands, above which, on a slight eminence, stands the village city, only two miles from Cardiff, to which it was proposed to translate the see in 1718. It is an oblong, embracing, under an uninterrupted line of roof, a NAVE, CHOIR, and PRESBYTERY, with aisles and a LADY CHAPEL—a village church of unparalleled size, plain, heavy, and flat. The peculiar arrangement is owing to the fact that a small building received successive enlargements, until it attained its present size, without any complete restoration from the ground. It was commenced by Bishop Urban, April 14, 1120, on the site of a church, measuring 28 by 18 feet, and 20 feet high, but the greater portion of the west front and lancet-work of NAVE and CHOIR must be attri-buted to a date not earlier than 1220. Henry de Aber-gavenny, 1193-1219, probably commenced them ; De Gold-cliffe, 1219-30, his successor, completing the fabric : the CHAPTER-HOUSE being somewhat later. In the presbytery is supposed to survive Urban's nave. The Cathedral con-sists of a NAVE of six bays, with aisles, Early English, choir of two bays ; PRESBYTERY of two bays, each with aisles ; a CHAPTER-HOUSE, Early English, south of the presbytery, and a LADY CHAPEL Decorated. William de Braose, 1266-97, and John de Monmouth, 1296-1323, are believed to have rebuilt the LADY CHAPEL with the presbytery aisles. John de Monmouth consecrated the church, 1296.

The WEST FRONT of the fine NAVE is composed of a gable, tasteful and unpretending, between a TOWER on the north and the fragment of another on the south. The latter, bold and meagre, was 89 feet in height, Early Eng-lish, with lancet windows. The two upper stories (which are Perpendicular) of JASPER's TOWER, still remaining, were built by Jasper Tudor, Duke of Bedford, in the 15th century. It is 105 feet high, of three stories, with an octangular turret-staircase on the south angle. Battle-ments have taken the place of its deep parapet and crocketed pinnacles. In the WEST FRONT, above the round double-headed door, in the head of which is an aureole containing the image of a bishop, is a fine triplet, with two blank lancet arches on either side of the central window, which is taller than the others: above this story is a series of eight round-headed trefoil niches, four on either side of a single large central light, and adapted to the slope of the gable, in which is a trefoiled arch with a mitred effigy and a plain cross above all. There is no triforium in the NAVE, which is of seven bays. The windows of the aisle have ogee mouldings with Perpendicular tracery. The clerestory is composed in each bay of two distinct lancets, each with a smaller arch on either side, divided by flat pilasters running into a corbeltable.

The floor has been laid with Minton's tiles. The arches of the CHOIR and PRESBYTERY have been opened out into the aisles. The PRESBYTERY is divided from the LADY CHAPEL by a wide Norman chancel arch, beneath which was discovered a beautiful screen built by Bishop Marshall 1480. The REREDOS, of Caen stone, triple gabled, richly carved, with columns of rouge-royal and emperor-red marble, has been erected by Rosetti, and a new pulpit by Pritchard and Seddon, with sculptures by T. Woolner, placed in the nave which, with the clerestory, has been rebuilt of Bath oolite. There are two rich Late Norman doorways, one in each nave-aisle; over the south doorway is a unique moulding like an Etruscan scroll. A small pair of doorways to the east are Decorated, of the same date as the windows.

The windows in the LADY CHAPEL, restored in 1844, at a cost of 1275l. which is Transitional, have Early geometrical tracery, and are of two trefoil lights, with a plain circle in the head; the groining of the vault is of five bays, simple and good, rising from Purbeck shafts. The CHAPTERHOUSE is square with a central shaft, and adjoins the south aisle of the choir. The five-light geometrical window was set up in 1844, with sedilia in the CHOIR, with rich mosaic panels and four shafts, alternately red and green, by Mr. John Pritchard, under the superintendence of Mr. T. W. Wyatt. The conventicle, erected 1751, by Mr. Wood of

Bath, was beneath contempt. The restorations have cost 8830*l.* On the south-west stood the Consistory Court.

The principal monuments are the following—

John de Monmouth, d. 1323, effigy; Paschal, d. 1361, effigy.

N. Choir Aisle.—David Matthew, standard-bearer to Edward IV., murdered at Neath, an alabaster effigy; Sir Christopher Matthew; effigies of a knight who fell in the civil wars and dame; Mr. Wyndham attributed these effigies to Cellini; Bishop Dubricius, effigy, and Bishop Bromfield, d. 1391, a cadaver.

N. Side Choir.—Bishop William de Braose, d. 1287, effigy.

Presbytery, S. Aisle.—Christian, wife of John Lord Audley, effigy.

S. E. Side of Choir.—S. Teilo, sepulchral recess of the date 1200, effigy. A cadaver is shown as that of a lady who died for love; at other cathedrals the cadaver is generally exhibited as that of a bishop who, by way of penance fasted forty days, and died of the experiment.

DIMENSIONS OF THE CATHEDRAL IN FEET.

	Length.	Breadth.	Height.
Nave	114	70	65
Choir and Presbytery	82	65	..
Lady Chapel	54	25	36
Chapter-house	23	21	8
Extreme length	245	..	..

All traces of the subordinate collegiate buildings are gone, with the exception of the castellated gateway of the 13th century, flanked by two huge square towers, with their angles chamfered off, characteristic of South Wales, and of the ivied walls of the palace, which was destroyed by Owen Glendower. There is a small house adjoining, with a geometrical hall and Elizabethan porch; and also an old ruin, called Black Hall, of two stories, with a two-light arch and foliated window in the gable. There is a village-green cross.

The Chapter is composed of a dean and three canons. There are two minor canons: there is neither organ nor choral service. There are only three week-day services. The Holy Communion is administered monthly. The income of the Chapter in 1852 was only 713*l.*; the expenditure on the fabric in 1844, owing to subscriptions, was

1275*l.* 9000*l.* in all have been spent. The library contains 95 volumes. The rebels compelled their Cavalier prisoners and the wives of the sequestered clergy to warm themselves, on a bitter winter's day, at a fire kindled at Cardiff with the books from Llandaff.

Llandaff numbers among its bishops SS. Dubricius, at whose desire Merlin translated the Giant's Dance to Stonehenge; Cymeliauc, seized by the Danes in his church, and ransomed for 40*l.* by the king; Kitchen, "who for ever spoiled the good meat of Llandaff;" Owen, who died in his chair at the news of Laud's death; Beaw, who fought for the king, and whom Tenison reminded that "at his age he should think of but one translation—to a seat above;" industrious Godwin; orthodox Marsh; princely Barrington and Van Mildert, and Watson, "the self-taught divine," who excused himself to the sceptic Gibbon for writing the book which drew forth George the Third's exclamation, "Apology for the Bible!—I never knew it wanted one," for thirty years non-resident, so that he could boast in his Westmoreland retirement, that, with the poorest bishopric in the king's books, he was the richest prelate in his dominions.

The palace is Bishop's Court, Llandaff.

Arms: Sa. two pastoral staffs in saltier or and arg. On a chief az. three mitres.

𝕸an.

THERE was an old tradition, that a mermaid along the shore meeting a young Manxman of great beauty declared to him her love, and, in revenge for his expression of revolt and disgust, obscured the Island and Cathedral with a veil of mist which made all vessels coming to it wander up and down upon its seas or wrecked them on the cliffs.

The ruined Cathedral of St. German, in Peel Castle, St. Patrick's Isle, has a position equal to the famous rock of

Cashel. The combination of military and ecclesiastical structures, within one enclosure, occurs at Dover, Porchester, and Exeter. It is a small cross church, with a short central tower, which has on the south-west angle a square belfry turret. The walls of red sandstone, and the general outline, give it a likeness to Carlisle. The CHOIR resembles St. Bees. The north and east windows in the SOUTH TRANSEPT are Decorated; on the west side is a lancet. On the west side of the TRANSEPT is the chief entrance from the sea, with a holy-water stoup. On the north side of the NAVE are two windows, Decorated. On the south side are four arches for a contemplated aisle. The east end resting on the edge of the precipice has a beautiful though small plain triplet, Early English. The five side-lancets are tall, but not acutely pointed; the bays are divided from each other by flat buttresses: on the north side are two arched recesses for tombs; on the south is a door to the crypt. The CENTRAL TOWER is Transitional Early English, or Early Decorated. The TRANSEPTS are also Decorated. Beneath the CHOIR is a fine CRYPT with barrel vaulting, diagonal ribbed, springing from thirteen dwarf shafts. In this desolate dungeon, reached by thirty steps— the dead above, the booming of the sullen sea below piercing through the crevices of the floor of rock—Eleanor, Duchess of Gloucester, on a charge of witchcraft was imprisoned, 1440-1454. Her spirit after death was supposed to take the form of a spectre hound, the Mauthe Dhoog of Peverel of the Peak. In this church Bishop Hildesley was enthroned. Bishop Simon of Orkney, 1232-49, was the founder of the Cathedral, he and Bishops Mark of Galloway, Hesketh, Phillips, Parr, and Rutter were buried in it.

DIMENSIONS OF THE CHURCH IN FEET.

	Length.	Breadth.	Height.
Nave	52 f. 3in.	} 20 f. 1in.	..
Choir	36 f. 4in.		
Transept.	68	19	..
Tower.	25 f. 11in	..	..
Crypt	29 f. 2in.	15 f. 2in.	..
Total length.	114 f. 6in.	..	..

The Arms,—Three legs conjoined at the knee, with the motto, " Quocunque jeceris stabit,"—were given by King Alexander of Scotland after his reduction of the island, 1266. They are now placed under an image of St. German, standing in a canopied porch, holding a church in his dexter hand—

Cardinal Fleury, from respect to Bishop Wilson's virtues, forbade the French privateers to make any descent on the island :

> That saintly name once had a thrilling tongue
> Which pleaded for thy sea-encircled strand,
> And still doth plead. . . . .

The island, originally subject to the King of Northumberland, was in the hands of the Danes or Norwegians, 1065—1266 ; the Scots then held it till 1334, when William Montacute, Earl of Salisbury, conquered it. Sir William Scrope held it 1393—1399 ; Henry, Earl of Northumberland, 1399—April 6, 1406 ; Stanleys, Earls of Derby, from that date to 1736 ; and the Dukes of Atholl, 1736—1763 ; but in 1825 (6 Geo. IV., c. 35) the right of nomination of the bishop was at last purchased by the crown.

Among the bishops occur SS. Amphibalus and Germanùs, who was consecrated, 447, by St. Patrick ; Wilmund, who became a buccaneer, and was blinded by the Scots ; John, who was burned accidentally to death ; Salisbury, who translated the Holy Bible into Welsh ; Philip, who made a Manx version of the Sacred Scriptures ; Rutter, who fought in the defence of Latham House ; Barrow, founder of King William's College ; Wilson, who, like Fisher of Rochester, refused translation in his words : " Because my spouse is poor, shall I desert her ?" and whose benediction was craved by a London mob ; Hildesley, who sang his Nunc Dimittus when he had finished his Manx translation of the Prayer Book ; luxurious Richmond, the first bishop who used a sedan chair in going to church ; and Baron Auckland.

𝔐anchester.

MANCHESTER, the Mancenion of the Britons, from " Main,"
stone, its hill of quarries, is the manufacturing metropolis of England, the great workshop familiar to Indian,
African, Turk, and Tartar by its fabrics. As natives or
residents it claims Dr. Dee, the necromancer ; Byron, Miss
Jewsbury, T. K. Harvey, and Charles Swain, poets ; the
first Sir Robert Peel ; the Duke of Bridgewater ; Dr.
Whitaker, E. Ogden, W. H. Ainsworth, De Quincey, and
Dr. Dalton, author of the Atomic Theory. It is situated in
a plain of great extent, girdled by a barrier of hills, from
which the view of flaming furnaces, canal and railway,
great flourishing towns and small villages, with patches of
moss-land, and the murmur of a dense population, is,
perhaps, the most extraordinary and busy in the kingdom. At the Palace-Inn in 1714 the Chevalier lodged.
The Chetham Library was founded, 1508, in the College
built by Delawarr in 1422 ; the hall, with dais and a dole
window, a double cloister, parlour, kitchen, and dormitory,
remain.

It is the office of sacred architecture to replace the loss
of the garden and pleasant field in cities, and possess us
with quietness of spirit, solemn and yet tender. It must
be a superficial mind that can overlook the advantages
of a cathedral to a busy commercial city ; the permanent
gifts which it abundantly bestows, and the influence it
constantly exerts by its daily offering of prayer, its recall
of worldly anxious hearts to a love of grandeur and beauty,
the assistance and strength it affords to the lively recol-
lection of GOD, His sublimity and mystery. Its quiet
solemn voice of sober reason reaches the heart at its
better hours, inspires respect for our ancestors, and thus
overcomes a natural propensity to overestimate our own
times and acts, and remind men how much of all they
most value was once without grudging sacrificed for a
higher cause. The cathedral of Manchester is in its
present state unworthy of the wealth of its merchant

princes, although a notable evidence of former piety, when it was the sole ornament of a town scarcely larger than an ordinary hamlet.

Sir George Head, in his Home Tour in the summer of 1835, said he heard the publication in this church of 197 banns of marriage on a single occasion. Col. Birch took away, after the siege by Lord Strange, the deeds of the college to London, where they were destroyed in the great fire of 1666. In 1642 the rebels used it as a storehouse during the siege by Lord Derby. In 1649 it was converted into a conventicle. It was by statute 1540-1 constituted a place of sanctuary.

Christ Church at Manchester, on the Strangeways Road, close to the Irwell, which serves for the twofold purpose of Cathedral and parish church, is composed of a NAVE of six bays and three aisles, two on the north and one to the south, with lateral chantries opeuing into that on the south. The south-west CHANTRY is ST. GEORGE's, the south-east ST. NICHOLAS' OR TRAFFORD; on the north-west is STRANGEWAY's CHANTRY; on the north-east is ST. JAMES's CHANTRY, which was a transept. The CHOIR of five bays has aisles and eastern procession-path; and on the north ST. JOHN BAPTIST's or the DERBY CHAPEL; and on the south JESUS' CHANTRY, with the OLDHAM CHANTRY on the north-east side. The CHAPTER-HOUSE, which is octagonal, with lights only to the south on four sides, is to the east of the former chantry. There is an insignificant eastern LADY CHAPEL, called Byron's. The TOWER, as at Bangor, is at the west end.

The College was founded by Thomas, Lord de la Warr, in the fifteenth century; disolved 1547, but refounded under Queen Elizabeth and Charles I. Ralph Langley, warden, in 1465 commenced, and Bishop Stanley in 1490 completed, the NAVE and aisles; ST. JAMES's CHANTRY, formerly the north transept, was built by John Huntingdon, 1440; the STRANGEWAYS' CHANTRY was built in 1508; and ST. NICHOLAS,' founded by Robert Chetham, was built by Sir George West; and the CHAPTER-HOUSE, by Bishop Stanley, about 1500, who added the clerestory roof and octagonal turrets of the CHOIR with the stall-work on the south. At the same time, Galley, a merchant of Manchester, built ST. GEORGE'S CHAPEL—he died 1505. The TRAFFORD CHAPEL was built in 1506. Richard Bexwith, iu 1506, added the JESUS' CHAPEL, founded by Ralph Hulme, and the Flemish stall-work on the north of the choir. Those on the south have the arms of Beck, West, and the Mercers' company. In 1513 Bishop Stanley built ST. JOHN BAPTIST'S OR DERBY CHAPEL, and the small ELY CHAPEL on the north, which contains a fine brass of this prelate, who added the parcloses. The LADY CHAPEL was altered by Warden West, and again in the 17th century. He added the clerestory and roof of the nave. The upper part of the tower was built in 1520. The SOUTH PORCH was built by one Bibby, 1520. The OLDHAM CHAPEL was built 1519. The TOWER and LADY CHAPEL were built about 1330, and it would appear without reference to the future intermediate structure. Huntingdon built the CHOIR and aisles 1440 designing a cruciform church.

The church does not hold a very high position; being built of soft red friable sandstone, deficient in ground-plan, and surcharged with ornament—yet its chief and sole beauty to soften, if it cannot conceal, the internal defects, otherwise painfully apparent. The three clustered pinnacles at the angles of the tower are, however, alike effective and unique. Externally it is 232 feet long by 130 in breadth.

The whole Cathedral is Late Perpendicular; neither the NAVE nor the CHOIR has any triforium ; the roof is of timber, panelled, with corbels carved into angels sounding on trumpets and musical instruments. The NAVE was filled with hideous pews in 1815. There are two organs of which the smaller, built by Father Smith 1684, bears a very high character; the other is dated 1724.

If the galleries and screens of tapestry were removed, the nave would resemble Chichester, with its lateral chantries, and the perspective present an almost Moorish aspect, like the mosque of Cordova, while the choir which is intrinsically beautiful, light, and pure in style, with its excellent roof and stall-work, would appear picturesque and remarkable. There is only a single range of stalls, so that clergy and lay vicars sit together.

The credence-table is of wood, unfixed, furnished with a leaf which is let down only during the office of Holy Communion. The tapestry, representing Ananias and Sapphira, was given in 1706. The colours of H.M. 41st Regiment are suspended here. Two glass windows by Edmonds have been set up in the south choir clerestory, 1858. The FONT has a beautiful canopy cover. In the CRYPT under the choir is the brass of John Huntington (died 1458). There is a statue of Humphrey Cheetham.

The Chapter consists of a dean and four canons. There are two minor canons, four vicars-choral, and four singing boys. There are two choral services daily at 11 and half-past 3 ; the Holy Communion is celebrated on Sundays and festivals. The capitular revenue in 1852 was 7599*l*. The expenditure in fourteen years previous 1199*l*. Bishop R. Lee was a warden, and Collyer, who refused to acknowledge the royal supremacy of Henry VIII.

Arms : Or, on a pale engrailed gu. ; three mitres arg. on a canton gu. ; three bends sinister of the field.

The see of Manchester was founded by Act of Parliament, 10 and 11 Victoria, c. 108 ; the present occupant, the Right Reverend James Prince Lee, who was consecrated in 1847, being, the first bishop. The palace is Mauldeth Hall, near Manchester.

Norwich.

NORWICH (North-wic, the "northern home," in allusion to the position of the deserted mother-town of Caistor) is a city of narrow streets diverging from its central castle, on a ridge sloping down to the river Wensum (*i.e.* winding water) on the east and north, and a valley on the south ;

so plentifully interspersed with gardens and trees as to
be known as the city in an orchard. Camden doubted
whether to call Norwich a city in an orchard, or an
orchard in a city. The hills are exaggerated in importance
by the flatness of the surrounding country.

Among its natives Norwich counts W. Beloe, Archbishop
Parker, Edward King, and Dr. Crotch. In the Grammar
School, Lord Nelson, Sir Edward Coke, and Rajah Brooke
were educated. It was taken by the Dauphin 1216,
plundered by the Flemings, and attacked by Wat Tyler.
Its royal visitors have been Henry I. who kept Christmas
1122, 1156; Henry III. 1272; Edward I. 1278, 1292;
Edward III. 1340, 1342, 1344; the Black Prince, 1350;
Henry IV. 1406; Henry VI. 1448-9; Henry VII. 1485;
Queen Elizabeth, 1576; Charles II. 1671.

No city has retained so many parish churches; they
are thirty-six in number. Among these are prominent
the tall towers of St. Giles and St. Peter Mancroft, a noble
structure, 212 feet long, 70 broad, and 60 in height, with
a panelled ceiling, built 1430-55, and interesting as the
burial-place of Sir Thomas Browne ; and the round towers
of St. Mary-Coslany and St. Julian's. In St. Giles's
is a lectern of brass made 1496. In St. Michael's-at-
Thorn an oak lectern ; in St. Swithin's a brass of a merchant, of the time of Edward IV.; in St. Laurence's a
brass of Prior Langley, d. 1437. St. Stephen's contains a
fine roof, a font of the 16th century, and glazing dated
1601 ; St. Mary-Coslany has a panelled pulpit. Like
All Saints, St. Giles's possesses a beautiful Decorated
font; there is another fine specimen in St. John's
Sepulchre. St. James's has an altar-cloth made from a
cope of purple velvet, richly embroidered, of the 15th
century; St. Michael-Coslany some glazing, dated 1610.
The Guildhall was built 1407-13. The Mayor's Council-
chamber retains its furniture of the time of Henry VIII.,
c. 1522; on the south side is a good Perpendicular door.
The Strangers' Hall has a porch of the time of Henry
VIII. and a Jacobean staircase. St. Andrew's Hall,
of 13 bays, 124 feet in length and 70 in breadth, was the

nave of the Black Friars' Church, built 1440-70; the choir is used as a place of worship for the inmates of the poor-house. There are also three alleys of a brick cloister.

The city walls, begun 1294, finished 1328, were fortified by Richard Spynk, 1342. At Sandling ferry, which commands the finest prospect of the Cathedral, is the Boom Gate, of black flint; a corresponding gate stood on the opposite bank, and between them a boom used to be drawn to impede the navigation of the river in times of danger. The Bishop's bridge, adjoining, of one arch, 43 feet in span, was built 1295. The grand quadrangular keep of the castle is 110 feet 3 inches by 92 feet 10 inches, and 69 feet 6 inches in height; the entrance, or Bigod's tower, is a rich specimen of Norman work. The Dungeon tower, an outwork, rebuilt 1390, is in St. Giles's Hospital meadow. In the Bridewell are some specimens of the famous Norwich flint-work, where this difficult material is reduced to octangular shape, and laid in courses as regularly as bricks.

The Cathedral Close, in which stands Milnes' statue of Lord Nelson, is approached through an open space called Tombland, perhaps, as at St. Alban's and St. Edmund's, a corruption of Romeland, the place of paying Peter's Pence and Romescot. On the west are two gates. One, built by Sir Thomas Erpingham, who died 1420, is a stately structure set between two demi-octangular buttresses, profusely sculptured, with thirty-eight small statues, shields, birds, and foliage, with the effigy of the founder over the portal. His motto, "Yenk," or thank, being misread pœna, gave rise to the legend that he built the gate as a penance. It is a very early specimen of Norfolk ornamental flint-work. He was a Wycliffite, and was imprisoned by the bishop; but Henry IV. reconciled them, and Sir Thomas became a fast friend to the church. The other, St. Ethelbert's, was built by the citizens in compensation for the injuries inflicted on the monastery, during a popular commotion in 1272; it has a chapel of black flint above the doors. On the north, in St. Martin's Plain, the exact synonym for the Italian Piazza

and French Place, is the St. Martin's or the Palace Gate,
built by Bishop Alnwick, 1430, with doors added by
Bishop Lyhart ; and a canopied niche containing the
effigy of a king. In the palace gardens are a ruined gate-
house, built by Bishop Salmon, and the remains of a
Decorated chapel, 130 by 30 feet, and the ancient hall,
110 by 60 feet, built 1299-1325, and destroyed by Cromwell. On the south were the refectory and kitchen, and
near them the infirmaries, of which three piers of the south
aisle remain : to the west are a guest-hall and cellarer's
apartments, while between them and the church intervenes
a Norman building, the purpose of which is unknown.
The charnel-house, now the free school, founded by
bishop Salmon 1316, was composed of a chapel, and the
actual bone-house, of two aisles, with a double row of
columns 14 feet high. In the palace are cellars and a
kitchen of the 13th century.

The church consists of a CENTRAL STEEPLE; a NAVE of
fourteen bays with aisles ; a TRANSEPT, each wing of three
bays ; an apsidal sacristy on the north-east side; a CHOIR
of four bays with an apsidal end, aisles, and a procession-
path : on the south side is the BEAUCHAMP CHAPEL; on
the north-east side JESUS' CHAPEL ; on the south-east is
ST. LUKE's CHAPEL ; and to the south of the nave is the
CLOISTER with each alley of eleven panes.

In 1096, Lozinga laid the foundation of the Cathedral,
and built the CHOIR, with aisles, TRANSEPT, and CENTRAL
TOWER ; Everard added, and John of Oxford completed,
the NAVE and aisles, 1121-1200. The Lady Chapel, since
destroyed by Dean Gardiner, to save the cost of repairs,
was built by Walter de Suffield, 1244-57. On Advent
Sunday, 1278, the church was reconsecrated by Walter
de Middleton, in consequence of a fire, and damage caused
in the feuds between the monks and townspeople. John
de Wakeling, 1416-26, built a chapter-house, destroyed
in 1298 ; Ralph Walpole built a spire of wood and lead in
1295, and commenced the CLOISTERS 1297, which were
completed in 1430. Bishop Salmon built greater part of
the CHARNEL-HOUSE, the PALACE-HALL, the SOUTH-WALK of

the CLOISTERS, and three bays of the gallery and a CHANTRY CHAPEL, 1299-1325. Bishop Goldwell constructed the vaulting of the choir after the spire had been struck by lightning, in place of the old wooden roof, destroyed in 1463; and to resist the thrust of that new stone-work, the flying buttresses of the CHOIR, 1472-99: he also masked the lower part of the choir, and added a clerestory in the Perpendicular style. Bishop Nix vaulted the TRANSEPT with stone, about 1500. Bishop Lyhart inserted the great WEST WINDOW, altered the Norman portal in the Pointed style, laid a new floor, added the STONE VAULTING of the NAVE, and built the ROOD-SCREEN. The spire of wood was thrown down by a hurricane in 1362; a new SPIRE of stone was finished by Bishop Percy, 1364-9, and repaired by Lyhart, 1446-72.

The first impression of the Cathedral of the Holy Trinity, when viewed from the south-west angle of the cloister, is very favourable: the lofty spire of the central tower, like a spear thrust into the skies, the noble transept and tiers of arcades along the south side of the nave, which is of unusual length and height, form a striking picture; the knots of ornament, as we retire to contemplate the entire structure, appearing faint and inconsiderable beside the buttressed pier, and fearless height of the spire, as the shadows steal back along the buttresses, like a receding tide leaves the ribbed sands, now chasing each other like the cloud-stains on the downside, and now flung in fantastic shapes upon the chequered cloister sward. But the decay of the stone, the dusky sombre hue of the building, and the absence of massive buttresses, detract fatally from the effect on a closer inspection. Two tall western steeples alone could redeem the enormous length and want of height.

With all the advantages of an open space and forest trees, the WEST FRONT lacks dignity and importance. We are before a large cathedral, but one not rising above the second class. It is composed of a gable between two turrets with spirelets and round-headed single panels. Above a recessed portal within a square head, and with four canopied

niches, is a rich Perpendicular window of nine trefoiled
lights, and good tracery, filled in 1854 with stained glass
by George Hedgeland, to the memory of Bishop Stanley;
a small light is set in the head of the gable, which terminates in a cross. The lateral ends of the aisles are
each of three stories, battlemented and similar to each
other, with an arcade interposed between a Norman door,
and a second threefold arcade with a single two-light
window under a round arch. The north-west arcade is
reticulated. The original Norman turrets flank either
angle of the front.

On the south side of the NAVE the aisle is of uncommon
height and three stories, the base tier is a blank arcade
of Norman arches with two Late Perpendicular windows
inserted; above, in each bay, divided by buttresses, is a
similar arcade, with a light, however, between a blank
arch on either side: the uppermost story has flattened
Perpendicular windows of four lights. The clerestory
resembles the middle arcade of the aisle; but windows
of two lights have been inserted in the centre of each
bay. An embattled parapet runs above the clerestory
and aisles. The SOUTH TRANSEPT is flanked by square
turrets, which are arcaded at the summit, and terminate
in pinnacles. Its Norman character is not materially
affected by some few innovations. The blank buttressed
wall of the vestry abuts the east wall. The upper portion of the clerestory, curiously rising from a Norman
base, alone is visible; it is Early Perpendicular, set between bold flying buttresses, which exhibit in their construction and application the extreme skill of the architect
who designed such ornamental supports, and below a
rich parapet embattled. The CHOIR terminates in a pentagon. The Lady Chapel is gone. The entrance double
arches beneath a trefoil remain; and three Pointed lights
above. Opening out to the south choir-aisle, is BISHOP
BEAUCHAMP'S CHAPEL, now the Consistory Court. To the
west of it was the prior's or St. Edmund's chapel; to the
south were the precinct gaol, now a dwelling-house, and
the dungeon. Corresponding to these buildings, on the

north side were the chapels of St. Stephen and St. Osyth, with a stone vault and a good Decorated window. In each of the first sides of the pentagonal apse is a chapel ; to the north the chapel of Jesus the Saviour, used by the bishop ; to the south the old prior's, or St. Luke's, now used by the parish of St. Mary in the Marsh, and with the treasury in an upper story. They are of uncommon form, two segments of circles intersecting. On the east side of the north transept is the ancient sacristy with a circular apse. The transept has no aisle. The south wing, or St. John's chapel, has been restored by Salvin, 1631. There is no chapter-house. It was apsidal, and of considerable size ; on the east of the cloister and south of the present passage to Live's Green, entered out of the east alley. To the south of the nave are the cloisters, of great size and considerable beauty ; the east door was the prior's entrance.

The Norman tower is the most lofty and rich in England. Square turrets, with their angles cut off, are at the corners. Four compartments divide it, consisting of the windows that light the lantern, a second arcade of intersecting arches ; a third, containing the round-headed windows of the belfry, with patterns of lozenges and circles alternately in the spaces ; and a double row of circles, five in each row on every face of the steeple. The Decorated battlements and crocketed spirelets are of the same date as the great octangular spire, which is of graceful form, richly crocketed, encircled with bands enriched with pinnacled buttresses at the foot, and terminating in a handsome finial. On Sunday, July 9, 1798, a sailor-lad, thirteen years of age, climbed up and walked three times round on this finial, to the terror of the spectators below.

Nowhere are the powers and grasp of the mind more sensibly felt than in a cathedral ; its marvellous dilation, and expansion by the genius of the spot, to contemplate without effort or pain these enormous structures ; which awe while they inspire, chastening not chilling, solemn but not sad.

> As the temple waxes,
> The inward service of the mind and soul
> Grows wide withal.

Here the vast tower lantern lifts itself indefinitely, the countless ponderous arches range and prolong themselves in ordered symmetry, till lost where a more goodly and softened work begins, charged with fair sculptures, and fluted shafts of delicate stone. There must be a profound sympathy between art and the mind to produce that strange charm, that keen delight, which is afforded by the mingled mystery and unity of the interior of a cathedral; intricate yet possessing a certain clue. Perhaps, we see something analogous to the change and chance of our own lives, for the pleasure of gazing down through the interlacings of the aisles is like that with which we hear the undersong flowing beneath the dominant strain of music, or see the crossing of the sailing clouds with their tresses interwoven, the braided twining of the forest branches, or the broken waves mingling their crests of foam.

The NAVE of Norwich is out of all proportion, as regards length, to the rest of the fabric; it is of fourteen bays, lofty with a superb vaulting of stone, and of vast extent and dimensions; the whole remarkable for massiveness, and an air of serenity and strength. There is but one fault —the triforium arches, heavy and circular, are too nearly of a height with those of the tier below: the same importance in fixing the expression of a church has been attached to the triforium as to the eyes in the human countenance. The piers of the nave are indeed

> Antique pillars massy proof,

with "high embowed" arches. Two cylindrical columns about the centre are observable from being channelled throughout with spiral mouldings. A billet moulding runs round each arch of the lower story, and a chevron moulding is continued throughout the church on the face of the arcade of the lofty and imposing triforium, which is entirely open. The clerestory Pointed windows, each of two lights, appear through the centre arch of an arcade, with three arches in each bay. The stone roof is elaborately designed, with 300 figures from Holy Scripture, ranging from the Creation to the Doom. That of the TRANSEPT is later and inferior in workmanship, but contains nearly 90 similar sculptures. The CHOIR is extended across the transept two bays into the nave: by an extraordinary and unecclesiastical arrangement, the choristers, who, except on festivals, wear purple gowns instead of surplices, are placed in the organ-loft, the screen of which was built by Bishop Lyhart, and had an altar of "Our Lady of Pity;" the sixty-two beautiful stalls of oak, canopied and pinnacled, do not extend further eastward than the lantern; the canopies are of the middle of the 15th century. The long vista of a PRESBYTERY, unencumbered with woodwork, loftier than the NAVE and TRANSEPT, with a noble triforium and an airy, graceful clerestory, occupying the length and circuit of the building, with the lightness and radiance of a lantern, and terminating in a circular apse, is strikingly imposing, while the grandeur of the lantern, with a triple arcade tier above tier and two galleries, adds, when the sunlight streams down through the windows behind the intricate arches of these corridors, inconceivably to the impressiveness of the choir. If the miserable stuccoed ceiling was removed, the whole view would be magnificent.

The clerestory windows of the CHOIR, each of four lights, are set between canopied niches now despoiled of their statuary. In the apse they are set in a pentagon, while the triforium is semicircular. A rich screen on either side of the PRESBYTERY conceals the pillars and aisles, with niches and canopies and open parapet to the floor of the triforium. On the north is St. Anne's chapel, on the south the chapels of St. George and St. James. The effect of the Lady Chapel opening behind the triforium is now lost. The feet of a Norman BISHOP'S THRONE still exists on the top of the wall over the altar; it was ascended by steps at the end of the choir; the altar formerly stood in front, and in the chord of the apse, as in the Roman basilicas. The rich Perpendicular FONT, with a representation of the sacrament, is in St. Luke's chapel; it was brought from St. Mary's-in-the-Marsh. In the north aisle of the choir is a small chamber, with a hagioscope, probably the hermitage of a recluse. A similar cell remains at Kells, Ireland, and in Wilbraham church tower. There was an example at Kilkenny. Henry III. is recorded to have confessed to the anchorite, who dwelt in the aisle of Westminster Abbey. Adjoining it, between the pillars, Queen Elizabeth's seat was set in 1578. In the south aisle is a clock with figures to strike the hours.

The CLOISTERS are the largest in England, and of considerable beauty, on the south side of the church; the bosses are carved with sculptured figures. The lavatories, built 1409. Over the west door are carved the Espousals of Adam and Eve; for at this portal the bride and bridegroom were betrothed, before they proceeded up to the altar to the actual service of matrimony.

Sir Thomas Browne says 100 brasses were stolen out of this church; and Bishop Hall describes, in animated language, the abominable excesses committed by the rebel musketeers, who converted the Cathedral into an alehouse, and sallied out sounding on the broken organ-pipe, habited in surplices and vestments, and parodying the Litany, burned the church books and records in the market-place. The aldermen were ranged on Sunday in the presbytery, and the mayor's chair occupied the site of the high altar. A retable, or picture on panel, is preserved, of the 14th century, 7 feet 5 inches by 2 feet 4 inches, and in five compartments, representing our Lord's scourging, bearing His cross, crucifixion, resurrection, and ascension. It is Italian in treatment of the heads, and elegant grouping, after the Siennese school.

The chief monuments are those of —

Jesus' Chapel.—Sir Thomas Wyndham, P. C. Vice-admiral, d. 1421, altar-tomb; Bishop Bathurst, statue, Carrara marble, by Chantrey.

St. Luke's Chapel.—Sir W. Boleyn, d. 1505, great-grandfather of Queen Elizabeth.

Choir, S. Side. St. George's Chapel.—Tombs of Bishop Wakeryng, d. 1426, and Prior W. Walsham, d. 1218. *St. James's Chapel.*— Bishop Goldwell, d. 1499, an effigy, altar-tomb, and canopy.

Choir before the Altar Steps.—Bishop Herbert, d. 1091, altar-tomb, modern, 1682.

N. Side of Choir Screen.—Sir Thomas Erpingham, low tomb.

South Side.—Lady Elizabeth Calthorp, d. 1582.

Nave.—Bishop Parkhurst, altar-tomb; Bishop Nix, d. 1536, flat monument arched over ; Chancellor Miles Spencer, altar-tomb, 16th century, on which the tenants formerly paid their rents.

North Side.—Sir J. Hobart, Attorney-General, d. 1507, altar-tomb.

N. Aisle.—Memorial window to Professor Smyth, of Cambridge, 1851.

DIMENSIONS OF THE CATHEDRAL IN FEET.

	Length.	Breadth.	Height.
Nave	230	97 f. 1 in.	73
Choir	165	45	83
Transept	191	36 f. 6 in.	73
Steeple	..	..	313
Cloisters { W. and E.	177	..	15
N. and S.	176	14 f. 9 in.	..
Lady Chapel was	57 f. 3 in.	36 f. 4 in.	..
Total length	411	..	..

The organ was built by Harris, and improved by Byfield and Bishop.

The Chapter is composed of a dean and four canons, two stalls having been suspended. There are four minor canons, eight singing-men, and ten choristers. There are two daily choral services at 10 and 4. The Holy Communion is administered monthly. The capitular income in 1852 was 7484*l.*; the expenditure in the former fourteen years was 10,230*l.* The library contains 4350 volumes.

Arms : Arg. a cross, sable.

The palace, originally built by Bishop Salmon, was restored by Bishop Reynolds, after suffering great injuries in the civil wars.

Norwich numbers among her bishops : Lozinga, the Simonist, the sorrowful penitent in his age ; John de Gray, the benevolent viceroy who divided Ireland into counties and brought in English laws—the brave soldier who took French castles, and the rich prelate to whom the king pawned his regalia ; Pandulph, who excommunicated John Lackland ;

W. Middleton, guardian of the realm ; John Salmon and William de Ermine, Lord Chancellors—the latter with the prelates of York and Ely present with an army of clerks, in the "White Battle" by the Swale, routed by the Scots ; Bateman, founder of Trinity Hall, Cambridge, who made Lord Morley, for poaching on his grounds, walk bareheaded and barefooted, with a burning taper in his hand, through the streets of Norwich, and do penance in the cathedral ; Henry Despencer, the bishop, with helm on head and hilt in hand, fighting for the Pope on shore, and as an English admiral at sea, easing the heavy Flemings of their good wine; Richard Courtenay, who died so sadly at the siege of Harfleur ; John de Wakering, Lord Privy Seal ; Nykke, the "blind bishop," the discovery of whose traitorous correspondence with the Pope caused the fine of 10,000 marks, which the king spent on the glorious glazing of King's College Chapel ; bad William Rugg, who deprived the see of its barony, so that his successors in Parliament sit as mitred abbots of Hulme ; Parkhurst, who loved to entertain Oxford scholars and dismiss them with light hearts and heavy purses; scandalous Scambler; John Jegon, the wag ; excellent Montague ; merry Corbet, the wit who would with his chaplain visit his wine cellar, and throw off doctor and bishop with hat and coat, begin his "Here's to thee, Corbet, here's to thee, Lushington," and yet kind-hearted withal, so that being without money and seeing a poor maimed scholar at Abingdon, he disguised his face and sang so sweetly in the market-place as to gather for the lad a bountiful alms ; saintly Hall; learned Overall and Sparrow ; Puritan Reynolds, who objected to the word "worship" in the marriage service, and was so sharply rebuked by King James, "Had you a good wife you would think all worship and all you could do well bestowed on her ;" George Horne, the commentator on the Psalms, whose sensibility to music was attributed to his father's humour of waking him as an infant with the soft tones of a flute,—consecrated so late in life that when he saw the steep flight of stairs in the palace he said, "Ah, I come here when I can neither go up or down these steps in safety;" and Bathurst, long the only bishop who spoke in favour of Roman Catholic emancipation, and said, as he left the House of Lords, "I have lost Winchester, but I have saved my conscience." Among the dignitaries occur three cardinals, J. Harpsfield, H. Prideaux, T. Sherlock; John archbishop of Smyrna, and Montgomery bishop of Meath.

Oxford.

Ye fretted pinnacles, ye fanes sublime,
Ye towers that wear the mossy vest of time
Ye massy piles of old munificence,
At once the pride of learning and defence;
Ye cloisters pale, that, lengthening to the sight,
To contemplation, step by step, invite;
Ye temples dim, where pious duty pays
Her holy hymns of everlasting praise,—
Hail, Oxford, hail!

OXFORD has been justly called a city of palaces : no town in England, and we may add in the world, can pretend to be its competitor. Sheltered by the heights of Shotover and the hills of Bagley Wood and Cumnor, watered by the lilied Cherwell and broad clear Isis, its streets lined with a succession of venerable and magnificent colleges—various in grandeur, beauty, and form—gateways, courts, embattled walls, interspersed with velvet lawns, over which breathes a spirit of peaceful yet cheerful seclusion ; rising from avenues, meadows, and woods of the richest verdure, with grey towers, domes, spires, and pinnacles ; the greatest university in the empire, the most renowned seminary in Europe, it is ennobled by its associations—over which its intimate connection with the national religion sheds a holy unction—more than by the attractions which it owes to the picturesqueness of its situation or the splendour of its buildings.   The impression is ineffaceable, the admiration and wonder without bound.

> Ye spires of Oxford! domes and towers!
> Gardens and groves! your presence overpowers
> The soberness of reason . . . to range
> Where silver Isis leads my stripling feet,
> Pace the long avenue, or glide adown
> The stream-like windings of that glorious street.

The High Street is a mile long, and in parts 85 feet broad; the street which crosses it is at the northern approach 146 ft. broad and upwards of 2000 ft. in length. No other city can produce so long and stately an avenue as the Elms of St. Giles.

Richard Cœur de Lion, King John, Sir William Davenant, Chillingworth, Antony à Wood, and Edward Pococke were born at Oxford.   Shakspeare used to lodge at the Crown Inn.   The first printer in England, Corsellis, set up his types here 1468 ; in the castle Queen Maud was imprisoned 1142.   Parliaments were held here 1185, 1203, 1207, 1258, 1263-4, 1625, 1644, 1681.   The royal visits were those of Henry II. and Stephen 1187, Henry III. 1264, Edward IV. 1481, Richard III. 1483, Henry VII. 1488, Prince Arthur 1496, Henry VIII. 1501, 1510, Elizabeth 1566, 1592, James I. 1605, Charles I. 1629, 1636, 1643, Charles II. 1665, the Allied Sovereigns and Prince Regent 1814.   The Black Assizes, in which the Lord Chief Baron, the sheriff, and 300 persons died within 40 hours, occurred 1577.

In such a profusion of architectural magnificence as the city offers, the Cathedral, which is dedicated to the Holy Trinity, SS. Mary and Frideswide, should hold the first place.   But neither in size nor character is it commensurate with its position.   Nothing can be more unfortunate than the general meagreness of this building ; for in Oxford there is no perception of that strangeness which a visitor often feels in passing from the modern dwelling-houses of a common town into a Cathedral, when he forgets that the building originally was built in the midst of a similar architecture.   The old effect, nearly everywhere except at Oxford, has suffered change, since the time when the familiar aspect of the streets was prolonged into the church, where it found its perfect development, and the superiority consisted in its greater gravity of ornament, its necessarily vaster size and more careful finish. It is this which makes them vivid records of the past, yielding a true portraiture and faithful memorials of the manners, costumes, arts, and industry of the cotemporaneous period, with an amount of information of absorbing interest to the artist, historian, and philosopher. The real secret of the impressiveness of a Cathedral, however, consists in its association with ideas the most hallowed to our imaginations, as the great central object of devotional regard; its beauties are heightened to our mind because they have received the assent of ages; and its sublimity owes much to that stillness which reminds us of our weak state, and raises up images of that great change which is but the momentary opening of the door to the awful immortality beyond. Devoid of grandeur, this church yet has details of considerable interest. The views through the Norman transept and choir to the lighter arches of the chapels of St. Frideswide and St. Mary, with the noble groining of late date, are impressive and beautiful; and the effect of the choir, when the canons, the clergy, and the white-robed scholars of the College of Christchurch, during the solemn evening services, fill the central space and line the sides up to the very altar, apparently an innumerable company of worshippers, is beyond description :—

> . . . The throng of beating hearts
> With all their secret scrolls of buried griefs,
> All their full treasures of immortal hope
> Gathered before their GOD.

The church was the minster of St. Frideswide's Priory of Augustinian canons : on June 9, 1545, it was constituted a Cathedral. The tower to the upper story appears to have been begun about 1004, with the base story of the lower south transept, which is of rubble, and contains small windows without columns. In the aisles may be seen the first approach to the pointed arch—that beautiful shape, more graceful and majestic than any mathematical figure. The semicircle formed by the diagonal ribs in the vaulting is elongated and raised vertically, to make the longitudinal and transverse arches of a height not exceeding their semidiameter. The contemporaneous spire—the beautiful symbol of the departed but deathless soul, and representing in its form a flame of fire—was added to churches when they became used as cemeteries. The Egyptian pyramid (and spires are anciently called by that name), during at least half a year, is lighted by the sun on every side at noon, so accurately was each set above the graves of Pharaohs by the old astronomer-priests. Great alterations and additions were made by Robert de Cricklade, prior 1150-80, to which date may be assigned the clerestory of the nave. The Chapter-house, the upper part of the tower, (c. 1220,) with the spire and St. Frideswide's chapel (c. 1289), are of the 13th century; the Lady Chapel and cloisters of the 14th century; the clerestory and vaulting of the choir were built by Wolsey.

The church consists of a CENTRAL STEEPLE, a NAVE of four bays with aisles, a TRANSEPT of two bays, a north wing of three bays, with a west aisle, and three chapels, each of four bays to the east; a south wing of two bays with an east aisle; a CHOIR of five bays, a CLOISTER, and CHAPTER-HOUSE.

The original west front, with four bays of the nave and the west alley of the cloister, was destroyed by Cardinal Wolsey, who intended to rebuild a Cathedral worthy of the illustrious college which is attached to it. His downfall defeated his design in 1529. The TOWER in its lower story, completed before 1172, is Norman, with circular turrets at the angles, which in the next story are arcaded and terminate in cylindrical pinnacles, with conical spires similar to those on the front of the north transept. The broach spire has on each side two belfry windows. When Bishop Westphaling was preaching here, an enormous icicle, which coated the spire, fell with a crash so tremendous that the congregation fled in terror: he knelt down one moment in prayer, reassured the fugitives, and completed his sermon. The belfry contains a peal of ten bells, celebrated in Dean Aldrich's famous glee, "The bonnie Christchurch Bells." The great bell was called Mary, after the queen, to whom Jewel was writing a complimentary letter from the university, when it first began to chime: "how musically doth sweet Mary sound!" exclaimed his companion, Dr. Tresham: "Alas!" observes old Fuller, "it rang the knell of Gospel-truth."

The east end of the CHOIR has two square Norman turrets; those on the fronts of the transept retain their pinnacles. The CHAPTER-HOUSE has five beautiful lancet lights, which within are divided by shafts of Purbeck marble. The use of transoms here is unique. It contains the foundation stone of Wolsey's college at Ipswich. A solid stone wall of Cromwell's time barbarously divides it into two rooms. This room was used us a council chamber by Charles I. in 1642. The vestry, formerly ST. LUCY'S CHAPEL, has an exquisite window of flamboyant character. In the coign of the buttress is a quaint altar, or reliquary, of stone, with sculptures of the Fall of Man, the Offering of Isaac, and the Doom. It was part of the old screen of St. Frideswide.

The pillars of the NAVE are alternately cylindrical and polygonal; the arches are semicircular and double, a lower one springing from corbels attached to the piers; and the capitals of composite architecture. Above a simple triforium is a clerestory of lights alternately pointed and round, between two round arches on short columns. The roof of the NAVE, restored 1816, TOWER, and TRANSEPT is of wood panelled. The vaulting of the aisles is Norman. The NORTH TRANSEPT has a west aisle; on the east are the CHAPELS OF ST. FRIDESWIDE and ST. MARY. The former is now called THE DEAN'S CHAPEL. The east window has stained glazing by Abraham Van Linge, representing Christ disputing with the Doctors, and is dated 1640. In the south choir aisle are two other stained windows by the same master—the story of Jonah, dated 1631, Sodom and Gomorrah destroyed, dated 1634; and Bishop King's window, interesting as containing a view of Oseney Abbey. In the north aisle is a window, the subject St. Peter and the Angel, painted by Isaac Oliver in 1700 at the age of eighty-four. The ancient glass was almost completely destroyed in 1651; some portions were preserved, and are in the west window: in the great north window is the Martyrdom of à Becket. The armorial windows were the gift of Alderman Fletcher. The vaulting of the CHOIR is Perpendicular, richly adorned and bound with carved pendants of stone from Oseney Abbey, like frost on drooping forest branches turned into pale marble. The choir arch is filled with canopied niches and statuary. The double arch in the lower story throughout the church is worthy of remark. The former ugly east window, designed by Sir James Thornhill, and stained by Price in 1696, was in 1854 replaced by glazing, designed by Hudson and executed by Alfred Gereute. It contains the events of our Lord's life. In 1856 the incongruous woodwork set up in 1630 was happily removed, the organ (built by Father Schmidt in 1680, and improved by Gray and Davison, 1848), set back in the south transept, and the choir prolonged three bays into the nave, under the superintendence of Mr. John Billing of Westminster, when a RELIQUARY CHAMBER, as at Ripon and Hexham, was discovered between the north and south piers of the tower, and a diaper pattern in colours found behind the altar. The altar has two candles, as at Durham and York, and Westminster and Wells.

The pulpit of wood is fine. It is a subject of hope that the rood-screen may be restored—that distinguishing feature of an English church—when so many fine specimens have been sacrificed abroad to the new "system of unity," which in the spirit of modern "Development" leaves the entire vista to the altar clear. At present it presents, although so small a church, an apparently boundless view.

When the shrine of St. Frideswide, who died Oct. 19, 740, was destroyed, the WATCHING CHAMBER was left. The screen, of three tiers, is rich, and Late Perpendicular, with

wood panelling, erected between 1480 and 1500, and tabernacle-work, the upper arches enriched with fine canopies.
At the shrine in 1264 Henry III. knelt, in defiance of the
tradition which denounced misfortune upon the English
king who entered the monastery. On Ascension-day, and
at Mid-Lent, the Vice-chancellor and university yearly
visited it in procession. In 1518 Queen Katharine of
Arragon paid her devotions to the relics of the saint. In
the chapel are two canopied monuments :—

A Prior, plain high tomb and canopy, of the early part of the reign
of Edward III., with an effigy; a knight, effigy, Sir John Noers, of
the date of Henry IV.,—arms (az.) a fess (arg.) between three
garbs (or); Lady Elizabeth Montacute, foundress of the Lady
Chapel, d. 1353, altar-tomb and effigy. William Baron Montacute
was buried here in 1320.

Choir, S. Aisle.—Bishop King, d. 1557.

N. Transept.—Dean Cyril Jackson, by Chantrey; high tomb of James
Zouch, d. 1503; Robert Burton, author of the Anatomy of
Melancholy, d. 1639.

Bishop Gastrell was buried in this Cathedral, and Bishop
T. Tanner of St. Asaph, 1775, Peter Elmsley the critic,
and Pocock the orientalist, and the learned Bishop
Berkeley of Cloyne in 1753.

The LADY CHAPEL is now called the LATIN CHAPEL, the
college prayers being daily said there in Latin, and sometimes the Divinity Chapel, from the lectures of the Regius
Professor being delivered in it. The stalls and desks,
chiefly of Wolsey's time, and very fine, were originally in
the choir. The north and west windows contain some
good decorated glazing removed from smaller lights. Two
bays of the south transept were merged by Wolsey in the
sacristan's house. The north alley of the cloister is the
muniment-chamber. The west walk has been destroyed.
The refectory over the east alley of the cloister was
subdivided into rooms in 1775.

Arms : Sa. on a cross, engr., arg. between four leopards'
faces, az., a lion pass. gules, on a chief, or, a rose, ppr.
between two Cornish choughs, ppr.

DIMENSIONS OF THE CHURCH IN FEET.

	Length.	Breadth.	Height.
Nave . . .	74	54	41 f. 6 in.
Choir . .	80	53 {with aisles 116 f.}	37 f. 6 in.
Transept . .	102		
Chapter-house .	54	24	..
Cloisters . .	54	..	..
Steeple . .	..	..	144

Total length   152 (it was 202 when complete).

The Chapter is composed of a dean and eight canons. There are eight chaplains, eight singing-men, and eight choristers. There are two choral services daily, at 10 and 4. Holy Communion is administered weekly and on festivals. The palace is at Cuddesden; rebuilt by Fell, after having been destroyed by Col. Legge and the rebels. Gloucester Hall, now Worcester College, was designed by Henry VIII. to form the bishop's residence. The bishop is Chancellor of the Garter.

Among the bishops occur—Curwen, Archbishop of Dublin; Corbet, poet and wit; Skinner, the only bishop who ministered holy orders during the rebellion, ordaining in one day more than 100 clergy in Westminster Abbey; Lord Crewe; Compton, the partisan of William of Orange; Fell, the cavalier-trooper—the loyalist's faithful priest in the rebellion, and learned classic; Parker, the pervert, intemperate, and mean; Timothy Hall, so contemptible, that no graduate would receive orders from him and no canon would instal him; noble Hough; learned Potter and Lowth; and earnest Secker. Among the dignitaries, &c., appear Wilkes of Oseney; Samuel Fell, the subject of the unmerited parody of Martial's epigram; accomplished Aldrich; learned Cyril Jackson and Gaisford; Peter Martyr, H. Hammond, Robert South, Edward Burton, E. Pococke, W. Buckland, Kennicott, and Goodwyn, and Lawrence, Archbishop of Cashel.

There are choral services at Exeter, New College, Magdalen, St. John's, and at Queen's College, daily.

The principal objects of interest in the University are

the Bodleian (1602)—the scene of the ominous traffic of
Charles I. and Lord Falkland with the Virgilian Lots,
prophetic of their fates—and Radcliffe (built by Gibbs,
1749), 100 ft. in diameter, Libraries; the Ashmolean
Museum, built by Wren ; the Clarendon, 1711, by Hawks-
moor, contains the famous Alfred jewel; the Theatre,
built in 1669 by Wren, on the plan of the Marcellus
Theatre at Rome, measuring 80 ft. by 70 ft., and capable
of holding 4000 people, once the scene of Heber's glory—
he was found on his knees praying after his triumph,
but his father died of the effects of joy; the Norman
Tower in the castle; the Tom-gate of Christ-church,
(founded 1525), built 1683 by Wren, with its great bell,
Tom of Oxford, a corruption of Grand Ton, weighing
17,000 lbs., and cast 1680—every night at 9 o'clock it tolls
101 times—the number of the students in the College—
warning under-graduates home ;—

Swinging slow with sullen roar.

The west front is 380 ft. long. The quadrangle is 264 ft.
by 261 ft. ; the vestibule of the hall, built 1640, is remarkable for its single supporting pillar and fan-tracery ;
the hall, 150 ft. by 140 ft. and 50 ft. high, with a carved
roof and pendants, built 1529, possesses a gallery of
portraits painted by artists from Holbein to the present
century : in it scenery and machinery were first employed
on a stage in England; the library, built 1716-61,
142 ft. by 30 ft. and 37 feet high, contains the Guise
collection of drawings of great masters, from Raphael to
Vandyke, and a noble picture by A. Caracci, and Wolsey's
Prayer Book, the last work illuminated in England; the
munificent benefaction of Archbishop Wake and other
distinguished scholars ; a fine collection of Oriental coins ;
and a gallery of portraits. Corpus Christi College (1527)
Hall, has a Late Perpendicular roof—the crozier of Bishop
Fox, the founder, is preserved ; on the gate of Brasenose
(1509), is the huge knocker which gave origin to the name.
The choir of St. John's Chapel, Merton College (1264), was
built 1300, the tower arches 1330, the tower and the tran-

septs 1417-24, with some fine glass and a roof restored in polychrome, and ancient tapestry in the choir ; the library is of the 14th century, and the treasury is of the 13th century. The hall of Wadham College (1613) has a good roof and screen of the early part of the 17th century, and Bernard Linge's glass in the chapel windows, 1621,—in the entrance tower the Royal Society held their first meetings 1652-9. In the superb chapel at New College (1370), of William of Wykeham, are preserved his crozier, and the ancient glazing, with a curious series of angelic choirs ; the original cloisters ; and hall with wainscot of the early part of the 16th century. The chapel, with windows by Hardman, cloisters, hall, tower, and stone pulpit of Magdalen College (1448), are of the latter part of the 15th century : in the hall, Hough made his memorable protest against James II. The painted Doom in the west window is by Fuller. The President's chambers, over the cloister-gate, are tapestried. The library and glazing of the chapel of Queen's College (1340), partly ancient and partly by Van Linge. St. John's Library (1555) possesses Laud's pastoral staff and the staff with which he walked to the block. The chapel of All Souls (1437) ; and library, 200 ft. by 30 ft., and 40 ft. high, built about 1720. The carvings in lime and cedar by Gibbons in Trinity College Chapel (1555.) The chapel of Lincoln (1427) has Italian glazing, bought in 1629. The hall of Exeter College (1315), with its fine roof, was built 1618, and its exquisite stone vaulted chapel of St. Peter, 95 ft. by 30 ft., and 60 feet high, by G. G. Scott, was consecrated Oct. 18, 1859. There are five Decorated three-light · windows on each side, and as many of two lights in the pentagonal apse, these having glazing by Clayton and Bell : the brass-work is by Skidmore of Coventry : at the west end is a Decorated rose window, with a two-light window above, supported on a double row of columns of Devonshire marble. A screen divides the chapel and antechapel ; over the latter rises a spiral turret, 150 ft. high—it cost 15,000*l.* The organ is by Hill. The glazing of Balliol College (1282) Chapel, Lombardic (rebuilt by Butterfield), was painted by Van Linge, 1637. The Divinity schools, and University Museum, were built by Deane and Woodward—the first stone was laid June 20, 1855; five statues, by Munro, of sages, were given by the Queen; it contains a central court with two windows, 128 ft. square; the front is 320 ft. 7 in. long, and in depth 178 ft. 4 in. The roof is by Skidmore of Coventry, and covers 5000 square ft. The Debating-room of the Union Society is by the same architects. Worcester College (1714), contains one of the finest works of Ruysdael. On the south side are four distinct ancient halls. The late 14th century White Hall, near St. Peter's le Bailey, Wolsey's almshouses, Kettel Hall, Broad Street, and Bishop King's House, in St. Aldate's Street, are observable.

Eminent men educated at Oxford:—Roger Bacon, William of Wykeham, Duns Scotus, Chaucer. *University College:* Dr. Radcliffe, Lord Herbert of Cherbury, Carte the historian, Sir W. Jones, Lords Stowell and Eldon, Langbaine, and Sir R. Chambers. *Balliol:* Wycliffe, Humphrey Duke of Gloucester, Tiptoft, Earl of Worcester, Coventry, L. K.; Kyrle the Man of Ross, John Evelyn, Adam Smith, Atkyns, Hutchins, and Rouse, the several historians of Gloucestershire, Dorsetshire, and Warwick. *Merton:* Wycliffe, Duns Scotus, Waynflete, Sir Henry Saville, Dr. Harvey, Jewell, Sir T. Bodley, Antony à Wood, Sir Richard Steele, Tyrrwhit, and Ruding. *Exeter:* Trevisa, Glanville, Tindal the historian, Borlase and Lewis, topographers; Frank Nicholls, and Walker, author of the "Sufferings of the Clergy;" Bishops Bull, Prideaux, Secker, and Judge Coleridge. *Balliol:* Lord Chancellor Shaftesbury, Lord Falkland, James Duke of Hamilton, Paulet Marquess of Winchester, James Norris, Brancker the mathematician, and Borlase. *Oriel:* Bishops Pecock and Butler, Cardinal Allen, Sir Walter Raleigh, Prynne, Joseph Warton, Anstis the herald, Longland, author of Piers Ploughman, Arnold, and Whateley. *Queen's:* Cardinal Beaufort, Bishop Tanner, the Black Prince, Addison, Wycherley, Collins, Tickell, Shaw the traveller, Horneck, Hyde the Orientalist; Rawlinson and Thwaites, Saxonists, Sir T.

Overbury, Halley the astronomer, Burns the lawyer. *New College:* Henry V.; Chichele, Fox, Ken, Huntingford, and Lowth, Grocyn, Harpsfield, Ayliffe, Sir Henry Sidney, Sir Henry Wotton, Somerville, Pitt, Spence, Dean Holmes. *Lincoln:* Bishops Sanderson and Hickes, Kettlewell, Dr. Radcliffe, Sir W. Davenant, Wesley, Sir George Wheeler, Hervey, author of the "Meditations," and Grey, of "Memoria Technica." *All Souls:* Bishops Heber, Jeremy Taylor, Sir Christopher Wren, Lynacre, Leland, Herrick, Sir W. Petre; Sydenham, physician; Sir W. Blackstone, John Norris, and Tindal the historian. *Magdalen:* Lilly, Foxe, Hammond, Heylyn, John Hampden, Addison, Dean Field, Wolsey, Dean Colet, Sir T. Bdleyo, Sacheverell, Camden, Lynacre, Cardinal Pole, Collins, Gibbons, Bishops Hough, Horne, and Latimer; John and George, Earls of Bristol; Arthur and Henry, Princes of Wales. *Corpus Christi:* Cardinal Pole, Jewell, Hooker, John Hales, Pocock, Fiddes, Basil Kennet, and T. Day, author of Sandford and Merton. *Brasenose:* R. Burton, Fôxe, Stradling, Sir W. Petty, James Earl of Marlborough, Lord-Treasurer; and the topographers Watson of Halifax, Burton of Leicester, Whittaker of Manchester, Prince of Devon, Ashmole of Berks; and Milman. *Trinity College:* Selden, Chillingworth, Sir James Harrington, Whitby, Aubrey, Ducarel, Sir J. Denham, Crashawe, Settle, T. Warton, W. L. Bowles, Merrick; J. Bampton, founder of the Lecture; Ludlow and Ireton, Anthony Earl of Shaftesbury, Lord Somers, Pitt Earl of Chatham, Montague Earl of Halifax. *St. John's:* Wheatley, Shirley the poet, Lord Northington, L.C.; Sir John Marsham. *Jesus College:* Archbishop Usher, Beau Nash, Herbert the traveller. *Wadham:* Bishops Wilkens and Spratt, Hody, Kennicott, Sir C. Wren, Admiral Blake, Harris, author of "Hermes;" Creech, Richardson, Persian lexicographer; W. Earl of Rochester, and Sir Charles Sedley. *Christ Church:* Charles the First, the King of Bohemia, the Prince of Orange, the Prince of Wales, (entered 17th day of October 1859,) Wycliffe, Sir Thomas More, Bishops Compton, Sanderson, Tanner, Smalridge, Wake, Potter,

Trelawny; Statesmen—Carleton, Lord Dorchester, Sir W. Godolphin; Sackville Earl of Dorset, Heneage and Daniel Earls of Nottingham, Bennet Earl of Arlington, Sir Wm. Wyndham, Carteret Earl Granville, St. John Lord Bolingbroke, Lord Lyttelton, Sir T. Hanmer, Lyttelton, L.K.; Murray, Earl of Mansfield, John Locke, Edward Pocock, R. South, Casaubon, Boyle Earl of Orrery, R. Friend, Busby, Adam Lyttelton, Browne Willis, Sir Andrew Fountaine, Camden; Drake, topographer of York; Sir Philip Sydney, Ben Jonson, Otway, Budgell, Bonnell Thornton, Colman, W. Penn, W. and Charles Wesley, Ruskin, Canning, Peel, and Gladstone. *Pembroke:* Camden, Beaumont, Pym, Dr. Johnson, Blackstone, Sir T. Browne; Morant, topographer of Essex; Durell, Whitfield, Shenstone, and Graves. *Worcester:* Dr. Nash, Sir Kenelm Digby, Thomas Allen, T. Coryat, Lovelace, and Foote the actor. *Magdalen Hall:* Sir Harry Vane, Sir M. Hale, R. Plot, Hobbes, Tyndal, Lord Clarendon, Dr. Sydenham, Sir Julius Cæsar, John Selden, Sir W. Waller, Sir T. Baker, C. J. Fox, Sackville Earl of Dorset, Archbishop Newcome. *St. Mary's Hall:* Cardinal Allen, Sandys the poet, Sir T. More, Sir Christopher Hatton. *New Inn Hall:* Sir W. Blackstone, Twyne the antiquary. *St. Alban's Hall:* J. Hooper, W. Lenthal, Philip Massinger, P. Elmsley. *St. Edmund's Hall:* Bishop Kennet, J. Mill, Oldham the poet, Kettlewell, Hearne, Sir R. Blackmore, Littleton and Onslow, Speakers.

Oxford has numbered among its Chancellors, Lord Grenville, the Duke of Wellington, and Lord Derby.

Among the churches the spire and tower (180 feet high) of St. Mary's, the University church, of the time of Edward II., and the porch with the statue of the Virgin, erected by Owen Laud's chaplain 1637—a fact brought against Laud at his impeachment. Here Bishop de Orlton preached before the Queen, "the she-wolf of France," on the artfully chosen text 2 Kings ix. 19, suggesting that the head of the King, as it was sick and diseased, should be removed. Some old glazing, and the

Saxon tower of St. Michael's ; the tower and spire of St. Aldate's of the 14th century ; and the south aisle, built 1318 ; and the ancient crypt and Norman choir of St. Peter's in the East are observable. Iffley Church (Norman) has been restored by Buckler. The west window is a memorial to Elliot Warburton. The Norman tower and crypt of St. George's chapel in the castle are deserving of a visit.

The memorial cross, 73 feet high, of the three martyr bishops—Cranmer, Ridley, and Latimer—who suffered at this site, was built by G. G. Scott in 1841. The statues are by Weekes. The Observatory contains an unrivalled heliometer. The most noticeable pictures are—Christ bearing his Cross, by Moralez, in Magdalen College Chapel ; the Noli Me Tangere, by Mengs, in All Soul's Chapel ; besides Fox Strangway's gift of specimens of the Tuscan school, 190 original drawings by Michael Angelo and Raffaelle in the Randolph Galleries ; a bronze cast of Flaxman's shield of Achilles, and busts and statues by Chantrey. The 129 Pomfret statues given by the Countess of Pomfret in 1754, are in the Taylor Institute, for the study of modern languages, built by Cockerell, with a centre 150 feet long, and the wings 70 feet ; and under the schools are the Arundel Marbles, including the famous Parian Chronicle. Inigo Jones built the gate of the Botanic Garden. Magdalen bridge, 526 ft. long, was built in 1779. Upon the top of Magdalen tower, every year on May-day at sunrise, in place of a mass for the repose of Henry VIIth, endowed with lands at Slymbridge, is sung the Eucharistic Hymn. Nor must Johnson's window at Pembroke, the groves of St. John's, the gardens of New College, Addison's water-path by Magdalen Park, the broad walk of Christchurch, or the alleys beneath the limes of Trinity, be unvisited. Some of the plate preserved in the colleges is of equal value and interest : the founder's jewelled salt-cellar, an exquisite gold chalice, patens, and charger at Corpus Christi ; King Edward IInd's cup at Oriel ; a gold grace-cup, 22 in. high, and salt-cellars, at New College ; the salt-cellars, jewels, and antique plate of

Chichele at All Souls'; and a fine drinking-horn and a silver horn for calling the Society together at Queen's. Some of the old customs are preserved to this day : the bellman yet rings a knell before the funeral procession of a gownsman ; at All Souls', on Jan. 14, is sung annually the song of the swopping mallard ; at New and University the fellows are summoned to Common-room by the blows of a wooden hammer, as in the Eastern monasteries ; at Queen's a horn sounds before dinner ; on Christmas-day the boar's head is borne up with an ancient carol, and bedecked with bays and rosemary ; and on New Year's-day the manciple presents to every member in hall a threaded needle, saying "Be thrifty."

Peterborough.

PETERBOROUGH, situated upon the river Nene, is the only city which has neither mayor nor corporation, whilst Ely is the only city not represented in Parliament. William Paley was a native. Queen Victoria visited Peterborough Sept. 6, 1858. At Longthorpe Manor is a fine Early English tower.

Several of the largest and most important monasteries were built among the fens and marshes—Ely, Croyland, Ramsey, Thorney, Kirkstead, and Oseney. Owing to the coldness of the place in winter, Pope Innocent IV. permitted the monks to put on their caps in church. Thus went the rhyming proverb :—

> Ramsey, the rich of gold and of fee,
> Thorney, the flower of many fair tree,
> Crowland, the courteous of their meat and drink,
> Spalding, the gluttons as all men do think,
>   Peterborough the proud,
>   Sawtrey, by the way, that old abbey
>   Gave more alms in one day than all they.

On one of the islands in the tract of the east marsh lands was built Medehamstede Abbey ("the Home in the Meadows"). Originally founded by King Penda in the 7th century, it was rebuilt for Benedictine monks by Ethelwold, Bishop of Winchester, and dedicated to St. Peter; and the name of the village changed to Burg, A.D. 970, which being incorporated with the apostle's name, is still called Peterborough, or St. Peter's town. It was a mitred abbey. In 1264, the abbot having joined the cause of the rebel barons, the minster was only saved from destruction by the king at the price of a large ransom. The abbey possessed this peculiar privilege, that a visit to its high altar was considered equivalent to a pilgrimage to Rome, and all of what degree soever, who entered its great gate, did so barefoot. It received the honour of a royal visit by Queen Philippa on New Year's-day, 1327.

The Cathedral of St. Peter is approached under a Norman gateway, with a chapel of St. Nicholas above it (now the music-school), built by Abbot Benedict: on the left hand is the chapel of St. Thomas à Becket (now the choristers' school), erected by R. Ashton, abbot 1438-1496. Ou the south side of the close is the GATEWAY leading to the BISHOP's PALACE, with the "Knight's Chamber" above it, built by abbot Godfrey de Croyland, in 1319. On the north side is the DEANERY GATE, built by R. Kirton, 1515, Late Perpendicular. The archdeacon's house is formed out of an Early English Hall.

The approach is eminently monastic, entering by the old grey gateway into a retired court filled with domestic buildings of the abbey ; from the quiet market-place appear the crosses over the deep pointed arches, the fine spires and the pinnacled turrets, while flights of birds sweep across the confused sculpture and intricate arcades—secluded in serene sublimity. Like most English Cathedrals which have either a commanding or engaging situation, this church stands in a green close with garden, flower, and evergreen shrubberies : whereas abroad the meanest buildings cluster against the walls, or the site is fixed in a narrow lane or crowded market-place. Few continental churches possess a good near effect from this cause, while in England most are so happily placed as to be retired yet not to be estranged from men.

The church consists of a GALILEE porch, a CENTRAL and two WESTERN towers, the latter, as at Lincoln, having each an eastern chapel; a NAVE of eleven bays with aisles; a TRANSEPT of three bays, with three chapels on the east of each wing; a CHOIR of four bays, with an apsidal termination; and aisles, and an eastern LADY CHAPEL.

The Danes in 870 slew all the monks, and burned the church; and again, in 1069, according to an extraordinary prophetic dream of Egelric, bishop of Durham, who had given up his mitre for the cowl. In 1116, Abbot de Seez cursed the house in a passion, and one of the brothers blasphemed and invoked the Evil Spirit; and, says the veracious Candidus, for their sins the church was burned a third time. On the 7th March, 1118, this same John de Seez, abbot (who died 1125), laid the foundation of the CHOIR; in 1143 the bishop of Lincoln consecrated it: the EASTERN CHAPELS of the TRANSEPTS were built by Martin of Bec, abbot 1133-55; the remaining portion of the TRANSEPTS and CENTRAL TOWER were built by William de Waterville, abbot 1155, together with two bays of the NAVE and the CLOISTERS. Benedict, abbot 1177-93, completed the Norman NAVE, which is built of Barnack stone, and added the painted roof of wood. The south aisle was built 1117-1143. The spire on the south-west turret, Early Decorated, was built 1320; the Perpendicular north-west spire c. 1470. The north-west tower was built for a belfry by John de Calais and Richard of London, 1249-74. Abbot Andrew, abbot 1193-1200, erected the WESTERN TRANSEPT; only one of the transeptal or BELL-TOWERS is complete—that upon the north-west; till the close of the 17th century it had a wooden spire. The stone of the church is from Barnack mill, near Stamford. The restorations have been made with Ketton stone.

The WEST FRONT, of the purest Early English style, with its three magnificent doorways and original wooden doors, was the work of Abbot Zachary and Robert of Lindsey, 1200-22; and the church was consecrated 1237, Oct. 4,

Non. The gables of the WEST TRANSEPT are of the same date. Great changes were cotemporaneously made. The Norman aisles were heightened, and in the lower tier windows of five lights inserted, three geometrical three-light windows, with three cinquefoils in the head, inserted in the three chapels of the south transept, a parapet of circular medallions added over the corbel table of the choir apse, and a LADY CHAPEL built parallel with the choir, and entered from the aisle of the north transept, by William Parys, prior 1272. There was a second entrance from the Presbytery in the north aisle, through a vaulted vestibule, in which were two chapels, one on either hand: that of St. Thomas had little windows opening into the old Lady Chapel; over it was the cell of an anchorite, Dame Agnes, with a window commanding St. Mary's Altar. Their sites are easily ascertained by marks in the outer walls. The transepts on the sides are of five stages; the upper arcaded. The aisles and clerestory have three-light Perpendicular windows; in the interior the arches of the blind story have billet mouldings; the triforium is composed of two round-headed arches, under a large arch, with a lozengy moulding in the spandril; the windows are of three lights. The parapet is quatrefoiled; the corbel table nebule. In the choir-aisles, apse, and south clerestory there are three-light windows. The tracery of the north choir clerestory is very peculiar. The north side of the church is very grand, rising in five stages in the nave, the triforium being parted from the aisles by a tier of small lights. The north transept has seven stages, three occupied by windows, two of arcades with blind arches in the battlemented gable, which is flanked by octagonal turrets. The clerestory of the choir and transept consists of a noble round-headed arcade. The variety of the tracery and mouldings in the windows and arches render the architecture as picturesque as it is imposing. Richard the Sacristan, before 1274, added the upper stage of the NORTH-WEST BELL-TOWER, with its panelling, parapet, and tracery: the CENTRAL TOWER, was erected with a wooden OCTAGON, by R. Ramsey, abbot 1353-61; the south-west spire and pinnacles of the flanking towers of the west portal, and a complete series of triforium Decorated windows had been added throughout the church by Henry de Morcot, his predecessor. The PARVISE, now the LIBRARY, was built about 1370, to provide against danger owing to the settlement of the central pillars of the portico, or, it has been suggested, it was erected as a Galilee porch with a Consistory Court above it, in order to restore its proper dignity to the central arch, which had been contracted to show as much as possible of the side doorways from without. Battlements were substituted for the conical cappings of the turrets of the transepts, and Perpendicular tracery inserted in the great Norman windows of the nave and transept, for their enrichment with stained glass, and the great west window ; the wooden screens of the transepts and vaulting of the choir were added at the close of the 15th century. The windows of the central lantern are of three lights, cinquefoiled with quatrefoils in the head. There are two in each face, set between three blank traceried windows. The New Building, or LADY CHAPEL, commenced by R. Ashton, abbot 1438, was completed by R. Kirton, about 1496 : this chapel was built in this lateral position, owing to the Martyr's Cross and stone of Hedda occupying the space to the east. It has five four-light Perpendicular windows on the east front. The CHAPTER-HOUSE, formerly the Hostelry Chapel, to the west of the SOUTH TRANSEPT, is of Transitional Norman. The ancient FONT, of Alwalton marble, is in the south-west transept. The organ was built by Allen, of Sutton Street, Soho, in 1809.

The WEST FRONT of the Cathedral consists of three arcades, the lower with three doors, the upper having three-light windows, recessed behind three lofty pointed arches, unequalled in the world for simple grandeur and majestic beauty; the gable and pointed arch, grouped, form the loveliest architecture. Behind these are TWO TOWERS, one unfinished above the roof on the south ; and in the central arch is a parvise or porch, which is indispensable to the stability of the structure: the front is flanked by two steeples with spires, and arcaded from the base-tier to parapet. The spandrils of the arches have niched saints. The mouldings are very varied. The porch has octagonal stair-turrets on either side, a battlemented parapet, and a six-light window with rich tracery. The steep gables have a trefoiled arcade over the great arches, with imagery; in the next tier is a rose of six lights in the lateral gable, and of eight lights trefoiled in the central gable, in the point is a statue in a niche; below a beautiful cross, octagonal, arcaded, and pinnacled turrets divide the gables. The solid masses of shadow, deep and diffused, thrown in colossal curves by the triple arches—strong as adamant, tall and deep like Horeb's cave, yet graceful as a bended bow—in contrast with the play of the sunshine, slowly changing from porch to porch, impart a gloom to these recesses that seems in sympathy with the sorrows of human life, that are carried within to a church, bright and sunny by the contrast to the worshipper, there to be laid down and find consolation. The short NORTH-WESTERN TRANSEPT, like the great NORTH TRANSEPT, is flanked with turrets; octagonal and battlemented in the latter instance, but in the former crowned with spires. The flatness of the wooden roof, though gorgeously painted, is the signal defect in the nave. But then how magnificent is that Titanic avenue of sombre richness and sublimity; wrought by vigorous intellect into enduring immovable firmness, like the everlasting nature of the Church, before she had put on the victor's crown of foliage in a new style of art, and in her soaring lines, as if unsatisfied with the world and its gifts, ever rose heavenward! What a triumph of human intellect to conceive the lofty grandeur and comprehensiveness of the whole design, to concentrate in one structure the idea of what is boundless and infinite, displaying wonderful mechanical skill, and yet combining with the utmost strength extreme delicacy of execution! The builders aimed at faultless perfection, and, therefore, their very shortcomings possess power and force; and in the leading lines and aspiring summits bear the impress of the Christian birth of Gothic architecture. We are conscious that the true exponent of the design in the receding aisle and exceeding loftiness, at which Wren scoffed, is their purpose to symbolize the universe—a whole as an infinite of parts—the endeavour to express the omnipresence of the Deity—"infinity made imaginable," says Coleridge. The great TRANSEPT has eastern aisles : in the south wing are a chapel of ST. BENEDICT, and the CHAPTER-HOUSE on the western side ; the CHAPELS OF ST. JOHN AND SS. PHILIP AND JAMES occupied the north wing, which contains a screen of good Perpendicular work ; and remains of the ancient stalls of the period of Edward III. with two curious wooden capitals of Early English. The tapestry, representing St. Peter's Deliverance from Prison, and the Healing at the Beautiful Gate of the Temple, in the NORTH TRANSEPT, is of the date of Henry VIII. A portion of the cope of John de Calais some years since was hung up above the tomb of Hedda. The massive piers are all alternately octangular and cylindrical, but without shafts, like the piers of the nave, which is of the Norman style, lofty, vast, solid, massive, yet without that overwhelming heaviness which appears in churches, where great circular columns are used. The absence of vaulting lends greater height to the tall narrow divisions of the nave. In these buildings the sense and consciousness of unlimited exulting power—the vast space, the freshness and vigour of art, the numberless beauties heightened by the pleasure of new discoveries—rouse and dilate the whole heart like the sound of the rushing waterfall, borne by a strong wind through the glade of the deep woods, or the sight of the eternal Alp.

> Get by heart
> The eloquent proportions, and unroll
> The mighty graduations, part by part ;
> The glory which at once upon thee did not dart.
> The fountain of sublimity displays
> Its depth, and thence may draw the mind of man,
> Its golden sands, and learn what great conceptions can.

The triforium arches have a chevron moulding : the clerestory is composed of a series of compartments of threefold semicircular arches, the middlemost being elevated. The aisle-walls are arcaded; cylindrical shafts are carried up from the floor to the roof between each pier, and are crossed by string-courses below and above the triforium. The CHOIR ends in a circular apse, having five windows with rich hanging tracery. The choir stall-work and organ-screen were erected in 1830 at a cost of 5021*l*., after the designs of Mr. Blore. In the windows of the apse are some fragments of Early English glass placed here in 1777. The brass eagle was set up by Abbot Ramsey, 1472. The original wooden roof of the NAVE is panelled in lozenges with figures painted in the centre. The choir and transept are ceiled with wood, the painting of which is in course of restoration by G. G. Scott. The groined stone roof of fan-tracery in the LADY CHAPEL, which is oblong, resembles that of King's College, Cambridge. Outside the buttresses end in statues, and the parapet is gracefully pierced and embattled. At the junction of this chapel with the choir rise square buttresses, which above the parapet become octangular, and terminate in spires. The battlemented CENTRAL LANTERN rises one story above the roof, and is flanked with four octagonal turrets, panelled and pierced below the battlemented parapet.

To the south of the cloisters are ruins of the Early English infirmary—CHAPEL OF ST. LAWRENCE, refectory, and lesser cloisters, built by John of Calais 1248-1274. The lavatory, in the south walk of the great cloister, was built by Abbot Lindsey, c. 1210; behind it are the arches of the fratry-room and infirmary; the abbot's lodge is the BISHOP'S PALACE. The hall is vaulted and parted by a range of columns into a double aisle. Two oriel windows mark the Heaven-chamber.

In July, 1537, Queen Katharine of Arragon was buried on the north side of the choir, and on August 1st, 1586, Mary Queen of Scots, under the doorway leading out of the choir into the south aisle; her body was removed, October 11th, 1612, to Westminster Abbey, which made the old folks shake their heads and say, "Stuart should not

prosper, since the dead had been moved in their grave."
After having sustained, on April 22nd, great injury at the
hands of Cromwell's ruffians on their way to Croyland, on
July 13th, 1643, again the ill-fated Cathedral was profaned
by sacrilege; the ancient monuments, the brasses, and
superb reredos were destroyed, with the exquisite stained
glass and chapter-house, a great portion of the palace,
and the whole of the magnificent cloisters, the glazing of
which was the finest in the realm. During a whole fortnight the church was in their hands; the lead was sold,
but the merchant-ship which was conveying it to Holland
foundered at sea. Chief Justice Oliver St. John, envoy to
Holland, procured the gift of the minster to himself, and
conveyed it to the inhabitants as their parish church,
having been used as a workshop since August 19th, 1651.
The Lady Chapel was totally destroyed to save the expense of repairs. In 1634 it was called Dame Amy's
Chapel, from an anchoress, whose adjoining cell was then
shown.

The principal monuments are the following:—

In the *Choir*, the effigy of Abbot Alexander of Holderness, 1222-26; in
the *Lady Chapel*, the remarkable Saxon monument of Abbot Hedda,
833, and monks slain by the Danes, and erected by Goodric, abbot,
1099-1103; and an effigy of William de Hotot, died 1250, abbot.

Nave.—R. Scarlet, d. 1594, aged 98. "He buried the two queens,
and the inhabitants twice over;"—truly a king of spades.

Aisle, North Transept.—Two memorial windows to the family of
Gates, by Clayton and Bell, 1858.

Morning Chapel.—Memorial window to J. H. Paley, by Hardman,
1859.

DIMENSIONS OF THE CATHEDRAL IN FEET.

	Height.	Breadth.	Length.
West Front (each portal)	82	..	156 f.
Nave . . .	81	78	266 f. 3 in.
Choir . . .	81	..	163 f.
Lady Chapel .	..	38	83 f. 5 in.
Transept . . .	81	..	184 f. 9 in.
Lantern Tower {within	135	..	..
Lantern Tower {without	150	..	..
Spires and Tower, W. Front	156	..	..
Total . . .	..	..	479

The Cathedral was constituted Sept. 4, '1541. The Chapter consists of a dean, four canons, with three minor canons, twelve singing-men, and sixteen choristers. Their income was, in 1852, 6892*l*. : the expenditure on the fabric in fourteen years amounted to 4813*l*. There is a grammar-school. The library contains 3000 volumes. There are two daily choral services, at 9 and 4, and Holy Communion is celebrated on the first Sunday in every month.

Arms.—Az. between two keys in saltier, three crosses fitchee arg.

Among the eminent bishops occur—Queen Elizabeth's " Dove with the silver wings ;" Lloyd and White, the non-jurors ; Cumberland, the orientalist, who learned his promotion from a newspaper in a coffee-room at Stamford ; White Kennet, the indefatigable antiquary ; and Marsh, the assertor of church principles in a lax age. Among the dignitaries are found—James Duport, Simon Gunter, and the learned Thomas Jackson, President of Corpus Christi College, Oxford.

Ripon.

" As true steel as Ripon rowels," was an old Yorkshire proverb, in allusion to the staple manufacture of the city, and is used by Davenant and Ben Jonson. Ripon stands on an eminence, within a short distance of the meeting of the Skell and the Ure: the latter flows through a vale teeming with corn, the woods of Studley Royal and the hills of Cleveland closing up the view. John Burton, Sterne's Dr. Slop, was a native of the town ; Archbishop Hutton and Bishop Porteous were educated in the Grammar-school. The city suffered much at various times : from the raids of the Danes in 950 ; during the revolt of the brave Northumbrians against the Normans, 1069 ; and in the incursions of Robert Bruce in 1323. Henry IV., during the plague, 1405, found a refuge here. King

James, in 1617, and Charles I., in 1633 and 1646, paid royal visits. The negotiations with the traitor Scots were commenced here Oct. 1, 1640. The rebels under Sir Thomas Mauleverer were dislodged, after a temporary occupation, by Sir John Mallorie and his brave cavaliers in 1643.

The city derives its name from its situation "ad Ripam," on the bank of the Ure, which has a noble bridge of 17 arches. On Saturday after Lammas, St. Wilfred, the founder's day, his effigy is drawn through the streets to the sound of music, in commemoration of his return from exile. At 9 P.M., the constable nightly blows three notes on his horn at the mayor's door, and sounds again at the obelisk in the market-place, 90 feet high, built in 1778 by W. Aislabie, M.P. The Town Hall was built by Wyatt, in 1801. The chapel of St. Mary Magdalene, attached to a Lazar-house, was built by Archbishop Thurstan, who died 1139. It retains a screen, an altar, a picturesque bell-gable, a Norman doorway, a stone altar-slab in the pavement, and a low side-window, through which lepers were communicated, or certain recluses made their offerings ; or for outer confession, or purposes of ventilation,—such are the conflicting opinions of the learned. A tesselated high place, 11 ft. by 3 ft. 8½ in., of a copy of Roman work in the 12th century. The chapel of St. John Baptist Hospital is of the reign of Edward II. ; that of St. Anne's is of the time of Edward IV. ; it retains its altar and a slab, on which a Scottish king's ransom was paid. Ailcy Hill is a barrow raised over Elsi and his brave Northumbrians, slain in battle with the Danes in 867.

Among the cathedrals set up like sacred standards in the land, hieroglyphics of the word GOD, lifting thought from its ordinary level, and attracting universal sympathy and veneration, whether in the densely-peopled city, or the remote country-town, in the village or the wild, that of Ripon holds a high place as an edifice. Like others, it fails, however, to secure that regard and stimulate those exalted feelings which are associated with buildings that form also the last home of the good and great.

> The quiet fortresses
> Where Piety, as men believed, obtains
> From Heaven a general blessing ; timely rains,
> Or needful sunshine, prosperous enterprise,
> Justice or peace.

The church of St. Wilfred was founded by Archbishop Wilfred, who was buried in it in 711. The minster received from King Athelstan a grant, like Hexham and Beverley, of frithstool and sanctuary. Sharow Cross is the only remaining boundary-stone of four that marked the precinct.

The Early English WEST FRONT, the CENTRAL TOWER, the TRANSEPT, with a portion of the CHOIR and aisles, were built by Archbishop Roger de Bishopsbridge, 1154-1181. Considerable repairs of the choir were made 1288-1300. The choir aisles were doubled in length by Archbishop Melton, 1319-40, after a fire in 1319 during a Scottish raid. Octagonal spires of wood, leaded, were set on the three towers in the reign of Edward III. ; the central spire fell in 1660, and the others were removed in 1664.

The Cathedral is composed of a CENTRAL and two WESTERN TOWERS, a NAVE of six bays with aisles, a transept of two bays, with four eastern chapels, two in each wing ; a CHOIR of six bays and aisles. On the south side is the apsidal CHAPTER-HOUSE, the south aisle of the Norman church, and a Lady Chapel above it. The WEST FRONT, a very fine specimen of bold Early English, plain, but elegant, and of good proportions, 103 ft. high and 43 ft. wide, consists of a lofty gable, set between two massive square towers of four stories, and somewhat higher. Above a portal of three arches, deeply recessed, are two tiers of two-light lancet windows, foliated with quatrefoils in the head, five in each row. There is a triplet in the gable, but the whole bears marks of restorations after the disastrous fire in 1319. The battlements and pinnacles were added by Dean Waddilove in 1797. The SOUTHERN TOWER contains a peal of eight bells, cast by Lester and Pack in 1762 ; a bell in the NORTH TOWER came from Fountains Abbey. The base tier has an arcade ; triplets fill each of the other stories, the central lancet being a light. The clerestory of the nave is Perpendicular, set under a battlemented parapet. The north transept has round-headed windows with Perpendicular tracery; the front is flanked by square turrets. The front of the south transept was left incomplete. In each gable is a three-light window. The doors have a trefoiled head rising from a corbel-like projection. The EAST END is Decorated; the window, 51 ft. by 25 ft., a fine example of early character, of seven lights, with geometrical tracery, was glazed at a cost of 1000*l*., by Wailes, in 1854; a window of the same character fills the gable. The old glass is in a window in the south nave aisle, near the octagonal Tudor FONT of blue marble. Massive double buttresses, gabled at the top, and terminating in octagonal spirelets, flank this front. The CENTRAL TOWER is of one story, and has angular pinnacles: like the nave it was partly rebuilt in Late Perpendicular. The appearance of the interior is remarkable; two of the arches being Norman, and the others cased with Perpendicular work, in order to harmonize with the nave, which is very light, and its composition fine. In each face are two Decorated two-light windows, under a battlemented parapet. There is a south-eastern spiral-turret. The weather mouldings show the original pitch of the roofs.

There is no entrance to the NAVE AISLES from the west. With the exception of the aisles of the NAVE and CHOIR, and the clerestory, which are of coarse sandstone and magnesian limestone from Smawse, near Tadcaster, the church is built of the latter material. The NAVE, which was in process of transformation from Early English to Perpendicular at the period of the dissolution, has no triforium; The roof is of wood panelled. The transept has a triforium. A beautiful SCREEN, 19 ft. high, of the date 1489-94, traditionally said to have been brought from Fountains Abbey, stands at the entrance of the choir. The CHOIR has three bays, built by Archbishop Roger, and two bays Decorated: there is a triforium. The vaulting is of wood, groined, and, like the roof of the nave and the REREDOS, was set up by Mr. Blore. Two brackets, 28 ft.

above the floor, once upheld the rood-beam. The south and eastern sides of the central, or St. Wilfred's tower, falling in 1459, necessitated the rebuilding of part of the south TRANSEPT. The STALLS bear the date 1494, and are not surpassed in lightness and delicacy by any tabernacle-work in the other cathedrals. They offer a forcible instance of the great innovation of Gothic art upon the old principles of symmetry and proportion of Grecian taste. Indefinite altitude was the grand object of attainment, and well-selected contrasts were to form a countervailing beauty in place of exact rules. Rich and minute tracery set against the plainer arch and massive pillar make the column appear more majestic, and the tracery finer and more delicate by the force of position. The sedilia are original; the reredos was erected in 1832. The throne was the gift of Archbishop Markham in 1812. In the NORTH TRANSEPT is part of a rich stone Perpendicular pulpit. The apsidal CHAPTER-HOUSE, built by Archbishop Thomas 1069-1100, and spared by Archbishop Roger when he rebuilt the minster, is on the south side of the choir, and contains some ancient paintings of sixteen kings on panel. Over it is the LADY CHAPEL, built 1482; a most extraordinary position—it is now the library. The ORGAN is by Booth of Leeds, 1833, but has some portions incorporated of Father Schmidt's organ of 1696.

There are two low-browed crypts: one is a CHARNEL under the chapter-house, lined and paved with the poor relics of humanity. The other, on the south side, is Norman, with buildings of the same style above it, probably of the time of Archishop Thurstan, now used as vestries. There is a Saxon cross, found in 1832, over the door: it contains some bosses of the old choir groining, but most have been replaced among those of the new vaulting. The TRINITY CHAPEL is under the central tower, and had an altar; it is approached by nine steps and a passage 45 feet long, and is of Saxon architecture, dark and cheerless as the grave, and cylindrically vaulted. On the north side is St. Wilfred's Needle, 13 in. by 18 in., possibly used as an Easter sepulchre in the services of Holy Week,

as a relic-chamber and a place of penance. It was reputed
to be an ordeal efficacious as the waters of jealousy.
"Those," says Fuller, "who could not thread the needle,
were pricked in their reputation."

The principal monuments are the following—

S. Aisle, Nave.—A lion, palm-trees, and a man kneeling; an Irish
crusader prince.

N. Transept Aisle.—St. Andrew's chantry; Sir T. Markenfield and
Dame Dionysia, altar-tomb and effigies, time of Richard II.; Sir
T. Markenfield and Dame Eleanor, effigies, 1483.

S. Transept Aisle.—*Mallorie chantry;* Sir William and Sir John
Mallorie the cavalier; W. Weddell, bust by Nollekens.

Choir, East End.—Seven sepulchral slabs of the 13th century.

DIMENSIONS OF THE CATHEDRAL IN FEET.

	Length.	Breadth.	Height.
Nave . . .	169 f. 5 in.	87	88
Chapter-house .	34 f. 8 in.	29	18 f. 8 in.
Vestry. . .	28	..	18 f. 6 in.
Choir . .	101	66 f. 8 in.	79
Transept . .	132	35 f. 11 in.	..
Crypt . .	11 f. 3 in.	7 f. 9 in.	9 f. 4 in.
Towers (the spires had an additional height of 110) 120 feet.			
Total length .	270	..	

On Nov. 18, 1569, the insurgents in the Rising of the
North heard mass sung at the high altar; and Richard
Norton and Thomas Markenfield displayed their memo-
rable banner.

The Chapter consists of a dean, five canons, two minor
canons, six singing-men, and eight choristers. There is
a daily choral service at 10 A.M. The capitular income
in 1852 was 5015*l.*; and in 14 years 3815*l.* were spent
upon the fabric. The library contains 1730 volumes; some
early books of Caxton and Wynkin de Worde, and a
"Book for Travellers," French and English, of unparalleled rarity.

By Act 2 Jac. I., Ripon was erected into a Colle-
giate-church. In 1839, by Act of Parliament 6 & 7
William IV. c. 77, it became the seat of a bishopric.
The first bishop was the Right Rev. Charles Thomas

Longley, D.D. ; and on his translation to the bishopric of Durham, in 1856, the Right Rev. Robert Bickersteth, D.D., the present bishop, was appointed. Eadhead, Bishop of Lindisse and Stow, 678—680, styled himself Bishop of Ripon.

The palace was built 1841 ; it is a mile distant from the city.

Arms : Arg. a cross saltier, gules, on a chief, gules, the Holy Lamb, nimbed or, bearing the cross-flag, ppr.

Rochester.

BEFORE the ancient bridge which spanned the noble stream of the Medway, with its ten pointed arches, built by Sir R. Knowles in the time of Edward III., was destroyed, no city presented a more romantic prospect than Rochester (the British Rorbis and Saxon Hrof Ceastre, though Bede says it is Hrof, a Saxon princess, Ceastre). But still the river runs broad and swift, bearing on it the strong ships-of-war, which may again be called to loose their thunders, though now lying idle and dismantled ; far beyond, as a background, are the lines of Chatham, forts bristling with the iron mouths of cannon, to protect the dockyard and arsenal, that are below the hill. Immediately in front, is the magnificent ruin of the Keep of the Norman Castle, built by Gundulph, 70 feet square, and 104 feet high, with towers at each angle of Kentish ragstone, and coigns of Caen stone, and rooms varying in height from 20 ft. to 32 ft. ; and in the centre, rising above the purple crowd of clustered houses, are the grey walls of the Cathedral, hoary and full of years. John de Salisbury, the friend of à Becket, was a native. The city was burned by Ethelred, 676 ; it gallantly resisted the Danes, 885, until relieved by Alfred. Ethelred II. was bribed by St. Dunstan to retire, having laid siege to it. William Rufus, in 1088, captured the castle, after a six weeks' siege. Robert, Earl of

Gloucester, in 1141 was a prisoner in the castle. In 1174, the city and part of the Cathedral was burned. John, 1215, took the castle after a siege of twelve months. Louis, the Dauphin, reduced it; Simon de Montford, in 1264, failed in an attempt upon it. In 1251, Henry III. held a tournament here. In 1264, the Earl of Leicester took the city and spoiled the church. Here Jack Cade's rabble rout dispersed themselves. In 1768 Christian VII. slept here. Queen Elizabeth visited the city in 1573. James II. was detained here on his flight from his throne. St. Augustine, whose robes were hung here with fish-tails, or à Becket, whose horses' tails were docked by the towns-folk, is said to have appended tails to the inhabitants.

In the George and Crown are some ancient Early English vaults; and there are remains of the city walls. Near High-street is the Norman apse of Bishop Gundulph's Hospital of St. Bartholomew. The Dockyard, established by Queen Elizabeth, and the Lines, made 1758-1807 at Chatham, deserve a visit. On June 12th, 1667, De Ruyter burned the English ships in ordinary then lying off Upnor Castle.

St. Catharine's Hospital was founded in 1315 for lepers, and Watts', in 1579, to entertain poor travellers, "not being common rogues or *proctors.*"

The church is composed of a central tower, a NAVE of eight bays, and aisles, a WEST CHOIR and TRANSEPT, each of one bay; and CHOIR, with solid walls interposed between it and the aisles; an EAST AMBULATORY, and a LADY CHAPEL of four bays, into which the altar has been removed, to the destruction of ritual and architectural effect. The Cathedral is dedicated to St. Andrew.

At the end of the 10th century, in accordance with the popular and universal superstition, all archives began with the words, "Now that the end of the world is approaching;" and when at last the panic passed away, the Church hastened to rebuild her buildings with enthusiastic devotion—of this period we have few remains in England. The nave of Rochester is the most ancient of any in the kingdom. With the tower, on the north-east side of the

transept, now unroofed, it was begun by Bishop Gundulph, who also built Rochester Castle, and St. John's
Church in the Tower of London. Its comparative lightness would show that it was not designed to bear a stone
vaulting. Many of the Norman cathedrals, and Rochester
especially, lost by being copies of foreign churches, built
long before the landing of William I.; and the consequent
introduction of an earlier, smaller, and less finely developed
scale of dimensions and mode of construction. Ernulph,
the architect of great works, while Abbot of Peterborough
and Prior of Canterbury, completed the church, and built
dormitory, infirmary, and chapter-house, and lengthened
the nave by two bays eastward, 1115-25. The Cathedral
was dedicated, May 7th, 1130, in the presence of Henry I.,
by the primate. The narrow Early English CHOIR, enclosed
by solid walls, rebuilt by William de Hoo, the sacristan,
was first used May 9th, 1227; he added the CHOIR
TRANSEPTS with the offerings made at St. William's shrine.
The NORTH AISLE was begun by Richard Eastgate, and completed by William Axenham in the 13th century: the
SOUTH AISLE, was built, 1240, by Richard the Sacrist. The
eastern arches of the north and south arcades of the
NAVE were rebuilt, probably with the intention of its
complete reconstruction. The north wing of the MAIN
TRANSEPT, Early English, was built by the monks, Richard
de Eastgate, sacrist, and Thomas de Meopham; and the
southern wing, by the monk Richard de Waledene,
about the year 1200. Haymo de Hethe added a window
in the south-west transept, the doorway, and lower walls
of the chapter-house, and a wooden spire on the great
tower in 1343; the refectory was built by Silvester, the
prior, after 1177. The murder by his servant, outside the
walls of Rochester, of a baker of Perth, who gave every
tenth loaf to the poor, and was on his pilgrimage to Jerusalem, A.D. 1201, led to the erection of a shrine of St.
William (canonized 1256) in this Cathedral, at which
great offerings were made towards the structure. Up to
that period the north choir aisle had been a parish church;
but now, not to interrupt the service, it was necessary to

build a Decorated little church of St. Andrew northward
of the transept.

The doorway of the WEST FRONT of the Cathedral
is unrivalled. A semicircular arch, deeply recessed and
enriched with beautiful mouldings of four orders, is encircled with ornamental bands, and crowned with capitals
of foliage, birds, and animals. The rich and fanciful leafage is quite Saracenic in character. On two of these
shafts are the effigies of King Henry I. and good Queen
Maud. The lintel bears reliefs of the apostles, with the
figure of the Saviour with an aureole in the medallion above;
cherubim and the evangelistic symbols surround Him.
The large eight-light window, of two orders transomed,
is of the date of Henry VII.: of the four arcaded octagonal towers which once adorned the front, only one retains its original pinnacle. On the front of the north-
west turret is a statue of Bishop Gundulph. The CENTRAL
TOWER, built by Bishop Shepey, 1352, and Haymo de
Hethe, has been rendered contemptible under the inno-
vating hand of Mr. Cottingham, in 1827, who removed the
spire, which had been erected in 1479. Earl Warren, in
1264, and the rebels in the civil wars, committed great
outrages in the Cathedral.

On the south-east side of the nave is St. MARY's
CHAPEL, of three bays, once the chapel of the infirmary.
On the east side of the south transept is St. EDMUND's
CHAPEL. The eastern transept has an aisle on the east,
composed of four chapels, and from the south wing, the
chapter-house is entered. To the east of the north wing
of the WESTERN TRANSEPT, is GUNDULPH's TOWER, 24 ft. by
24 ft. on every side, and with walls 6 feet in thickness. It
very probably formed a transept tower, as at Exeter,
while the corresponding tower on the south has been
destroyed. A passage at the side led the pilgrims to St.
William's shrine. In the south-east transept, in the thickness of the wall, are stairs to the penance and indulgence-
chambers, now blocked up. This transept was parted
from the choir by tapestry-hangings, representing Noah's
entry into the Ark. A door, in the south wall of the

church, led into the porter's watching chamber. The
CRYPT is partly Early English and partly Saxon, as appears
by rude groins, plain shafts, and heavy-pillared capitals.
No new crypt was built in England later than this, which
was completed 1227; some ancient specimens were restored.

While we rejoice in our simpler worship—

> In beauty of holiness with ordered pomp—
> Decent and unreproved—

we cannot be insensible to the loss which has accrued to
the effect of the vast interiors of our Cathedrals, by the
removal of altars, and hangings, and lights. There is a
coldness too perceptible in the grand naves, which can
only be taken away by supplying the windows with stained
glass, peeling off the disfigurement of whitewash, and still
better, by the use of them for special services and frequent
sermons. We have happily been ridden of those super-
fluous ornaments which throw a blemish on the happiest
efforts of sculptor and architect, and having no lamps or
burning of incense, which render the churches of the
Continent warm and pleasant, we must thus, by constant
acts of adoration, throw life and vigour into the buildings
which are our precious inheritance. Architecture, sculpture, and painting are sisters—the three Graces of the
visible arts. The tesselated colours on the floor, the
frescoes blazoned on the vault, the variegated marbles,
and gilding on the wall, the chequered mosaic, the blaze
of bright stained glass in the storied windows, now happily
introduced gradually into our churches, will be an appre-
ciable increase of beauty, while they will not diminish
the intrinsic majesty, nor be out of harmony with the
character of our daily services, to which music, in its
highest form, lends grandeur and sublimity. We shall
only feebly represent the divinely-ordered worship and
architecture of the Tabernacle and the Temple.

A popular author describes the repugnance persons fee
at the very thought of spending a night in a church—
within a few years churches have looked so sepulchral.
Our forefathers were of a different mind. Formerly—

Our ancestors, within the still domain
Of vast cathedral or conventual church,
Their vigils kept, where tapers day and night
On the dim altar burned continually,
In token that the House was evermore
Watching to GOD.

Chevron mouldings enrich the arches above the piers of the NAVE, which, on either side, are dissimilar in design as well as those of the triforium, the arches of which open into the aisles : the triforium only extends along the six western Norman bays of the nave, above which rises a lofty clerestory. The open timber roof is supported by corbels in the form of angels bearing shields of arms. It is very rich ; and the arches below the tie-beams are semicircular where they come in contact with the Norman arches of the lantern, to adapt the two to each other. There are two transepts, as at Lincoln and Salisbury. The triforium of the CHOIR and MAIN TRANSEPT is composed of three unequal lancets, divided by shafts of Petworth marble, a decoration which is profusely employed in the choir : so beautiful with dark brilliance, its stains of subterranean fire, its dappled veins and lines, the legend of the mystic story of the mountainous kingdom of its origin. In the east wall, a recess marks the site of St. Nicholas' Altar. On the west side of the southern wing is ST. MARY'S CHAPEL, now the Consistory Court, and on the eastern side is the MUNIMENT-ROOM. The only reason assignable for this extraordinary position of a Lady Chapel is either that it was the infirmary chapel, or that the monks, on seeing the designs of Henry VIII., expended their revenues on this new chapel, and other buildings, to disappoint his avarice and deter him from seizing their revenues, with the higher motive of preserving the church as long as possible. The old Lady Chapel was then thrown into the choir. Eastward of the high altar stood St. Paulinus' shrine.

A flight of ten steps leads up to the CHOIR. In a loft over the poor mean screen designed by Rev. W. Olive is an organ built by Green in 1792, and enlarged by Hill in

1835. The pavement, of Bremen and Portland stone, was laid down in 1743, and the stalls and bishop's throne reconstructed. The vaulting of the CHOIR and EASTERN TRANSEPT is of stone; plain Early English groining. The oaken roof of the south-choir transept is of the date of Edward I., that of the CENTRAL TOWER 1840. The CRYPT, which once contained nine altars, was built by William de Hoo. It extends under the whole length of the choir, and contains some specimens of fresco-work with these arms— *Or*, an eagle displayed *sa.* The cloister was in an unusual position, the south-east side of the choir: except at Lincoln, where it is on the north of the choir, no cloister adjoins that part of a cathedral. The Norman west front of the destroyed chapter-house is very beautiful, and elaborately carved, with zodiacal signs. Beneath three round-headed windows, with chevron mouldings, is a rich central doorway set between two highly-sculptured arches. There are three doors adjoining, possibly those of the slype, dormitory, and infirmary: to the south wall of the cloister was attached the refectory, and there are remains of the wall passage to the pulpit, as at Chester and Beaulieu.

There is a fresco at the back of the pulpit; and by the throne, erected by Bishop Wilcocks, a fine Early English corbel of Petworth marble, with foliage and masks. There was an altar-piece of the Apparition of the Angels to the Shepherds, by West. The doorway of the chapter-house, built by Bishop Shepey, 1352, restored 1830, represents the Church as a Prelate, and the Jewish Synagogue as a woman blindfolded—her crown fallen, her flag-staff broken, and the Two Tables reversed: above are Bishops Gundulph, Ernulph, St. Martin, and Haymo de Hethe, or the four great Latin Fathers SS. Augustine, Jerome, Ambrose, and Cyprian; purgatory and a ransomed soul: a similar design is painted in fresco at York. At the east end of the nave is an incised slab, with an axe, to the memory of Bishop Fisher.

The principal monuments are the following:

N. E. Transept.—Walter de Merton, drowned 1278—effigy and two pyramidal canopies, partly original, of Limoges work, and partly restored by Hussey, 1849; Bishop Lowe, d. 1467, a table tomb; and the tomb of St. William, whose shrine was in the centre of this chapel.

N. Side of Choir.—Bishop Shepey, d. 1361, effigy and canopy with original colouring, discovered in 1825. The three Decorated sedilia on the south side, restored 1825, mark the ancient place of the high altar, before the old Lady Chapel was thrown into it in the 15th century. In the spandrils are the arms of Canterbury and Rochester, and a St. Andrew's Cross.

S. Side, Presbytery.—Bishop Gundulph, stone cist., 1107; Bishop Inglethorpe, canopied effigy, Petworth marble, 1291.

N. Side, Presbytery.—Bishop Laurence, effigy, 1274; Bishop Glanville, coped tomb, Petworth marble, 1214, with medallions.

S. Choir Aisle.—Bishop Bradfield, d. 1283, canopy and effigy.

Nave.—Lord Henniker, d. 1803.

DIMENSIONS OF THE CHURCH IN FEET.

	Length.	Breadth.	Height.
Nave	159	65 f. 4 in.	55
Choir	110 f. 6 in.	..	..
Lady Chapel	44	28 f. 8 in.	..
West front	94	..	..
Tower	..	..	156
Main Transept	122 f. 3 in.	..	..
Choir Transept	92	..	..
Gundulph's Tower	24	24	95
St. Mary's Chapel	45	30	..
Total length	310	..	..

'Three gates remain: the Prior's, an embattled tower on the south-east; the Deanery or Sacristy, adjoining the north transept; and the College Yard, or Cemetery Gate, which led from the market cross to the west door. Of the three precinct gates, the North, or St. William's, with the cloisters, has been destroyed. The palace, the last occupant of which was Bishop Fisher (and Erasmus tenderly entreated him to leave it, so damp and unhealthy was it), has long been abandoned as an episcopal residence. The embattled tower arch of the south cloister gate remains. The almonry on the south-west was converted into the prebendal house.

The Chapter is composed of a dean and four canons.

There are four minor canons, six lay-vicars, and eight
choristers: two services-choral daily, at 10½ o'clock, A.M.,
and 3¼ o'clock, P.M., and monthly celebration of the Holy
Communion.   The   capitular   revenues   were,   in   1852,
10,000*l.*; and the expenditure on the fabric in fourteen
previous years, 7479*l.* The library contains 1100 vols., the
Textus Roffensis 1120, and Custumale Roffense, A.D., 1320.
The palace is Danbury Court, Chelmsford.

Among the bishops occur Putta, who on his deposal went
about Mercia teaching plain song; St. Paulinus; Gundulph,
the architect; Arnulph, the compiler of Textus Roffensis;
Walter, the lover of the chase; Galeran, compelled to take
his pastoral staff from the altar of Canterbury in sign of
subjection; Glanville, whose exactions compelled the
monks to coin the silver shrine of St. Paulinus; Walter de
Merton, the keen huntsman, Lord Chancellor, and founder
of a college at Oxford; John de Shepey, Lord Chancellor;
munificent Rotherham; Russell; Lord Chancellor Alcock,
founder of Jesus College, Cambridge; Cardinal Fisher,
who escaped poisoning by his cook to die by the executioner—his life cost him by the scarlet hat, which Henry
swore he should carry on his shoulders, for he should have
never a head to wear it: Ridley, burned at the stake;
Young, who refused Norwich, saying it was a hard seat
for an old man since the base Scambler took away the
cushion—its revenues; ambitious Neile; brave and
generous Warner; Sprat, the wit and time-server; eloquent Atterbury, Garth's "Urim," the Jacobite who proved
the faithlessness of princes, of whom Lord Bathurst said
his enemies were like wild Indians, "who think to inherit
the goods and abilities of the man they kill;" Pearce, who
vainly implored to be relieved of his mitre, saying every
wise man would desire an interval of repose to prepare to
die; and learned Horsley, the staunch opponent of the
slave trade. One cardinal, Barnard, bishop of Raphoe, and
T. Plume were canons. The best palfrey, the best cup,
and the kennel of the bishops in their diocese became in
old time the property of the primate.

Arms: Arg. on a saltier, gules, the letter R of the field.

St. Asaph.

St. Asaph, formerly Llan-Elwy, "the Church of the Elwy," though of unpretending dimensions, has all the effect of a Cathedral; seated on the brow of a gentle slope, with the village-city clustering below, in the vale of Clwyd, watered by the rivers Clwyd and turbulent Elwy. At the entrance of the valley is Rhuddlan Castle, the scene of an ancient battle, still commemorated in the air of Morva Rhuddlan, and of a Parliament in 1283; the resting-place of Richard II. on his way to Flint, 1399 : and in 1850 distinguished by the meeting of the Eisteddfod. In the street is a mark on a black stone, which the folks say is the print of the hoof of St. Asaph's horse when he leaped hither from Onan Hassa two miles distant, a legend resembling that of the Magdetreppe of the Hartz. From its situation on the great road for the march of armies, the church was constantly exposed to loss and injury during war ; and as their goods escheated to the Crown, the bishops never made wills, but the best clothes, horse, book, falchion, knife, ring, and purse of every beneficed clergyman fell to the bishop, until the time of Fleetwood. The ground-plan of the church is cruciform : it was built by Bishop Anian II., in 1284. He had threatened King Edward I., to whom he had been confessor in Holy Land, with a ban : the king replied by confiscating his temporalities and burning his cathedral in 1282. In 1490, after having lain eighty-eight years in ruins, having been burned by Owen Glendower, 1402, because Bishop Trevor revolted from Richard II. to Henry Bolingbroke, Bishop Redmayne roofed it anew, set up the east window and choir-stalls, which are traditionally said to have been carved by an idiot, and repaired the tower. The exterior is very simple and plain. The NAVE of five bays and TRANSEPTS are Decorated; the west window is of six lights and elegant in form. There is no triforium. The clerestory of the nave has small square apertures, with portions of ancient tracery. The CHOIR is modern Perpendicular, by J. Turner, 1783. Bishop Owen added the pulpit throne and stalls in 1631-5. Bishop Short, in 1849, set up two good stained glass windows. There are two couplets and one triplet on each side of the CHOIR, which was extended under the tower in 1833. The east window, 27 ft. by 18 ft., which was rebuilt in 1744-5 and in 1780, is a copy of that of Tintern Abbey; it was glazed by Egginton, in 1780, after a picture of Albano. Good Decorated windows are in the TRANSEPT and WEST FRONT, and in each face of the short square TOWER, which is embattled, and has on the north-east angle a turret, square staircase, and one bell. The SOUTH TRANSEPT, once the LADY CHAPEL, forms the chapter-house; the NORTH WING is occupied by vestries. The vaulting of the CHOIR is plaster; the central TOWER, of one story, commands a view of the whole sweep of the vale of Clwyd, the grand mountains beyond, and the Irish sea. The organ was built by Hill in 1831, and the Cathedral is noted for giving sonorous effect to music.

> From the arms of silence, list, oh, list !
> The music bursteth into second life ;
> The notes luxuriate, every stone is kissed
> By sound or ghost of sound in mazy strife,
> Heart-thrilling strains, that cast before the eye
> Of the devout a veil of ecstacy.

The spectator will hardly fail to be sensible of a regret, when he looks at such poor feeble Cathedrals as St. Asaph, Bangor, Llandaff, Oxford, or Bristol, that, in their place, cannot be transposed the magnificent churches of Beverley, Christchurch, Tewkesbury, Sherborne, St. Mary Overy, St. Alban's, and Selby, now mere parish churches, and destitute of the solemn services once celebrated daily within them. The first sermon in Welsh was preached March 6, 1630, by Rev. Morris Jones, a vicar-choral, in the parish church.

The chief monuments are those of—

S. W. pier of the Tower.—Bishop David Owen, altar-tomb, effigy, 1512.
Under the Lantern.—Bishop Griffith, d. 1666.
Before the W. Door.—Bishop Isaac Barrow, d. 1680, with the
  inscription : " O ye who pass by into the house of the Lord, the

house of prayer, pray for your fellow-servant that he may find mercy in the day of the Lord." Felicia Hemans, (who lived at Bronwylfa and Rhyllon).

South Transept.—Dean Shipley.

North Transept.—Bishop Luxmoore, d. 1830, sitting effigy, white marble, by Tamouth.

DIMENSIONS OF THE CHURCH IN FEET.

	Length.	Breadth.	Height.
Nave	119	68	60
Choir	60	32	40
Transept	108	33	..
Tower	34 f. 8 in.	29 f. 9 in.	93
Extreme length	179	..	..

The Chapter is composed of a dean and three canons-residentiary, and ten cursal canons, four minor canons, six lay vicars and six choristers. There are two daily services, 10 A.M. and 3 P.M., which are choral on Sundays and twice in the week. Holy Communion is administered monthly and on great festivals. The library contains 1600 volumes; the income of the Chapter, in 1852, was 1408*l.*

Arms : Sa. two keys in saltier arg.

Among the bishops occur SS. Kentigern and Asaph; Geoffrey of Monmouth, the Welsh Herodotus; Anian, the Black Friar of Schonau ; the Crusader John de Trevor, who pronounced Richard II's. deposal at Flint Castle ; Edmund de Birkenhead, and Goldwell, who sat in the Council of Trent ; Pocock, the Wickliffite; Davies, one of the translators of the Holy Bible ; W. Hughes, who held with his see eight cures and nine sinecures ; Owen, who introduced sermons in Welsh ; Griffith, the author of the Form of Adult Baptism ; Isaac Barrow, the good Bishop of Man ; Jones, the Simonist; learned Beveridge, the restorer of primitive piety, who would not accept Ken's see; Tanner, the historian of monasteries; Maddox, once a pastry-cook, who used to recommend tarts to his guests, " though not of his own making ;" and Horsley. N. Marsh, Bishop of Ferns, was a canon.

The episcopal palace was rebuilt by Bishop Carey.

St. David's.

Most beautiful, most desolate,
It was St. David's ancient pile, chancel, nave, tower, and windowed
    aisle,
And skirting all the western side a palace fair in ruined pride;
With storied range in order set, and portal, arch, and parapet,
There hiding from the haunts of men, in hollow of the mountain glen,
Religion's venerable hold, with wrecks and ruin manifold,
Burst full on the astonished eye, hoar in sublime antiquity.

THUS sweetly does the poet describe the scenery of ancient
Menevia, on the little river Alan, not a mile from the sea :
from the broken cliffs of slate and granite adjoining may
be seen, on clear days, the shores of Ireland. Once an
archbishopric, the city is now only a hamlet, poverty-
stricken and apparently deserted. The country on every
side is wild, desolate, and barren ; and in a ravine of the
hills is set the Cathedral, buried in the shadows of its
departed greatness. Ruins, shapeless heaps, unroofed
walls, and mouldering remains of great extent, riven and
strewn far and wide, render the scene profoundly gloomy
and romantic, without meadow or tree, except a few
gnarled stems and weather-beaten tops in the hollow.
There is a bleakness and a chill about this secluded church
oppressive and monotonous ; in concord, however, with
the wail of the wind sweeping along hills steep and sombre,
and the dreary moaning of the restless Atlantic, beating
against the iron-bound coast and bleak headland, like an
eternal and powerless despair—all is inexpressibly melancholy, decay, and loneliness. Yet two pilgrimages to
St. David's shrine were declared by Pope Calixtus equivalent to one visit to Rome, and now it is a rock deserted
by the tide—the tide of population ebbed for evermore.
" On the east," says Defoe, " the hills darken the air with
their height." It was here the Red King boasted—" I will
bring all my ships hither and make them a bridge for my
army," when he saw the dim outline of Ireland beyond.
Prince Murdach, of Leinster, paused when the speech was

related to him, then asked, "Did he add to his mighty threat, if GOD will?" "No," was the answer. "Then," said the prince, "since that man trusts to human and not divine power, I fear not his coming."

The road to the church was known by thousands of pilgrims as Meidr Saint, the Sacred Way. Druidical remains and relics of chapels on the hills evince the religious character of the neighbourhood at various eras. King William came in 1079, and Edward III. and Queen Eleanor on Nov. 26, 1284. Over the brook once lay the Lech lavar, "the talking stone," which cracked in sunder when a dead body was carried over it. On it, as Henry II. in 1171 crossed to the cathedral, a Welsh woman, disappointed in her petition, invoked his death, according to Merlin's prophecy, by a man with a red hand. The church stands in a Close, walled in, with a compass of nearly one mile in extent. To the north is the ruined College of St. Mary, built by Bishop Gower, with a tower 70 ft. in height and a chapel 69 ft. by 45 ft. On the east hill is the Tower-gate, 60 feet high, with double turrets. To the south-west lie the remains of the once magnificent palace, which Bishop Barlow unroofed in 1536. The quadrangle was 120 feet square; the south-eastern and western walls remain: the hall was 67 ft. by 25 ft.; King John's hall 96 ft. by 33 ft.

The Cathedral, dedicated to SS. Andrew and David, was built by Archbishop Sampson in the tenth century, and rebuilt after 1176 by Bishop Peter de Leia. The church consists of a CENTRAL TOWER, a NAVE of six bays with aisles, SOUTH PORCH of two stories, a TRANSEPT, each wing of two bays with an eastern aisle to the south arm, and the east chapel of ST. THOMAS, with the old CHAPTER-HOUSE above it, in the north arm; a CHOIR of three bays, one being formed by the lantern, with aisles; a PRESBYTERY of two bays, the TRINITY CHAPEL of a lower level, each with aisles, an ante-chapel with aisles projecting on the north-east and south-east; and a LADY CHAPEL of two bays. The material employed is sandstone from Caerfai for the parts previous to the Perpendicular period;

subsequently Somersetshire oolite was used. The cloisters
were on the north side. The exterior, which, if ornamented, would have lost its beauty, owing to the sea air
and climate, is now dilapidated: the chapels of the transept, the choir-aisles, and Lady Chapel are roofless.

The tower is of three stages: the lower Norman, the
second Decorated, on each face it has a long two-light
window between two niches, with loops above; the uppermost storey, Perpendicular, added by Bishop Gower, is plain
and mouldering; it has an open parapet and pinnacles, and
polygonal clustered shafts at the angle, a flat octagonal
shaft divides the loops on either side. The west front
was rebuilt miserably by Nash in 1793; the north side of
the nave was built in 1180. The NAVE is highly ornamented, spacious, and massive; the round arches are
enriched with a chevron-moulding; above these is a string-
course, which is joined by delicate mouldings continued
from the arches abovo a deeply-recessed clerestory of
round-headed windows, curiously amalgamated with a triforium of couplets in each bay, under alternate ornamented
circles. The windows of the clerestory are Decorated,
those of the aisle Perpendicular or Decorated. The roof
of Irish oak, built by Owen Pole, treasurer, about 1508, is
flat, and panelled with carved Tudor pendants. Three of
the lantern arches, Late Norman, are pointed, whilst the
third is round; the sides of the next story are enriched
with an arcade. A beautiful Decorated ROOD-SCREEN, erected
by Bishop Gower, stands before the choir. It is of five
compartments, and retains the stair to the loft. The
cornice was added in 1847. The CHOIR, according to
Bishop Tulley's arrangoment of the twenty-eight stalls
which he erected 1460-80, occupies only the space under
the lantern. Bishop Morgan, who died 1488, gave the
throne. The organ, built by Schmidt, was improved by
Lincoln in 1848. The painted roof of the CHOIR was completed about 1492. The pavement is of tiles. The clerestory is composed of lancets: there is no triforium. A
Late Decorated screen, an unique feature, parts off the
PRESBYTERY, which is of three bays, built in 1220. It is

rich and graceful, and simple in composition. The altar
stands under a rich triplet. The Perpendicular window
above has been cut in two to admit the TRINITY CHAPEL on
the east, Late Perpendicular, built by Bishop Vaughan
1509-23, and elaborately adorned with fan-tracery and
pendants. The LADY CHAPEL, Early Decorated, was built
by Bishops Beke and Martyn, 1290-1328. It is parted
off from the aisles by a couplet of Early English arches.
It retains its sedilia.

The TRANSEPT was built in 1220: the north wing was
St. Andrew's chapel, and is lighted by a large pointed
window, inserted 1844. The SOUTH TRANSEPT, Transitional
Norman, was St. David's chapel; it is called the Chanter's,
(a corruption of chancellor's) Chapel, and was converted
into a parish church in 1843-4. · It has two tiers of double
four-light Perpendicular windows, under a round arch. The
CHAPEL OF ST. THOMAS, built about 1220, contains a graceful Early English drain. It was first used as a Chapter-
house, July 25, 1829. The foliage in the transepts bears
a remarkable similarity to that of the same period in Wells
Cathedral. In the north is a Perpendicular screen, and a
stone table-tomb under a round arch, which marks the
ancient shrine of St. Caradoc.

The Cathedral is peculiarly rich in incised slabs. The
principal monuments are the following :—

Choir, North Side.—St. David's shrine, died 542, a plain tomb, with
four quatrefoil apertures for offerings, and three niches emptied of
the images of SS. David, Patrick, and Denys; Rhys ap Gruffyd, died
1196, small effigy; Rhys ap Grygg, his son, died 1233, Prince of
South Wales; Bishop De Leia, died 1192, effigy; S. Lloyd, treasurer, died 1612, altar-tomb, canopy, and effigy, cinque-cento.

South Side.—An armed knight, effigy of the latter part of the 14th
century; Bishop Anselm, died 1248, effigy; Bishop Gervase, died
1229, low tomb, effigy; priest, effigy under a Decorated recess.

Choir, Centre.—Edmund Tudor, Earl of Richmond, father of Henry
VII., died 1456, altar-tomb of Purbeck marble.

Chapel Aisles, South Side.—Bishop Fastolfe, died 1361, effigy.

North Side.—Archdeacon Hiot, died 1419, with a sculpture of the
Crucifixion on the wall, effigy; a knight, Wogan, of 13th century,
effigy; Canon Wogan, 15th century, effigy under a Decorated recess.

Lady Chapel.—Bishop D. Martyn, died 1238, altar-tomb, canopied.

Rood-Screen.—Bishop Gower, died 1347, altar-tomb and effigy ; *South Side.*—A treasurer; D. Barret, a chancellor; J. Gome, effigy, contemporaries of Gower.

Nave, South Side.—A priest, effigy, called that of Giraldus Cambrensis, in a decorated recess, with a stellated canopy like those in Bristol Cathedral ; Bishop Morgan, died 1504, altar-tomb and effigy ; a Flemish brass.

DIMENSIONS OF THE CATHEDRAL IN FEET.

	Length.	Breadth.	Height.
Nave . . .	127 f. 4 in.	76	45 f. 8 in.
Choir and Presbytery	80	..	..
Transept .	120	27 f. 3 in.	..
Tower . .	..	..	116
Total length .	290, externally 306 feet ..		

The Chapter is composed of a dean and four canons : there are three minor canons, three vicars-choral, and six choristers. There are two daily services, at 10 and 3 : on Sundays and Saturday evenings they are choral. The Holy Communion is administered fortnightly. The capitular income, in 1852, was 1529*l.* ; and in the fourteen previous years, 2000*l.* had been spent on the fabric.

Arms : Or, on a cross, sa., five cinquefoils, or.

Among the bishops occur SS. Dubricius and David; Adam Houghton, Lord Chancellor ; Gilbert, Lord Treasurer ; Archbishop Chichele ; Lyndwood the canonist ; Martyn, Chancellor of Ireland ; Laud ; Ferrar, the first bishop consecrated according to the English Ordinal, and burned a martyr at the stake ; Middleton, deprived for the triple crime of bigamy, forgery, and simony ; Rudd, who boldly reproved Queen Elizabeth and warned her of death ; Mainwaring, on whose grave his faithful dog lay down and died ; Watson, deprived for simony ; the learned George Bull ; Horsley ; Hon. W. Stuart, primate of all Ireland ; and Burgess, founder of Lampeter College.

St. David's was once an archbishopric, ruling over Hereford, Worcester, Llanbadarn, and Margam, and the other three Welsh sees ; with them the primate met St. Augustine, at Augustine's accession. The palace is at Abergwili.

St. Paul's, London.

Let my path
Lead to that younger pile, whose skylike Dome
Hath typified, by reach of daring art,
Infinity's embrace; whose guardian crest,
The silent Cross, among the stars shall spread
As now, when she hath also seen her breast
Filled with mementoes, satiate with its part
Of grateful England's overflowing Dead.

SIR CHRISTOPHER WREN, on determining the place of the foundations of the new Cathedral, lighted on a piece of Bishop King's gravestone with the one word, Resurgam! The phœnix over the south portico comemmorates the augury. It is a matter of congratulation that he was not suffered to depart from the Christian cruciform plan in its erection—a Gothic conception expressed in Italian details. Of its style it may safely be pronounced the noblest effort of human genius. It is, however, a proof that had the old abbeys and rich foundations stood, church architecture at their dissolution being in decline, and shortly after Italianized, we should have had the same barbarous additions of vitiated and degenerate taste to deform our cathedrals, as those which spoil continental churches.

It is impossible, however, to fail to recognize the exceeding beauty of the dome of matchless curve, everywhere appropriate, by its suggestiveness of durability, perfection, and repose, elevating and influencing the imagination; a vast hemispheric globe swelling into the air, the type which rose before the eyes of Martin as he designed the celestial city dawning on the enraptured gaze of the pilgrim. It is that legacy of Byzantine art which appears from the temple palace of the Kremlin, to the Alhambra of Granada; reaching from the banks of the Ganges and the mosque at Bozrah, through Cairo and Damascus, to Saracenic art in Sicily; from Santa Sophia to St. Peter's, and here in St. Paul's, the characteristic feature of the mother-city of an empire on which the sun never sets. Without one single good approach, from the neighbouring streets, or the silent highway of the Thames, the church is seen like an alp through a dusky gorge, crowning with superb grace the vast accumulation of buildings below; but from a distance, when the lower parts are lost in the smoke-cloud, the cross and cupola seem to hang midway suspended in the air: the cross itself burning in the sunlight against the deep blue firmament, more gloriously than the jewelled illumination which kindles on high days the gloom of the Venetian dome of St. Mark. Yet there is no type here of a heavenly counterpart, a glass to see heaven through, except in the ground plan, which was forced upon the architect. No lowly western door, introduces to an increasing grandeur and beauty in the interior, to find its height and completion in the eastern sanctuary. Art here is not the handmaid of Religion which sanctifies it. It is not in the pediment, that rests calm, secure, and passionless, in self-complacent beauty on earth; not in the bow of the half orb spanning the horizon like a martial arch of triumph, and exulting over earth—the symbol of an arrogant claim of universal supremacy; this effect can be seen only in the spire and pinnacle, diminishing as they rise from the earth towards heaven, of which the material church is but the gate. The huge western portal here is only the entrance to a building, in which the sanctuary is the meanest portion, and an unworthy adjunct. This Cathedral was finished in 1710, during the episcopate of one bishop (Compton), by one architect, and the same master mason, (Strong): the first stone was laid on June 21, 1675. It was built at a cost of 736,752*l.* by a tax levied on coals, and subscriptions, equal to 1,222,437*l.* present money. The iron balustrade of the yard (5 feet 6 inches high), cast at Lamberhurst in Sussex, and designed by M. Tijoue, cost 11,202*l.* Sir Christopher Wren, in consideration of his labour, received 200*l.* a-year for the pleasure, as the Duchess of Marlborough expresses it, of "being dragged up in a basket three or four times a-week;" and we may add some mortifications, for it is said he wept when compelled to add aisles to the church, and peevishly exclaimed upon the erection of a balustrade round the exterior, "Only ladies think nothing well without an edging." In his latter days, when the feeling of his dismissal from office weighed heavier upon him than the infirmities of years, Wren would have his chair carried before St. Paul's and gaze on his magnificent handiwork until his eyes ran down with tears. Sir James Thornhill was paid for his paintings at the rate of 40*s.* the square yard, and Bird 1100*l.* for his carvings.

It is built of Portland stone, and comprises a NAVE of five bays, a TRANSEPT of one bay in each wing, and CHOIR of four bays with aisles, a WESTERN TRANSEPT, CENTRAL DOME, and two WESTERN TOWERS with a magnificent portico at the west end, and a semicircular portico in either face of the transept. The WEST FRONT is approached by a double flight of steps of black Manx marble, from Polvash, and is composed of a range of twelve coupled columns, and eight above, and a pediment 64 ft. by 17 ft. filled with sculptures of St. Paul's Conversion, by Francis Bird. Over the doors are sculptures of the Apostle's acts, by the same artist. On the summit is the statue of St. Paul, on either hand are those of St. Peter and St. James. At the angles of the towers are the four Evangelists. On the south-west is the CLOCK-TOWER, remarkable for a geometrical staircase of 110 steps, and for the great bell, 10 feet in diameter, weighing four and a half tons, and cast by Robert Phelps 1716, and only tolled at the death of a member of the royal family, the diocesan, the dean, or the lord mayor. The metal is principally that of the Great Tom of Westminster, which the sentinel heard on the terrace of Windsor Castle strike thirteen times, and so saved his life when charged with sleeping on his post. The clock dial is 18 feet 10 inches in diameter ; the works are by Langley Bradley : it cost 300*l.* In the centre of the yard, before the church, is a statue of Queen Anne, by Bird, 1712, and satirised by Garth.

There is no triforium in the Cathedral. In the north-west transept is the morning chapel, with screens and woodwork by J. Maine ; in that of the south-west the

Consistory Court, and above it the library 50 ft. by 40 ft.;
its floor parqueted with 2376 pieces of oak. Supported
on eight vast arches, with keystones carved by Gibbons,
and piers, four of the latter being 40 and the rest 28 feet
broad, the glorious dome rises from the whispering gallery,
a peristyle of thirty-two pilasters, reached by 260 steps;
the immense vault above opening with an overpowering
effect. The whole space occupied by these piers and
covered by the dome contains upwards of half an acre of
ground. In the centre is a great circle of light and dark
marble, arranged like the mariner's compass. Above an
attic is the exterior dome (its base surrounded by the stone
gallery), which is surmounted by the outer golden gallery,
reached by 560 steps (the inner golden gallery is at the
base of the lantern), from which rises the stone lantern,
reached by 616 steps, crowned by a mound and colossal
cross avellane, 15 feet high: the former, 6 feet 2 inches in
diameter, will hold eight persons, the latter weighs 3,360
lbs. The exterior dome, only of timber covered with lead,
contains 16,087 square feet. The lantern, 700 tons in
weight, is supported by a brick cone. The inner dome, of
brickwork, two bricks thick, has stone bandings at every
rise of five feet, and a wrought-iron chain, weighing 95 cwt.
cemented into a course of Portland stone with melted
lead. At early morning the intense grandeur of the prospect from the summit is inconceivable—the sight of a world
as from a world beyond: the river, broad and shining, the
most ancient and most modern thing in the landscape;
with its numerous craft asleep or stirring on its laden
bosom; the sounds too of the habitations of two millions
of human beings—every house, square, theatre, court, and
church, with towers and steeples like some great navy
moored—a canopy of vapour hiding the swarm, and showing
only the outskirts of their works; a mighty heart throbbing beneath; innocence, guilt, joy, grief, passion, thought
and deed, felt or acted in that labyrinth of streets—under
that maze of roofs, spread over a circuit of miles, in amount
too great for grasp of intellect—distinct, but such, that
the eye, ranging over it, cannot calculate the vast ex-

tent. At evening it is unutterably imposing, when the river is garlanded with chains of light by unseen hands, and night like a pall drops on the murmuring city. The view extends from Epping forest to Richmond—from Hampstead and Highgate to the hills of Reigate and Wrotham.

The interior of the dome was painted with eight pictures of the acts of St. Paul, which have been restored in chiar'oscuro by Paris 1854. 1. The Conversion; 2. Elymas the Sorcerer; 3. The Cripple at Lystra; 4. Gaoler at Philippi; 5. Paul at Athens; 6. Burning of the magic books at Ephesus; 7. Agrippa; 8. Shipwreck at Melita. They narrowly cost Thornhill his life, but for the presence of mind of his attendant, who daubed one of the figures as the painter was stepping back to the edge of the scaffold to mark its effect. Mr. Gwyn, while taking measures on the exterior of the dome, slipped, and his life was saved by his boot catching in a piece of lead.

Bishop Berkeley's passage is too long for quotation, in which, while walking in St. Paul's, he meditates on the analogy between the building itself and the Christian Church, "the divine order and economy of the one emblematically set forth by the just plain majestic architecture of the other." A fly upon one of the pillars suggests the narrow glance of the freethinker; its prospect confined to a little part of one of the stones of a single pillar, "the joint beauty of the whole, or the distinct use of its parts, being inconspicuous."

Round the dome were hung some of the flags taken at Louisburgh, 1758; and at Valenciennes, by the Duke of York, 1793; and others captured by Howe, Nelson, Duncan, and Keith—

"Endless ensigns ravished from the foe—"

shaking out their shot-rent folds as though the breath of conquest again waved them into motion: they have been removed to Chelsea Hospital. "Destitute of all internal variety, decoration, splendour of colour," Von Raumer characterised this church as "a vast white solitude;" and Addison made his Indian princes believe that it was hewn out of a hill of stone. It looks indeed cold and poverty-stricken ; with a pompous ambitious grandeur, an imitation of a foreign original, without its internal completeness ; pretentious in style, but deprived of the gorgeous gilding, costly marbles and mosaics, which lend an appropriate and necessary splendour to its Italian prototype. The light wants to be subdued, warm colouring and decoration are absolutely required to enliven the chilliness of the interior ; the union of the sister arts to blend and harmonise the building with doubtful lights and a rich mysterious gloom. The present excellent bishop and accomplished dean have sanctioned enrichments under the care of Mr. Penrose. It is to be hoped that the east end will be rendered a prominent object. On October 1, 1773, the Royal Academy delegated Angelica Kauffmann, Sir Joshua Reynolds, Cipriani, Benjamin West, Dance, and James Barry, to fill the church with paintings and sculptures, but the primate, diocesan, and dean superstitiously refused their introduction. In consequence of this the intended east window was transferred to New College Chapel, Oxford, where it figures as the " Washy Virtues."

The organ, built by Bernard Schmidt at a cost of 2000*l.* in 1694, and repaired in 1802, stands on a Corinthian screen (for each pillar E. Strong received 52*l.*), with a Latin inscription to this effect, " Beneath is buried the architect of this church and city, Christopher Wren, who lived above ninety years, not for himself, but for the public good; if you inquire for his monument look around." How humiliating is the contrast this affected epitaph bears to the words that gird the dome of the eternal city— the charter of the Bride of Christ—perverted though they be in intention there, yet still the words of the Rock of Ages : " On this Rock will I build my church." A new organ is to be erected by Mr. Hill, at a cost of 2000*l.*

On each side of the CHOIR, opened December 2, 1697, are fifteen stalls, with the lord mayor's seat and the bishop's throne, carved by Grinling Gibbons with fruits and foliage in his exquisite manner; in fact there are three thrones, all alike, except in some minute minor details—a monstrous piece of absurdity. He received 1,333*l.* The east end terminates in an apse. The pulpit, designed by Mylne and carved by Wyatt, was set up in 1802. The brass lectern is an eagle, as if bearing the Bible into all lands upon its wings.

To St. Paul's, Queen Anne came in solemn thanksgiving for the victories of Marlborough, 1702, 1704; June 27, 1705; December 31, 1706; May 1, 1707; August 19, 1708; King William III. in 1697, for the peace of Ryswick; George III. on his accession, Jan. 20, 1761, and on his recovery, April 23, 1789; and again on December 19, 1797, for victories at sea; the Prince Regent, July 7, 1814; and Queen Caroline for her deliverance, November 29, 1820. The anniversary of the charity children in June has been pronounced the most imposing spectacle in the world. On this occasion trumpets and drums are employed to swell the choruses: it is the only instance remaining of the use of musical instruments to assist the organ, practised even in the reign of Charles II.

St. Peter's at Rome is 669 feet long, and to the top of the dome 432 feet high. The area of St. Peter's is 227,069; St. Mary's, Florence, 84,802; St. Paul's, 84,025 superficial feet; St. Sophia is 360 feet long. The great domes of Europe are of the following dimensions, external diameter and height from the ground line: St. Peter's, Rome, 139,330; St. Maria della Fiore, Florence, 139,310; St. Sophia, Constantinople, 115,201; St. Paul's, London, 112,215; The Pantheon, Rome, 142,143.

In the crypt, which extends under the whole church, rest side by side, under the dome, the great Duke of Wellington—in a mausoleum hewn out of a solid boulder of chocolate-coloured Luxulyan porphyry, which weighed 70 tons, and was polished on the Treffry estate at a cost of 1100*l.*—and the immortal Nelson, in a coffin made out of the mainmast of the " L'Orient," and in a marble sarcophagus made for Cardinal Wolsey. Here also are buried Lord Collingwood, Sir Thomas Picton, Earl of Rosslyn, Sir

Christopher Wren, Sir Joshua Reynolds, Dr. Boyce,
James Barry, 1806; John Opie, 1807; Benjamin West,
1820; Sir Thomas Lawrence, 1830; Lord Northesk, H.
Fuseli, R. Mylne, 1811; J. Rennie, 1821—the architects,
one of Waterloo the other of Blackfriars Bridge; and J.
M. W. Turner, 1851. In the Cathedral were buried Bishops
Brian Walton of Chester, Thomas Newton of Bristol, and
F. White of Ely.

In the crypt are the effigies of Sir N. Bacon, Sir Thomas
Heneage, and Sir Christopher Hatton, the bust of Dean
Colet, and the shrouded effigy of Dean Donne by Nicho-
las Stone, which were saved from the burning of the old
Cathedral.

The principal monuments are the following; most are
unworthy of a place in a Christian temple, and simply im-
pertinences, too ludicrous for grief or reverence :—

Captain Westcott, fell at the Nile, died 1798, cost 4200*l.* (T.
   Banks); General Crauford and General Mackinnon, fell at Ciudad
   Rodrigo, died 1812, cost 1200*l.* (Bacon); Lord St. Vincent, died
   1823, cost 2100*l.* (Baily); Admiral Sir Pulteney Malcolm, died
   1838 (Baily).

North Transept.—Lord Rodney, died 1794, 6300*l.* (C. Rossi); Sir T.
   Picton, fell at Waterloo, 3150*l.*, buried here 1859 (Gahagan); Gen.
   Hay, fell before Bayonne, 1814, 1575*l.* (H. Hopper); Gen. Dundas,
   died 1794, 3150*l.* (Bacon); Gen. Hoghton (Chantrey); Col. Sir W.
   Myers (Kendrick), fell at Albuera, 1811—each cost 1575*l.*; Gen.
   Mackenzie and Langworth, fell at Talavera, 1809, 2100*l.* (Manning); Gen. Gore and Skerrett, fell at Bergen-op-Zoom, 1814, cost
   2,800*l.* (Chantrey); Sir W. Ponsonby, fell at Waterloo, 3150*l.*
   (E. H. Baily); Lord Duncan, died 1804, conqueror at Camperdown,
   2100*l.* (Westmacott); Capt. Mosse and "gallant good" Riou, fell
   at Copenhagen, 1801, 4200*l.* (C. Rossi).

N. E. Ambulatory.—Gen. Bowes, died 1812 (Chantrey); Gen. Le
   Marchant, died 1812 (C. Rossi); each 1575*l.*—they fell at Sala-
   manca.

N. Aisle.—Dr. Samuel Johnson, died 1784, 1575*l.* (J. Bacon).

Choir Arch.—Marquess Cornwallis, Governor-General of India, died
   1805, 6300*l.* (C. Rossi); Capt. J. Cooke, died 1805 (Westmacott);
   Duff, (Bacon); each 1575*l.*—they fell at Trafalgar; Lord Nelson,
   died 1805, 6300*l.* (Flaxman).

S. E. Aisle.—Bishop Heber, died 1826 (Chantrey).

South Aisle.—Gen. Sir T. Jones, R.E., died 1794 (Behnes); John Howard, the philanthropist, the first statue erected in St. Paul's—" He trod an open but unfrequented path to immortality." (J. Bacon).

S. E. Ambulatory.—Gen. Ross, fell at Baltimore, died 1814, 1575*l.* (J. Kendrick); Col. Hon. H. Cadogan, fell at Vittoria, 1813, 1575*l.* (Chantrey).

South Transept.—Lord Howe, conqueror June 1, died 1799, 6300*l.*; (Flaxman); Lord Collingwood, died 1810, 4200*l.* (Westmacott); Lord Heathfield, the defender of Gibraltar, died 1790, 2100*l.* (Rossi); Gen. Hon. Sir E. Pakenham, fell at New Orleans, 1815; Gen. S. Gibbs, 2100*l.* (Westmacott); Gen. Gillespie, fell at Kalunga, 1814, 1575*l.* (Chantrey); Sir John Moore, the hero of Corunna, died 1809, 4200*l.* (Bacon); Sir Ralph Abercrombie, died 1801, of his wounds received at Alexandria, 6300*l.* (Westmacott); Capt. Sir W. Hoste, R.N., died 1829 (T. Campbell); Sir Astley Cooper, died 1842 (E. Baily); Capt. Burgess, R.N., fell at Camperdown, 5210*l.* (Banks); Capt. Faulkner, R.N., fell in action with La Pique, 1795 (C. Rossi); Capt. Miller, R.N., fell at the Nile (Flaxman); Capt. G. N. Hardinge, killed in action with La Piedmontaise, 1808 (C. Manning); Dr. Babington, died 1833 (Behnes); Gen. Sir J. Brock, fell at Queenstown, 1812 (Westmacott).

Nave.—Bishop Middleton, (Lough); Sir William Jones, died 1794, (J. Bacon); Sir Joshua Reynolds died 1792 (Flaxman); Capt. M. Lyons, R.N., died of wounds received before Sebastopol (Noble). The memorial of the Coldstream Guards, by Marochetti, with the flags of the regiment.

DIMENSIONS OF THE CATHEDRAL IN FEET.

	Length.	Breadth.	Height.
Nave	212	102	
Choir	147	..	100
Transept	223	126	
The Cross (dome, outer diameter)	145 inner 108		365
W. Towers	..	..	220
Extreme length	462	..	..
W. front	..	180	180

The Chapter is composed of a dean and four canons, there are twelve minor canons, six lay-vicars, and twelve choristers. There are two daily choral services, at a quarter to 10 and half-past 3, and a weekly celebration of the Holy Communion. The capitular revenue in 1852 was 12,746*l.*, and the expenditure, within fourteen previous years, on the fabric, 8000*l.*

Arms: Gules, two swords in saltier ppr. in chief the letter D or.

The CHAPTER-HOUSE is on the north side of the yard. The stair-foot money, established by Jennings, the carpenter, 1707-11, for the relief of workmen injured in building the church, was the origin of the present admission fee.

Among the bishops occur—Wina, who purchased the mitre, and was the first simonist in the English church; St. Erkenwald, the patron saint of the see; William the good bishop, to whose tomb the mayor and citizens went in annual procession, in grateful acknowledgment of charters and privileges obtained through his influence; Roger, who died from eating poisoned grapes; Foliot, who defied pope and primate, the first bishop who had a canonical translation—loud and insubordinate before he gained the mitre, silent after; Fitzwalter and Fitzneale, who wrote on the Exchequer, the latter being, like Falconberg, Lord Treasurer; Roger Black, who defied a king when tyrannical; Fulke Basset, who said, "My mitre, pope and sovereign, stronger than I, may remove unjustly, my helmet will remain;" de Wengham and Chichele and Baldock and Waldon, Lord Chancellors; de Bynteworth, and Braybrooke and Clifford, Lord Keepers; Sudbury, massacred by a London mob; Courtenay, Lord Chancellor; Bubwith, Lord Treasurer; Warham; gentle-hearted Tonstal; Stokesley and Bonner, whose names are written in blood; Ridley, who died in the flames at Oxford with heroic courage; Aylmer, whom Elizabeth threatened to fit for heaven, to walk thither without his staff and leave his mantle behind him; Fletcher, whom she suspended because he dared to marry; Vaughan, who believed in exorcism; Laud, Juxon, and Sheldon; Henchman, who aided King Charles to escape after the battle of Worcester; Compton, who put on uniform and jack-boots, and talked more like a colonel than a clerk; Robinson, Lord Privy Seal, the last bishop who held a civil office of state; learnèd

Gibson, whom his enemies called the "English Pope;" Sherlock, Pope's " plunging prelate," and Bentley's Cardinal Alberoni; Lowth, who refused the primacy; and Porteus, who suppressed Sunday entertainments. Among the dignitaries, &c., are found Colet, founder of St. Paul's school; Nowel, Donne, Barwick, W. Sherlock, and Milman; three cardinals; Francis, archbishop of Constantinople, bishops Hodgkin of Bedford and Young of Callipolis, Ralph de Diceto, Peter de Blois, Adam Murimuth, Polydore Vergil, John Harpsfield, Jortin, Waterland, Calfhill, Joseph Warton, W. Beloe, R. Nares, R. Tyrwhitt, W. Crowe, Paley, J. Davison, Sydney Smith, and Barham (Ingoldsby).

The old Cathedral of St. Paul in 1309 was of the following dimensions : 629 feet in total length; the transept, finished A.D. 1256, was 130 feet long; the NAVE, completed A.D. 1283, was 102 feet in height.; and the CHOIR, of the date 1252, 188 feet in length; while the STEEPLE, completed A.D. 1221, was 534 feet high, the tower being 260 feet, and the spire 274 feet high. Inigo Jones added a classic portico, 200 feet by 50 and 40 feet high, set between TWO WESTERN TOWERS. It was commenced by Bishop Maurice, 1087-1107; and Bishop Niger repaired it after a great fire, January 1135. It was composed of a nave, transept and choir, a presbytery and Lady Chapel, each with aisles, the end being square; and the vaulting of the same height. The east aisle of the transept was occupied by chantries. On the south-west side of the nave was St. Gregory's church, to the west of the south transept was a small but beautiful double CLOISTER of two open alleys, one above and one below, with an exquisite CHAPTER-HOUSE in the centre. The choir had a superb east marigold window. The CENTRAL TOWER was remarkable for its lofty triplets of lancets and eight flying buttresses, two at each angle of an unique form. The undercroft was St. Faith's Church.

Several interesting associations were connected with the church. King John of France offered at St. Erkenwald's shrine; King Henry III., on the Feast of St. Paul's conversion, gave 1500 tapers to the church and fed 15,000 poor in the garth. St. Baude, in lieu of twenty-two acres, bequeathed a fat doe in winter, and a buck in summer, which was received at the altar crowned with roses, by the Chapter annually, till the reign of Queen Elizabeth. Even in Queen Mary's reign the choir, on great festivals, sang anthems after vespers high up in the spire. In it, in 1299, Baldock cursed all who had searched for a hoard of gold in St. Martin's le Grand. From the altar the mob tore Walter de Stapledon, bishop of Exeter, and beheaded him at Cheapside Cross, Oct. 15, 1326. In 1458 the Duke of York, leading Queen Margaret, and a Yorkist leader hand in hand with a Lancastrian, came in procession hither to pretend a hollow reconciliation. In it Richard III. appointed the supple Doctor Barnes to hail him king as he entered, but the duke was delayed, and the preacher had to repeat his oracular witness, to the amusement of his audience. In it Jane Shore did penance ; in it Wycliffe was tried for his doctrines, 1376 ; and at its altar Dean Colet's boy-bishop ministered till the Reformation was accomplished. At PAUL'S CROSS, Bishop Fisher February 14, 1538, exposed the famous Rood of Grace, from Boxley Abbey ; and from his attendance there as a preacher, Richard Hooker dated the miseries of his married life. On Sept. 8, 1559, were celebrated the commemorative obsequies of Henry II. of France—the only time such a service has been observed since the Reformation. In 1600 Bankes and his famous horse mounted to the top; and a similar feat at Rome cost him his life as a magician.

So early as 1400, Bishop Baldock excommunicated all who made its aisles a thoroughfare; in the reign of Philip and Mary the Common Council ordered that henceforth no cattle, porters or hucksters, should pass through it. In 1569 the first lottery known in England was drawn at the west door. Yet Bishop Earles tells us of its thronged Paul's Walk—remarkable as the fashionable lounge and merchants' change ; where the domestic stood to be hired at the serving-man's log, as Bardolph by Falstaff, and

every serjeant-at-law had his pillar to hear clients; and
infamous for rufflers, quacks, ballad-mongers, masked women, stale knights, and captains out of service, as Captain
Bobadil in Jonson's play. Bishop Hall satirizes the pro-
fane use of the East Alley with the Si Quis door for
advertisements; Decker says the south alley was for
usurers, the north for simony, the horse-fair in the midst,
and the font for the payment of money. On the base of
one of the pillars was sculptured the foot of Algar, the
first prebendary of Islington, as the standard measure for
legal contracts in land, just as Henry I., Richard I., and
King John furnished the iron ell by their arms.

Its bell-tower had been gambled away by Henry VIII.
to a dissolute knight; its Chapter-house and cloister, with
its Machabre or dance of death, had been destroyed by
Somerset the Protector; in June 1665, it was used as
a magazine of arms in the civil wars; in the plague-year
as a pest-house, and three hundred pallets filled the aisles.

> A phantom form three several nights appeared,
> Sitting upon a cloud-built throne of state
> Right o'er St. Paul's Cathedral. On that throne
> At the dead hour of night he took his seat,
> And, monarch-like, stretched out his mighty arm
> That shone like lightning. In that kingly motion
> There seemed a steadfast threatening, and his features,
> Gigantic 'neath their shadowy diadem,
> Frowned, as the phantom vowed within his heart
> Perdition to the city.

In September 1666, it was destroyed by the Great Fire:
with the tombs of Kings Seba and Ethelred; Lacy Earl of
Lincoln, 1310, from whose house Lincoln's Inn derives its
name; John of Gaunt; the Duchess of Bedford; Dean
Nowell; Sir Philip Sidney, 1586; Sir Francis Walsingham,
1590; Sir Christopher Hatton, the position of whose ponderous tomb caused Stow's epigram—

> Philip and Francis have no tomb,
> For great Sir Christopher takes all the room;

Lynacre the physician, 1524; Sir Nicholas, father of the

great Bacon, 1579; William Lily, 1522; and Vandyke, 1641.
One monument, that of Sir John Beauchamp, who died
1358, was mistaken for Duke Humphrey's tomb, so that
dinnerless loungers were said to dine with that prince.
Cromwell's horses were stabled in the aisles. Books to
the value of 150,000*l.* were burned in the crypt of St.
Faith's when the Cathedral was destroyed.

> Nor could thy fabric, Paul's! defend thee long,
> Though thou wert sacred to thy Maker's praise,
> Though made immortal by a poet's song,
> And poets' songs the Theban walls could raise.
> The daring flames peeped in and saw from afar
> The awful beauties of the sacred choir;
> But since it was profaned by civil war,
> Heaven thought it fit to have it purged by fire.

There are several ancient buildings worthy of a visit.
The choir of the Priory church of *St. Bartholomew the
Great*, Smithfield, built by Prior Rahere, the minstrel, in
1102; the entrance-gate is Early English. In Middlesex
Passage are remains of the crypt and refectory. In *St.
Giles', Cripplegate*, are buried Milton, Speed, Fox and
Frobisher. In *St. Giles'-in-the-Fields* are buried Chapman,
Lord Herbert of Cherbury, Shirley, R. l'endrell, Sir R.
L'Estrange, and Andrew Marvell. St. Etheldreda's or *Ely
Chapel*, Holborn, built over a crypt, has a fine door and
large Decorated east window. Windows of the same
period light the Dutch conventicle, formerly the *Chapel
of the Austin Friars*. *St. Helen's, Bishopsgate*, a Benedictine
Priory church, retains some fine 15th and 16th century
brasses, the nuns' stalls, and the effigies of Sir J. and
Dame A. Crosby, who built, in 1466, the adjoining Crosby
Hall, 54 ft. by 27 ft., and 54 ft. high, with its superb chestnut
roof. The porch of *St. Sepulchre's, Snow Hill*, is of the
middle of the 15th century. The Perpendicular *Gate-house*
of the Hospital of the Knights of *St. John* in Clerkenwell,
was long the abode of "Sylvanus Urban." For the
church of *St. Mary Overye*, see Walcott's "MINSTERS" in
this series. *St. Mary's, Lambeth*, recently restored, was built
1347; the north aisle 1504, the south aisle in 1505, the

Howard and Leigh Chapels in 1522. On the retention of the figure of a Pedlar, a rebus on a benefactor named J. Chapman, in the window depends the tenure of certain lands. Here are buried Ashmole, Dollond, and Archbishops Parker, Tenison, Secker, and Bishop Thirlby. *St. Mary le Savoy* was built in 1505, the roof was blazoned by Willement in 1843, the altar-screen restored by Smirke. G. Douglas, translator of Virgil, and G. Wither are buried here. *St. John's* in the *White Tower* was built by Bishop Gundulph, 1078. In *St. Peter's-ad-Vincula*, mostly Perpendicular, were buried Queen Anne Boleyn, Queen Catherine Howard, Sir T. More, John Duke of Northumberland, Cromwell and Devereux Earls of Essex, Lady Jane Grey, the Duke of Monmouth, Lords Kilmarnock, Balmerino, and Lovat. There are also the effigies of Sir R. Cholmondeley and Sir R. Blount of the 16th century. *St. Mary's, Temple*, has a choir, Early English, 86 ft. by 59 ft., dedicated 1540, and a round vestibule 59 ft. high and 69 ft. in diameter, consecrated 1185, by the Patriarch Heraclius. There are only three other round churches in England—at Northampton, Cambridge and Maplestead. The Templars built this church after the form of that of the Holy Sepulchre at Jerusalem; it is significant that a circular shape was adopted in early times for baptisteries and that great building. The architecture is Transitional Norman. The triforium of the round church consists of interlaced arches; the clerestory of six windows filled with glass; on the staircase is a penitential cell, in which Walter le Bachelor, grand preceptor of Ireland, was starved to death. On the pavement are freestone effigies of Knight Templars and Crusaders, restored by Richardson; they include Geoffry, Earl of Essex, 1114; William 1219, William 1231, Gilbert 1241, Earls of Pembroke; and Robert Lord de Ros, 1245. This part was formerly used by lawyers to receive their clients. The floor is laid with Minton's tiles. The choir, of three alleys, is Early English, and lit with triplets. It was restored by Savage and S. Smirke in 1839-42. The organ, by Schmidt, was the cause of a year-long contention on the merits of their respective instruments by Schmidt and Harris, when Judge Jeffries decided in favour of the former. Harris's organ was divided between St. Andrew's, Holborn, and Christ Church, in Dublin. The vault is painted with Eastern arabesques in polychrome. The stall-work is modern; the glazing by Willement. At the west end are painted rude effigies of the three first Henries, Richard I., and John. Here are the monuments of Bishop Eversden of Carlisle, died 1255; an effigy of Selden, 1654; Hooker; and Lord Thurlow, (died 1806,) by Rossi, in the choir; and in the triforium those of Plowden, Howell, and Gibbon. Hooker, Gibson, and Sherlock were masters of the Temple. The choral service on Sundays at 11 and 3 is of remarkable excellence. The great gate is Jacobean; the cloisters are by Wren. Beaumont and Cooper, Littleton, Coke, and Selden, were members of the Inner Temple.

Middle Temple Hall, 100 ft. by 40 ft. and 60 ft. high, was built 1562-72. It has a fine timber roof, pictures of Charles I. by Vandyke, Charles II., James II., Queen Anne, William of Orange, and George II., and busts of Lords Eldon and Stowell, by Behnes. Goldsmith and Dr. Johnson lived in this Inn of Court, which claims among its members Sir W. Raleigh, Ford, Wycherley, Congreve, and Southerne; Plowden, Lord Clarendon, Somers, Ashburton, and Stowell; Sir W. Blackstone, Burke, and Sheridan.

The gate-house of *Lincoln's Inn* was built by Sir T. Lovell, K.G., 1578; the doors were set up 1564; the Old Hall, 71 ft. by 32 ft., was erected 1506, and its screen 1565. The chapel was built 1621-3, by Inigo Jones, above an open crypt, but the windows are Perpendicular. The glass is Flemish, the stalls are Jacobean. Donne, Usher, Tillotson, Warburton, Hurd, and Heber have been preachers here, and Fortescue, Sir T. More, Lambard, Spelman, and Selden occur among its members. The chapel-bell was brought from Cadiz by Lord Essex.

The *White Tower*, N. and S. 176 ft. by 96 ft. E. and W., in the *Tower of London*, the prison of King John of France, was built by Bishop Gundulph, 1098, and repaired in the 13th century. The stone walls were added by Bishop Longchamp, 1190. The entrance is by the S.W. or Middle Tower, and under the Byward Tower; the South Tower is St. Thomas', with Traitors' Gate below it. On the S.E. are Cradle, Well, and Iron-Gate Towers. In the Inner Ward, on the west, are Bell, S.W., tower, the prison of Bishop Fisher and the Princess Elizabeth; the Beauchamp Tower, the prison of Lady Jane Grey, Dudley Earl of Leicester, and Raleigh, with the walls traced with devices of the poor prisoners; on the N.E. is Martin Tower, the prison of the "Seven Bishops;" on the E. are Broad Arrow Tower, and Saltpetre Tower, a circular tower with a dungeon; on the S., facing St. Thomas's Tower, are the Record and Bloody Tower, the latter infamous for the murders of George Duke of Clarence and the Boy Princes; the gateway is of the time of Edward III. The other towers have been modernized, or destroyed by the Ordnance. Among the prisoners in the Tower occur Bishop Flambard, King John Baliol, Charles of Blois, and the twelve citizens of Calais; Chaucer, Duke of Orleans, 1415, the poet-Earl of Surrey, Cranmer, Ridley, and Latimer, Bacon and Coke, Earl of Strafford, Laud and Hall, and Jeremy Taylor, Sir J. Harrington, Pepys, Lord W. Russell and Algernon Sidney, Duke of Monmouth, Judge Jeffries, Penn, Duke of Marlborough, Sir R. Walpole, Atterbury, Wilkes, and Lord George Gordon. The Armoury contains a fine collection of English armour, from 1450 to 1685; Greek, Chinese, Mogul, Italian and German armour; and in Queen Elizabeth's armoury is a curious collection of Tudor arms and Spanish instruments of torture, and oriental arms. Some Tudor cannon lie in front of the White Tower.

Lambeth Palace has a Great Hall or Library, 93 ft. by 38 ft., built by Archbishop Juxon; the Gate-house by Archbishop Morton in 1490, the Lollards' Tower by Archbishop Chichele in 1434, with a prison 15 ft. by 11 ft. and 8 ft. high. The Chapel, mainly Early English, built by Archbishop Boniface, 1262, and a crypt of the same date; the Guard-chamber, 58 ft. by 27 ft., with a fine Perpendicular roof, and portraits of Laud by Vandyke, Herring by Hogarth, Secker by Reynolds, Sutton by

Beechey, Howley by Shee. In the Picture Gallery, built by Cardinal Pole, is a portrait of Tillotson by Beale. The collection of MSS. and early printed books is very valuable.

There are several crypts remaining : one Norman under Bow Church ; one of the 14th century at Garraway's Coffee House ; one at the Guildhall, built 1411 ; one Norman at St. James' or Lamb's Chapel, Monkwell Street ; one under Leather-Sellers' Hall, and that of St. Stephen's, Westminster, built by Edward I. in 1292.

Salisbury.

GAY, in his Epistle to Lord Burlington, apostrophises Salisbury—

> Who can forsake your walls, and not admire
> Your proud cathedral and its lofty spire ?

No two neighbouring cathedrals can be more dissimilar than those of Winchester and Salisbury. The one grave massive, solemn, awe-inspiring, a patriarch not yet weary, with years ; the other queenly, aspiring, unearthly, a very poem graven in stone. It is full of suggestive thought to stand on the shapeless heaps of the Norman keep, now even with the ground, of the dead city, where the sheep feed and sleep above the turf which overlies the altars of Old Sarum, and looking over the deep fosse of the Roman and the half-buried fortifications of Alfred, across the faint lines of the mother-church, drawn by the summer heat on the corn-field—to see the fairer daughter lift her pale spire high among the sailing clouds, which capriciously fleck it with fleeting shadows, herself embosomed among the trees. In 1834 the intense heat showed the dimensions—a nave 150 ft. by 72 ft., a transept 150 ft. by 60 ft., and a choir 60 ft. in length, in all 270 ft. The coarse jeers of the Norman garrison, the despotism of the

governor, combined with the bleak air and narrow space
of the enclosure, determined the monks to remove to a
kindlier shelter. In the year 1220, Pandulph, the papal
legate, laid the first stone of the new church in Merrifield,
on April 28, to the great joy of the canons, who compared
their late residence to "the ark of God shut up in the
temple of Baalim," or set "beneath the tower of Siloam."
The old legend says that the site was determined by the
fall of an arrow in Merrifield, shot by a stalwart archer
from the ramparts of Old Sarum.

Sear-byrig, "the dry city," has lost the significance of
its appellation in New Sarum. The streams of the Avon
and Bourne ripple along in sparkling channels, cut in
1338, by the side of the streets, which are laid out in
squares, as at Old Winchelsea and Chichester. It is
situated in a green vale, among the breezy downs, extending bare and unenclosed for miles upon miles. Pepys,
in his journey from Hungerford, records that he rode many
a league by the distant spire, which was probably designed
as a landmark over their monotonous and almost track-
less extent. "An instinctive taste," observes Coleridge,
" teaches men to build their churches in flat countries with
spire steeples, which, as they cannot be referred to any other
object, point as with silent finger to the sky and stars, and
sometimes, when they reflect the brazen light of a rich
though rainy sunset, appear like a pyramid of flame burning
heavenward." Addison was educated in the grammar-school.
James Harris (Hermes), Henry Lawes, P. Massinger, Pitt
Earl of Chatham, and John of Salisbury, Bishop of Chartres,
were natives of the city;—which has been honoured with
the following royal visits: Henry III., 1258; Henry VI.
1457; Edward IV., 1478; Henry VII., 1486; Henry VIII.,
1516, 1535; James I., 1608, and on seven other occasions;
Charles I., 1625, 1635; James II., 1688; George I., 1722;
George III. and Queen Charlotte, 1778; and Queen Victoria. Parliament sat here 1297 and 1328. In honour
of the staple manufacture, the cathedral is said to be built
upon wool-packs. Henry Duke of Buckingham was beheaded opposite the Saracen's Head in 1483. There are

several objects of interest in the city: the chief are an old hostelry, formerly the George Inn, where Pepys lodged, in High Street, a good 15th century timber house, with an outer gallery; a distemper painting of the Adoration of the Three Kings is in a house in New Street; the banqueting-hall of John Hall, a merchant of the staple, of the 15th century, with a fine timber roof, and stained glass of the time of Edward IV. or Henry VI., on the canal, built 1470, and restored by Pugin; Audley House, in Crane Street, is of the latter part of the 15th century, with a gate-house and bay-window; in Brown Street is a house with rich stone chimney-pieces; and a market cross of the 14th century, erected by an Earl of Salisbury by way of penance, at which, according to custom, the vicar of Malmesbury had to flog nine poachers, stripped to a single garment of linen, and doing penance for two days, having stolen Bishop Mortival's bucks at Ramsbury; some portions of the hospitals of St. Nicholas and Vaux, near Harnham Bridge, founded 1227; the Early English chancel and brass lectern of St. Martin's church, and St. Thomas, (30 ft. by 70 ft., in which is the tomb of the Duke of Buckingham, beheaded at Salisbury 1483,) and St. Edmund's, Perpendicular. Dahl's picture of Queen Anne and Hoppner's portrait of an Earl of Radnor are in the Guildhall, built 1788-1795. The whole appearance of the town is light and cheerful.

In the Close, which occupies an extent of half a square mile, there are the king's house, a palace of Richard II., and the royal wardrobe. There are three gates, the South or Harnham, the East or St. Anne's, and the Close or North, with a statue of Henry III., built, like the walls, between 1327 and the accession of Richard II. The Cathedral possesses every advantage of site and space. The ample sward and magnificent trees give it effect and importance: an uninterrupted view is obtained on every side. On the north-east side it affords the best prospect of a cathedral in England, fortunate in its site and in its solitude. Upon the delighted observer, whether it is bathed in sunshine or capriciously lit up on a moonlight night, its beautiful

symmetry of outline, its fine dimensions, consummate
unity of effect, incomparable disposition of parts, its
exquisite grace and simplicity, its uniformity of architecture in the purest period—the spring season of the
art—and unrivalled spire, like a soaring pyramid of silver,
inlaid with diamond fret-work, and touched with points of
pearl, produce an indelible impression.

> The heaven was so darkly blue, the sun so full and glowing bright,
> When rose the Minster's stately pile, expanding in the golden light;
> Seemed the cloud resplendently, like wings to bear it up alway,
> And on the blessed depths of heaven, its spired tower to melt away.

The ground-plan of the Cathedral is perfect, embracing
a NAVE of ten bays, with aisles; a NORTHERN PORCH; a
MAIN and a CHOIR TRANSEPT of four and three bays each,
with an aisle once containing chapels; to the east, a CHOIR
and PRESBYTERY, each of three bays, and LADY CHAPEL, all
having aisles. A CLOISTER is on the south side, and on
the eastward of it the CHAPTER-HOUSE. An octangular
MUNIMENT ROOM is to the south of the south-east transept.
It is entirely built of Chilmark stone, quarried about
fifteen miles from the city. Its pyramidal disposition
externally at once strikes the eye. The only ancient cathedral completed on a uniform and well-arranged plan, and
in one style, it seems to have sprung into being at once,
clean and perfect.

> Beautiful queen! unlike thy high compeers,
> Thou wast not cradled in the lap of years;
> But like celestial Pallas, hymned of old,
> Thy sovran form, inviolate, and bold,
> Sprung to the perfect zenith of its prime,-
> And took no favour from the hand of Time.

On Sept. 29, 1225, the first service was celebrated in the
new Cathedral of St. Mary of Sarum, a church in a style
hitherto unequalled, and which no generation perhaps shall
see surpassed, when Archbishop Langton consecrated it.
Bishop Poore, 1217-28, its founder, was translated to display his architectural talents in the northern diocese of

Durham. Elias de Dereham was clerk of the works.
Bishops Bingham, 1229-47, William of York, 1247-56, and
Giles of Bridport, 1256-63, continued the erection of the
fabric, which, after a cost of 40,000 marks, or about
26,666*l.* sterling, was consecrated Sept. 30, 1258, by Archbishop Boniface. In the episcopate of Walter de la Wyle,
1263-70, the CLOISTERS and CHAPTER-HOUSE were completed. The TOWER, from within a short distance of the
ridge of the roof, was built by Bishop Wyville, who succeeded 1329, in the best period of the Decorated style.
The SPIRE, begun in 1335 by Nicholas de Portland, was
completed in 1375 by Richard de Farleigh, the architect
of the abbeys of Bath and Reading. Bishop Beauchamp
1450-82, built the BEAUCHAMP CHAPEL, now destroyed, on
the south side of the Lady Chapel, and the great hall in
the palace. Bishop Audley, 1502-24, built the CHANTRY
CHAPEL on the north side of the choir. The CHANTRY OF
LORD HUNGERFORD, now destroyed, was built 1476. The
CLOCHARD, which stood on the north-west of the church,
had a peal of eight bells.

The WEST FRONT is composed of a screen of the highest
beauty. No verbal description, however minute, could
convey any impression of its intricate and minute composition. The principal bay is composed of a steep gable,
with an arcade of two couplets, with chevron mouldings
and quatrefoils in circles above each pair, and the upper
lozenge-shaped spandril is filled with a foliated aureole.
Below an intervening quatrefoiled band are three tall
lancets, shafted and with chevron mouldings, the central
the highest; beneath them is a canopied arcade of trefoiled arches, which surmounts three pedimented deeply-
recessed porches, the middle forming the chief entrance.
Two similar porches are in either face of the lateral
screen, which is sculptured with four arcades of lancet
arches from the base to the parapet; the square towers
on either angle are arcaded, terminate in pinnacles,
and are crowned with spires. There is a quatrefoiled
band above the line of the triforium; the gabled buttresses are niched, and retain their statues; couplets light

the aisle and triforium. On the north side is a lofty PORCH, richly arcaded within, and having a parvise above, in no way inferior to its competitor at Hereford. The gable is crocketed and set between shafted turrets terminating in spires. The aisles throughout the whole extent of the buildings are lighted by couplets in each bay ; the clerestory is in triplets of lancets, and a graceful open parapet and a trefoiled corbel table surround the whole church. Dr. Heylyn notes the curious calculation that there are in the church as many windows as days, pillars as hours, and gates as months in a year. The superiority of the early masonry over succeeding styles is very perceptible—with such close joints as if the fabric were but of one stone. The TOWER is of three stories at the crossing of the great transept. Four canopied two-light windows, trefoiled with a quatrefoil in the head, fill each face in the two upper tiers, divided by buttresses and mullions, and enriched with tracery and niches. At each angle is an octangular turret crowned with a short crocketed spire. The octangular SPIRE springs from the midst of four pinnacles, with canopied spire-lights to the points of the compass : three rich quatrefoiled bands divide it; and the angles, with their ball-flower ornaments beaded on the sides, give a slightly broken outline against the sky. It is 24½ inches out of the perpendicular on the south, and 16¾ inches on the west ; but it was braced with iron by Sir Christopher Wren, and no perceptible further settlement has been observed since 1681. The flying buttresses on the south side of the CHOIR were built by Bishop Beauchamp 1450-81. During the Whitsun holidays it was, years ago, the custom for daring spirits among the town's people to ascend the spire to some height; but when an adventurous lad, during the visit of George III., mounted by the iron rings—the only mode of ascent for the forty-two upper feet—and stood on his head on the capstone, the king very properly refused to give him any reward, saying he was bound to provide for the lives of his people. Great skill and boldness are evinced in the curious and ingenious timber-framing within the spire. The number of niches—many of them emptied of their statues—which decorate the exterior of the church have been calculated at 160. On the west front there were 123.

The fronts of the MAIN and CHOIR TRANSEPTS consist of four arcades, a triplet in the base tier, three two-light windows, with a quatrefoil in the head in the second stage: in the MAIN TRANSEPT then occurs an arcade of six lancets under a quatrefoil: in the gable, are two 2-light windows, each with a quatrefoil, and under a foliated circle. In the CHOIR TRANSEPT the gable is filled with a triplet, above four lancets with a quatrefoil included under a pointed arch.

The east part of the CHOIR consists of a steep gable set between two octangular turrets with lofty spires ; an arcade of seven lancets, the central triplet being windows, fills the space above the string-course. In the choir aisles the east end has in the base tier a triplet ; in the gable a triplet in an arcade of five lancets. In the east end of the LADY CHAPEL the composition is similar, but the gable is crocketed, the upper triplet is set under a pointed arch between two trefoiled niches ; the aisles have single lancets below, and a trefoiled couplet under a quatrefoiled circle in the upper story.

The piers of the NAVE of ten bays are of four clustered columns, with as many shafts, of Purbeck marble : one large column, the single centre of animation, strength, and unity, girt by lesser shafts, bound fast together, one inseparable company. The triforium is of four trefoiled arches in each bay, in couplets, with a quatrefoil in the head ; the clerestory is of triplets of lancets ; the vaulting is plain ; a chevron-moulding ornaments each of the lower arches. In the NORTH MAIN TRANSEPT are a double aumbry and a lavatory; in the SOUTH TRANSEPT there are a double aumbry and double piscina. Time, while it slowly destroys, if it removes the sharpness of outline, adds a dignity to the mass; the changes which deface the memorials cannot evaporate the spirit which created them.

> There is a charm about the building—
> Deceived by its gigantic elegance,
> Vastness which grows, but grows to harmonize,
> All musical in its immensities.

Unhappily James Wyatt the Destructive has made a wreck of Salisbury, at the price of 26,000*l.* What years and fanatics had spared he utterly swept away. Horace Walpole was scandalized at his wholesale demolitions. Besides the obliteration of paintings on the roofs of the choir and choir transept, the Beauchamp, with its roof of Irish oak, and ,Hungerford chapels, on either side of the LADY CHAPEL (their fragments now form the organ screen), the reredos, two north and south porches, the screens of nine chapels in the transept, and the detached ancient BELFRY on the north-west side of the church, were utterly hewn down. The ancient monuments were removed, and set in two formal rows down the NAVE; and the LADY CHAPEL, which is divided by three lancet arches under a triplet from the PRESBYTERY, thrown into it by the removal of the screen in 1789-90. The visitor, however, may take advantage of these series of sculptures of the middle ages, and observe the serene graceful attitude, the vertical sweeping draperies of the lady, the chastened countenance of the ecclesiastic, the impetuous knight or resolute crusader, his hand upon the sword-hilt, only to turn away with contempt or pity from the hideous tablets and statues of recent times. Lord Radnor preserved all the iron-work of these tombs, and arranged it round his pew on the site of the Hungerford chapel.

A remarkable feature is presented by the four-centred BUTTRESSING ARCHES under the TOWER built by Nicholas Wayte, in 1415 : similar precautions have been rendered necessary at Canterbury, Wells, and Hereford ; but here the tower, six feet in thickness at the base, narrowed to walls only two feet solid at the summit, yet upon them the spire was erected. It was struck by lightning, June 1741. An east window, representing the Resurrection, once in the LADY CHAPEL, was designed by Sir Joshua Reynolds and painted by Egginton. In the CHOIR, the theatrical east window, by Pearson, after the designs of S. H. Mortimer, and the gift of Lord Radnor, represents the Brazen Serpent. In the west triplets of the NORTH MAIN TRANSEPT, the west windows of the NAVE, the east windows of the CHOIR aisles, and in the south windows of the MAIN TRANSEPT, are fragments of glass, Early English, set up 1240-80. The west triplet is filled with glass brought from Dijon during the French revolution. The church covers 55,000 square feet. The altar stood to the eastward of the CHOIR TRANSEPT, beneath the figure of the Saviour, within an aureole on the groin above. Bishop Ward renewed the stalls (the canopies are by Wyatt) and laid down the marble floor in the choir. The poppy-heads, fleurs-de-lys of the bench-ends, are of the date of Henry VII. From the neighbouring parsonage of Bemerton, George Herbert came usually twice every week on certain appointed days to the service, and would say at his return that "his time spent in prayer and cathedral music elevated his soul and was his heaven upon earth." The organ, by Green, 1792, was contributed by George III. as "the subscription of a Berkshire gentleman." The church is rendered interesting by the fact that the Sarum Costumale, instituted by Bishop Osmund in 1077, formed the standard order of musical service; and to this day the bishops are styled the precentors of the Episcopal College. Its missal, by the same author, held a chief place in the south of England, while the Uses of York, Bangor, Hereford, and Lincoln, were observed in the north-west and eastern dioceses. In the muniment chamber are preserved an episcopal ring, a paten and chalice, and a wooden pastoral staff of the 13th century.

The CLOISTERS, repaired by Bishop Denison, are of considerable dimensions. The CHAPTER-HOUSE is octangular, supported by a central shaft; in the spandrils of the arcade are sculptures of Scripture subjects, from the Creation to the Exodus, restored by Philip. The Psychomachia of Prudentius, the battle of the Virtues and Vices, is represented in polychrome on the west door; and the story of Reynard the fox between the bases of the shafts of the central pillar. The iron ties are original. The building has been restored by H. Clutton, in 1856, as a memorial to Bishop Denison, and the roof painted by Hudson. It contains the original tiled floor, a chair of the time of Henry VI., and an ancient wooden table : over the east side of the cloister is the library, built by Bishop Jewel, and furnished with books by Bishop Gheast. The bishop's palace contains a series of portraits from Duppa to Burgess, a chapel and good tower, Early Perpendicular. The palace hall was built in 1460. In Mr. Wyndham's garden is the old doorway of the north transept.

The principal monuments are the following :—

Nave, N. Side from E. to W.—Sir John Chèney, standard-bearer at Bosworth, died 1509, effigy of alabaster; Walter, Lord Hungerford, altar-tomb; Bishop Osmond, altar-tomb; Hon. John de Montacute, who fought at Cressy, d. 1388, altar-tomb and effigy; William Longspée, first Earl of Salisbury, d. of poison 1220, altar-tomb and effigy; the chorister bishop, basso relievo, a miniature figure in episcopal vestments 13th century, found 1680 near the pulpit, perhaps the effigy of Bishop Wykehampton, d. 1284.

S. Side E. to W.—William Longspée, second Earl of Salisbury, a crusader, killed near Cairo 1250, buried at Acre, effigy; Bishop de la Wyle, d. 1270, effigy; Lord Stourton, hanged for murder with a silken halter (the privilege of a peer), 1556, at Salisbury, altar-tomb; Robert, Lord Hungerford, d. 1459, effigy of alabaster: Bishops Beauchamp, d. 1482, altar-tomb; Roger, d. 1139, basso relievo; Joscelyne, d. 1184, basso relievo.

Nave.—Edward Thomas Lord Wyndham of Finglass, d. 1745, (Rysbrach); Sir R. Colt Hoare (Lucas).

Main Transept, N. Wing.—Bishop Woodville, d. 1484, altar-tomb; Bishop Blythe, d. 1500, altar-tomb; Benson Earle and Walter and William Long (J. Flaxman); James Harris, author of Hermes (J. Bacon); the 1st Earl of Malmesbury (Chantrey). *S. Wing.*— Bishop Metford, d. 1407, effigy and canopy; Lieutenant Fisher, killed at Moodkee (Pugin).

N. Side Presbytery.—Bishop Audley, d. 1524, chantry; Bishop Bingham, d. 1247, under a canopied arch; a cadaver; the indent of the brass, a cross fleury with a demi-figure, is perhaps the most ancient extant in England. *S. Side.*—Bishop William of York, d. 1256, canopied arch.

Choir Transept, N. Wing.—Bishop Poore, d. 1241, altar-tomb and effigy of Purbeck marble; Bishop Wyville, d. 1375, incised brass, representing Sherborne Castle. Bishop Jewell is buried here. *S. Wing.*—Bishop Bridport, d. 1263, tomb, effigy, and small chantry, with biographical sculptures. Two memorial windows to 62nd Regiment, by O'Connor.

Lady Chapel. N. Aisle.—Sir T. Gorges, d. 1510, effigy; Bishop Mortival, d. 1375, slab with a floriated cross; Sir T. Mompesson, d. 1701, and dame, effigies; Bishop Capon, d. 1555, altar-tomb. *S. Aisle.*— Earl of Hertford, d. 1621, and his Countess, d. 1563, effigies; W. Wilton, Chancellor of Sarum, d. 1506, altar-tomb.

DIMENSIONS OF THE CATHEDRAL IN FEET.

	Length.	Breadth.	Height.
West Front	112	..	87
Nave	229	78	81
Choir	151f. 5in.	78	91
Main Transept	206	57	81
Choir Transept	145	44	81
Lady Chapel	69f. 5in.	37	40
Cloister	182	18	18
Chapter-house	diameter	58	53
Steeple	..	..	404
Total length	450	..	..

The Chapter is composed of a dean and four canons; two stalls were suspended. There are four vicars-choral, seven lay vicars, eight choristers. There are two daily choral services, at half-past 10 and 3; and a weekly administration of the Holy Communion. In fourteen years, previous to 1852, 10,000*l.* were spent on the fabric. The capitular revenues, 1852, amounted to 2539*l.* The library contains 2872 volumes, many valuable MS. service-books, a cotemporary MS. of Geoffrey of Monmouth, and a Gregorian Ritual with an Anglo-Saxon version.

Arms of the deanery: Az., the Blessed Virgin and Holy Child Jesus; in chief the letter D, sable.

Salisbury numbers among its bishops Osmund, the compiler of the famous Sarum Use; Roger the Chancellor, who won his mitre by singing a hunting mass quickly before Henry II.; Poore, the great architect; Wyville, who sent his champion clothed in white to try wager of battle with Montacute, Earl of Sarum, for Sherborne Castle; Waltham, Lord Chancellor; Cardinal Hallam ; Ayscough, whom Jack Cade, one of his tenants, murdered at Evenden ; Woodville, who died of sorrow at the downfall of his family ; Blyth, Master of the Rolls ; Cardinal Campeggio ; studious Jewell, whose pack provided him with venison ; Seth Ward, who could not refrain from a run with the beagles if he met them on the plain ; the Whig Burnet ; the troublesome Hoadly ; Sherlock ; Douglas, the friend of Goldsmith ; and the learned Burgess. Among the dignitaries, etc., occur eleven Cardinals, quaint Fuller, N. Spinkes, W. Lisle Bowles, and John Bampton, founder of the Bampton Lectures at Oxford.

Wells.

WITHIN a few miles of the Vale of Avalon, and the ruins of the Abbey of Glastonbury, "the town of the Glassy Isle," so called from the lake which surrounded it, within shelter of wavy hills, stands the Cathedral of St. Andrew at Wells, which derives its name from the ancient well in the bishop's garden, dedicated to that apostle. From each of the high-roads, the three glorious towers of the Cathedral, silver-grey in the distance, form a conspicuous object. With the magic of sun and shadow, the back-ground of harvest-field and meadow, bounded and girdled in by the blue hills, and a faint streak of sea far away, together with the stillness and repose, broken only by the sheep-bell, the peasant's song, and the hum of the summer-insect in the chalice of the wild flower, it forms a picture so dreamy and fairy-like, that we could almost fancy the fabric in its beauty would dissolve and float away like an autumn cloud. The Mendip Hills, bold and steep, some richly wooded, others bare and rugged, girdle the town ; and to the south is seen the High Tor, on which R. Whiting, the last devoted Abbot of Glastonbury, was hung by the savage Henry VIII., 1539. Savaric assumed the title of Bishop of Glastonbury, 1192-1218. Queen Anne visited the city in 1613. On Lansdowne, near Bath, still

remains the hostelry chapel of St. Lawrence, used by pilgrims to the minster. To this day, Wells alone, of English Cathedral towns, has preserved its ancient seclusion
and calm, which has continued unbroken for centuries.
Its quiet streets are divided into four verderies, quarters
once presided over by the verderers, or officers of assize, of
the bishop's forest of Mendip.

The ground-plan of the church, which is built of Doult
ing stone, a shelly limestone quarried seven miles from
Wells, is 'perfect. It consists of a NAVE of ten bays, with
aisles ; a TRANSEPT of two bays with aisles ; in the north
wing Holy Cross Chapel, in the south the chapels of St.
Calixtus and St. Martin ; and a CHOIR of six bays with
aisles ; a LADY CHAPEL of two bays, with aisles, once the
chapels on the north of St. Stephen, on the south of St.
Catharine, and two lateral chapels, which form an EASTERN
TRANSEPT—St. John's being to the south.

Bishop Jocelyn built the west front of the Cathedral
1206-44 ; he did not touch the nave. He dedicated the
church, Oct. 23, 1239. The CHOIR was originally square at
the end, with a processional path and Lady Chapel. The
NAVE, WEST FRONT, TRANSEPT, and a portion of the CHOIR, are
Early English, except that portion of the latter which was
elongated in the Decorated style, the three westernmost
arches being identical with the transept. The Early English part of the CENTRAL TOWER ends at the roof. The upper
part, Late Decorated with a mixture of Perpendicular,
was built 1318-21 : within fifteen years it began to settle,
and buttressing arches were added 1337-8. The stall-work
of the CHOIR was erected, 1325, of wood from Middleton,
each canon paying for his own seat. The church westward from the PRESBYTERY was consecrated as St. Andrew's,
October 23rd, 1239. Bishop Harewell, 1366-86, built the
upper part of the SOUTH-WEST TOWER, above the third row
of statues, and glazed the west windows ; Bishop Bubwith, 1407-24, erected the upper portion of the Late
Decorated NORTH-WEST STEEPLE. The LADY CHAPEL was
built 1326, the PRESBYTERY was completed 1242-46, the
CRYPT of the chapter-house in 1286. The Decorated

CHAPTER-HOUSE and CENTRAL TOWER were built by Bishop de
la March, 1293-1302. The eastern side of the CLOISTER
was built by Bishop Bubwith, the western by Bishop
Beckington, and the south walk, with its Perpendicular
tracery, completed by Thomas Henry, the treasurer.
Thomas Beckington, about 1505, built three gateways.
Ralph of Shrewsbury, 1329-63, moated and walled the
palace, and built the residence of the vicars-choral. The
library was founded by Bishop Lake, 1620.

The palm must be awarded to this unrivalled Cathedral,
which distances all competitors, both in the completeness
of its ground-plan, the richness and profusion of its sculpture, the delicacy and grace of its architecture, the almost
perfect preservation of its three gates, palace, college, and
conventual buildings, the extent of grassy lawn, and harmonious and picturesque accessories. Flaxman, Stothard,
and Cockerell—sculptor, painter, and architect—have all
borne enthusiastic testimony to the superb west front,
entirely covered with sculptures, one hundred and fifty-
three of the size of life and larger, including 21 crowned
kings, 8 queens, 31 mitred ecclesiastics, 7 knights, 14
nobles and princes, all drawn by Carter in 1784-6; and
upwards of four hundred and fifty of smaller figures, in
niches, subjects from the Holy Bible, embodying the
whole Christian scheme, from the creation of the world to
the day of final retribution, which crowns the central gable,
while in the third tier are designs from the Old Testament traditionally arranged on the south side, and those
drawn from the New Testament to the north of the
western portal; a plan or idea the same as was followed
by Raffaele and Michael Angelo. In the first arcade are
the early missionaries to England, next angels jubilant,
holding crowns of glory. Above these are two tiers of
kings and queens, on the north ; bishops, saints, and
religious, on the south, from the foundation of the church
to the reign of Henry III.: while in the sixth tier, in the
upper niches, and on the south and north fronts, are
portrayed the dead rising from the grave, in the attitude
and with the expression betokening their various emotions

at meeting the great day—rapturous joy, and wonder and despair. There are 92 figures. In the seventh are the orders of angels, in the eighth apostles, in the ninth the Eternal Judge. All is grand, simple, earnest. For artistic skill and excellence, they are not surpassed by any contemporaneous sculptures on the Continent : they are accurate transcripts of nature—simple, faithful, and sublime ; the figures are carefully and gracefully draperied and full of action : the details of costume are minute, and the whole composition chaste and dignified. Although in parts severe and rude, and anatomically incorrect, yet piety, fine sentiment, and taste, shine irresistible through the whole. It was the achievement of an English artist, working at the same period as Nicolo Pisano, in Italy, and completing his labour two years after the birth of Cimabue. Cockerell estimated the cost of production at 20,000*l*. sterling ; and it cannot fail to have been a subject of remark, that here, as in so many other instances, the workman is nameless—for although we have assigned the fabric to a bishop or a prior, it must be understood that it does not follow that they were the architects, but rather that to their alms or efforts they are mainly to be attributed, while in some cases, the reason has been, that it was the most convenient method for defining a date.

> Who builds a church to GOD, and not to fame,
> Will never mark the marble with his name.

Those works, wrought with the fire of life, and in which whole lives were summed, bear no impress of personal vanity. Coleridge says truly : " Gothic art depended entirely on a symbolical expression of the infinite—which is not vastness, nor immensity, nor perfection, but whatever cannot be circumscribed within the limits of actual sensuous being. Accordingly sculpture was not attempted by the Gothic races, till the ancient specimens were discovered, while painting and architecture were of native growth among them . . . no artificial emblem could satisfy the Northman's mind ; the dark wild imagery of nature, which surrounded him, and the freedom of his life, gave his mind a tendency to the Infinite; so that he found rest in that which presented no end, and derived satisfaction from that which was indistinct. . . ."

The WEST FRONT is composed of a central bay with a double doorway beneath; above which are three distinct lancet arches, pedimented, divided by niches and shafts, piers of masonry nearly as broad as themselves; while above and below are arcades of niches: the gable is fronted with a similar screen rising from boldly-projecting buttresses of extraordinary breadth, which terminate in circular pinnacles and spirelets. These projecting buttresses, covered with statuary, form also a distinctive feature of the two splendid towers, in each face of which are set two lofty trefoiled windows, with simple tracery, side by side. The towers in the lower arcade have two-light trefoiled windows, with a quatrefoil in the head; in the middle arcade pedimented lancets; in the upper story trefoiled panels, with two-light windows above, a battlemented parapet, and panelled buttress turrets. The buttresses are shallow, and never arched; the windows of the nave and transept, with the exception of two in the latter, are of two-lights, with plain tracery. The west front is later than the nave. At Lincoln, Ely, and Salisbury, there is a pervading similarity of style, originally French or Burgundian, and resemblance of work, as if that of one simultaneous school of art; but at Wells, which is a contemporaneous building, the architecture is but improved Norman, a local body of masons working on in their old fashion, careless of adjacent innovations. The arrangement of the nave, transept, and north porch, all present an Early English arrangement, not very common, differing much from Salisbury, and yet full of simplicity and elegance. It is curious to observe how each severy—with its wide apertures, its lengthened supports of pillars with the angles only facing the cap, its removal of all solid wall as far as possible, its diagonal outline in perspective, each part perforated and subdivided, and its vault, coved inward like the inverted pod of the Egyptian bean (the emblem of resurrection)—conveys the same idea to the mind as was intended by the eastern Ciborium, the suspension of the vast mass above made to hover in air by an almost magical deception, without an apparent resting-place, or with the slightest stay of earth.

The beautiful PORCH, with a parvise, is on the north side of the nave, as at Hereford and Salisbury; in the foliage of the capitals are sculptured the acts of the martyrdom of St. Edmund. The gable is panelled with lancets, and flanked by octagonal turrets and spires. Over the aisles and clerestory, a graceful double trefoiled parapet and corbel able are continued round the church. On the east of the TRANSEPT is a gallery of communication, which passes across the CHAIN GATE to the Vicar's college; and to the eastward, parallel with the choir, is the CHAPTER-HOUSE, here exceptionally detached from the cloisters. The FONT in the south transept is of a date contemporaneous with the erection of that work. The triforium consists of couplets in each bay. On the west angle of the NORTH TRANSEPT is an astronomical clock, constructed in 1325 by Peter Lightfoot, a monk of Glastonbury; on the summit are five mounted figures, who revolve when the hours strike; two are knights, one is a hooded jester, the other has a Jacobæan costume. It was removed hither on the dissolution of the abbey. The seated figures strike the hours and quarters with their feet; they are in armour of the 15th century, of the period of Henry VI. or Edward IV. The front of the NORTH MAIN TRANSEPT is of four stages; the first has two-light windows; the uppermost have arcades of lancets; the buttresses are arcaded above, tapernig upwards, and end in spires. The windows in the adjoining staircase are of four lights, with five circles in the head. The CENTRAL TOWER has its first story arcaded with lancets; the second has trefoil panelling; the third, three two-light trefoiled windows, transomed, with a quatrefoiled canopy. The buttresses are pinnacled; the parapet is battlemented. The SOUTH TRANSEPT has a front of four stages— the base tier a triplet, the second arcading of lancets, the third and fourth a triplet. The three west bays of the CHOIR have a clerestory of two-light windows with plain tracery : the east have three-light canopied windows, with quatrefoils in the head, like those in the aisles. The CHOIR TRANSEPT has a four-light trefoiled window, with quatre-foiled tracery ; the aisles of the PRESBYTERY similar five-light windows ; and the LADY CHAPEL five-light cinquefoiled windows, with four orders of trefoils in the head. The east choir gable has a traceried lozenge.

The interior of the NAVE opens out a magnificent view of this

> Fit abode, wherein appear enshrined
> Our hopes of immortality.

On the south side of the nave, above the triforium, is a MINSTRELS' GALLERY.

The lofty pointed arches, with their graceful columns and capitals of foliage ; the unrivalled range of lancets, three in each bay, composing the triforium, which is here of extreme height, equal to that of the story below, the effect being increased by the plainness of the openings ; the deeply-recessed clerestory ; and the stone roof, simple and grand, springing from short columns of fine design, when the colours of the western window are projected on the pavement by a setting sun, form a superb vestibule to the more enriched eastern portion of the church—

> The very light
> Streams with a colouring of heroic days,
> In every ray, which through each arch and aisle
> A path of dreamy lustre wanders back
> To other years ; and the rich-fretted roof,
> And the wrought coronals of summer leaves,
> Ivy and vine, and many a sculptured rose,
> The tenderest image of mortality,
> Binding the slender columns, whose light shafts
> Cluster like stems in corn-sheaves ; all these things
> Tell of a race that nobly, fearlessly
> On their heart's worship poured a wealth of love.

At either angle of the TRANSEPT is a chantry, and against a pillar on the south is a stone pulpit of the 15th century, the gift of Bishop Knight. It has a legend (2 Tim. iv. 2). The choir-screen is simply panelled. The roof below the

CENTRAL TOWER is highly carved with fan-tracery, and in each great arch of the four arms of the crossing are double-curved stone braces, with circles in the spandrils, of wonderful boldness of design and massive construction.

On entering the CHOIR, the ornament, luminousness, and delicacy of the three easternmost severies are conspicuous. It is—

> ' . . . . . One grand romantic whole
> Which charms the fancy and exalts the soul.

The three westernmost bays are similar to the NAVE, while beyond the altar are seen the graceful arches and clustered pillars of the LADY CHAPEL; for a triforium appears a range of cinquefoiled and canopied niches. Great restorations, as at Hereford and Ely, have been effected here. The forty-one STALLS, of an unusual material, and in a peculiar position, were set up by Salvin in 1848, during the memorable decanate of Dr. Jenkins. They are of stone: five gabled canopies, with sub-ogee arches, richly carved by J. B. Philip and J. Forsyth, and divided by crocketed pinnacles and Purbeck shafts, occupy the space between the piers of each arch, while the curious misereres are worked up in the new wood-work. The MISERERES, which only occur between the 13th century and the Reformation, are common to the Continent. The sculptures, seldom of scriptural or religious subjects, are—1, Illustrations of a popular romance, such as Reynard the Fox; 2, or, of Bestiaries—books of animated nature and monsters; 3, of the fabulous Aristotle, or Æsopean fables, the Ysoprets and Avynets; 4, or of illuminated kalendar portraitures of the works of each month; 5, allegorical, legendary, and heraldic carvings; 6, games and pastimes in which monks and nuns figure; and, 7, grotesque fantastic sketches taken from the margins of old MSS.

The stone ornaments on the outside, partly decorations, partly talismans, the lions and griffins, are typical of the twofold nature of the Saviour, and the strength of the Church: the beasts of prey, figurative here of evil, were adopted as crests by cities, and are retained as supporters of escutcheons ; for heraldry is the last remnant of ancient symbolism, and a true branch of Christian art

The high pace is laid with Minton's tiles ; canopied sedilia, with Purbeck shafts, a new reredos, floriated and diapered, and a new pulpit of stone, have been added. The roof has bosses and ribs relieved by trefoiled and quatrefoiled panels. Three pointed arches open into the choir transept behind the altar ; the east window is in three compartments, and of seven cinquefoiled lights, with geometrical tracery. The organ, by Father Schmidt, 1664, was rebuilt by Green, 1786.

The LADY CHAPEL was restored by Ferrey in 1842, the ancient glazing, of the date 1320, in the five stained windows rearranged by Willement, and a tesselated pavement introduced, with some slight and tantalizing additions of polychrome. The cinque-cento ·glass of the west window of the nave is of the date 1507. Some Perpendicular fragments remain in the windows of the nave and transept. The brass lectern was given by Bishop·Creyghton.

The manner in which the junction of the Lady Chapel with the choir is effected, is most masterly. The CLOISTERS are on the south, of 12 panes east and west, and 13 to·the south, with Early English entrances into the nave and south transept, but have no north alley. The old Chapter-house was made into a chapel. In the centre is the ancient lavatory ; and over the east walk is the LIBRARY. The CHAPTER-HOUSE (Early English, verging on Decorated), which is approached by a fine flight of forty-eight ·stairs, being 20 ft. higher than the floor of the cathedral, is octagonal, and supported by a central column, of small dimensions, channelled into eight lesser shafts of Purbeck marble. The groined roof springs from it, expanding like the boughs of a palm-tree, and is enriched with bosses of foliage. There are seven four-light Decorated windows, with segmental tracery. The walls have an arcade of fifty-one canopied niches. In the staircase is a penitential cell. In the gloomy CRYPT or SACRISTY, which is of earlier date, below, there are an ancient record-chest of oak, a bena-ture, and a stone cresset for a lamp. The ancient machinery of Lightfoot's clock is preserved here.

The PALACE at Wells resembles an old baronial castle, with its strong military gateway, bastions, broad moat, embattled wall, built by Bishop de Salopia in 1329, and an area of seven acres. The garden front is of the 13th century: a house of the 14th century is in ruins: a conduit in the garden was built by Beckington. The hall, of the time of Edward I., has a window of the period of Henry III., and a fireplace of the reign of Henry VII. The north-east tower is called the Virgin's Tower. The gate-house was built by Beckington. The CHAPEL, Early Decorated, was built by Bishop Jocelyn in 1236, and restored by Bishop Bagot; Bishop Law gave the east window. The now roofless HALL, with nine windows, a nave, and two aisles, 120 feet long and 70 feet wide, was built by Bishop Burnell, 1274-92; it was the scene of the trial of the last Abbot of Glastonbury, Whiting, in 1539. The chair of the Abbot of Glastonbury is in the GALLERY, 80 ft. long with a vaulted roof, carved door, panelled wainscot, and a collection of episcopal portraits. The entrance is through a crypt, built 1293. The ancient lantern preserved here was originally hung in the CRYPT, under the CHAPTER-HOUSE. In the hall Bishop Ken on every Sunday entertained a certain number of poor guests. A pastoral staff is preserved in the deanery, with a head of Limoges enamel jewelled, and representing St. Michael; it is supposed to have belonged to Savaricus, bishop 1192-1205. The DEANERY, on the north-west, a magnificent specimen of architecture, was partly built by Gunthorpe in 1472, who here entertained King Henry VII. The VICAR'S COLLEGE, founded by Bishop Jocelyn in 1230, a charming oblong court, half domestic, half ecclesiastic, on the north of the Close, contains a chapel, muniment-room, library, hall, and 42 two-roomed dwelling-houses, 21 on either side, and a covered gallery over the gate to the church. It is now occupied by the students of the Theological College. It was built by Ralph de Shrewsbury, Erghum in the reign of Richard II., and Beckington. In the hall are observable, the reader's pulpit, the fire-dogs, fireplace, and a curious painting of Ralph de Shrewsbury and the Vicars.

The Close-Gate, on the west side, is known as Penniless Porch, and, as well as the gate of the Palace, was built by Bishop Beckington : some architecture of the same period remains on the north side of the market-place; to the south are several Tudor houses. The Close Hall, or Chaingate, extending from the Vicar's Close to the Cathedral on the north, was also his addition. Bubwith's almshouse and chapel were built 1424.

The principal monuments are the following :—

N.E. Chapel. — Bishop Creyghton, d. 1672, effigy, mitred and with pastoral staff; Bishop Berkeley, d. 1581, altar tomb; near it is the effigy of Friar Milton.

St. John's Chapel.—Bishop Bitton I., d. 1264, effigy: the earliest incised slab in the country.

Presbytery, S. Aisle. — Bishop Drokensford, d. 1329, table-tomb canopied.

Choir, S. Side.—Bishop Beckington, d. 1465, chantry, effigy, and cadaver; Bishop Bitton II., d. 1274, effigy; Bishops Barwold, d. 1008; Ethelwyn, d. 1023; and Brithwyn, d. 1024—mutilated effigies; Bishop Still, d. 1607, effigy in parliamentary robes.

N. Side.—Bishop Ralph de Shrewsbury, d. 1363, effigy; Bishop Giso, d. 1088. effigy; Bishops Brithelm, Kinewald, Alwyn—mutilated effigies.

N. Transept (Holy Cross Chapel).—Bishop Cornish, Provost of Oriel College, d. 1513, altar-tomb and canopy; Dean Forest, d. 1446, effigy.

S. Transept (St. Calixtus' Chapel). — Bishop Harewell, d. 1386, effigy of alabaster; Dean Husee, d. 1305, effigy of alabaster; altar-tomb, with effigies under an arch. (*St. Martin's Chapel.*)—John Storthwaite, precentor, d. 1454, effigy; Bishop de la March, d. 1302, effigy; Joan Viscountess de L'Isle, d. 1464, low tomb.

Nave, N. Side.—Hugh Sugar, treasurer, d. 1489, chantry.

S. Side.—Bishop Bubwith, d. 1424, chantry; Bishop Haselshaw, d. 1308, brass stolen; Bishop Erghum, d. 1400, brass stolen.

Besides these are a slab in the Nave, said to cover King Ina's ashes; a brass to Dean Goodenough, by Waller; and a coped tomb of Dean Jenkins. John Philips of Montacute (Chantrey); memorial window to Archdeacon Brymer; a window in the south choir aisle is by Ward and Nixon; the Dean, Mr. F. H. Dickinson, M.P., and the students of the college, gave others in 1846. The brass effigy of Bishop Jocelyn, who died 1247, now destroyed, was one of the earliest specimens of the art on record.

DIMENSIONS OF THE CATHEDRAL IN FEET.

	Length.	Breadth.	Height.
West Front	235	..	..
Nave	191	67 with aisles	67
Choir	108	..	..
Presbytery	22	..	..
Lady Chapel	47	33	..
Transepts	135	..	..
Central Tower	..	..	160
Western Towers	..	..	130
Cloister, South Alley 155 E. 159 W.		..	164
Chapter-house	55	42	65
Extreme length	371	..	..

The Chapter is composed of a dean, and four canons. There are four minor canons, seven lay vicars, eight choristers. There are two choral services daily, at 10 and 3, and a monthly celebration of the Holy Communion. The library contains 2348 volumes. The income of the Chapter in 1852, was 4717*l.* 14*s.* 4½*d.* The expenditure on the fabric during twelve years 12,951*l.* 11*s.* 4*d.*, inclusive of subscriptions to the amount of 8155*l.*

Arms: Az. a pastoral staff in bend dexter, arg., between two keys, addorsed and interlaced in bend sinister, or.

Among their bishops, Bath and Wells number John de Villula, who obtained the mitre "by anointing the king's hand with white ointment;" Burnell, Lord Chancellor, at whose manor-house was passed the statute of Acton Burnell; De la March, Lord Treasurer; Drokensford, Lord Keeper and Viceroy; Beckington, Lord Keeper; Stillington, Lord Chancellor; Cardinals De Castello and Wolsey; Fox; Clerk, Master of the Rolls, who aided Henry VIII. in the treatise which procured for him the title of Defender of the Faith; Barlow, who made the gravest matters a jest, and his preferments opportunities of sacrilege; Bourne, President of Wales; Godwin; Still, who avowed that after a violent thunderstorm in 1596, the marks of a cross were printed on his wife and others of the congregation; Montague ; Laud ; Piers, who, in the rebellion, had to entreat for a curacy ; Creyghton and Mews, who fought as Cavaliers ; saintly Ken, who obtained a mitre for "refusing poor Nelly a lodging ;" Kidder, killed in his bed by a fall of a stack of chimneys ; and John, Baron Auckland. Among the dignitaries occur De la Knole, the ambassador ; four Cardinals ; Cromwell, Earl of Essex ; Weston, Lord Justice of Ireland ; William, Bishop of Tusculum ; Cheam, of Glasgow ; Francis, of Constantinople ; Peter of Blois ; Polydore Vergil ; Edwyn Sandys, the traveller ; and Anthony Horneck.

The fine parish church of St. Cuthbert, Late Decorated, has a Perpendicular tower, one of the most beautiful compositions of the style, a nave of eight bays, and chancel, with aisles and a transept: the arches of the nave are Early English. There are two lateral chapels—Trinity chapel on the north and Coward's chantry on the south; and two Sacristies. There are remains of a Jesse altar, 1470, in the south aisle, and a tabernacled altar of the 15th century in the north transept. Bubwith's Hospital is on the north side of the churchyard. They were added to by Bishop Stillington, 1592-3.

Winchester.

John Taylor, the water-poet, in the reign of Charles I., described Winchester as "an ancient city, like a body without a soul, almost as many parishes as people." It undoubtedly had fallen from its high estate, when, in the reign of Henry I., it boasted a Cathedral, two royal minsters, sixty churches, a palace, two castles, and a mint, and reached from St. Cross to Worthy, from St. Mary Magdalene down to Weeke ; but now it by no means wears a dull air, although there is the quiet about the Close and College peculiar to religious and academical retreats. Its memories and associations would require a volume. Winchester,

(the Caer Gwent, White City, of the Briton, and by corruption Wenta-Ceaster of the Saxon) is situated on a
hill sloping down to the Itchin, in a wooded valley sheltered
by high downs, and was the capital of the Saxon, the
Norman, and early Plantagenets. It has derived a popular
celebrity as the resting-place of St. Swithin, the removal
of whose remains, during a heavy rain, has given rise to
the belief, that, if it should · rain on his feast, it will con-
tinue to fall in a deluge for forty days after, as Gay
sings—

> If on St. Swithin's feast the welkin lowers,
> And every penthouse streams with hasty showers,
> Twice twenty days shall clouds their fleeces drain,
> And wash the welkin with incessant rain.

Oliver's Battery commands a fine view of the guarded
down.

> Where Cromwell's rebel soldiery kept guard o'er Wykeham's town,
> Beneath their pointed cannon all Itchen's valley lay,
> Saint Catherine's breezy side, and the woodlands far away;
> The huge Cathedral sleeping in venerable gloom,
> The modest college-tower and the bedesman's Norman home.

The romance of King Arthur makes him a familiar guest
at Winchester.

The original bushel, called the Winchester measure, is
still preserved in its ivy-mantled west gate. The tribute
of the wolves' heads, paid by the Welsh, is commemorated
in Wolvesey Castle. Easter was kept in its palace by
William I. and Rufus, Christmas by Henry III., 1289, and
Edward II. Earl Godwin's sudden death occurred here,
1066. The famous massacre of the Danes, known as
"Hock," commenced here on Nov. 13, 1002. Henry II.
and Stephen were here in 1184 ; John was here fifty-two
times ; Edward and Queen Eleanor, Jan. 12, 1276 and 1279 ;
Edward II., 1308 ; Richard II. and Queen Anne, 1388 ; and
Henry VI., visiting the College as his example for Eton,
1440, 1444, 1449 ; Princess Anne, 1684 ; James II. 1685.
Waltheof, Earl of Northumberland, was beheaded here
1307 ; and Edmund of Woodstock, March 14, 1329. The

iniquitous trial of Sir Walter Raleigh took place, 1603. Henry III. bore the name of his birthplace (October 1st 1207), as Harry of Winton. Pace, Warham, and Lingard were natives of Winchester. In 1184, Prince William, the ancestor of the house of Hanover, was born here, and Prince Arthur in 1484. Parliaments were held in its hall, 1265, 1268, 1270, 1276, 1285, 1329, 1354, 1392, 1403, 1405, 1449.

The WEST GATE is of the age of Henry III. ; outside of it Guy of Warwick vanquished Colbrand, the gigantic Dane. The King's Gate, of the 13th century, forms the entrance to College Street; over it is built St. Swithin's Church.

The PALACE, now the Barracks, was built by Sir Christopher Wren for Charles II., and was subsequently a refuge for the emigrant clergy during the horrors of the revolution in France.

The great ST. STEPHEN'S HALL of the KING'S PALACE was built by Henry III., and consists of three alleys : since the 16th century it has been used as a court of justice. In the Nisi Prius Court is the round table, dating certainly six centuries back : it is 18 feet in diameter, and was painted in the Tudor colours, green and white, on the occasion of the visit of the Emperor Charles V. It represents King Arthur, and has the names of his paladins on the edge. It is as interesting a relic as the Mappa Mundi at Hereford, and the Rota Fortunæ of Rochester. In the Bailey, Edmund, Earl of Kent, was beheaded in the reign of Edward II., waiting a whole day till an executioner could be found. The CITY Cross, of three stories, erected by the Fraternity of the Holy Cross in the High Street, is 43 feet in height, and of the earlier part of the 15th century ; in the second story is a statue of St. Lawrence. East Bridge stands near the site of the last gate, of which Wolstan records the legend that a belated citizen, before he could enter, was stricken down and paralysed by three terrible water-spirits, two dark and bare, one gigantic, clad in white, who immediately sank into the Itchin. In St. John Baptist's Church is an Easter sepulchre, in the north chancel aisle ; the parcloses and bench ends are of the 14th century, the screen is Perpendicular. The sandstone font is of the 12th century. Some curious frescoes were discovered on the north wall recently. The aisles are wider than the nave; the arches are Transitional Norman; the wall and corbels of the roof Early English; the tower on the south-west Perpendicular. St. Peter's, Cheese Hill, forms a parallelogram Transitional Norman: the lower part of the tower is Norman, the upper portion Early English. At St. Michael's, Kingsgate Street, is a wall-dial of the 13th century. St. John's Hall, 62ft. by 28ft., contains a portrait of Charles I. by Lely. In St. John's Hospital is an Early English chapel. At St. Giles' Hill was the scene of a famous mediæval fair. The gateway and monk's walk of Hyde Abbey remain. Bishop Morley's College for widows of clergymen, in the Close, was founded 1672. The museum in Jury Street deserves a visit. St. Thomas', Southgate, was built 1847; the spire was added in 1856. There is a Russian gun at the foot of High Street.

The COLLEGE of ST. MARY WINTON, the parent of Eton and model of Westminster, and standing on the site of a school in which King Alfred was taught, is entered by a gateway, with a figure of St. Mary and the Holy Child in a niche. On the southern face of the MIDDLEGATE TOWER is represented the Annunciation, and the founder, William of Wykeham, in prayer. The peculiar junction of the turret with the parapet is observable: it was a peculiar arrangement of Wykeham. The quadrangle is 110 ft. long and 140 ft. in breadth. The various chambers, distinguished by sculptured symbols, are allotted to the fellows and scholars. On the south are the chapel and hall. The CHAPEL of six bays, 93ft. long and 30ft. broad and 57ft. in height, was consecrated on St. Kenelm's day, 1394. It is approached through a PORCH 29ft. by 12ft. 6in. which was, in 1857, arcaded on the west side 16ft. 6in., high by Field, from designs by Mr. Butterfield, with cinquefoiled panels, 8ft. by 4ft. 6in., shafts and mosaics of English marbles, as a MEMORIAL to the Wykehamists who had fallen in the war in the Crimea. The oak roof is by Norris of London, and the iron gates at either end by Potter. The floor is laid with Minton's tiles. The roof of the beautiful and solemn chapel is fan-traceried in Irish oak, and the east window glows with its ancient glazing. Some carving by G. Gibbons is over the altar. The TOWER was built by Warden Thurburn. The HALL is 63 ft. long and 30 ft. in breadth, and has a timber roof and wainscot dated 1540. At the entrance of the kitchen is the famous wall-painting of the Trusty Servant, which dates back about two centuries, and was copied probably from a French original. Over the entrance of the great SCHOOL, built 1692, 90 ft. long and 36 ft. broad, is a statue of the founder in bronze, by Cibber. The well-known school-table is painted on the west wall—" Aut Disce, aut Discede, manet sors tertia cœdi," with the mitre and staff as the rewards of learning, the sword and ink-horn for those who would not study and must therefore leave ; the famous Wykehamical rod of four twigs being the only alternative. On the east wall are the school rules. The CLOISTERS form a square of 132 feet ; in the centre is a CHANTRY of the early part of the 15th century, now the LIBRARY, restored 1856 ; in the cloister-roof of Irish oak no spider will build. The visitor should come in July and hear the Dulce Domum sung, and witness that most characteristic gathering of Wykehamists old and young, proud of their royal school, the most ancient of any in these dominions, and one which has contributed at least its proportion of worthies in church and state. Among those who have been members of one or other of the two St. Mary Winton Colleges, occur Henry V., according to Stow ; Waynflete, founder of Magdalen College ; Chichele, of All Souls' ; Fox, of Corpus Christi College, Oxford ; the Speakers Onslow, Cornwall, Sidmouth, and Eversley ; the Admirals Keats and Warren ; the Generals Guilford, Dalbiac, Myers, and Seaton ; Judges Redesdale, Erle, and Cranworth ; Warham, Grocyn, Norris, Shaftesbury, and Harris ; Daubeny, Holmes, Buckland, Arnold, and Moberly; Sir J. Browne and Sir H. Wotton ; Barrow, Gunning, Ken, Bilson, Burgess, Butson, Lowth, Maltby, and Mant ; Otway, Young, Collins, Somerville, Philips, Spence, Whitehead, Dibdin, Crowe, Russell, and Bowles.

Adjoining is Wolvesey Castle, built by Bishop de Blois, 1138 : the Norman arch and window of the hall and the courses of narrow, square, and round stones, are the most observable objects in the ruins of the keep, which formed a square of 250 ft. long by 160 ft. in breadth ; it was destroyed by Cromwell's orders in 1646. Portions of the city wall still remain. The bishop's palace, now the Diocesan Training School, was begun by Sir C. Wren in 1684, and completed in 1706, it contains a Perpendicular chapel, gallery, and some good rooms of the period. It has not been occupied for years, however, by the bishops of Winchester. Bishop North demolished a large portion of the buildings in which Queen Mary lodged and held her marriage-feast.

At the distance of a mile across the water meadows is the Hospital of St. Cross at Sparkford ; founded by Bishop de Blois in 1132, and augmented by Cardinal Beaufort in 1444. It is beautifully situated on the river bank, and enclosed on the south with noble trees. At the porter's gate a horn of beer and manchet of bread are offered to every traveller. On the east side of the entrance court is the Hundred Men's Hall, where once daily that number of almsmen were fed. Over the great gate is a statue of Beaufort; in the lateral niches stood a holy cross and St. John. On the labels are represented Henry IV. and V., John of Gaunt, and Wykeham. In the great quadrangle on the south is the refectory, retaining its timber roof and minstrels' gallery; in it now the thirteen brethren, who wear a black robe and silver cross over the heart, dine only on high days. It contains a triptych of the Adoration of the Magi. Their rooms are to the west. In the founder's rooms are carved oak presses of the 15th century, set up by Bishop Sherborne; on the east, over an ambulatory 135 feet long, are the nuns' chambers over the cloister, once occupied by three sisters who tended the sick, and the infirmary, with a window opening into the church, which is on the south side. It is cruciform, with a central tower of a single story, nave of three bays, choir, transept, each of two bays, with aisles and a north porch ;

150 ft. long, 120 ft. broad at the transept. At the east
angle of the choir aisle and south transept is a curious
triple arch with aumbries, probably used for issuing doles
to the poor. The west front and doorway were built
1292. The rest of the building is Transitional Norman ;
the north porch Early English. The encaustic tiles, the
piscina, wooden parcloses, the credence-table of stone, and
glazing of the Decorated period are all observable. The
stalls are Tudor. There is a fine brass to Archdeacon
Campden, d. 1382. Under the tower in the south nave
aisle is a monument to Mr. Speaker Cornwall. The stall-
work is Cinque-cento.

There is a curious mize maze, 86 feet square, on St.
Catharine's Hill (which was a Roman camp, still perfect);
it is supposed to have been of ecclesiastical origin, like the
labyriuths on church floors, by threading which persons
compounded their vows to a pilgrimage to Holy Land. It
adjoined an ancient chapel destroyed by Wolsey.

One gate of the monastery, St. Swithin's, remains; it is
at the west side of the Cheney Court, so called from the
administration of justice, in old times, to the servants of
the church, beneath an oak-tree (chêne). The whole
precinct is kept in the finest order, with lawns and noble
trees. A magnificent avenue leads through the Close to
the western door. The exterior of the Cathedral, with the
exception of the panelled east end, is sombre and plain,
but that, with its rich buttresses, its domed and panelled
turrets flanking a large seven-light window, foliated pinnacle, crocketed gable, and interwoven tracery is like a
coronal lifted by giant hands above the inner Sanctuary.
The north side offers a fine view, as there are crocketed
flying buttresses with tracery in the spandrils, pinnacled
buttresses, and a pierced parapet. The tower is deficient
in height and importance ; and the nave, redeemed from
baldness by an outline fringed with pinnacles, is of the
formal period of the Perpendicular, the inventor of which
was time-honoured William of Wykeham, whose name
meets us at every turn, immortalized by his glorious
works in stone and existing monuments of munificence

and learning. "Environed with objects proper to exalt the imagination" (to adopt the words of an accomplished Frenchman), "the walls of this church impress the mind with the respect due to the sanctuary of GOD! they are open books of science, arts, and morals, all speaking and all animated with the same spirit, every angle and even remote corner ever presenting its lesson or precept with the most admirable harmony." Within, the long-drawn nave, its massive yet graceful piers, combining the solemnity of the massive Norman with the buoyancy and aspiring lines of Perpendicular work, its bossy vaulting, its choir-screen, approached by a noble flight of stairs; above it the matchless reredos, and the glowing east window in the far misty distance, constitute a view with which no interior of any Cathedral can compete; while the magnificence of its numerous and elaborate chantries raise it to the first rank for richness and variety of ornament. The chapels of the NAVE and CHOIR-SCREEN, themselves beautiful and lost in the grandeur of the entire building, yet serve as standards to measure its space, magnified indefinitely to the mind's eye by distance, and exalted in every element of splendour by the obscure backward beyond. With the sublimity of age and association, patient toil, genius, and exquisite taste, Winchester Cathedral scarcely seems the effect of mechanic agency. The effect is that of immensity; the building, never to be seen as one by a single or many glances, can only be constructed as a whole by the imagination, and the attempt to comprehend it employs at once the keenest and most pleasurable operations of the mind, memory, and anticipation. If the exterior of Lincoln surpass that of York, few would hesitate to prefer the interior of Winchester to every other church in England, from the majesty of the choir, with its canopies of dark and finely-carved old oak, the massive chandeliers swung from the illuminated ceiling, the deep arches of the aisles thickly set with clustered pillars, the traceried vaulting, and the niches of the reredos like lacework wrought in stone.

The ground plan is composed of a NAVE of eleven bays,

a TRANSEPT of three bays, a CHOIR of five bays, a PRESBYTERY of three bays, and a LADY CHAPEL of three bays, each having aisles. The whole church has been called a school of architecture, embracing the stern Norman arches in the TRANSEPT, the exquisite proportions of the Early English, and graceful traceries of the Decorated period in the PRESBYTERY, and the last effort of Tudor architecture, elaborate in ornamental detail, in the LADY CHAPEL, before architecture fell into utter decline. It is the venerable patriarch among cathedrals. Here, indeed, we have

> The solemn gloom
> Of the long Gothic aisle and stone-ribbed roof,
> O'er-canopying shrine, and gorgeous tomb,
> Carved screens and altar glimmering far aloof,
> And blending with the shade; a matchless proof
> Of high devotion, which hath now waxed cold.

On the site, according to tradition, of two former churches a Cathedral was built by St. Birinus in 647; a second was dedicated on October 20th, 980, by Bishop Ethelwold; and a third on April 8th, 1095. The mounds on the north-west angle of the Close mark the site of St. Swithin's Chapel, and on the south-west side was the great minster gate. The west front of Walkelyn's Cathedral stood 40 ft. in advance of the present front. So close, till 1127, was St. Mary's Abbey that the bells and organs jarred.

The WEST FRONT, 118 feet in breadth, which is composed of a panelled gable, set between hexagonal turrets, crowned with spirelets, with the first compartment of the north, and two bays of the south aisle, was the work of Bishop Edyngdon, who died 1366. In the canopied niche of the panelled gable is the statue of William of Wykeham : the vacant brackets which flank the central portal were filled with images of St. Peter and St. Paul. In the GALLERY above, the bishop gave his solemn benediction on high festivals. The GREAT WINDOW is of six orders, and in three compartments, each of three foliated lights; the parapet is simply moulded; that of the west portion of the church is plain, but has a corbel table, which in the TRANSEPT is round arched ; the LADY CHAPEL has a panelled battlement. In the NAVE the windows are of three lights, those in the aisles are transomed. The north front of the TRANSEPT is of four stages, and retains its round Norman windows with billet mouldings divided by three massive buttresses, but with Perpendicular tracery inserted. In the gable is a marygold. The south front has similar windows, but is flanked by square turrets, the gable has an intersecting arcade. In each face of the TOWER are three noble Norman windows, with chevron mouldings.

In the interior, in each bay of the TRANSEPT the triforium consists of round arched couplets under a large round arch, the clerestory is composed of three round arches, the central being light and very lofty. The walls are arcaded. Upon entering the NAVE, over the north-west door, is the TRIBUNE, formerly used by minstrels on occasions of high ceremonial, when tapestry was hung from the large hooks along the nave. There is no triforium ; a panelled arcade supplies its place. The FONT, of black marble (and probably the gift of Bishop Walkelyn), represents, in its sculptures, the acts of St. Nicholas of Myra. Above the CRYPT, extending from the east end to the second pillar, westward of the tower pier, is a raised platform, approached by a flight of ten stairs. The SCREEN, at the entrance of the choir, by Mr. Garbett, replaced a cumbrous Grecian screen by Inigo Jones. The statues are those of James I. and Charles I. Near Bishop Morley's tomb may be seen a portion of the double tier of Norman arches, which was converted into a single bay by William of Wykeham, the chief benefactor of Winchester, who began the work of transformation of the nave, the groining of which was completed by his successors, Cardinal Beaufort and Waynflete, whose devices are on the bosses of the vaulting.

The CHOIR reaches from the eastern tower-piers to the first west piers of the nave, and is approached by two fine flights of stairs, the aisles are reached by stairs from the transepts. The TOWER was built in the 12th century. The beautiful carved and canopied stalls, of black Normandy oak, were erected about A.D. 1296. In 1632 there was a magnificent series of sculptures in relief of wainscot, with stories from the Old and New Series along either side. The upper tier of desks are dated 1545, and bear the initials of Henry VIII., Bishop Gardiner, and Dean Kingsmill; the pulpit has those of Silkstede, prior from 1498 to 1524. The organ by Willis, which cost 2350*l*., was opened on June 3, 1854. In 951 one of the earliest organs built in England was set up here by Bishop Elfsy.

The SANCTUARY, built c. 1320-50, extends from the brass eagle or lectern to the sumptuous reredos, which is far superior in size to those at St. Mary Overy, St. Alban's, or Christchurch-Twyneham; it is the finest specimen of tabernacle-work in England, and vies with the screen of Seville. The large cross, now a blank, was covered by a superb jewelled rood, above which was hung the crown worn by Canute when he rebuked his courtiers. The niches, in all the three tiers, were filled with images of saints and canonized bishops of Winchester. Over the doors are sculptures of the Visitation and Annunciation of the Virgin. On this spot have been crowned Egbert in 827, Edward the Confessor in 1042, Henry II. and Queen Margaret in 1172, Richard his eldest son in 1176, and Richard I. on April 17, 1194; Henry IV. and Joan of Navarre on January 7, 1404; and Mary and Philip of Spain on July 25, 1554, celebrated their nuptials here. In 1140, before the assembled bishops, the cardinal prelate in the Cathedral excommunicated all who refused obedience to Matilda, to whom he pointed as queen regnant. The marble pavement and chancel rails were the gift of Prebendary Harris, A.D. 1700. The altar-piece is Benjamin West's best work, " The Raising of Lazarus." The aisles or processional paths, dated 1525, and the vaulting from the lantern to the east window, glazed with the characteristic beauty of its age, (when glass painting attained its highest perfection as an art,) were the work of Bishop Fox, whose initials, R. W. (Richard Winton,) and badge, the pelican, with the motto, " Est Deo gracia," are observable on every side.　The letters H. B. and legend "In Domino confido," commemorate Cardinal Beaufort.　The initials W. F. are those of one Fleming, whose motto was "Sit laus Deo."　The tracery of the east window has the glazing of Fox's time that; in the north-west clerestory is of the reign of Henry VI.; the timber roof is of his period, covered with heraldic charges, but over the sanctuary with emblems of the "Passion," and the faces of the Apostles, Pilate, and Herod.　Above the fine stone parcloses are six MORTUARY CHESTS in the Cinque-cento style, containing the remains, among others, of Egbert, Canute, Queen Emma, and Rufus, set here by Bishop Fox.　The Roundheads of Sir W. Waller, in December, 1642, used these poor relics to break the painted glass.　The grey marble tomb of Rufus stands in front of the bishop's THRONE, which was designed by Mr. Garbett, the architect employed to set up the flat transept ceilings (copied from St. Alban's Abbey) and carry on the great repairs made between 1812 and 1828.　The vaulting of the LANTERN was completed in Charles I.'s reign, and has on the central boss a chronogram for 1634.　In 1643 Cromwell's troopers committed abominable excesses in this church; but, owing to the interposition of Colonel Nathaniel Fiennes and Nicholas Love, the tomb of the founder and Wykeham's College were preserved from injury.　The clerestory and aisles have four-light Perpendicular windows transomed.　There is a screen of quatrefoils, in front of the clerestory, in place of a triforium.

The TRANSEPTS, built 1079-93, have each aisles, and an aisle of two arches at either end raised to the level of the pier-arch.　Towers at each angle were to have completed the grandeur of the exterior.　In the NORTH TRANSEPT, which once contained five altars, is the episcopal throne given by Bishop Trelawny.　On the east wall are frescoes of St. Christopher.　In the north-west angle is a fine Norman arch; in the north wall a niche for an altar-tomb: there are two curious responding niches in the north-east piers.　The entrance to St. Ethelwold's triple CRYPT, now choked up with earth, is in the south-east angle. Like those of Canterbury, Gloucester, Rochester, and Worcester, it was built before 1085, and is one of the earliest specimens in England. Under the organ-loft is the CHAPEL OF THE HOLY SEPULCHRE, enriched with frescoes of the 12th century, representing the Passion of the Redeemer. The roof has been barbarously injured to make places for the lower apparatus of the organ-bellows. In the SOUTH TRANSEPT, the west aisle, now the chapter-house and library, which was furnished with books by Bishop Morley, was the SACRISTY, being approached by the Norman doorway, now walled up. The presses for robes bear the rebus of Prior Silkstede. The door in the south wall led to the inferior conventual offices; the flight of stairs on the east, to the dormitory of the monks. The east aisle is divided into three portions: 1, a calefactory, the chamber for lighting the censers; 2, the CHANTRY OF SILKSTEDE, which contains a beautiful specimen of a mediæval lock and some frescoes; and, 3, the CHAPEL OF VENERABLE BEDE, marked by elaborate iron-work. The screen on the south was placed here by Dean Rennell in 1816. There is a bench which may be contemporaneous with the transept. Domesday Book was originally kept in the Treasury here, and was in consequence called " the Book of Winton."

Behind the reredos is the high-pace, where, at King Edgar's silver shrine of St. Swithin, the early conventual mass was sung. On the east side of the screen which parts it from the presbytery are nine decorated tabernacles, once filled with images of St. Birinus, Kings Alfred, Egbert, Canute, and others; the central brackets supporting the images of the Saviour and St. Mary. The low arch beneath led to the " Holy Hole," where reliques were preserved. The PRESBYTERY, built by Bishop Lucy about 1202, has its central alley of three bays elevated, and graceful arcading along the walls of the aisles. On the exterior it has an arcade of four lancets in each bay, the central couplet being glazed. The LADY CHAPEL, begun by Prior Hunton 1470-98, and completed by Prior Silkstede, who died 1524, retains traces of twenty-four frescoes of legends of the Virgin: the chair in which Queen Mary sat at her marriage with Philip of Spain, on July 23, 1555, is still shown. The Purbeck shafts at the entrance, the desks, stalls, panelling, frescoed vaultings, and parcloses, both in this chapel and in LANGTON'S CHANTRY, are deserving of minute attention. The parapet on the exterior is panelled, and at the east end battlemented, with a round arched corbel table. The walls of the aisles have two trefoiled arcades above the lower arcade of lancets. The three windows of the east bay are of seven lights, transomed, and of three orders, the base tier has an arcade with blind geometrical tracery. The southern CHANTRY is that of Bishop Langton: the colours in the altar-screen are almost perfect; the rebuses carved on the vaulting—a long, a hen, a vine conjoined with a ton—stand for Langton, Hunton, Winton; as a skein of silk and a horse do for Silkstede. He died when elect to Canterbury, hence the arms of that province on the panelling; his motto was " Laus tibi Christe ;" that of Silkstede " In gloriam Dei." The memorial window is that of Mrs. Garnier, wife of the dean, and was put up by Nixon and Ward in 1847. The northern chantry was the Chapel of the Angels; the window is a memorial of the Rev. Chancellor Garnier.

Nave, S. Aisle.—Dr. Joseph Warton (Flaxman); Bishop Tomline; the chantry of William Wykeham, founder of the two St. Mary Winton Colleges, effigy; Bishop Willis (Cheere); Sir George Prevost, K.B. (Chantrey); chantry of William de Edingdon.

N. Aisle.—Bishop Morley, his crozier and mitre suspended above the tomb; Elizabeth Montagu, the authoress, died 1800; Dr. Littlehales (Bacon); Miss Jane Austen, the authoress, died 1817.

In the *Nave* are memorial windows to Charles Morley, 1851, Canon Poulter, 1853, by Evans, and to the 97th regiment by Gibbs, with their colours on the wall.

N. Transept.—Rev. Frederick Iremonger, died 1820, table-tomb and effigy by Chantrey.

S. Transept.—Izaak Walton (Silkstede's Chapel).

Choir.—Bishop Cooper, brass.

S. Aisle.—Bishop Courtenay; Bishop Fox's chantry, effigy and
cadaver; Prince Richard, son of William I., killed in the New Forest.

N. Aisle.—Bishop Gardiner's chantry, effigy and cadaver—in it King
Edmund's grave-stone; King Hardicanute.

Presbytery.—Prior de Basyng, died 1295; Cardinal Beaufort's chantry,
effigy; Sir J. Clobery, died 1687 (William Wilson); Bishop
Levinz (Sodor), died 1692; Sir Arnald de Gaveston, died 1302,
effigy—the front of the tomb is now built into the east wall of the
so-called Guardian Angels' Chapel; Bishop de Lucy; Bishop Ethel-
mar; Bishop De Rupibus, effigy; Bishop Waynflete's chantry,
effigy; Prior Silkstede.

Lady Chapel.—Bishop North, d. 1820 (Chantrey).

Langton's Chantry.—Bishop Langton.

Angels' Chapel.—Bishop Mews, a mitre and crozier suspended above;
Richard Earl of Portland, Lord Treasurer, died 1634.

DIMENSIONS OF THE CATHEDRAL IN FEET.

	Length.	Breadth.	Height.
Nave	250	86	78
Transept	208	78	..
Choir, &c.	138	43	..
Lady Chapel	54	..	..
Tower	50	48	138f. 6in.
Presbytery	70	..	..
Total length	560	..	..

The Cloisters were 180 by 174 feet square.

The Chapter-house, approached by the dark archway
southward of the south transept, leading into the paradise
or cloister-close. The cloisters were destroyed in 1570 by
Bishop Horne; the injury done by the rebel troopers in
1644 was in comparison slight. The slype is the passage
on the south-west side of the nave; on the buttress is
a Latin anagram, Illâc precator, Hâc, viator, ambula, and
on the wall, 1668, Sacra sit illa choro, serva fit ista foro,
pointing out that one way lies to the church, the other to
the market-place.

The Chapter consists of a dean and eight canons (there
will be only five stalls spared); four minor canons, sixteen

vicars-choral and ten choristers. There are two choral services daily, at 10 and 3 in winter, and 4 in summer. The Holy Communion is administered every Sunday and on festivals. The income in 1852, was 22,878*l.*; the expenditure within fourteen previous years 7809*l.* The library contains 3500 vols. The palace is Farnham Castle.

Arms: Gules, a sword, arg., hilted, or, between two keys addorsed in bend dexter ; in chief the letter R, or.

Winchester numbers among its bishops, St. Birinus, who, on his voyage home, walked back for his slippers to France on the sea, and recovered the ship before it reached port ; St. Headda ; St. Swithin the rainy ; St. Brinstan, who sang Dirige at midnight, and the ghosts answered Amen ; Elfsin, frozen on the Alps as he went for his pall to Rome ; St. Athelwold, who coined the church plate during a famine ; Brithelm, the patron of Brighton ; Walkelyn, who, when he obtained the right of cutting wood in the king's forest of Hempege, to the king's disgust left not a tree standing ; Giffard, Lord Chancellor ; the princely De Blois ; Toclive, Grand Justiciar ; De Roche, the chancellor who was knighted for service in the field by Cœur de Lion ; Rayleigh, " a coward among men-at-arms, a hero against clerks ;" D'Ely, Chancellor and Treasurer ; Sandal, Lord Chancellor ; Orlton and Stratford ; Edingdon, who refused the primacy, alleging that Canterbury had the highest rack, but Winton the deepest manger ; time-honoured Wykeham, founder of New and Winton Colleges ; Beaufort and Waynflete, Lords Chancellors ; Waynflete, founder of Magdalen College ; Fox, founder of Corpus Christi College ; Wolsey, founder of Cardinal College, Oxford ; cruel Gardiner, Lord Chancellor ; White, who lost his mitre by applying to Elizabeth the text, " a dead lion is better than a living dog ;" Horne, the most unprincipled and wanton of bigots ; Watson, who bribed Leicester to save him from the mitre ; learned Bilson, Andrewes, and Neile, whom King James consulted whether he might tax episcopal revenues—Neile replied, "Surely your majesty is the breath of our nostrils," and Andrews, " Sire, you can take brother Neile's, for he offers it;" Morley, founder of the Matrons' College; Mews, like Dolben, Fell, Beaw, Lake, and Creyghton, a Cavalier officer, and killed while in a faint by an overdose of hartshorn; Trelawny; Trimnell; the heretic Hoadly; Thomas, one of two contemporary bishops of the same name, who both squinted, and rose simultaneously as city rectors and royal chaplains; and Tomline, so sorely handled in the " Probationary Odes." Among the members of the church occur the Emperor Constans and Richard of Devizes; Ellis, Bishop of Kildare; Dr. Joseph Warton; and Francis Earl of Guilford.

The entrance to the DEANERY, once the prior's lodgings, consists of three arches and a vaulted passage of the age of Henry III. The hall is of the 15th century, with a fine timber roof. In the garden, the area of the CHAPTER-HOUSE, 86 ft. by 37 ft., its north Norman arcade, and west arches open to the Close, are observable to the south of the transept, with an Early English door. In the chapter-house, July 12, 1203, King John was absolved by Cardinal Langton; and Eleanor, the heroic queen of Edward I.; admitted into the fraternity of St. Swithin, Jan. 12, 1276. Here in 1044, Queen Emma, "the pearl of Normandy," walked over eight ploughshares, red-hot, to vindicate her innocence. The convent prostrated themselves in the dust before Henry II., complaining that their bishop had cut off three dishes from their table; ten only had he left them, they said. " I have but three myself," replied the king, "and I enjoin my lord to reduce you to that number."

On the west side of the paradise, next to Dr. Williams' House, are the vaults beneath the old Guesten Hall, which was 41 ft. long, 23 ft. broad, and 40 ft. in height, the scene of the coronation-feast of Richard I., accompanied by the King of Scotland. In the kitchen, 36 feet by 24 feet, is an Early English table. The dean's stable, once a barn, retains the oak roof of the age of King Edward I. A

cloister, 90 feet in length, led from the great cloister past
the south transept to the infirmary. The barge boards on
the porter's lodge by the Close Gate deserve notice.

Worcester.

THE city of Worcester, situated on the Severn, and famous
for its china manufactures, has borne more names than
any town in England. It is the Wiga-erne, the Warrior's
Lodge of the Saxon, with the affix of Ceaster, a town. Not
one has suffered more considerably or frequently from civil
wars and border feuds along the marshes; but it prides
itself on the loyal appellation of " the faithful city," as it
was the first in which a mayor proclaimed Charles II. at
the restoration. In College Green, on the south side of the
Cathedral, is Edgar's tower, of the latter end of the reign
of Edward III.; in it is preserved Shakspeare's marriage
bond. The spire of St. Andrew's church, was built,
1751, by W. Wilkinson, a stonemason of Worcester;
the roof is 95 feet, the spire 155 feet high. There is a
water-gate by the river. St. John's Bedwardine and St.
Peter's are the more interesting Mixed churches. St.
Clement's is Norman. Henry I. kept Christmas here 1129,
King John in 1214, Henry III. 1232 (Whitsuntide also in
1234), Edward I. in 1276. The other royal visits were
those of Edward I., who was here seven times; Henry IV.
1407, Henry VI. 1459, Edward IV. 1471, Henry VII. 1485;
Elizabeth 1575, 1585; Charles I. 1644. From a timbered
house, built 1572, in the corn-market, Charles II. escaped,
1651. James II. 1687, George III. 1788, Prince Regent
1807. Parliament sat here 1281. Lord Somers and Butler,
author of Hudibras, were natives of Worcester.

There is a great resemblance in the churches of the west
of England, offered by the absence of western towers, and

by the central highly enriched tower common to Bristol,
Hereford, Gloucester, and Worcester. Its appearance is
most beautiful when seen from the hills of Malvern, where
at one point the towers of Gloucester and Hereford are
also discernible.

The Cathedral of St. Mary, like Chester and Carlisle,
built of red sandstone patched with a whiter material, has
but a plain exterior, and a mutilated west front destitute
of a portal, yet possesses height, extent, good proportions,
light and beautiful outline, and effect. The ground plan
is composed of a CENTRAL TOWER, NAVE of nine bays, CHOIR
of four bays, PRESBYTERY of one bay, the breadth of the
choir transept, and LADY CHAPEL of four bays with aisles—
one bay of the latter is, however, aisleless—and of equal
breadth; a MAIN and CHOIR TRANSEPT, each of two bays,
without aisles, CLOISTERS of seven panes in each alley,
CHAPTER-HOUSE, and NORTH PORCH.

The CRYPT, and Early Norman portions of the NAVE and
TRANSEPT were built by St. Wolstan, 1084, on the site of a
church built by King Offa in 983. It is recorded of St.
Wolstan that he wept when he saw the foundations laid.
" We destroy our father's works," he said, " to get praise
to ourselves : happy was their age which knew not of
stately churches; any roof sufficed for them to offer them-
solves living temples to GOD ; and they wrought on others
to do so likewise : we neglect souls to heap up stones."
The Perpendicular great WEST WINDOW was built, 1378,
and the NORTH PORCH by Bishop Wakefield, 1386. In the
episcopate of Bishop Roger, 1164-80, the two western towers
were blown down. That part of the WEST END of the nave,
which is Transitional, was repaired 1202-14; the Early
English CHOIR was begun by Bishop William, 1224, completed about 1280, vaulted 1376 ; and the Early Decorated
eastern portion of the NAVE in 1320, and vaulted 1377 by
Bishop Wakefield. The Decorated TOWER was built 1281-
1374 ;—the CHAPTER-HOUSE, semi-Norman, by John de Page-
ham, 1113, and finished 1220. The GUESTEN HALL, now
the audit-house (68 ft. long), at the east of the CHAPTER-

HOUSE was built by Walter de Braunsford, prior in 1320; the Decorated REFECTORY (now the College Hall), parallel with the south walk of the cloister, in 1372. The CLOISTERS, Late Perpendicular, are probably the work of De Liliis in 1500; the WATER GATE, LIBRARY, and DORMITORY, 1378.

The Cathedral was dedicated June 9, 1218, by Bishop Sylvester of Evesham, in the presence of Henry III. King Stephen offered his ring at the altar, 1139; Henry II. and his queen in 1159 offered their crowns; King John made a pilgrimage to St. Wolstan's shrine in 1203. George III. visited the Cathedral in 1788.

On the north side of the NAVE in the clerestory the pilasters are flat, the parapet is plain, and the windows, like those of the aisles, have late tracery inserted. A CHAPEL and PORCH with a parvise occupy the eastern portion; plain flying buttresses support that to the west. The MAIN TRANSEPT has Perpendicular windows on the north and east, and is flanked by buttresses terminating in pinnacles. The CHOIR TRANSEPT retains its Early English triplets in the base tier and clerestory; in the latter stage they are longer, and the central light is the tallest. It is also flanked with pinnacled buttresses, and like the rest the gable is lighted by loops. The clerestory and aisle-windows of the CHOIR and LADY-CHAPEL, have Perpendicular tracery. The parapet has a shallow machicolation. The WEST FRONT has no doors; the west window is Early Perpendicular, of eight lights, and richly traceried, flanked by square buttresses, which terminate in octagonal turrets crowned by pinnacles. A Perpendicular window lights each aisle; above each is a Decorated window of two lights under a round arch. The walls of the aisles slope and are flanked by buttresses, with loops to light the internal staircases, and crowned with pinnacles. The east end is very similar, a gable flanked by buttresses, with tall plain and slender pinnacles, and strengthened by simple flying buttresses; but there is a good gable-cross. The east window is Decorated, of nine lights.

The TOWER, of two stories, contains eight bells ; it is of noble design, the lowermost arcaded with pointed trefoiled arches, and lighted by two belfry windows ; a band of quatrefoils is introduced below the upper story, in each front of which are two belfry windows, of two lights, of double the width of those beneath, and like them canopied ; on either side are three statues : on the north, two bishops and the Virgin ; south, King Henry III. ; west, a king ; east, Edward III. A perforated parapet and four octangular turrets complete the graceful structure.

In the west portion of the NAVE the lower circular arches, having been injured, were replaced by pointed arches of the semi-Norman period. The NAVE is broad and spacious, unencumbered with chantry or chapel ; lofty wide windows shed in such light that it appears cheerful, almost gay : simple to bareness, yet with its giant procession of columns—bars of light set against the darker recesses of the aisle—it is singularly impressive ; it is the work of men happy while they worked. ·

> They dreamed not of a perishable home
> Who could build thus.

It is observable, that in the clerestory to the east are triangular-headed arches ; but to the west are round-headed central windows, with small lancets to the gallery on the side. In the west triforium below are three open round triplets, two in each bay, with graceful chevron mouldings and rosettes ; in the east triforium are couplets. The triforium is large and Early English—simple, elegant, and light ; the clerestory was intended for triplets of lancets : both have chevron mouldings.

The Early English pinnacles have been recently rebuilt on the turrets of the church ; and the triplet in the south-west transept been fitted with a memorial window to Queen Adelaide, the glazing by Rogers. The Cathedral, like Durham, York, Norwich,

Wells, and Peterborough, is open to the public. The altar-screen was built 1812; the EAST WINDOW (45 ft. by 27 ft.) of the CHOIR was remodelled in 1792; the WEST WINDOW (45 ft. by 24 ft. 6 in.) of the NAVE in 1789, and both mutilated.

The rood-screen is of three bays with canopied ogee arches. The organ is by Hill, 1852. There is a fine Early English CHOIR, with rich canopied stalls, a handsome groined roof, and the capitals of the pillars are noticeable for the delicacy of their mouldings and freedom in the foliage. The stalls of oak are of the date 1397. The stone parclose of Prince Arthur's chapel shuts off the SOUTH CHOIR TRANSEPT; that on the north is divided by a stone wall. The triforium in the CHOIR is formed of couplets; the clerestory has a screen of triplets behind the exterior triplets in each bay of the LADY CHAPEL. Purbeck marble is freely used for the shafts, and the arches are more sharply pointed than in the CHOIR. The triforium is not open, but is arcaded behind the screen arches. In the spandrils of the triforium, throughout the church and in the trefoiled aisle-arcades, figures are introduced. The REREDOS is of carved stone, and there is an octangular stone PULPIT, with a sculpture of the New Jerusalem behind, and evangelistic symbols in the sides. On the wall of the NORTH CHOIR AISLE, adjoining a gracefully foliated arch in front of a window, and a shafted triplet before that which succeeds, is a rood-solar, or sacrist's balcony, from which the light burning constantly in the church was watched. The transept has pointed panelling in place of a triforium. The NORTH CHOIR TRANSEPT has triplets filled with Perpendicular tracery, with a screen of three insulated clustered shafts inside, occupying the space of the clerestory and triforium in the upper tier. The walls have a trefoiled arcade. The double transept, common to Wells, Salisbury, and Rochester, an ordinary feature in Byzantine churches, yet never seen in England till a period subsequent to the passage of the Crusaders through Constantinople, suggests a clear but hitherto unsuspected intercourse and familiarity with the art of the great metropolis of the Eastern Empire.

The CRYPT extends under the choir from the east wall of the main transept to the centre of the choir transept. It consists of an apsidal nave of four alleys, with lateral aisles, a second aisle to the south, all subdivided by pillars, of plain but bold bases, and cushioned capitals, from which rises a massive round vaulting.

The CHAPTER-HOUSE, on the east side of the CLOISTER, is a decagon with a central shaft, the oldest so formed in the kingdom. It has a range of fine intersecting arches. The windows have Late tracery insertions. The Guesten Hall has a fine open roof of the 14th century, and some frescoes above the dais. The cloisters have rich quatrefoil panelling in the jambs of the arches, and peculiar square apertures.

Near the lavatory, which is still supplied with water from Henwick Hill, in the west walk, is a door which led to the dormitory. The DEANERY was built in 1225 by W. Bedford, the prior. Near the NORTH PORCH, which has a parvise above, is the CHARNEL-HOUSE, with a chantry over it, built by Bishop Blois, 1218-36, to receive the remains which were dug up in the repairs. An octagon belfry, which stood on the north of the Lady Chapel, was pulled down, 1647.

DIMENSIONS OF THE CATHEDRAL IN FEET.

	Length.	Breadth.	Height.
Nave	180	78	66
Choir	120 }	74	68
Lady Chapel	60 }		
Main Transept	128	32	66
Choir Transept	120	25	..
Cloisters W. S. N. 120 E.	125	18	..
Refectory (King's School)	120	38	..
Chapter-house, diameter	55	55	45
Crypt	67	30	..
North Aisle	63	15	..
South Aisle	55	16	..
Crypt under Vestry	45	15	..
Extreme length	394	..	..

In the presbytery are buried Bishops Stillingfleet, (epitaph by Bentley,) Gauden, and Hurd; and the Duke of Hamiltou, killed Sept. 3, 1641, in the battle of Worcester.

The principal monuments are :—

Before the Jesus Chapel, Nave, N. Side.—Sir J. Beauchamp, beheaded 1388, and Dame, effigies of alabaster. *S. Side.*—Colonel Sir H. Ellis, killed June 20, 1815 (by Bacon), altar-tomb; Judge Lyttleton, d. 1481; monument to 29th Regiment, by Westmacott.

Cloisters, N. Alley.—A stone marked "Miserrimus," perhaps that of Rev. T. Morris, a nonjuror, who died in 1749.

> " Miserrimus, and neither name nor date,
> Prayer, text, or symbol graven upon this stone;
> Nought but that word inscribed to the Unknown;
> That solitary word to separate
> From all, and cast a cloud around the fate
> Of him who lies beneath."

Main Transept, S. Wing.—A priest, effigy under an arch (F. Baskerville); Bishop Johnson, by Nollekens.

Main Transept, N. Wing.—Bishop Hough, d. 1743, (by Roubiliac).

Choir Transept, or Bishop's Chapel, N. Wing.—Mrs. C. Digby, d. 1820, an exquisite monument by Chantrey.

Dean's Chapel, S. Wing.—Chantry of Prince Arthur, built 1504, very rich in statuary; Sir G. Ryce, altar-tomb and effigy; Sir W. Harcourt, altar-tomb, effigy; Bishop Giffard, d. 1301, altar-tomb and effigy; Maud Longspée, altar-tomb, Perpendicular, and effigy, of 13th century; Lady De Clifford, d. 1301, effigy.

Choir.—King John, effigy of grey stone, formerly the lid of the stone coffin; on the sides of the head are SS. Wolstan and Oswald.

Presbytery, or Lady Chapel.—Bishops St. Oswald, d. 1061, effigy; St. Wolstan, d. 1062, effigy; Sylvester De Evesham, d. 1216; J. De Constance, d. 1198, effigy; Abbot Hawford, of Evesham, dean, effigy, d. 1557; a Lady, effigy of 12th century; a Knight, effigy, c. 1292; Bishop Hemenhale, d. 1338, a coffin lid; Bishop Thornborough, d. 1641, with an epitaph drawn from the Pythagorean philosophy.

The Chapter consists of a dean and four canons (six stall are suspended). There are three minor canons, eight singing-men, and ten choristers. There are two daily choral services, at quarter past 10 and 3, and a weekly administration of the Holy Communion. The capitular revenues in 1852 were 10,609*l.*; the expenditure on the fabric within fourteen previous years 6244*l.*; the library contains 3600 volumes. The palace is Hartlebury Castle.

Worcester numbers among its bishops SS. Wolstan, Dunstan, and Oswald; Roger of the iron nerve, who continued High Mass when the west end fell and the congregation fled in terror; Cantilupe, enthroned in the presence of the king and the queen of England and Scotland; Giffard, Lord Chancellor, who travelled with a retinue of one hundred knights; Cobham, the good clerk; Cardinal Bourchier; Alcock; Pope Clement VII.; brave Latimer, who prophesied at the stake, "We shall this day light such a candle, as shall never be put out in England;" Bilson; Prideaux, who drew crowds of foreigners to his Oxford lectures, and would say of his disappointed boyish ambition, "Had I been parish clerk of Ugborough, I had never been bishop of Worcester;" Fleetwood, who carried off Prince Charles in safety from Edgehill; Stillingfleet, Hough, and Hurd. Among the dignitaries occur one cardinal, Bishop Hicks, T. Inett, and John Davison.

Arms : Arg. ten torteauxes 3.3.2.1 on a canton, az. the Blessed Virgin and Holy Child, sceptred and nimbed, or.

York.

What could be
Of earthly structures, in God's honour piled,
Of a sublimer aspect? majesty,
Power, glory, strength, and beauty all are aisled
In this eternal ark of worship undefiled.

York, a corruption of the Celtic Eborac, "the Town at the Meeting of the Waters," is situated on the Ouse, in one of the richest and most fertile of English valleys, enlivened by the busy traffic of a navigable river. Alcuin, Constantine the Great, Sir T. Herbert the traveller, Conyers Middleton, Elizabeth Montagu, Bishop Porteus and Flaxman were natives of York. Here Malcolm IV. did homage to Henry II., and in 1171, William, laying in token on St. Peter's altar, spear, and saddle, and breast-plate, and again, August 10, 1175, with his barons, prelates and abbots. In 1230, Henry III. kept Christmas; and in 1251, the marriage feast of his daughter Margaret with Alexander III. of Scotland was celebrated here. In 1327, Edward III. kept Christmas, and, January 24, 1328, was married to Philippa of Hainault. Henry II., in 1160, Edward I., and Richard II., held parliaments in the city. Edward IV. was crowned in the minster with the regal abacot; and Richard III., in 1483; Henry VII. and James I., each twice visited York, and Charles I was fre-quently within its walls.

The embattled walls of York, 12 to 17 ft. high, extend two miles and a half, from Clifford's tower to Fishergate postern, with twenty towers and bastions on the brow of a high bank, with a terrace walk on the inside: where the river intersected the lines there were forts and a chain-boom. There are four gates and five posterns still remain-ing: Goodram—now called after the General, Monk Bar—is good Decorated, the handsomest and most imposing, on the Scarborough-road; Micklegate Bar, on the London-road, 53ft. high, 26ft. broad, 54ft. 7in. deep, has tall circu-lar turrets at the angles, often deformed with the ghastly heads of noble and knight, according to the Lay of Towton Field; Richard Plantagenet 1461, Earls of Devonshire and Wiltshire 1462, and the Jacobites 1746; Botham Bar, 46ft. by 26ft. 6in. on the north, with a Norman archway and portcullis, the upper portions of the fourteenth century, with additions of the period of Henry VIII.; Walmgate Bar, principally of the fourteenth century, with a barbican projecting 56ft. from the gate erected in 1648; Fisher-gate Postern is an earlier structure. Outside the walls on Severus' hill, in 210, the emperor was burned on his funeral pile. The wall and the tower by the Fossbridge, near Peasholme Green, are of the time of the Edwards. The turret is curiously corbelled out. St. Anthony's Hall, 81ft. by 27ft., built 1440, has an open timber roof. The Guildhall, where Charles I. was sold by the Scots, built 1449 (96ft. by 43ft.), has a nave with aisles, divided by wooden pillars, with an oak open roof. There is a house in Newgate Street of the fourteenth century. At the end of the pavement is a house with a stone base of the 14th century, and a timber upper story of the 15th century. Merchants' Hall has a Perpendicular chapel. There are twenty-three churches. In Holy Cross is an Early Perpendicular lectern, with a book chained to it. In St. Mary Bishophill the tower was rebuilt after the twelfth century, and the south wall of the chancel, with Saxon materials. In All Saints', North Street, the east window of the north aisle has a Decorated window, and there is some glazing of the time of Henry VI. In St. Martin's Church, Coney Street, the west window in the north aisle is Decorated; another of the same period, with some Early-English glass, is in St. Denys'. Near St. Helen's in the Wall, Camden records the discovery, at the period of the Reformation, of a supposed tomb of Constantius Chlorus, which had a lamp burning. A similar light was found in a Roman sepulchre at Baena, near Cordova, in Spain, in 1833: it is believed that the lamp was filled with combustible materials which kindled on the admission of the outer air into the closely-sealed vault. In the Castle is the noble ancient keep, on a mound— Clifford's Tower. In All Saints Pavement is an octagon lantern, in which a large lamp was placed as a beacon to guide travellers over the forest of Galtres. St. Michael's bell still rings at 6 A.M., a relic of a similar purpose. In St. George's yard is buried "Dick Turpin," 1739. The entrance-gate of Trinity Priory is built up with modern erections. In the grounds of the Yorkshire Philosophical Society, established 1822, (the museum was built by Wilkins 1830, which contains a most valuable collection of ancient and scientific curiosities), are on the lawn, the beautiful transitional Early English ruins of St. Mary's Abbey, of the time of Henry III., rebuilt by Simon de Warwick, used to build a palace by Henry VIII., a gaol by William III., and Beverley Minster by George I.; a portion of the Roman wall, and a Roman multangular decagonal tower; a guest-house of stone and timber of the fourteenth century; some Norman work in St. Mary's Gate; the ruins of St. Leonard's Hospital, the entrance-door and ambulatory Transitional Norman, with a portion of an Early-English Chapel.

While Lincoln Minster is solid, abounding in picturesque variety, the Cathedral of York is lofty, spacious, rich, and vast,' a giant's step towards heaven. The one absorbs every sense of time and place; the piety of the builders is the paramount sensation; the splendour of the detail is lost in the impressiveness of the whole; the observer feels dwarfed into insignificance, in a temple worthy of the service of the Invisible: the other is majestic, magnificent, full of genius, fit for the worship of mortals. It will generally be found the case, that both the spot and objects contained in these memorable churches will seldom fall short of the most sanguine expectation; while the immediate impression produced by them on the spectator, who has come to revere what is venerable, and has a sense of what is glorious, is inconceivable.

The king of Cathedrals, it towers like a giant over all the city; its three towers, above the parish steeples, like forest oaks among an underwood; the profusion of crocketed pinnacles gives a picturesque variety to the outlines; the proportions are harmonious and noble;

> This outshining and o'erwhelming edifice
> Fools our fond gaze.

It is indeed remarkable the effect produced by the exterior of imperial York, which addresses itself immediately to

the intellect, and would almost persuade us to believe
that the works of man rival, in grandeur and perpetuity,
those of Nature herself. There is an instinctive sense of
awe and veneration, rising from a perception of the glory
that attaches to such prayerful and sublime aspirations of
the men who reared a pile so magnificent in magnitude
and extent; the long, difficult, often interrupted work of
centuries; the evidence of a rare self-denial; where the
first architect displayed his best art, and built his portion
solidly, while he bequeathed it for completion to successors
animated by the same spirit. Within, the idea of infinity
perfectly marvellous is produced, simply by an elongation
and multiplication of a continued series of aisles and
arcades.

On the site of a wooden church, in which St. Paulinus
baptized King Edwin, 627, Archbishop Albert, 767, erected
a cathedral, of which some fragments of early masonry
remain in the crypt, and an image of the Virgin in the east
wall of the presbytery. Archbishop Thomas, after a fire
in 1069, rebuilt the NAVE aisles and TRANSEPT with a large
central TOWER, and substantially repaired the choir. In
1171, Archbishop Roger rebuilt the CHOIR, and added to
the CRYPT. Archbishop Gray completed the SOUTH TRAN-
SEPT in 1240, and John le Romayne, the treasurer, the
NORTH TRANSEPT immediately after, re-facing also the upper
part of the LANTERN TOWER. Archbishop John le Romayne, son of the treasurer, laid the foundation of the
NAVE, in 1291. In 1338, Archbishop Melton glazed the
great WEST WINDOW, which was filled with stained glass, by
Thornton of Coventry, 1405-9. In 1355, Archbishop
Thoresby ceiled the NAVE with wood. Simultaneously
with the nave, the CHAPTER-HOUSE, was built and completed about the middle of the fourteenth century, and
leaded 1370. Archbishop Thoresby laid the foundation-
stone of the PRESBYTERY or Lady Chapel, July 1361; and it
was completed in 1372. The CHOIR was built, 1373-1400,
and roofed in 1405. About the year 1409, the central tower
piers were recased with Perpendicular work, but the TOWER

was not completed, in its present appearance, until 1470. The south-west BELL TOWER was begun by John Berningham, treasurer, 1432, and finished, 1456. The NORTH-WEST TOWER was completed, 1456-1472. The rood-screen was built 1475-1505, W. Hyndley being master mason. Dean Andrew added the battlements and buttresses of the south side of the choir. The dedication of the church was held July 3, 1472. The crypt was paved with Flemish tiles, 1415; in 1399, it was used as a storehouse for the fabric.

The peculiarities of the church are, that its eastern and western limbs are equal in length; the CHOIR is narrower than the NAVE, and the MAIN TRANSEPT of three bays still narrower, being one half of the total length of the nave and choir: and the east and west ends are both square. The MAIN TRANSEPT has lateral aisles. The ground plan is only broken by some chapels on the south; those upon the north having been destroyed. The NAVE is of eight bays, while the CHOIR is of nine. There is a short choir transept. The NAVE is mainly Decorated with geometrical tracery, but has flowering tracery at the west end. The TRANSEPT is Early English; the CHOIR and the three TOWERS are Late Perpendicular; the PRESBYTERY is an early specimen of that style. The SHRINE of ST. WILLIAM stood behind the reredos, the same position occupied by the shrines of their patron saints at St. Alban's, Winchester, Westminster, and other minsters.

The chief defect is the want of relative proportion of the great width to the length: and the span of the arches makes the interior open in every direction, and robs it of the charm of intricacy and indefinite perspective. Pinnacles and flying buttresses were designed to bear up a vault of stone. As in the octagon at Ely and the choir of Winchester, the design was superseded by an imitation in wood of admirable construction, with simple grandeur and appearance of stability owing to the radiation of the ribs from shafts which extend direct from the floor. It was. this timber construction which, in the ceilings, gave a depth and boldness, and contrived ribs and boss richly carved, and rendered this feature of English churches unsurpassed by any nation, and at length was transmitted to stone, and the greater cost fatally diminished the extent of their dimension.

When it was found that the Early English transepts were out of harmony with the new work, a pier arch was removed on either side, and Decorated arches were built on Early English bases. The triforium is Early English. The engineering was faulty, for the arches began to yield, and the architect was compelled to build up a pier on either side with solid masonry.

A peculiar interest has been awakened in this Cathedral from the occurrence of two fires which threatened its destruction within a very recent period : the first the act of an incendiary and maniac, Jonathan Martin, a brother of the great painter, on Feb. 2, 1829, when the stalls and roof of the choir were burned ; the second in May 1840, when, by the carelessness of the plumbers, the south-west tower, with its fine peal of bells, was reduced to a shell and the whole of the central alley of the roof consumed.

On the west door and lower and upper windows is geometrical tracery, but in those in the middle tier, over panel, buttress, niche, canopy, parapet, and finial, beams an exuberant display of tracery and enrichment which renders this the most elaborately gorgeous mass of masonry in England. An open battlement crosses the entire front, spans the towers, and is continued along the nave and choir. This is pierced by the canopy of the great window, which is filled with open tracery ; behind it rises the actual gable of the roof, which is richly adorned, and finished with graduated open battlements on the sides, and a pinnacle on the summit. The WESTERN FRONT is splendid. Great Peter in the north-west tower, which cost 2000*l.*, and weighs 10 tons 15 cwts., was cast by Mears in 1845. In the south-west tower is a peal of bells, the gift of Dr. Beckwith. The central porch is divided into two portals by a shaft with six foliated triangles ; in the head above this rises the superb canopied west window of eight lights, 54ft. by 30ft., richly canopied. In each of the TOWERS there are three tiers of single windows, the upper and lower being canopied, above the lateral doorways: double buttresses, of great boldness, add dignity to their elevation: the upper portion is richly battlemented, and has eight pinnacles. The clerestory has five-light windows, foliated with quatrefoiled circles in the head; the aisles have canopied three-light windows, trifoliated with three quatrefoiled circles: the grandeur of the aisles is unequalled in England. On the north side of the NAVE, where the archbishop's palace abutted on the Cathedral, there are neither pinnacles nor canopies, and the buttresses are large, broad, and massive. On the south the tall pinnacled buttresses are tripled in each bay of the aisles, with projecting gurgoyles, foliated finials, and tabernacles filled with statuary; in the clerestory there are flying buttresses pinnacled. On the west side of the south transept is the commonplace Record-office. In either TRANSEPT is an arcaded clerestory, with three lancets out of five in each bay glazed; the aisles have an arcade, with couplets as lights. In the interior in the triforium, in each bay under a pointed arch, are four lancets with rich foils in the head. The roof is of wood, but resembles that of the nave and choir by its bosses and groining ribs. The north transept contains the five lancet windows known as the Five Sisters, under five lancets graduated to the gable. The East End consists of the great east window set between huge panelled buttresses which end in pinnacles with crowns at the base; parapets of open work surmount the front and aisles, which are flanked by pinnacled buttresses. The aisle windows of the CHOIR are of four-lights canopied; in the clerestory the windows are of five-lights trefoiled. The CHOIR TRANSEPT of one bay has a five-light south window, with three transoms. Pinnacles enrich this side. The battlemented LANTERN TOWER rises on arches 109 feet high, only one story above the roof; it has two canopied three-light transomed windows on each face. At an angle of the great tower, on a little turret, the Duke of Buckingham in 1666 erected a beacon, taken down December, 1803, to alarm the country in case of an invasion by the Dutch or French. This it was intended to replace to give notice of any landing in the last French war, but the plan fell to the ground. The traceried roof is 180 feet from the pavement. The CHAPTER-HOUSE is on the north side: the cloister appears to have adjoined it.

Under the east window, and on either side of the west door, are the statues of Sir Robert de Vavasour, who gave his quarries at Tadcaster, and Sir Robert Percy, who gave his woods at Bolton to the rebuilding of the nave in the 14th century. Over the central west door is the statue of Archbishop Melton, restored by Taylor: at the east end is the effigy of Archbishop Romaine. The SOUTH TRANSEPT has a magnificent front of three stages in the purest period of architecture. Over a double arcade, the upper · pierced with couplets and a three-gabled porch, are three lancets, and in the gable is a double rose window, 30 feet in diameter, of 20-trefoiled lights, with three outer circles filled with toothed mouldings, under a triangular window. The front is approached by two flights of steps, and flanked by octangular turrets: over the gable is the "Minstrel's Turret" of a later date. In the west aisle is the FONT, of dark shelly marble.

The NAVE-triforium consists, in each bay, of five trefoiled arches canopied; each central arch had a statue; the lateral arches are pierced; on the north side is a great beam, carved like a dragon's head curved back, which supported the font cover. On the opposite side is the "Soldier of Christ," in allusion to the Baptismal Vow. In the central light of each bay was a figure; some remain. In the spandrils of the lower arcade are the shields of benefactors. The gorgeous WEST window, the extreme height of the vaulting, the play of light and shade, vastness, breadth, and spaciousness of the aisles, with their canopied arcades, impress the mind with a sense of grandeur and admiration, which is increased almost pain-

fully upon standing beneath the soaring vault of the
central lantern, with the colours of the stained glass dyeing
the pavement on either hand, and the superb SCREEN of the
CHOIR, 25ft. high by 50ft. broad, so light and beautiful,
with its niched statues of kings, representing the line from
William I. to Henry VI., the period of its erection. The
last figure was the work of Michael Taylor. The organ, by
Elliot and Hill, 1837, the gift of the Earl of Scarborough,
is most unhappily set upon it. The fifty-two canopied
STALLS and REREDOS were restored in 1830, after the fire,
under the care of Sir Robert Smirke, Mr. Wild, and
Mr. Mackenzie, carved in London out of Dutch oak. The
brass EAGLE was the gift of Dr. T. Croft, 1686. The ROOF
is of teak supplied from the royal dockyards. The pillars
of the CHOIR have each a bracket and niche for a statue,
and the sides of the windows are niched. The EAST WINDOW,
76 ft. by 32 ft., has been called "the wonder of the world"
for glazing and stonework; it has 115 scriptural subjects,
each about 2 ft. 2 in., high, in the lights, finished with the
delicacy of a miniature, transparent and gleaming as the
rainbow-tinted spray of the sea-foam, the blossoming of
the ocean. In the ancient CHAIR at the north side of the
altar have been crowned several of the Saxon kings,
Richard III. and James I.

The greater part of the old glass is Early English, about
the date of 1220, being a portion of a Jesse window; and
in two windows from the west, on the north side of the
nave clerestory. The Five Sisters, each 54 ft. 3½ in., by 5 ft.
in the north transept, are glazed with glass of the latter
half of the 13th century : the window above is modern,
by Peckit. There is a melancholy legend attached to the
window—Five sisters dwelt at York, wards of St. Mary's
Abbey: one died a young widow, and was buried in the
southern transept of the Cathedral: the survivors agreed
to fill the five lancets to her memory with patterns taken
from their broidery-frames long in sorrow laid aside. By
the stone marked with the name of Alice, bright in the
stream of coloured light, they walked or knelt for many

hours in each day; one by one they passed to the land where the loving in death are not divided, and the single stone long bore this only epitaph, five Christian names. In the CHAPTER-HOUSE the glazing is Early Decorated; but the window facing the entrance is modern, by Barnet. In the NAVE, the magnificent great west window, with flowing tracery of surpassing beauty, is of the time of Edward III., about 1330: the superb east window of the choir was glazed by John Thornton of Coventry, 1404; above it on the exterior is the effigy of Archbishop Thoresby. The second and fourth windows from the east of the choir clerestory, on the south side, are Decorated. The aisles eastward of the SOUTH TRANSEPT, and the lancets on the east of the MAIN TRANSEPT, have glazing of the reign of Henry IV.: that of the rest of the choir is of the date of Henry V. and VI. These windows were preserved from destruction through means of Thomas, Lord Fairfax. The south-east window of the south CHOIR aisle was brought from St. Nicholas, Rouen—a gift of Lord Carlisle—in 1804; it is a copy of a picture by Baroccio, and is of the latter half of the 16th century.

The fine Norman CRYPT is of four aisles, each of three bays, and situated under the choir. The piers are 7 feet high, circular, and of enormous dimensions; the capitals are sculptured. In the PRESBYTERY east of the choir transept, the clerestory, in order to give effect to the glazing, has a screenwork of stone of three trefoiled arches, transomed, before and behind the windows. The tiles and two water-drains. remain. The arches have chevron mouldings, which retain their original glazing.

The library, by Dean Markham, was removed into the old chapel of the archiepiscopal palace. In the octagonal CHAPTER-HOUSE one of the piers has a Latin inscription to this effect ("inserted in golden Saxon letters by one lately coming into this kingdom," says a MS. of 1634; probably Gondomar); "As the rose is flower of flowers, so this is the structure of structures." It has forty-four stalls, and was restored 1845. The shafts are of Petworth marble, the windows are of five-lights trefoiled, with three foliated circles in the head.   In the entrance pillar is an exquisite effigy of the Virgin and Holy Child.   In the windows is perceptible the ingenious method by which circles were fitted to the pointed arch ; they are piled up to fit the form : the next and immediate step to the introduction of flowing tracery, was the employment of spherical triangles.   It is the only chapter-house of the style which wants the central shaft, the cause being that the roof of wood did not require this support.   York and Lincoln alone retain their spire-like high-pitched roof.   Of the early prayers at 6 A.M., in the Lady Chapel, a legend is told of an aged maiden lady, a constant attendant, rising too soon on a bright summer morning and finding the doors closed, when suddenly the portals opened, and instead of an empty nave and silent choir, a few worshippers and the simple service, a glorious vision, like the gates of heaven, burst upon her eyes, the stalls filled with devout priests chanting to divinest music a sublime and magnificent service, crowds kneeling along the aisles, the altar blazing with lights and veiled with clouds of incense, till her soul fainted within her and she swooned away on the threshold.

In 1189 the gentry of the county, who were all deeply indebted to them, during a massacre of the Jews, ran to the Cathedral, where their bonds were kept, and made a solemn bonfire of the papers before the altar.

In the inner vestry, in a large press, are preserved a spear-head, helmet, and spur, a pastoral staff of silver, 0 feet long, given by Catharine of Braganza to her confessor, Smith, and presented to York in 1699 ; the mazer bowl, given by Archbishop Scrope to the guild of Corpus Christi in 1398 ; an alms box ; record chest, with sculptures of the story of St. George, of the time of Henry V. ; an ancient cope chest with iron scroll patterns ; a chair in which King Richard III. was crowned, Sept. 8, 1483 ; three chalices of silver ; the rings of Archbishops Sewel, Greenfield, Bowet, Neville, and Lee; and Ulphus' horn of ivory, of the 11th century. He was Prince of Deira, and bequeathed his lands to this church, the tenure of which is secured by the possession of this relic, as the forest of Inglewood is by Henry II.'s horn at Carlisle, and the Pusey estates by Canute's horn. There is also here an ancient coronation chair. On August 11, 1617, King James I. visited the Cathedral, and finding St. William's monument destroyed, commanded that his bones, "which were large and long," should be preserved in the vestry. The Norwich Captain, in 1634, mentions here sumptuous church-plate lately given by the king, a gorgeous canopy, copes of embroidered velvet, cloth of gold, and tissue of great value and worth; and "St. Peter's chair, wherein all the archbishops are installed, two double gilt coronets, the tops with globes and crosses to set on either side of his grace, which are called his dignities."

DIMENSIONS OF THE CHURCH IN FEET.

	Length.	Breadth.	Height.
Nave	264	104½	99½
Choir, Presbytery, &c.	223½	99½	102
Transept	223½	93½	92
Lady Chapel	64	100	101
Chapter-house, diameter	57	57	67 f. 10 in.
Central tower	..	65	213
West tower	32	32	202
West front	..	109½	..
Extreme length	486	..	..

The chief monuments are :—

Lady Chapel.—Archbishop Frewen, effigy; Archbishop Matthew, effigy; Archbishop Sharp, 1713, mitred effigy.

N. Aisle.—Archbishop Sterne, 1683, mitred effigy.

S. Aisle.—Archbishop Bowet, a superb canopy with three lofty tabernacles, mutilated by the fire, 1829; Wentworth, Earl of Strafford, d. 1695, statue of the earl and his wife; Dr. Burgh, by Westmacott; Archbishop Scrope, beheaded 1495, table-tomb, the sides quatrefoil.

Presbytery, S. Aisle.—Archbishop Lamplugh, d. 1691, mitred effigy, with a pastoral staff, standing; Archbishop Hutton, d. 1605, effigy recumbent; Archbishop Dolben, 1686, standing mitred effigy; Archbishop Savage, d. 1507, effigy under a panelled arch, with a screen; Archbishop Harsnet, effigy, in a cope and alb, mitred, and with a pastoral staff, brass.

N. Transept.—Prince William de Hatfield, d. 1344, effigy and canopy; Archbishop Greenfield, canopied tomb, 1315—the brass is one of the few surviving of 120 which in 1612 were entire; Dr. Beckwith, d. 1843, effigy.

W. Aisle.—Treasurer Haxey, d. 1424, table-tomb of Purbeck marble and cadaver—on it to this day certain rents are paid; Archbishop Harcourt, d. 1847, recumbent effigy, by Noble.

S. Transept.—Archbishop Grey, d. 1255, canopy of two tiers of tre-foiled arches, and effigy—the upper shrine-shaped story has crocketed gablets, the finials have sculptured birds, foliage enriches the spandrils and capitals of the eight slender shafts; Archbishop Kimton, d. 1264, table-tomb under a canopy of trefoiled niches.

Nave, N. Aisle.—Archbishop Roger. *S. Aisle.*—Memorial to Colonel Moore and the heroic soldiers of the Europa.

Choir, N. Aisle.—Two ancient stone coffins brought from Clifton; Charles, Earl of Carlisle, time of Charles II.; effigies of knights, Mauley, of the 14th century. *S. Aisle.*—Memorial of Parian to 33rd Regiment, 1859, by Richardson.

The burial-places of King Edwin, 7th century; King Egbert, 757; and Tosti, Earl of Northumberland, 1066, are not known.

The Chapter is composed of a dean and four canons. There are five minor canons, fourteen lay vicars, and ten choristers. There are two daily choral services, at 10 and 4, and celebration of the Holy Communion on all Sundays and great feasts. Since the time of Mason, the organist, the Nicene Creed has never been sung here. The library contains 8000 volumes. The capitular revenues in 1842 were 3041*l.*, the fabric fund, 2144*l.*, and the expenditure on the fabric since 1829 (including subscriptions 71,590*l.*,) was 106,560*l.*

Arms: Gules, two keys in saltier, in chief a mitre or.

Among the primates of York occur SS. Paulinus, Chad, Wilfrid, and St. John of Beverley and Oswald; Aldred, who made the Norman invader kneel for pardon when his servants had been robbed by the king's sheriff; Thurston, who won the Battle of the Standard; St. William, who died from drinking a poisoned chalice; Roger, the enemy of à Becket; the gallant Geoffrey Plantagenet, Henry II.'s only affectionate child, and chancellor, the brave soldier who fought with Scot and Frenchman with distinction; Gifford, Lord Chancellor; De la Zouche, who took David Bruce and Melton prisoners in the battle of Beure Park; Thoresby, Lord Chancellor, who said to hear God's word in English was better than to listen to a hundred masses; Scrope, cruelly beheaded, whose coat of mail Henry IV. sent to the pope, saying, "See if this be thy son's coat or no." Bowet, Lord Treasurer, carried in a litter to battle against the Scots; Neville, Lord Chancellor, who for his pains in showing his treasures to Edward IV. was despoiled, and saw his mitre melted into a royal crown; Cardinal Rotherham, Lord Chancellor, founder of Lincoln College, Oxford; Savage, who delighted to wind the horn and listen to the baying of hounds at Scroby and Cawood; Cardinal Baynbridge, poisoned by his valet; Wolsey, who introduced the crown into the arms in place of the ancient pall; Heath, for whom the ungrateful Elizabeth suggested the use of torture when he was eighty years of age; Sandys; Hutton, who, as Elizabeth said, in his sermons "pinned her shroud about her face;" Matthew, the punster; Monteigne, who suggested his preferment to James I., who asked him what was the greatest act of faith. "Say, Sire, unto this mountain, Be thou cast into that sea;" Neile, who burned a heretic for the last time; Williams, the pluralist Lord Keeper, who was a diocese in his own person; Frewen, author of "The Whole Duty of Man;" Dolben, who in Westminster Abbey, when the preacher fell ill, continued the sermon in all its heads and divisions;

Sharp, who said he owed his mitre to an alternate study of the Holy Bible and Shakspeare; and Blackburne, the buccaneer. Among the dignitaries occur eleven cardinals, Thomas Stubbs, Elias Bishop of Auxerre, Theobald of Liege, John and Christopher of Elgin, William of Derry, and Bramhall of Armagh.

The archbishop's palace is at Bishopthorpe, the birth-place of Guy Faux.

IRELAND.

INTRODUCTION.

THE PERIODS OF IRISH ARCHITECTURE.

I. NATIVE or Celtic style, much anterior to the incursions of the Danes or the Norman Conquest:—Churches of small size, like a Roman basilica shorn of its apse; rude massive buildings oblong in plan, with triangular-headed small windows; pyramidal-shaped doors; and Cyclopean or Pelasgic masonry. This and the following style occupied the interval between the fifth and sixth centuries, and the year 1176. The early Scottish, Anglo-Saxon, and French churches of the sixth century were all parallelograms. It is remarkable that the Greek oblong temple, composed of a nave and shrine, like the Temple of Jerusalem, also consisting of oracle and nave, 116 ft. 3 in. by 37 ft. 6 in., and 58 ft. 1½ in. in height, were both derived from an Egyptian original. The architect of the temple on Zion was of Tyre, a Phœnician colony; and while the legend of Cadmus, a Phœnician and the civiliser of Greece, denotes a correspondence between those countries, the commerce of Tyre with the western isles is boldly asserted by many writers. These early churches, rather oratories than capable of holding a congregation, range from 20 ft. to 60 ft. in length; they are aisleless, rectangular, have no apse, and are never found in a circular form; sometimes they are provided with a small chancel, and occur in groups. On Mount Athos, in other parts of Greece, and in Asia Minor, churches were usually built in groups of seven, in remembrance of the seven churches of the Apocalypse. The *round towers* are of this period, which lasted till the 11th century, but are continued until the 13th century. Their form was adopted in consequence of the difficulty of obtaining cut limestone for the corners. Their purposes were various: they have been variously represented as serving for a belfry, a beacon, a treasury, and a retreat for the priests. In the 14th and 15th centuries, they were replaced by tall narrow square central towers. In the earlier towers the parapet is plain, with a range of holes instead of gurgoyles for letting off the water; in later buildings there are stepped battlements resting on corbels.

The *Saints' houses*, the beehive houses of Connemara, and the oratory of Gallerus, are of " Cyclopean masonry," built of masses of rock, and vaulted with stone roofs; but the latter are of a later date, and are provided with chambers. In St. Kevin's, Glendalough, the lower structure is of the 7th century. The upper tunnel vault was provided with ribs, on which were laid the horizontal courses of the outer roof, which was built up straight to throw off the rain; this plan was also adopted in Cormack's chapel, Cashel, built 1127-34. The vault, upper chamber, and belfry are of the 12th century.

The cathedral of Glendalough is full of interest as one of the earliest Irish structures. The east window and south door, however, are of the beginning of the 13th century. In the succeeding style of native architecture, the roof became flattened, chevron mouldings were introduced, the arches received semicircular heads in place of triangular pediments or square lintels; windows became larger, and chamfered beadings ran round the inner arch, and the masonry was inferior. The peculiar cairn-like shaped door, formed of three stones, two jambs sloping upward towards a horizontal lintel, lasted throughout the various styles, and took its origin, like the round tower and Cyclopean masonry, in the stubborn nature of the building material. Within the pale the

English introduced the Early English, after the Norman style. But the early architecture of the Isles, Northumbria and North Wales, bore a great resemblance to each other. Dublin appears to have been the architectural school of North Wales still later.

II. Norman and Ostmen's style :—remarkable for the absence of enrichment, and frequently of aisles, and the presence of continental features ; and lasting longer in Ireland than in any other country. St. Bernard tells us, that when St. Malachy (O'Magair, bishop of Connor, 1124), in the 12th century, replaced a wooden structure in Ulster by a church of stone, the Irish protested against it as a Norman and extravagant innovation. The bishop, however, merely introduced the use of hewn, in place of rough stone, and of mortar instead of mud. The earliest Irish churches were of timber.

III. The Lancet :—found mostly on the eastern side of the island, having been introduced by the English, though on the western side it seems to have been a native discovery, or a developed or Transitional Norman style. At Kilconnel a small cloister, 48 ft. square, resembles cloisters in Spain and Sicily.

IV. The Later Pointed—has many continental features.

The churches and monasteries were fortified, and rooms built above the vaulting and in the roofs. At Cashel Cathedral, of the 13th century, the Castle forms the west end of the building, and passages communicate from it with the vaulting and the central tower. Holy Cross, on the road to Thurles, was at once castle and minster. A similar combination of a baronial and ecclesiastical structure is found in St. Mary's Abbey, Crossraguel, in Scotland, where a rough square tower immediately adjoins some very delicate architecture. The lesser cathedrals commonly appear to be of the 12th or 13th century.

CATHEDRALS OF IRELAND.

Achonry.

St. Crummatha's. This is now only a poor parish church in a small hamlet; but it boasts a dean, precentor, archdeacon, and three prebendaries.

Aghadoe.

St. Canice. There are here the remains of a Cathedral 80 ft. by 20 ft. Dr. Ledwich, Vicar, 1772, says, that his predecessor pulled down most of it to wall-in his demesne. The *nave*, of the 8th century, was lighted by two round windows, one on each side; there is a good doorway, composed of a semi-circular arch, with double zig-zag mouldings and beading in the interval, which springs from small round pillars, 3 ft. high, with plain capitals. The *choir*, of the 13th century, has a south window, a couplet in the east wall, and contains three tombs. The *Ogham stone*, rendered famous by Weld and Vallancey, is at Aghadoe House. There is the base of a *round tower* of the 12th century, called the Bishop's chair, and a smaller structure named the pulpit.

Ardagh.

THERE are a few ruins of a small Cathedral.   Here Goldsmith was directed to Fetherstonhaugh House as an inn, an incident which he has introduced in his play—"She Stoops to Conquer."   The learned Dr. Graves was dean of this church.

Ardfert.

ST. BRENDAN'S.   The parish church is a portion of the cathedral, which was burned in the wars of 1641; principally Early English or Transitional Norman, with a few Decorated windows.   It consisted of a nave and choir, 78 ft. by 30 ft., with aisles.   On the north-west are two detached chapels.   At the east end is a triplet, and there is an arcade of nine trefoiled arches on the south wall of the *choir*.   The effigy of a bishop remains.   A west tower of dark marble, 100 ft. high, fell down in 1770.

Ardmore.

ST. BRENDAN'S.   A small church, with ancient imagery and bas-reliefs.   The round tower is 91 ft. high, and 15 ft. in diameter.

Armagh.

ARMAGH means "the High Place;" it was anciently called "the City of Saints."   The Cathedral is magnificently seated upon the crown of the "Hill of Sallows," a steep which falls away rapidly on the sides.   The first church was founded by

St. Patrick, but destroyed by the Danes, 832-839; it was rebuilt; burned 1020; restored 1125-1145, and again burned in 1404; once more in 1566 by Shane O'Neal, from some supposed insult offered by the primate Loftus; and for the last time by Sir Phelim O'Neil in 1643. The old church was a parallelogram, 140 ft. long. The present structure is 183 ft. 6 in. by 119 ft. broad at the transept; the central tower, low and solid, rises 110 ft. high, with a spire 40 ft. It has been repaired by the archbishops Boulter, Robinson, and Lord John Beresford, at a cost of £30,000, since 1835. Cottingham was the architect employed, and, as at Rochester, perpetrated every form of monstrous absurdity. The chief monuments are those of Dean *Drelincourt*, by Rysbrack; Archbishop *Robinson*, bust, by Bacon; *Stuart*, effigy, by Chantrey; William, Viscount *Charlemont*, died 1671; William, Baron *Caulfield*; and Sir T. *Molyneux*, statue, by Roubiliac. The chapter consists of a dean and four canons; there are two vicars choral, four choirmen, and four choristers. There are daily services at 10 and 3.

St. Bernard says that the Irish thought no man could be rightful primate without St. Patrick's cross and canons. The see boasts St. Patrick, Usher, Bramhall, and Marsh.

The nave is of five bays with aisles; the choir of three bays and transept are both aisleless. The choir screen includes the easternmost bay of the nave. In 1782 Primate Robinson intended to build a west tower like that of Magdalen College, Oxford, 101 ft. high, and employed I. Cooley as architect; only 60 ft. of the entire height were completed, when there were signs of a settlement; and at the request of some elderly ladies who became alarmed, the works were stopped. In 1786 Johnston, another architect, reinstated the original central tower, but with a single window instead of a pair as heretofore. The choir is seated under the lantern, which has a flat ceiling; the organ is ingeniously arranged on the east and west walls of the north transept, which is Early English with Decorated windows. A stone pulpit, canopied, stands on the north-east, and a throne of oak, canopied, at the south-east angle of the lantern. The east window is Decorated, and of three lights; in each of the side walls are three two-light windows. The east window is filled with stained glass by Warrington; two upon the sides by Ward and Nixon; a third by Willement; the fourth is the work of a lady amateur. The pillars and clerestory of the nave are Late Transitional Decorated; the west window, which is a triplet, and the west windows of the aisles, Perpendicular, contain glass by Warrington. The roof is a flattened cove; the font octagonal. Some statues are of great interest; those of SS. Andrew and George have the characteristics of the German school of Late Gothic sculpture. Two statues of bishops of the early half of the 16th century are simply treated, and have graceful drapery.

Arms: same as Canterbury.

Cashel.

Yet do we love these ancient ruins;
We never trod upon them, but we set
Our foot upon some reverend history;
And questionless here in this open court
(Which now lies naked to the injuries
Of stormy tempests) some men sleep interred
Who loved the church right well, gave largely to it,
And thought it should have canopied their bones
Till doomsday. But all things have their end;
Churches and cities, which have decease like men,
Must have like death that we have.

KILLABN and Doddry, two swineherds, had kept ward on the Hill Drumpava—"the woodlands,"—for several months, when on a sudden appeared a vision, bright as the sun, which with a voice sweeter than any music, prophesied of St. Patrick's coming, and consecrated the hill. Upon it Cork, King of Munster, hearing of the apparition, built his palace, called Lis na Chree—"Fort of Heroes,"—and, as his tribute was paid here, named the name Cios ail—"Rock of tribute-money."

With its commanding situation, its massive proportions and singular variety of outline, the range of buildings is the most

remarkable in Ireland, perhaps in Europe. The Cathedral
stands on a huge limestone cliff, partly precipitous and wholly
isolated, conspicuous for miles round, in the midst of the
Golden Vale, with the tall dark Galtee mountains on one side,
and in every other direction the open plain without a tree.
Within the ruined wall of enclosure, are these limestone
buildings—the *hall of the vicars choral*, the *old palace*, a strong
castle at the west end—both were repaired by Archbishop
O'Hedian, 1421; *McCormack's chapel*, built of sandstone, and
the *round tower*, of freestone, which is 50 ft. round, 90 ft. high,
with a door 12 ft. from the ground, and four apertures at top.

The CATHEDRAL, begun 1169, by King Donald O'Brien of
Limerick, and completed in the 13th century, consists of a
nave, choir, and transept without aisles, and a square central
tower. The windows are lancets. It is 210 ft. long, and
170 ft. broad at the transept. Archbishop Price, not being
able to drive up to the doors, procured an Act of Parliament
to change his see to the church of St. John, and unroofed them
the cathedral 1744-1752. On the south side of the choir are the
monument and mitred effigy of Primate *Miler Magrath*; on
the south side of the cathedral is the effigy of St. Patrick on a
slab, said to be the original tribute-stone: on it the kings of
Munster were crowned. In 1101, there was a meeting of all
Munster here, when Murtough made a great offering on the
altar. In 1172, King Henry II. received the homage of
Donald O'Brien, and the bishops in synod conferred the kingdom upon him. In a chapel of the north transept is the *font*
and the tomb of the founder McCarthy, which was removed
from the north wall between the doorway and tower, in
McCormack's chapel. In the wars of the Butlers and Fitz-
Geralds, the Earl of Kildare burned the cathedral, 1495, and
excused himself to the king, on the plea that he should never
have committed such a sacrilege, but he was told that of a
certainty Archbishop Creagh was inside: the king answered
the bishop of Meath, who complained of his turbulence
—"If all Ireland cannot govern this man, who so fit as he to
govern her?"—and he constituted him viceroy, August 6, 1496.
In 1647, Lord Inchiquin and the Parliamentarians summoned
the citizens to pay him £3,000 to retire; but they bravely

took to the rocks, and numbers, with twenty monks, were slain at the storming. McCarwell, assassinated with a skeine by a competitor for his throne, from Rome; Nicolson, the Earl of Normanton, and Lawrence, have been archbishops; and among the dignitaries occur the names of Dean Cotton, author of the "Fasti Hibernici;" Sir Harcourt Lees, and C. Forster, the author. There are five vicars choral.

McCormack's chapel, which after 1169 was used as the chapter-house, was built by Cormac M'Carthy, a priest-king, who had been deposed 1127 : it was consecrated 1134 by the archbishop and prelates, in the presence of the assembled Irish nobility. It stands between the choir and south transept of the cathedral. It is 55 ft. long, and composed of a nave 18 ft. by 29 ft., and chancel 12 ft. square, and at their junction on either side is a slender square tower, like an outer transept. The *north door* is the chief entrance, and has a curious sculpture between a centaur and a lion; there is a corresponding south, but no west door originally. The *south tower* is ornamented with eight projecting bands, without a roof, and is 55 ft. high, 10 ft. long, and 6 ft. 8 in. broad. The upper stories were used as apartments, and a spiral stair leads to crofts above the nave and chancel, which were dormitories. The *north tower* has a pyramidal roof, and is 50 ft. high. The walls of the chapel are decorated with arcades, both within and externally; in the choir, on the inside, they rest on columns, but in the nave on square pilasters, with chevron mouldings; above them in the north and south sides is a series of stunted columns, resting on a string course, and from the capitals spring square ribs, as in the crypt at Repton, to support the semicircular roof, which is of stone, high-pitched, and supported on external corbels. The chancel has an intersecting vault, the nave a tunnel vault with transverse beams. In place of an east window is an arched quadrangular recess for a throne or altar. The chancel-arch is of four orders, with two spirally-fluted pillars. The great "Magician of the North" was on his way to London, when, astonished by the unexpected magnificence of the ruins, he forgot his intended journey, and was found at midnight wandering through the lonely aisles.

There are some beautiful ruins in Cashel of St. Mary's Abbey, and remains of the Franciscan Priory, of the time of Henry III.: four effigies of the 13th century, which were rifled from the crypt, are now built into St. John's Church-yard wall.

Arms: Gules, two keys addorsed in saltier or.

Clogher.

The Cathedral of this poor remote village was built in 1041, rebuilt by Bishop M'Cathasaidh 1295, who gave it bells; considerable alterations after a fire, 1396, were made by Bishop M'Cannæil. It is a poor plain building, dedicated to St. Macaslin, and cruciform. Among the bishops occur the names of St. Patrick, Spottiswoode, Leslie, Boyle, and Sterne, founder of the University press, Dublin.

Arms: Az. a bishop pontifically habited or.

Clonfert.

The Cathedral of St. Brendan, a dingy, small building of the time of Henry II., is situated in the midst of a miserable hamlet of poor cabins, on a gentle rise, near an expanse of bog, a dreary waste scarcely relieved by some woods: the name well describes the situation—"a place of retirement;" near it are the ruins of St. Brendan's Abbey.

Arms: Az., two crosses addorsed in saltier or.

Clonmacnoise.

Clonmacnoise, Cluan mac nois —"the secluded retreat of the noble's sons," was the site of a Culdee monastery, and the great school of the Irish nobility. In the midst of a dreary sameness of red bog, on the ridge of low hills which bisect it and slope down to the slowly-flowing Shannon, is this Iona of Ireland. Where there is only the call of the curlew and heron to break the silence, rise two round towers, churches, a cell, chapel, cross, palace, and castle, from the earliest Irish style of architecture to that of the close of the 12th century, extend in desolate ruin. One round tower, near Macarthy's church, is very perfect, 55 ft. high, and 7 ft. in diameter, and has a spiral staircase to the top. The second, or *O'Rourke's tower*, is of ash-grey limestone, covered with lichen and many-tinted mosses, 55 ft. high, with a tier 10 ft. higher of rough masonry; the walls are 3 ft. thick, and the door 14 ft. from the ground :—

> Those lonely columns stand sublime,
>   Flinging their shadows from on high;
> Like dials which the wizard Time
> Had raised to count his ages by.

St. Keran's cell has an octangular belfry. The *Temple M'Dermot* possesses a good west entrance, and on the north a Pointed door, one of the most ornate in the country, of hard blue limestone, repaired 1645, with three figures in alto-relievo, and a group above. Near the west door is a fine stone *cross*, 15 ft. high, with rude but elaborate carvings. The moated *palace* is built of rounded pebble stones.

Arms : Az. between three mitres ; a pastoral staff in bend sinister, debruised by an inescutcheon arg.

The Cathedral of the diocese of Meath, dedicated to St. Keran, was built at the beginning of the 14th century by Bishop Tornillach M'Dermot, who died 1336. The north door is of the 15th century, built by Dean Hugh ; it retains three statues of SS. Patrick, Francis, and Dominic. The great western doorway of sandstone has been destroyed. Near it is a cross 15 ft. high. The church is a small venerable building, utterly spoiled and shuttered up.

Arms : Sa., three mitres labelled or, 2 and 1.

Cloyne.

In a rich and fertile valley stands the Cathedral of St. Colman, Cloyne, from Cluaine, a cave, in allusion to the neighbouring limestone rocks. It is a plain heavy cruciform building of the latter part of the 13th century. The central tower has fallen; on one of the piers is a benatura. The *nave*, with aisles, 120 ft. long, is of six bays, with square massive pillars. The *choir*, 70 ft. long, is lighted by three small windows on either side, and a Late Decorated east window. The *north transept* was the chapel of the Fitzgeralds; the *south wing* that of the Longfords. Bishop Agar, in 1776, raised a blank wall at the east end of the nave, and fitted up the choir with Italianesque details. The *organ* bears date 1813. On the north-west is a *round tower*, now embattled, 92 ft. high and 10 ft. in diameter; it was used as a belfry, 1683-1749, when its conical roof was destroyed by lightning. The Cathedral contains the monuments of Bishops Woodward, Warburton, and Bennett; and of Susan Adams, with an epitaph by Mrs. Piozzi. The see has been held by Crowe, whose care redeemed it from the title of the " Bishopric of five Marks ;" Berkeley, to whom Pope attributed " every virtue under heaven ;" Frederick, Earl of Bristol: Ash, the friend of Swift and Addison ; Brinkley, the astronomer ; and Woodward, who when arguing with Father O'Leary on the subject of purgatory, was slily reminded that " he might go farther and fare worse."

Arms : Az. a mitre labelled or between three crosses pattée fitchée arg.

Connor.

The parish church of St. Saviour serves as the Cathedral.

Cork.

THE Cathedral of St. Finan Barr is wholly unworthy of the beautiful city which it deforms. This plain, dull, tasteless, Doric oblong was built, 1725-35, with money raised by a coal-tax. The tower and west door of the ancient church alone remain; the former has an octagonal spire; the latter, deeply recessed and richly moulded, has an inner freestone arch, and an external arch of seven foliations of limestone. The *round tower* was destroyed by Marlborough's fort on Barrack Hill. Cromwell confiscated the bells, adding, with a gloomy humour, that "as a priest invented gunpowder, bells should go for cannons."

There are four vicars choral.

Arms: Arg. a cross pattée gu. charged with a pastoral staff in pale, enfiled with a mitre labelled or.

Derry.

THE city of Derry, " the place of oaks," or " a sandy hillock in a boggy plain," covers a hill, round which, for the most part, flow the waters of Lough Foyle. The Cathedral, which was dedicated to St. Columba, was originally 90 ft. long, and built 1164, but was destroyed partly by an explosion of gunpowder, 1568, and utterly by Docura in 1600. The present structure, 114 ft. by 66 ft., and 46 ft. in height, is an imitation of Perpendicular by Sir John Vanbrugh, 1633, built at a cost of £4,000. The tower, which is 32 ft. square, was originally 66 ft. high, but in 1778 the Earl of Bristol added 21 additional feet, and an octagonal spire 178 ft. high, repaired in 1802 by Bishop Knox; the entire steeple being now 228 ft. to the top of the vane. The church consists of a nave and chancel with hexagonal pillars, long aisle galleries, and roomy pews. Among the bishops occur Bramhall, King, Nicholson, and Hervey Earl of Bristol.

The walls and gates remain, but are modernized; from Bishop's Gate the garrison under the heroic Walker made their sorties in the ever-memorable siege.

Arms: Gu. two swords in saltier arg., hilts and panels or; on a chief az. a harp of the third, stringed of the second.

Dromore.

THE Cathedral of Dromore, Druim-mer, "the great chine of the hill," is a poor, mean, modern building, not cruciform. It contains, however, the dust of the admirable Jeremy Taylor. The old cathedral was destroyed 1641. The ballad-loving Percy as well as Taylor were bishops of the see. The woods round the palace are planted on the model of Shenstone's Leasowes. At the north-east of the town is a Danish rath 60 ft. high with entrenchments, and a passage 260 ft. long to the Lagan. Through Dromore, William of Orange marched to the Boyne, June 24, 1690.

Arms: Arg. semée of trefoils slipped over a cross pattée gu. on a chief az.; a sun in splendour ppr.

Downpatrick.

THE ancient Cathedral was the burial-place of SS. Patrick, Bridget, and Colomb, and after being spoiled by the Scots and Edward Bruce, 1316, was destroyed, 1538, by Lord Deputy Leonard de Grey, and the sacrilege formed one of the charges which led to his beheadal. The present cathedral, 100 ft. long and 52 ft. broad, is composed of a nave and choir with aisles, and a western tower having angular square turrets embattled and pinnacled. The east end has a window of two orders of five-lights; in the head is geometrical tracery, above it are three Pointed niches which held images of the three

Saints, the only remains of the structure built 1412. The belfry, 66 ft. high, was destroyed 1783. Among the bishops occur Leslie, Taylor, and Mant.

Arms : Az., two keys addorsed in saltier or suppressed by a lamb, in fess. arg.

Dublin : Christchurch, or Holy Trinity.

THIS Cathedral, consisting of an Early English nave with a north aisle ; a transept Transitional Norman ; choir, Lady Chapel, and central tower, the spire of which was blown down 1316, is picturesquely situated on the declivity to the river, and on the south side upheld by gigantic buttresses. It was commenced by Sitricus the Dane and Archbishop Donat, 1038, for secular canons ; they built the nave and aisles, St. Michael's chapel, and St. Nicholas Chapel on the north side. Archbishop Donat was buried here 1074. Archbishop O'Toole, in 1163, introduced canons regular and added the choir, tower, and two chapels of SS. Mary and Edmund, and of St. Laud, and in the south aisle the Chapel of the Holy Spirit. Only the original north wall of the nave remains, and the north aisle is almost a ruin. The *nave* is of six bays ; the pillars are 6 ft. in diameter and 10 ft. 6 in. high, composed of a central column with eight clustered shafts. The arches on the north side are very beautiful ; the capitals have graceful foliage, but the bases of the piers are sunk below the floor. The clerestory is composed of triplets ; the west door is Norman. The stone roof fell in 1562, and destroyed the south aisle ; the south wall and west end were badly rebuilt, and a wooden roof set up. The *transept* is aisleless ; the Norman door of the north wing has been re-moved to form a south entrance. The *tower*, with a chapter-house, was burned down January 11, 1283 ; the present structure, ordinary and square, with angular turrets, is of the early part of the 14th century ; the pillars of hewn stone are 9 ft. in diameter. The east window of the *choir* was glazed with the armorial bearings of the chapter, now removed to the west window. The altar slab is of green scagliola. The organ was built, 1751, by Byfield : the former instrument, by Harris, is at Wolverhampton. The throne and stalls are of Grecian design, incongruous and bad. The pews are enormous and unsightly. On March 25, 1395, four Irish kings received knighthood before the altar from Richard II. ; Lambert Simnell was crowned here with a coronet borrowed from St. Mary's image, 1487. In 1559 parliament sat in the chapter-house ; in 1508 St. Patrick's staff was brought hither from Armagh and fanatically burned. The *choir* was rebuilt by Archbishop St. Paul, 1349-62. The *Lady Chapel*, on the north side of the choir, is used by the parishioners of St. Michael's.

The principal monuments are the following :—

Nave.—Strongbow, Earl of Pembroke, d. 1177, and his Countess, Eva, effigies repaired 1570, by Sir H. Sidney ; Thomas Prior, d. 1756, by Van Nost, epitaph by Bishop Berkeley ; John Lord Bowes, L.C., d. 1767, by Van Nost ; James, Viscount Lifford, L.C., d. 1789 ; Bishop Ellis, of Kildare, d. 1705.

Choir.—Robert, 19th Earl of Kildare, d. 1745, by Cheere ; Gen. Sir Samuel Auchmuty, d. 1822 ; Bishop Fletcher, of Kildare, d. 1761.

Here also were buried Archbishops John de St. Paul, died 1362, Luke, 1255, Comyn, 1212, F. Marsh, 1693, and Parker, 1681 ; and Primates Margetson, 1672, and Lindsay, 1724.

DIMENSIONS OF THE CHURCH IN FEET.

	Length.	Breadth.	Height.
Nave .	103	38 it was 51	..
Choir .	105	28	..
Transept .	90	25	..
Tower .	..	..	..
Lady Chapel.	60	26	..

Archbishop Brown in 1541 converted the priory into a deanery. There are daily services at 11 and 3 ; on Sundays 11.15 and 3 ; six vicars choral, five stipendiaries, and four choristers.

St. Patrick's.

DUBLIN (Dubb linn " Blackwater "), like London and Chester, contains two cathedrals ; Rome being the only instance abroad of such an arrangement. St. Patrick's is situated on the south side of the Liffey, on ground so low as to be subject to inundations, in the midst of the poorest and most squalid quarter of Dublin. The first church was built here in the 5th century, on the site of St. Patrick's well. In 1190 Archbishop John Comyn founded a collegiate church, which, jointly with Christchurch, Archbishop Henry de London, in 1213, erected into a cathedral. On April 6, 1362, it was burned and suffered greatly owing to the carelessness of John the Sacristan. In 1364 Archbishop Minot commenced its restoration. Dean Keating in 1820 made many repairs; but more are now imperatively demanded.

The church is composed of a nave of nine bays with aisles, a choir of five bays with aisles, Early English, a Lady Chapel with an antechapel of two bays, and a transept,—the north wing forming the parish church of St. Nicholas-Without, rebuilt by Archbishop Magee; the south wing, Early English, was St. Paul's Chapel, and once formed the *chapter-house* with sacristies to the east; the triforium and clerestory are original; the flying buttresses were built in the 16th century. On the south side of the nave is the *consistory court*. In the south-east angle of the south aisle are some fragments of stone vaulting. On the north-west is the *tower*, built by Archbishop Minot, 1370, who compelled all the vagabonds of Dublin to assist. It is of blue limestone, of four stories, with square projecting flat turrets at the angles; in the upper story is a Perpendicular belfry-window under a battlemented parapet. There are eight bells. The spire of granite was added in 1750 through the benefaction of Bishop Stearne. It is a great ornament to the city. In the lofty *nave* the aisles are separated by octagonal pillars 10 ft. high and 5 ft. in diameter. The west window, Perpendicular, was added by Dean Dawson. The roof is of wood, open to the timbers, restored 1816; the passages only of the triforium remain. Lord Strafford, the famous lord-deputy, cut down all Shillela wood, because the O'Beirnes could not prove their title to its possession, and gave some of the timber to roof St. Patrick's. The floor is 3 ft. above the original level. On the north side the clerestory is of two-light windows, Decorated, of the 14th century, under a battlemented parapet; the aisle presents a blank wall; at the east end is a good, Decorated window. The *south transept* has a triplet on the south and two lights set in a steep gable; it has an eastern aisle; the clerestory has a lancet and three Pointed arches under a round arch. The *choir* extends across the transept; the roof is of stucco. The clerestory is composed of triplets above a good triforium, large and simple; the piers are octangular, tall, and graceful, with foliaged capitals of the 13th century. At the east end are two tiers of five lancets. Bold flying buttresses panelled and terminating in spirelets project on the exterior. Within, on the south side, there are three sedilia with a piscina, the shafts being of Turbet marble, the capitals of Caen stone; and on the north is an altar-tomb used once as the Easter sepulchre. The stalls, throne, and pulpit are of oak; the western stalls being allotted to the knights of St. Patrick, whose banners and helmets are suspended above. The organ stands on the basement of the ancient rood-screen, the staircase of which still remains; the instrument was built by the elder Harris at Rotterdam, 1697, for a church at Vigo; but fortunately the Duke of Ormond captured the ship which carried it during the siege of the place in 1702, and presented it to St. Patrick's. It was rebuilt by Byfield. On Sunday afternoons, when the choral service is sung with an exquisite taste and power which has rendered its excellence proverbial, and the grey of approaching evening sheds a soft gloom over the sacred walls, the lines of the poetess will come into mind,—

Never have I dreamed

Of aught so beautiful. The happy faces,
The banners, and the knights, and then the sun
Streaming through the stained windows, even the tombs
Which looked so calm, and the celestial hymns
Which seemed as if they rather came from heaven

Than mounted here.   The bursting organ's peal
Rolling on high like an harmonious thunder,
The white robes and the lifted eyes, the world
At peace ! and all at peace with one another.

"The majestic harmony of effect," says Mrs. Hemans, in a
note to these well-known lines on St. Patrick's, "produced by
voice, organ, and scientific skill, is not a little deepened by
the character of the church itself, which seems all filled and
overshadowed by the spirit of chivalrous antiquity."

It must be indeed a poor imagination which cannot repress
a painful impression in this mutilated building, and in fancy
elevate what is unworthy, and disguise what is discordant,
whilst there remain such richness of memory, such exquisite
beauty, and costliness of workmanship.

The choir aisles retain their stone vaulting ; at each end is a
triplet.   The *chapter-house*, once the Lady Chapel, and formerly, after 1665, used for the religious worship of Huguenot
refugees, has an eastern triplet and lancets on the sides.   It
was almost rebuilt by R. C. Carpenter in 1846-49.   The
ceiling is covered with plaster ; it has a peculiar corbel-table
of trefoiled arches.   It was built, 1271, by Archbishop Sandford.   It was allotted in 1821 to the Knights of St. Patrick.

Edward Bruce, in 1315, plundered the Cathedral.   In the
year 1313, Archbishop Lecke founded a University within its
walls.   In the reign of Henry VIII. the partisans of Lord
Deputy Kildare and the Earl of Ormond undertook to confer
amicably in the church, but words grew to blows, and the
fabric was injured by the arrows which flew briskly.   The
mayor, until the Reformation, every Corpus Christi day,
walked barefoot to church as a penance.   In Dean Swift's
time the Musical Society of Dublin held their meetings
here.   In the reign of Edward VI., 1548 and 1554, the
cathedral was made a law court, and Cromwell's Roundheads
and James II.'s troopers stabled their horses in the aisles.
The choir is cumbered up with the most hideous large pews,
arranged in the most unecclesiastical and unsightly manner
conceivable.

The principal monuments are the following :—

Choir.—Duke of Schomberg ; his skull is kept in the Chapter-house.

The grave-stone was laid down by Dean Swift. Near the altar, suspended by a chain, is the cannon ball which killed General St. Ruth at the battle of Aughrim, 1691. Archbishops Jones, d. 1619, effigy, and Smith, d. 1771, epitaph by Bishop Lowth. Roger Viscount Ranelagh; Richard, first Earl of Cork, d. 1631: this huge monument Archbishop Laud removed from its monstrous position behind the altar, and so provoked the fatal revenge of the family.

Nave, S. Side.—Dean Swift, d. Oct. 19, 1745; Hester Johnstone (Stella), d. Jan. 27, 1728.

Nave, N. Side.—Earl of Cavan, d. 1778; Archbishop Treguny, d. 1471, effigy; Bishop Meredith, d. 1597.

S. Transept.—Archbishop N. Marsh, d. 1713.

In the cathedral were buried Archbishops Talbot, 1449, Rokeby, 1521, Inge, 1528, Loftus, 1605, and Cradock, 1772; and Primate Boyle, 1702. While only one sepulchral brass is known to exist in Scotland, and that is at Glasgow, the only two specimens on record in Ireland are in this church. The floor tiles are Flemish, and resemble those at Bebenhausen in Suabia, and some pavements in Normandy.

DIMENSIONS OF THE CATHEDRAL IN FEET.

	Length.	Breadth.	Height.
Nave	130	67	..
Choir (ritual)	90 the architectural choir is only 60 ft.		
Transept	157	..	..
Lady Chapel	55	..	..
N. Transept	32	29	..
S. Transept	50	32	..
Tower	..	..	120
Spire	..	..	103
Extreme length	300	..	..

There are four minor canons, thirteen vicars-choral, and six choristers; and choral services at 3 P.M. on Sundays, Wednesdays, and Fridays.

Among the prelates occur St. Rumbold, the first bishop of Mechlin, martyred there 775; De Bickner and Minot, Lord Treasurers; and Wikefold, Waldby, Crawley, and Inge, Lord Chancellors of Ireland; Fitz-Somers, Lord Deputy, Viscount Bulkeley, and Charles Earl of Normanton.

Arms: same as Armagh.

Elphin.

ELPHIN, "the stone of the clear fountain," from the legend of the fall of a meteoric stone, 675, possessed the barn-like parish church of St. Mary, 80 ft. by 28 ft., with an old square tower, narrow, tall, ragged, and plastered; but being situated on the brow of a hill and in the centre of only miserable cabins it can be seen miles distant rising over the trees. It contains some old tombs and has round-headed windows.

Arms: Sa. two pastoral staffs addorsed in saltier or, in base a lamb couchant arg.

Emly.

THE parish church of this inconsiderable village is the Cathedral, built 1827. There are a few ruins and a large churchyard cross. Among the bishops occur Mackinede and Cœnfelad, Kings of Cashel. Dr. Hales, the chronologist, was chancellor of the cathedral.

Ferns.

ON the side of a hill covered with the ruins of a castle, and to the north-west of the rivulet Bauna, amid some poor thatched cabins, a mean building, built 1816, and dedicated to St. Edan, serves as the parish church. It contains the Early English effigy in marble of St. Edan, the founder (who died 632), under a niche. Near it are the remains of the abbey, of which two sides of a cloister and a narrow chapel lighted with lancets, an oblong square tower of red sandstone, a broken font and stone cross are only preserved. The castle was built by the

Don Roderick of Ireland—Dermot McMurrough, King of Leinster, whose abduction of Dearbhorgoil lost him his country, a fact so plaintively commemorated by Moore in the " Song of O'Ruark."

The most eminent bishop was Elrington.

Arms : Az. two keys in saltier, over all a mitre arg.

Glendalough.

GLENDALOUGH, " the glen of the two lakes," is the Irish Balbec. The solemn, impressive valleys of Glendaron and Glendalough are parted by broad gates of rock,—dark-coloured, wild, and bare ; in the gloomy solitude where all is stern, desolate grandeur, locked in by grey cliffs, and huge mountains seldom unveiled by the dark brooding clouds, in the vale of the meeting of the waters, lie the low ruins of the ancient city, burned by the English in the summer of 1398 : and in one of the two glassy lakes, immortalized by lay and legend, is mirrored the one lonely, lofty column, the famous Round Tower, lonely as Pompey's pillar amid the sands of Alexandria.

The Cathedral, the see of a bishopric long united to Dublin, is composed of a nave and choir. The *choir* was built between 886-997 ; the whole church is 55 ft. by 37 ft. The Irish architects thought neither of size nor elegance, but built at one time a number of churches in one place as here, the mystical number of seven being the average. The south side is lighted by three small windows. At the east end was an arch, 17 ft. 6 in. wide, behind which extended a chapel, 37 ft. 6 in. by 23 ft., with an east window ; on the north there are two small windows, on the south, one. Another door in the choir, 3 ft. 8 in. wide, opens into a chapel, 16 ft. by 10 ft. ; under a small window in the choir on the south side is a tomb of freestone. The chief door is 7 ft. 4 in. high, 3 ft. 6 in. in breadth a top, and 3 ft. 10 in. at the base. The *tower* is now 100 ft. high, with a round-headed arch for the doorway, hewn out of one stone and filled with masonry : with its conical

roof, the tower was 132 ft. high ; it is attributed to the famous
Goban Saer, and the date 610.   The walls of the cemetery
are 4 ft. thick, and the enclosure 52 ft. round the church.
There are some remains of crosses, one a solid block of granite,
11 ft. high.   Thackeray said, " The clergy must have been
the smallest persons, with the smallest benefices and littlest
congregations ever known ; as for this cathedral, what a
bishoplet it must have-been that presided here !"   Bishops
filled the see, 612-1192, those of Dublin being then their suffragans.   There are remains of a detached *sacristy*.

Our Lady's Church, the westernmost and most ancient of
the churches, is nearly opposite the cathedral ; it is little more
than a mass of ruin, with walls of hewn stone, and the other
materials rude mountain ragstone.   But it appears to have
been built with more architectural taste than the others, and
the lintel of the doorway still shows a cruciform ornament.
The dedication dates only from the 12th century, when the
Irish abandoned their ancient custom of giving the names of
national saints to their churches.

The *Ivy Church* is utterly roofless and ruined.   The round
tower beside it fell 1818.

Rhefeart, " the sepulchre of the kings," contained the
gravestone of King McThuil, or O'Toole, who died 1010, but
it has been broken up by tourists' guides.   Scarcely a vestige
of the church remains standing ; the ruins are overgrown
with thick underwood, and most romantically situated.

Beneath the frowning cliff of Lugduff, on a little patch of
arable land, almost inaccessible, except by water, lie the ruins
of the *Priory of St. Saviour*, the most eastern church, of the
9th or 10th century, called the Team-pull-na-Skellig, " the
priory of the rock ;" and also the Abbey of SS. Peter and
Paul.   The *chancel* is 15 ft. 6 in. by 11 ft. 5 in.   At the
end is a stone bench, probably the abbat's 'throne, and 2 ft.
from it was an isolated stone-altar, 5 ft. by 2 ft. 11 in. and
4 ft. high.   In the south wall are three niches.   The *nave*
was 42 ft. by 26 ft.   On the north side were the priests'
rooms.   Of the chancel arch, three receding pillars, 10 ft. in
breadth and 11 ft. high, with scuptured capitals and bases,
remain.   There are some chevron-mouldings of later date.

The *Holy Trinity Church* stands on rising ground to the north. In the front of it is a circular belfry on a square base. The chancel arch is 9 ft. broad, 10 ft. 6 in. high, and semicircular. The *chancel* has one round-headed window, deeply splayed inwards. There are some triangular-headed windows still remaining. The entrance-door was square-headed.

St. Kevin's Kitchen, as the most perfect of the seven churches is called, is of the 7th century, with additions in the 12th century, and resembles St. Columb's house at Kells. St. Kevin died 618, at the age of 120 years. The church is 31 ft. high to the ridge of the roof, the walls measuring 11 ft. in height, and having a projecting string-course. The gables form an equilateral triangle. The lower or vaulted chamber is 20 ft. high, the *upper croft* 7 ft. 6 in. The quadrangular west door remains, of mica slate, with a lintel and a semi-circular arch 2 ft. 8 in. wide at top, 3 ft. 2 in. at bottom, 6 ft. 8 in. high. There were three windows, two in the east wall and one of later insertion in the south wall. The *belfry,* entered from the upper croft, is 9 ft. high from the roof ridge to the top of its conical head, 46 ft. from the ground, and 4 ft. 6 in. in diameter; it has four lights, one to each point of the compass. The *chancel* is 11 ft. 3 in. by 9 ft. 3 in. and 12 ft. high, lighted by two windows; the chancel arch measures 8 ft. 10 in. by 5 ft. 3 in. The *sacristy* is 10 ft. by 7 ft. 9 in., and 12 ft. high, lighted by a round-headed window, and entered by a door 5 ft. by 2 ft. wide. The belfry, chancel, and sacristy were built after 1163; they were roofed with stone; that of the church, composed of thin flags, neatly laid, and with a very high pitch, is still perfect. St. Kevin's Kitchen is one of the few remaining stone-roofed buildings in Ireland; the finest specimen being Cormac's chapel on the rock of Cashel. The nave measures 30ft. by 22 ft.

The east precinct-gate fell in the summer of 1848. It was 16 ft. 6 in. by 16 ft., the outside arches composed of twenty-four stones, 9 ft. 7 in. wide, 10 ft. high, of mountain granite, the inner arch of twenty-seven stones 2 ft. 6 in. deep. On the south side of the lake is *St. Kevin's bed,* a cave hewn in the solid rock, which will just hold three persons, and rendered famous by the fate of Kathleen :—

> By that lake whose gloomy shore
> Skylark never warbles o'er;
> Where the cliff hangs high and steep,
> Young Saint Kevin stole to sleep.
> Ah! you saints have cruel hearts!
> Sternly from his bed he starts,
> And with rude repulsive shock
> Hurls her from the beetling rock.
> Glendalough! thy gloomy wave
> Soon was gentle Kathleen's grave.

Kildare.

> I slowly wandered through the site
> Of crumbling walls, half-falling tower,
> Mullions and arch, which darkly cower
> And o'er the intruder seem to frown ;
> Putting on size beyond their own,
> Like giants in enchanted tale,
> As dimly seen through misty veil.
> 'Tis here the midnight tombs around
> Strange floatings by were said to sound,
> And through the aislèd stillness deep
> Strains indistinct were heard to sweep.

KILDARE, "Chilledara, the wood of oaks," once boasted of St. Bridget's Cathedral, only inferior to Kilkenny and St. Patrick's, but the tower, nave, and transept were reduced to ruin by the Parliamentarians, 1641. The west end and the walls of the south aisle of the *nave* remain: the latter of six bays was pierced with lancets under pointed arches, with flat pilaster-like buttresses intervening: in the third bay was the door. The *tower* rose two stories above the roof, with two lancets below and three lancets above: the *south transept* has three single lancets, and contains the tombs of *Sir Maurice Fitzgerald* of Lackugh; an effigy of a knight in armour; and that of Bishop *Edward Lane*, mitred, with his staff, 1522. The *choir* is still used. The cathedral is known to have been repaired by Ralph of Bristol, bishop, 1232, and by Bishop

Lane. In it were buried Gerald Lord Offaley, died 1286, and John Earl of Kildare, died 1316. At a distance of 100 ft. from the west door is the most highly finished *round tower* in Ireland, 132 ft. high, of white granite for 12 ft. from the ground, and for the remainder of blue stone; the door is 14 ft. from the earth. The church was haunted by a legendary hawk of St. Bridget which reached an untold age.

Aodh Dubh, Black Hugh, King of Leinster, was a bishop of the see, 638.

St. Bridget, born 458, having received the veil from St. Patrick, founded an abbey of monks and nuns who had a common church. Her narrow stone cell remains, the *fire-house* of St. Bridget, on whose altar the sacred fire was kept constantly burning.—

> The bright lamp that shone in Kildare's holy fane,
> And burned through long ages of darkness and storm.

Arms: Arg. a saltier engrailed sa. on a chief az., an open book clasped and garnished or.

Kilfenora.

THE parish church of St. Fachnan, in this mean hamlet, composed of a nave and chancel, serves as the Cathedral ; in the chancel is the alleged tomb of the founder.

Kilkenny.

> Thou for thy worshippers hast sanctified
> All place, all time.
> Yet must the thoughtful soul of man invest
> With dearer consecration those pure fanes
> Which, severed from all sound of earth's unrest,
> Hear nought but suppliant or adoring strains
> Rise heavenward. Ne'er may rock or cave possess
> *Their* claim on human heart to solemn tenderness.

THE Cathedral of St. Canice, in the diocese of Ossory, would have proved a national ornament of Irish taste, owing to the praiseworthy exertions of Dean Vignolles, had he not encountered opposition in a quarter from which he might naturally have looked for encouragement and support. The church is composed of a nave of six bays with aisles, a choir with lateral chapels, a transept with eastern chapels, a south porch and a low central tower. Felix Delany, bishop, 1180, began the structure; Hugh Rufus, in 1114, rebuilt it on an enlarged scale, but again only of timber. Bishop Hugh Mapleton, 1251-6, commenced the present building of stone, and Geoffrey St. Leger completed it in 1260. Bishop Ledred filled the windows with rich glazing 1354; so exquisitely beautiful was the glass in the eastern lancets, that in 1645 Rinuccini, Archbishop of Fermo and papal nuncio to the confederate Catholics, offered £700 for it, the subject being the Life of JESUS; unfortunately, as the event proved, Bishop Roth refused to sell it, for the regicide Colonel Axtell, in 1650, being governor of the city, destroyed it, with the exception of a few fragments now in the west windows.

The *west front* is composed of a high gable with a cross, which is said to have been preserved by a swarm of bees which stung and drove away the iconoclasts who had mounted on ladders to destroy it. This is flanked by two turrets with conical spires. There are three lancets, the central being shorter than the side-lights has a panel pierced below, which lights a small gallery within. Over these is a circular window, filling the space above the large double doorway, which has two cinquefoiled arches and a quatrefoil in the head, under an arch with two lateral shafts. The clerestory of the *nave* is composed of quatrefoils; black marble piers form the pillars. The roof was rebuilt 1795. The aisle windows are couplets with a quatrefoil above.

There is an Early English *font*, cylindrical and fluted, standing on five short columns. On the exterior the masonry is of cut stone, and spawled rubble with groins of limestone, and sandstone brought from England or some distant quarries. Situated on a hill, its battlemented tower and stumpy spire acquire height, seen through the rich foliage of surrounding trees, and the tall shaft of the round tower on the south, with a long flight of marble stairs, built 1614 before the west entrance, lend to the main building a beautiful and picturesque effect. On the south side is an unusual feature in Irish churches, a *porch* of two orders, pedimented, with a quatrefoil in the gable. The *south transept* has a lofty couplet in each of the west and south walls. Adjoining it is the *round tower*, of eight stories, with a door 8 ft. 6 in. above the ground, and a shingled roof. It may have served as a belfry, a watch-tower, a place of refuge, and treasury: under some similar structures very rarely have been discovered graves. The *choir* has two square-headed windows next the tower, and then three round-headed lancets eastward. The *Lady Chapel* was lighted by three triplets, but the central triplet is now blocked up. The *north transept* is disfigured by an ugly colonnade erected by Bishop Pococke; but the north door, of soft yellow sandstone, consists of a round arch with bands at intervals, and fillet and roll, of sandstone, set under a pointed arch with a quatrefoil in the spandril. On May 22, 1332, the central tower fell and broke down great part of the choir and side chapels. The present *central tower* contains six bells, two recast 1724, and four in 1851. Through the vaulting, which was set up by Bishop David Hacket, the architect of Batalha, 1460, the belfry ropes are let down as at Holy Cross, Kilkooly, Dunbrody, and Jerpoint, and in the cathedrals of Exeter and Bristol: by an ingenious contrivance the bells can be chimed by one person. The choir arch is blocked up by an ugly blank wall. The Italianesque walls of the choir were set up by Bishop Pococke, 1756. Like Rochester Cathedral solid walls enclose it. On the north side of the choir is a chapel; at the east end are the foundations of an anchorite's cell; it had three steps, a low side window, and a hearth; the poor recluse had no door. On the east of the north transept is the parish church, restored 1850. On the east side of the south wing is the *Lady Chapel* and sacristy; and on the south side of the choir is the *chapter-house*.

The principal monuments are the following :—

Bishop Walsh; he was murdered with a skean by James Dulland, a man of infamous character whom he had cited, in 1585. The ruffian joined banditti at Troy Wood, who discovered his villainy, and hung him on a tree. Bishops Roger of Wexford, d. 1289, effigy, and Richard Talbot; Pococke the traveller; Piers Butler; "the Red Earl," 8th Earl of Ormond, effigy black marble, and his countess, Margaret Fitzgerald, famous in the wars of the Butlers and Geraldines; Walter, 11th Earl of Ormond; James, Earl of Ormond, d. 1546, effigy and tomb with images of saints; effigy of a lady, 16th century; Richard, Viscount Mount Garret, effigy, and his two successors; James, Marquis of Ormond, d. 1838; John, Marquis of Ormonde, d. 1854, effigy by Richardson; Bishops Otway, d. 1693; Kearney, d. 1813; Fowler, d. 1841; Sir Denis Pack, d. 1823, with the colours of the 71st Highlanders above the tomb; and Cox, Archbishop of Cashel, d. 1779. He left a compartment vacant on his wife's tomb for his own name, and a wag affixed to it these lines—

> Tis well-known truth, by every tongue confessed,
> That by this blank thy life is best expressed.

Besides some incised slabs in various parts of the cathedral, there is in the north transept *St. Kieran's chair*, Early English, with foliage of Kilkenny marble; the stone seat is modern work: it was probably part of a canon's stall.

DIMENSIONS OF THE CHURCH IN FEET.

	Length.	Breadth.	Height.
Nave	107	63·9	..
Choir	73·10	27·6	..
Transept	117·8	..	..
Lady Chapel	28·7	20·8	..
Chapter-house	29·8	15·11	..
North Chapel	48·6	15·10	..
Porch	15·7	13·3	..
Vaulting of lantern	26	26	44
Round Tower circumference	46·6	..	100
Extreme length	212·3	..	..

In 1367 a parliament was held here. The foul-mouthed Bishop Bale did great injury to the church; in 1641 the Irish septs pillaged it, and on March 25, 1651, Cromwell stabled his horses in the aisles, and committed great devastation; but in 1660 Bishop Williams restored it. In 1646, August 18, Roth fulminated an interdict from the altar. The market-cross, built 1355, was destroyed 1771; there Father Clym

saw pilgrims for the Holy Land branded with the cross;
there the Puritan bigot, Bale, in 1552, taught the prentice
lads to act religious dramas on Sunday; and the Viceroy
in 1578 condemned two poor creatures to be burned as
warlocks, on the site of a similar auto da fé of Lady Alice
Kylelar by Bishop Ledard in 1324. St. John's Abbey, the
"lantern of Kilkenny," is a parish church. The Franciscan
Friary is a tennis-court; and the Dominican Abbey of the
14th century has been restored as a Roman Catholic Church.
Kilkenny was the birth-place of Banim.

The good works begun by the present dean will be remem-
bered as long as the bells which he set in order have a voice:—

O'er the startled city, as in the olden times,
Bursts forth the music of the grey cathedral chimes;
They are heard in rural villages like fairy tinklings clear,
They swell in loudest changes o'er the fields and gardens near;
Old men and youths are listening to their soft melodious spells,
And maiden's eyes are glistening at the pealing of the bells.

Arms: Gules, a covered chalice ensigned with a cross
pattée or between five crosses pattée fitchée of the last.

Killala.

THE ancient Cathedral of St. Muredarch, in this pleasant
straggling village at the mouth of the Morg, was modernized
in 1817 into a common-place parish church. Here, in 1798,
landed General Humbert and the French troops, only to be
defeated ignominiously shortly after.

Arms: Gu. a pastoral staff in pale or, surmounted by a
book.

Killaloe.

The Cathedral of St. Lua (which gives name to the place, Kil or church of St. Lua, Killaloe by corruption) is cruciform, with a low massive central tower, and 200 ft. by 50 ft. It is Early English and rude Norman ; was built by Brian Boromhe 1014, and added to, in 1160, by King Donald O'Brien of Thomond. The west door of the *nave* has a billet-moulding. In the south wall is a rich Norman doorway, called popularly the tomb of King O'Brien, who died 1120. The windows throughout the church are of narrow lancets splayed inwards ; the east window of the *choir* is a triplet, a central round-headed window between two lancets, and flanked by two pilaster buttresses. The *north transept* is used as a school-house ; under the stair is the ancient font. There is also an ancient *crypt*. Near the church is the stone-roofed cell of St. Molua, of the 7th century. No wood is employed ; the tunnel vault has a pointed roof of steep pitch over it, with a slab covering. The west door is round-headed, with two short columns : on their capitals are sculptures of an ape and an elephant ; a round-headed window fills the gable. In the east wall is a triangular-headed window. On an island of the Shannon (which is crossed by a picturesque bridge of nineteen arches with gateways to either shore) is another stone-roofed church, with Cyclopic masonry of large polygonal stones. The door is of pyramidal shape, with a lintel formed of a single slab.

At Killaloe, Sarsfield interrupted the march of the artillery of William of Orange.

Arms: Az. a cross gu. between twelve trefoils slipped vert, on a chief az. a key in pale or.

Kilmacduagh.

On a stern cold bed of limestone stands the ruined Cathedral of St. Colman M'Duagh, died 610. The parish-church is modern. St. Colman's Abbey has a leaning tower 7½ ft. out of the Perpendicular.

Kilmore.

In the small village of Kilmore (the great church) stood the plain ancient church of St. Feline, constituted a Cathedral 1454 by Bishop Andrew M'Brady, and which also served as the parish church. Among its prelates occurs the venerated name of Bedell. The present cathedral is 103 ft. long, and cruciform with a central tower : the nave is 46 ft. by 37 ft. 6 in., the choir 34 ft. 6 in. by 23 ft., the lantern 20 ft. by 20 ft., and 57 ft. high; the throne and stall-work are of oak, the east window is of five lights ; the style employed by Mr. Sclater, the architect, is Early Decorated. It is observable that the two great cathedral restorations in Ireland have been achieved in both instances by a prelate bearing the honoured name of Beresford.

Arms : Arg. on a cross gu. a pastoral staff enfiled with a mitre or.

Leighlin.

Leighlin, the " half-enclosed valley," seated in a recess of the Clogrenan hills, is an assemblage of poverty-stricken cabins. The cathedral of St. Laserian consists of a nave 84 ft. long and a choir 60 ft. by 21 ft. The font is 5 ft. in height. It was built by Bishop Donat 1185, and rebuilt by Bishop Saunders 1527. The matrix of the brass of the latter, who died 1549, remains. The belfry tower is 60 ft. high, with a slated spire and an internal staircase of sixty-two stairs. Bishop Maurice Doran was murdered by his archdeacon Kavanagh, who was summarily hanged on the spot.

Arms : Sa. two pastoral staffs addorsed in saltier or, suppressed with a mitre.

Limerick.

THE Cathedral of St. Mary, built on the site of the palace of O'Brien, King of Limerick, 1142-80 with additions in the 13th century. It is cruciform, 156 ft. long, 114 ft. broad at the transept, and has a square embattled tower 120 ft. high. In the memorable siege, it had a large gun placed on it and plied so successfully, that although the gunner was killed, Ginkle did not care to fire any more upon the church. It was used as a barrack. In the south aisle is a Gothic monument, and in the choir a monument of Lord Thomond, president of Munster, who died 1624. The wooden roof has been restored and the east window glazed as a memorial to Mr. Stafford O'Brien, M.P., by Mr. Slater of London. The cathedral bells were cast by an Italian for a monastery near his home which was destroyed. Years after, a childless man, for his three sens fell together on the fatal field of Pavia, he came an exile to Ireland; on his reaching the Shannon he left the ship which had brought him and entered a boat. Evening was closing in, when from the distant tower of St. Mary rang out a soft chime: the oarsmen paused in their talk as they saw tears on the aged stranger's cheek, joy and grief struggling for the mastery, while with arms folded over his beating heart, he leaned forward to catch the faint music; he continued motionless, and when they reached the landing-place they stepped forward to lead him out: it was the well-remembered sound of his own dear bells with their thousand agonising memories that had arrested his ear—he was dead.

There is a daily service at 3 P.M. There are six vicars-choral. Among the bishops occur Elrington, Viscount Glentworth, and Jebb.

Arms: Az. in dexter chief a pastoral staff, in sinister a mitre labelled in base; two keys addorsed in saltier or.

King John visited the town in 1210. Ireton died under the castle walls 1651. In 1690 Sarsfield gallantly repulsed William of Orange; and on October 3, 1691, St. Ruth capitulated to Ginkle after a long siege : the garrison marched out with the honours of war ; and 11,000 men sailing to France formed the famous Irish Brigade.

Lismore.

LISMORE, " the Great Fort," once the ecclesiastical Athens of Ireland, is situated on a terrace above the steep rocky banks of the Blackwater before it mingles with the Owensheaded. The suburbs are most beautiful, rich in parks and woodland scenery, with a noble avenue and picturesque bridge ; the grey massive castle built by King John 1185, with marks of its ancient grandeur, on the verge of a perpendicular cliff, and the tapering spire of the Cathedral of St. Mochuda, form a charming landscape. The church, which was Early English, plain and simple, built by Edmund Fitzgibbon, the White Knight, 636, was almost rebuilt 1663 by the Earl of Cork, and has received great additions in the present century. It was designed to be cruciform, but has only one transept. The walls are of sandstone resembling Portland stone ; the choir has stained glass and stalls, and pulpit of dark oak. Among the dignitaries occur R. Pococke, the traveller ; Dr. Miller, afterwards dean of Exeter ; Ryland, the historian of Waterford ; and John Lord Decies. The cross, made by Nectan 1112 for Bishop Nial Aeduccan, is now in the possession of the Duke of Devonshire. There are five vicars-choral.

Old Ross.

THE old Cathedral of St. Mary was destroyed by the insurgents in 1799 ; it was replaced 1800 by a parish church.

Raphoe.

THE Cathedral, cruciform and plain, with a tower of the 18th century, serves as the parish church.

Arms : Ermine, a chief party per pale ; dexter side azure a sun or ; sinister, gules a cross pattée or.

Tuam.

THE Cathedral of St. Jarlath is a very small parish church. It was built originally, with the aid of Turlough O'Connor, King of Ireland, by Archbishop Acoh D'Hirsin 1128-56. Some few portions of this early building remain. The *chancel*, a square of 36 ft., has at the east end three circular-headed windows, 5 ft. high with a splay of 5 ft., with chevron mouldings and a rich arcade of six round-headed recessed arches, the outer 20 ft. 6 in. wide and 19 ft. high, the inner 15 ft. 8 in. by 16 ft. high ; the shafts have rectangular capitals, and the arches chevron, billet, and nail-head mouldings. The organ is by Bevington. The cross of sandstone, the finest monument of its class in Ireland, 13 ft. 8 in. high, is lying prostrate in the market-place.

Arms : Az. under three canopies in tabernacles an archbishop, dexter side ; an angel holding a lamb, sinister ; the Blessed Virgin with the Holy Children in the midst.

Waterford.

THE town—exquisitely beautiful, with its bridge across the Suir, its noble quay a mile in length, and the loveliness of the slopes of wood and river banks—has lost its venerable Cathedral, built 1096, by the Ostmen, with a nave 66 ft. by 45 ft.,

a choir with aisles 66 ft. long, a southern chapel of St.
Saviour, and a northern chapel of St. James and Katherine.
The chapter demolished it in 1772. The modern church, which
was restored 1815-18, has a nave 90 ft. long and 40 ft. high,
the entire structure measuring 170 ft. by 58 ft. A suit of
vestments found in the old cathedral walls is now at Oscott
College. Among the bishops occurs the name of Butson.

There are ruins of a Franciscan Friary, and on the quay a
round tower built by Reginald the Dane, 1003.

Arms: Az. a saint nimbed, holding a crucifix in pale with
his outstretched arms, and standing on three steps or.

SCOTLAND.

INTRODUCTION.

THE earliest churches in Scotland were, probably, constructed of wicker-work.

Four great periods of architecture are distinctively marked. The first period extends from the arrival of St. Columba in 565, to the marriage of St. Margaret and King Malcolm in 1070. It has many features in common with Ireland; for instance, its round towers, sculptured crosses and tombstones, with the small size and the combination of buildings in one enclosure. Brechin, Abernethy, and Iona, offer the most remarkable specimens. At Iona there is a priest's chamber over the aisle, a common feature in early Irish architecture.

The second period has at an early period—the twelfth century—a Norwegian character. The round arch is not peculiar to this style, but lingered on to the latest date, and is found in connection with the richest ornament of the subsequent periods. The influence of England prevailed from 1070 to 1371, as in ecclesiastical synod, constitution, and liturgy. The Round style extended from the accession of King David I., 1124 to 1165. The best examples of the style are found in the nave of Dunfermline, St. Margaret's Chapel in Edinburgh Castle, and the small churches of Leuchars (Transitional) and Dalmeny, all of which have semicircular apses; and also at Kelso. In the transition to the succeeding style, very minute mouldings are employed.

The Lancet, or Early English, style, common to both sides of the Tweed, lasted from the accession of William the Lion in 1165, to the death of Alexander III. in 1286. The germ of Scottish tracery will be found to consist in the ingenious adaptation of the bays of an arcade to windows. At Elgin the earlier forms actually appear over windows of the succeeding style at the east end. In the nave of Glasgow there is not a specimen of foliage, while the mouldings are elaborate; in the choir the reverse is observable. Of this style the finest specimens are the Cathedrals of St. Andrew's, Brechin, Dunblane, Dornoch, Elgin, Galloway, and Kirkwall. It is found in considerable portions of the abbeys of Aberbrothock (very Early), Dryburgh, Paisley, and Pluscardine Priory Church; in some parts of the abbeys of Dunfermline and Jedburgh; in the Transitional tower of Cambus Kenneth, built indeed in 1147; in the gable of the south transept of Kilwinning Abbey, and the vaulted chapter-house of St. Columba's, Inchcolm. At Kelso and Paisley the nave was shorter than the choir. The choirs as at Dunkeld, Dunblane, Whitherne, Paisley, and Sweetheart, were destitute of aisles. Sweetheart, Elgin, Pluscardine, St. Andrew's, Aberbrothock, Dryburgh, and Melrose, had only an east aisle to the transept; Brechin, Dunblane, and Whitherne had no transept.

The transition from Early English to Decorated was gradual, and is as difficult to be traced or defined as that of the gentle method in which the Norman became merged in the Lancet style. Haddington Church offers the best opportunity for the study. There the west door and the triplet in the tower retain the Norman semicircular arch, but have enrichments of a later period. The nave pillars, although clustered, have shallow mouldings, and the flowering of the capitals is slight. The toothed and nail-head ornaments are found at Melrose, mingled with the latest forms of the next style. Effect is produced by the use of chamfers; but the splay of the arch was still moulded.

The Decorated style began about 1286, the period of the death of Alexander III., and lasted to the middle of the 14th century, maintaining an English aspect; but in 1371, when the Stuarts ascended the throne, and maintained a close correspondence with France, the architecture assumed a decidedly continental or flamboyant character until 1567. Among the more interesting specimens of the style, occur the Cathedrals of Edinburgh, Aberdeen, Fortrose, and Lismore; the abbeys of Melrose and Sweetheart; the collegiate churches of Lincluden, St. John's Perth, Roslyn, and King's College, Aberdeen; the churches of Costorphine, Haddington, Linlithgow, and Seton; and portions of Elgin, Iona, Brechin, Dunkeld, Dunblane, and Glasgow. The features of the later style consist of the intricate flamboyant tracery; the saddle-back tower, as at Pluscardine and Sweetheart abbeys; the polygonal apse; the crow-stepped gable; the richly-crocketed pinnacle, the angular turret; and the pointed arch enclosing a double doorway with flattened heads. The porch is a distinctive feature, as at Aberdeen, Dunfermline, and Paisley. Some of the most interesting specimens of doorways will be found in those on the west and south-west of Dunkeld; those of the north cloister and south transept, Melrose; and the west, and sacristy doors, at Iona. Aberdeen offers the only instance of two western towers: the central tower is rarely elevated more than one story above the roof, and seldom dignified; the spires are poor, and sometimes horizontally divided by bands, as at Aberdeen, Dunfermline, and Glasgow. An imperial crown is found at St. Giles's as the termination of a steeple. The great characteristics are the varied dimensions of columns in the triforia, the profusion of niches, the elaborate ornament, and a tenacity of retaining forms whilst the details were debased. In the 14th and 15th centuries the hanging tracery was common to the baronial and ecclesiastical architecture, as seen in Roslyn and Holyrood, at Linlithgow Palace and Stirling Castle. The capitals, seldom good, and rarely elaborate, are either octagonal or round. The growth of window tracery is most observable: the earliest form is that of lancets, included within semicircular arches; or of foliated lancets under a foliated circle. The other designs are the following:

1. The pear-shaped loop, a circular head of two foliations, as at Melrose. 2. A combination of two two-light windows with such tracery under one arch, as in the north transepts of Paisley and Jedburgh, and the west end of Brechin. 3. A head filled with three feathered loops like a spur wheel, as the east window of Iona, and the south transept of Melrose. 4. The net pattern, as in the east belfry window, Iona; the north side, Dunkeld; and the refectory, Dunfermline. 5. The diverging mullion. 6. The spherical triangle, as at Roslyn and Pluscardine. The elliptical Early English window was developed into the Decorated marygold of twelve cusps.

The largest cathedral was that of St. Andrew's, 358 ft. long, thus exceeding all the Irish and Welsh cathedrals, and those of Bristol, Carlisle, Hereford, Manchester, Oxford, Ripon, and Rochester, while Brechin was only 114 ft. long. Glasgow measures 319 ft.; the other churches of Scotland are all considerably short of 300 ft.

The establishment which has usurped these beautiful buildings, finds them uncongenial to the grim Genevan mind, and unfitted for its cold bald services. Every man of taste would rejoice to see them restored to the exiled Church, which the heirless House of Orange persecuted, but which has since assisted signally in evangelising America. Mutilated by Knox and Covenanters, barbarously misused in even later times, left to ruin, or deformed by the most hideous enclosures, there are few who would not be glad to find the prophecy of a writer across the Atlantic fulfilled :—

In *Edin's* high cathedral, no more the fishwife's voice,
In *Glasgow's* crypts and cloisters, no more the rabble's noise;
Oh! then *St. Andrew's* crozier once more shall be upheld,
And the Culdee mitre glisten in *Brechin* and *Dunkeld;*
See and see uprearing once more the shattered cross,
Once more a bishop treading the heathery braes of *Ross,*
Fair *Elgin's* choir unfolding the *Moray's* shepherds' rest,
And *Aberdeen* from ruins uprising bright and blest.
One heart in Gael and Saxon, in cotter and in thane,
One creed, one church, in Scotland from *Kirkwall* to *Dunblane.*
Bide thou thy time in patience, the sons of thy bold foes
Shall build thine old waste places *Dunfermline* and *Melrose.*

There is a striking lament over the state of the Scottish Churches in " Peter's Letters to his Kinsfolk."

Blessed be that day which shall see restored these ancient churches, with sacred altar and comely lectern, and storied pane, episcopal throne and prebendal stall; a service full of nobility and majesty; a nave thronged with kneeling worshippers; a choir echoing with the sublime and magnificent music of the organ, and the glorious solemn sound of chanting choristers and devout-looking men singing the praises of God, that ascend like incense to heaven. As we look on the huge gallery and cumbrous pew, the pulpit standing where the altar was, and the new forms which have supplanted the ancient worship, and hear the acknowledgment that the merest barn would be sufficient for a kirk, we cannot but say with him of old, who also saw his own church in the dust, " Quousque Domine, quousque?"

CATHEDRALS OF SCOTLAND.

𝕬berdeen.

> It was a pile of simplest masonry,
> Of narrow windows and vast buttresses,
> Built to endure the shocks of time and chance;
> Yet showing many a rent, as well it might
> Warred on for ever by the elements.

NEAR the " Queen of the North," the type of modern activity and enterprise, remain the ill-fated ruins of its ancient pride, begun in 1357—the Cathedral of St. Machar, the contemporary of St. Columba. It is an impressive building, 200 ft. long, without a sign of decay in its rigid outlines, though for centuries—

> Exposed to the tumultuous seas,
> And scourged by the wind's tempestuous sway;

but from its material, granite, has a stately, but stern, gloomy look. The church, however, appears to advantage, rising over a group of venerable trees, which follow the windings of the Don.

At the west end are two symmetrical and simple machicolated *steeples* of castellated design, 112 ft. high, and at a height of 52 ft. terminating in spires. These are octagonal, with two embattled bands, having crocketed pinnacles on the angles, and a profusion of spire-lights. There is a window, plain, unmoulded, and round-headed in each face of the square base of either spire. The *west front*, imposing and bold in design, Decorated, was, with the walls of the nave, begun between the years 1420-1440, by Bishop Leighton, but not completed till the first quarter of the 16th century. Seven long equal one-light windows divided by stone shafts, and round-headed but trefoiled, stand over the great entrance, a double doorway of two pointed arches, with an aureole in the spandrils under a round-headed arch. In the gable are two round-headed but foliated windows, surmounted by a small square window and a cross. There is a large gabled *south porch*, crowstepped, and having a parvise with a foliated circle in the gable. Bishop Lyndsay, 1441-1459, roofed the nave of seven bays, which is nearly perfect.

The pillars in the interior are round, and have mere mouldings for capitals. The *clerestory* is composed of very narrow trefoiled lights, framed on the inside between short massive columns. There is no triforium. The aisle windows are of three lights with geometrical tracery. The *wood ceiling* is flat, but very richly carved, gilded, and coloured; panelled in saltiers and squares, with flowered crosses of elegant design at the intersection of the saltiers, and heraldic bearings of kings, and ecclesiastics, and laymen, at the crossing of the main ribs, which part it into forty-eight longitudinal divisions; for the blazoning James Wintoun, of Angus, received £8 Scots from Bishop Gawain Dunbar, 1515-1531, who built the south transept. The flowered capitals and clustered pillars at the east end once supported the arch of the square central tower, like the choir and transept, being of freestone, it has long since perished. A fragment of the walls of the transept has been suffered to remain: in the south wing are embedded two superb freestone tombs, in monumental recesses—one of Bishop *Leighton*, 1422-1448, who built this transept: a panelled altar-tomb, with an effigy under a round arch trefoiled in grand curvilinear sweeps, beneath a rich cornice. The other monument is of Bishop *Gawain Douglas*, an altar-tomb, panelled, under a round arch, with a vignette and Tudor ornaments.

Arms: Az. a temple arg. St. Machar, pontifically vested, in his sinister a pastoral staff; his right hand extended over three children in a boiling caldron.

The choir was destroyed by a furious mob from New Aberdeen, who would have demolished the entire structure had not the Earl of Huntley, and Leslie of Balquhar, seasonably arrived at the head of their retainers. The rabble carried off the bells and unroofed the church. The Covenanters destroyed the altar. The church was unroofed 1568. In 1649 the exquisite carved work was hewn down, and only a beautifully-carved pulpit was left. Cromwell took away a great part of the stones to build a fort at Aberdeen. The great central tower, with its wooden spire 150 ft. high, built by Bishop Elphinstone, 1487-1514, having been undermined by Cromwell's troopers, fell May 9, 1688. The bells formerly hung on trees, a custom not extinct in Scotland a century since.

The Use followed by Aberdeen, Caithness, and Elgin, was that of Lincoln, whilst Glasgow and Dunkeld adopted St. Osmund's Rule. The bishopric was founded by King David. Among the prelates occur W. Elphinstone, founder of King's College and Lord Chancellor, Matthew Scot, L. C., Greenlaw, L. C , Spence, Privy Seal, and W. Stewart, Lord Treasurer, Jolly and Skinner. Barbour, the poet of Bruce, was a canon. Bishop Seabury, first bishop of the church of America, was consecrated at Aberdeen. The cathedral contains the monument of Bishop Scougall.

The bridge over the Don is a fine specimen of ancient work. The College of the Holy Trinity and St. Mary, now known, in commemoration of James IV., under the title of King's, was founded in 1505 by Bishop Elphinstone. The tower, 100 ft. high, erected 1515, and rebuilt 1636, is of four stories, embattled, and crowned with a lantern, of circular ribs crossing, which is surmounted by a crown : the window of the library is round-headed, and filled with flamboyant tracery. The ceiling is of wood, richly carved. In the chapel the open screen, and a double range of canopied stalls, are exquisitely carved, infinite in variety of design, luxuriant fancy, and of extreme delicacy. They were preserved by the gallant conduct of Hector Boethius, the principal, who armed the students and checked the assault of the barons of the Mearns, who came down furiously flushed with the sack ot the cathedral.

Brechin.

Though Time
Has hushed the choral anthems, and o'erthrown
The altar, nor the holy crucifix
Spared, whereon hung outstretched in agony
The Eternal's visioned arms, 'tis dedicate
To prayer and penitence still; so says the hush
Of earth and heaven unto the setting sun,
With a profounder meaning than the burst
Of hymns in morn or evening orisons.

THE Cathedral, 114 ft. long, which is of the 12th century, is
now a parish kirk. Until 1806, it remained perfect externally, but in that year the transept was destroyed, new aisles
were built, and a roof stripped off from the nave, which had
been framed in a wood among the braes of Angus, with
timbers, as in Styria, steeped in some chemical preparation.
Part of the Lady Chapel remains. The nave of five bays is
late and plain Early English, mixed with Decorated work.
The north-west tower is Decorated, square and massive, of
three stories; the undermost being rib-vaulted with corner-
shafts; the capitals and bases are Early English. The rich
west window, slightly flamboyant, is set under a crow-
stepped gable. In the tower, which is crowned with an
octagonal spire, having dormer windows, are three bells. On
the south side of the nave is a detached round tower of the
12th century, 80 ft. high, with a spired roof 23 ft. in height,
lighted with dormer windows; the diameter ranges from 16
to 20 ft. This tower slightly tapers upwards; the side to
the church is straight, the other forms with it an obtuse
angle. The whole structure has been seen to sway in a heavy
wind. The only other instance in Scotland of a similar
building is at Abernethy. The choir is Early and pure Early
English, plain outside but rich within; it was 84 ft. 4 in.
long, but now measures only 30 ft. 10 in.

The Maison Dieu, Early English, was built in 1256.

Among the bishops occur P. de Leuchars and G. Shores-
wood, lord chancellors.

Arms: Arg., three piles meeting at the points in base, gu.

Dunblane.

Inexorably calm, with silent pace,
Here Time hath passed ; what ruin marks his way !
This pile, now crumbling o'er its hallowed base,
Turned not his step, nor could his course delay.

DUNBLANE, on the banks of Allan Water, derives its name from Dun, a hill, and St. Blaan, a native of Bute and the founder of a Culdee monastery here. The cathedral is 216 ft. long by 76 ft. broad and 58 ft. high. The aisleless *choir* of six bays is Norman and Early English, and lighted by tall windows. It retains a unique feature in Scotland, its stalls of black oak canopied, 32 in number, with the Dean's seat and bishop's throne, and its lofty vaulted roof. There never was a transept. The architecture is mainly pure Early English, with the exception of the Norman Tower. The *west front* is very grand: a steep gable with a rose window rises above three magnificent lofty lancets with trefoiled lights: each, long and narrow, is of two lights; in the head of the central is a cinquefoil, and a quatrefoil in the heads of the other two ; above these, in the gable, is an aureole within a bevelled fringe of bay leaves, arranged like chevrons, with their points in contact. The west door is superb, flanked by two lesser doors and two projecting pedimented buttresses.

The *nave* of eight bays, with arches of unequal span, has long Decorated windows and a battlemented parapet. The south aisle is roofless. The clerestory in each bay has two two-light foliated windows with a quatrefoil in the head, set between flat pilaster-buttresses, crocketed. The north aisle, being continued eastward, formed a chapter house, which is beautifully groined. The aisleless *choir* is of six bays with pointed three-light trefoiled windows. The east window is a triplet, the lateral lancets being very narrow ; that in the centre is of double their breadth, of four-lights foliated, with a band of quatrefoils in the middle, and of similar tracery in the head. The choir will remind the visitor of the Lady Chapel at Lichfield.

The Norman *bell-tower*, 128 ft. high, stands upon the south side of the south aisle; the upper story is later; it has two-light windows, three of them one above the other on the west side, angular turrets, a battlemented parapet, and a short spire.   There remain the effigies of a lord of Strathallan, Bishops *Michael Ochiltree* and *Finlay Dermot* of the 15th century, and in the chapter-house *Malise*, Earl of *Strathern*, died 1271, and his Countess, the figures of gritstone. There are also three blue slabs to the memory of *Margaret*, *Euphemia* Lady Fleming, and *Sybilla*, the daughters of John Lord Drummond, who were poisoned by the courtiers of James IV. at a breakfast in 1501.

The Cathedral was built by Bishop David 1142, and restored by Bishop Clement in 1240. It received great injury in 1559. When Laud rode past in 1633 he observed that this was " a goodly church." " Yes, my lord," said a bystander, " before the Reformation it was a brave kirk." " What, fellow !" cried the primate, looking at the havoc, " Deformation not Reformation."

Adjoining is the " Bishop's Walk," named after Leighton, who here repelled adroitly the widow who told him that she had a revelation to marry him.

Among the bishops of this see occur S. Gilbert Moray, Lord Chamberlain ; Alan S. Edmunds, and N. de Balmarle, Lord Chancellors ; A. Stewart, Lord Treasurer ; and devout Leighton, who died, as he long desired, " a wayfarer in an inn."

Arms : Arg. a saltier engrailed az.

Dunkeld.

Around the cross the flower is winding,
  Around the old and ruined wall,
And with its fragile blossoms binding
  The arch from which it soon must fall.

The solemn shrine is now laid lowly,
  Shivered its wondrous rainbow-panes,
Silent its hymns ; that pale flower solely
  Of all its former pride remains.

Hushed is the ancient anthem, keeping
  The vigil of the silent night,
Gone is the censer's silver sweeping,
  Dim is the sacred taper's light.

True, the wrapt souls' divine emotion
  The desert wind to Heaven may bear :
'Tis not the shrine that makes devotion,
  Nor place that sanctifies the prayer.

DUNKELD, " the castle on the hill," was the scene of the romantic escape of Mary, Queen of Scots, from death by an infuriated stag. There was a Culdee monastery founded here 570, for brethren from Iona. In 1127 King David I. introduced canons regular, and commenced the cathedral. Abbat Mill, of Cambuskenneth, who wrote early in the 16th century, attributes the nave to Bishop Cardeny, who laid the foundation April 27, 1406, (but the nave piers are certainly of an earlier date and look like Norman work,) and the completion of that portion of the building to Bishop Lauder, who consecrated it in 1464, and built the great tower and chapter-house, 1469-1477. This bishop lived in rough times ; for while celebrating high mass at Whitsunday, he was compelled to find shelter among the rafters of the choir roof from the arrows of the clan Donnoquhy, led by an Athol chieftain. The Chapter was constantly exposed to the raids of the Highland lairds, who carried off their cattle and despoiled the treasury.

The west front is composed of an octagonal south turret,

flanking a deeply recessed portal of three orders, with a Pointed side door; the canopy of the great window is deflected to admit a circle filled with geometrical tracery in the gable under a cross of good design. The windows of the aisles are Decorated or flamboyant. The roofless nave, full, even in ruin, of dignity and character, is of seven bays, and measures 120 ft. by 60 ft. and 40 ft. in height; the piers are circular, the arches Pointed; the triforium has semicircular arches, divided by mullions enclosing trefoils; the clerestory, rude within, but with a look of Early English, consists of Pointed windows of two-trefoiled lights with a trefoil in the head. The *choir*, aisleless and of four bays, was built 1318-1337, by Robert the mason, repaired by the Murrays in 1691, and rebuilt by the Duke of Atholl in 1820, at a cost of £5000. The north-west tower, Decorated, is of three stories, 96 ft. high, with a south-east octagonal turret; the parapet is plain, the windows are of two lights, trefoiled, with a trefoil in the head. The chapter-house, rectangular, is of the same date, and is the burial-place of the Duke of Atholl, who died in 1833. In the vestibule is buried P. Alexander, Earl of Buchan, " the wolf of Buchan," who burned Elgin cathedral. In the south aisle of the nave is the effigy of Bishop Cardeny, under a richly crocketed canopy; on the sides of the tomb are canopied angels bearing shields, and in the enclosing arch stand images of saints. There is also a mutilated effigy of Sinclair " the warlike bishop," whom Robert Bruce called " his own bishop." He led the troops to battle against the English, crying out, " Let all who love Scotland follow me!" In the garth is buried Colonel Cleland, who fell, at the head of his Cameronians, under the broadswords of the Highlanders in 1689. Near his grave two Swiss larches, the earliest introduced into Scotland, are observable.

The Cathedral is beautifully situated on the banks of the Tay, winding clear and rapid below; the river is spanned by a magnificent bridge, and goes down to the sea flashing like a bar of opal, under ranges of dark wooded hills, and washing the base of the fir-crowned mountain-top of Coragtinean. The red masses of the town contrast well with the round swells and bright green of coppices of hazel, birch, and oak, opening into avenues of stately trees in the valley, or receding into pale colourless distance, or yet nearer, barred by a deep glen of craggy rocks, and heights rich with purple heath. The see has been presided over by W. de Bidun, M. Scot, J. Peebles, J. Bruce, and J. Livingstoun, Lord Chancellors; M. Moneymusk, Grand Chamberlain; W. Turnbull, J. Raulston, and G. Crichton, Lord Keepers; A. Inglis, Keeper of the Rolls; Hugh, " the poor man's bishop," and G. Douglas, translator of the Æneid. Bishop Douglas went to entreat Cardinal Beaton to interpose between the Hamilton and Douglas factions at Edinburgh, 1520: the archbishop was clad in mail under his robes, and laying his hand on his heart, said, " On my conscience, I cannot help what happens:" " Methinks," retorted the bishop, hearing the ring of the armour, " your Grace's conscience clatters." Bishop Gawain Douglas was compelled to take possession of his see by force in 1516 under a shower of shot from the steeple and palace. A strong reinforcement enabled him to succeed.

Arms: Az. a cross Calvary sa. between two Passion nails gules.

Durnoch.

THE Cathedral, which was the see of Caithness, is now the parish kirk. The tall square western tower of the bishop's palace serves as a jail and court-house, the remainder was burned 1570, by Murray, the master of Caithness, and Mackay of Strathnaver, and recently removed. The cathedral was built by Gilbert de Moray, bishop 1223-1260, the founder of Elgin cathedral. It was restored, about the year 1837, by the Duke of Sutherland. It consists of an aisleless nave, choir, transept, and low central tower with a short spiked spire. The west window is of four lights with geometrical tracery.

The east window is a triplet with a lancet in the gable. The transepts have triplets; the remaining windows are lancets.

Alan St. Edmunds, Lord Chancellor, was bishop of this see.

Arms: Az. a crown of thorns or, between three saltiers arg.

Edinburgh.

THE cathedral of St. Giles, huge, sombre, and irregular, was rebuilt externally, 1830, by Burn. It was a cell of Dunfermline Abbey till James III., 1466-1483, made it a collegiate church. The old church was burned, 1384, by the Duke of Gloucester. The Cathedral consists of a nave with double aisles, a transept, built 1390-1413, which was the most ancient portion, a choir with five chapels, built 1387, on the south side, and four, built 1437-1451, on the north. The rest is of the period of James VI., and the arms of the benefactors are carved upon the pillars. The choir alone is in a state of preservation, the remainder of the church having been rebuilt in a motley style, and being in a wretched condition. Four plain octagonal pillars at the west end divide the central alley from the aisles; two more, one a respond, occur at the east end. The pier arches are obtusely pointed, the easternmost being of greater span. The western arches are of three plain chamfered orders. The roof is groined, and enriched with ribs and large round sculptured bosses. The roofs of the aisles are vaulted. The tracery of the windows is modern. The ground-plan is of French design; the main transept, which has aisles, scarcely projects beyond the line of the nave and choir. In the south wing external buildings give it a cruciform shape. On a line with the end of the nave is a transept with a flat roof. The High Church or Holy Blood aisle was built by Preston of Craigmillar. The interior was divided into four kirks previous to the late repairs. The nave was the tolbooth, the choir the high kirk, and the south transept the old kirk; while the north transept, being desecrated as a court-house and police office, was known as the

" den of thieves." The great Earl of Montrose was buried here May 11, 1661; the Regent Murray, 11 February, 1570; near the centre of the south aisle, and on the outside of the north wall, is the monument of John Napier of Merchistoun, the inventor of logarithms. John Knox was buried in the cemetery. Among the eminent provosts of the College occur Gawain Douglas, the translator of the " Æneid " and author of the " Palace of Honour," an anticipation of the " Pilgrim's Progress." The see was founded by Charles I. 1633, and ranked after St. Andrew's and Glasgow. The first prelate was the learned William Forbes. John Knox here used to fulminate Calvinism, as if he would beat the pulpit into matchwood; here the Regent was assailed by Hamilton, and King James I. in 1596 was greeted as wicked Haman by the Presbyterian teachers. When Laud and Andrewes attended him, he here, amid the sobs of the congregation, bade his Scottish subjects farewell, promising that he would visit them at least once in every three years. On July 23, 1637, the English Service was first read here by Dean Hannay, on Stoning Sunday or Casting of Stools-day, when Jenny Geddes, a low disreputable kail-wife, immortalized by the Covenanters, hurled her stool at the clergyman's head; and Bishop Lindsay, courageously ascending the pulpit, vainly attempted to preach in the face of the most brutal violence. Charles I. was frequently here. On December 1, 1638, the solemn League and Covenant was publicly read in the church. On August 25, 1822, George IV. occupied the chair of the Lord High Commissioner of the General Assembly.

The *lantern* forms a mural diadem, the crockets are the pearls, the pierced parapet is the circle of the crown. Eight ribs of stone springing from corbels meet to support an airy gallery and a tall pinnacle. When this beautiful structure was illuminated on festival eves with coloured lamps the effect must have been most rich,—tracery and arch, every graceful outline standing out dyed with every prismatic hue. The silver lamp of St. Eloi, rescued from the sack of Jerusalem, and its four supporting brazen columns, which stood within the canopy, have been melted down into cannon. The effigies of prelate, noble, and knight, with the rich glazing, have all disappeared, and gallery and every hideous incumbrance block up the once-majestic interior. The central *tower* is of three stories, having on each face a plain Transitional Early English two-light window, above which are three equal trefoiled lancets, under a very rich parapet pierced with quatrefoils, and richly crested; from buttresses spring eight crocketed ribs, which, at the point of meeting, support a central pinnacle. The *east window* is of two orders, of five trefoiled lights, with geometrical tracery in the head. The vaulting is simple, and the ribs of the groining meet in central bosses: there is no triforium; the pillars are clustered, and the easternmost capitals carved: the rest are octagonal and plain. The clerestory has a splayed pointed arch within; the windows are of two trefoiled lights. The whole building has been miserably modernized; indeed the choir and lantern are all that remain of interest.

Blair, the author of the well-known sermons, and Henry the historian, have been preachers in this church.

DIMENSIONS OF THE CATHEDRAL IN FEET.

	Length.	Breadth.	Height.
Nave . .	110	26·7	..
Choir . .	88	{S. Aisle 22·7} {N. Aisle 18·2}	..
Transept .	129	20	..
Tower . .	..	..	161
Extreme length	206	..	..

Among the bishops occurs Rose, who came to London to intercede for the preservation of his order, 1688.

Arms: Az. a saltire arg.; in chief a mitre of the last.

The large octagon tower which overhangs Cowgate was part of the old archiepiscopal palace. *Heriot's Hospital*, a school for poor and orphan boys (Laureston Place), designed by Inigo Jones, and founded by George Heriot, court jeweller to James VI., is quadrangular, 162 ft. by 92 ft., with four square towers and domed turrets: it resembles Fredericksburg in Denmark. It was built, 1628-1660, at a cost of £27,000; the chapel on the south side has stained glass. Heriot is buried in the Old Grey Friars churchyard, where also lie George Buchanan, Black the chemist, Allan Ramsay, Blair, Mackenzie, and Robertson. The Tolbooth, Canongate, was built in 1591 ; Moray House, St. John-street, in 1618 ; Panmure House was the residence of Adam Smith, who is buried near Dugald Stewart in the Canongate churchyard. In Whitehorse Inn Close, Dr. Johnson resided in 1773. Smollett resided in 1766 in St. John-street; and Lord Monboddo lived at No. 13. In the castle is a Norman chapel, built by Queen Margaret, wife of Malcolm Canmore ; it has been restored by Mr. Billings. It consists of a chancel 16 ft. 4 in. by 10 ft. 4 in. and a semicircular apse 10 ft. 4 in. by 9 ft. 8 in. ; the east window is a square head trefoiled. Near it is Mons Meg, a hooped gun, cast at Mons in 1486. On Salisbury Crags are the remains of St. Anthony's hermitage chapel, well known to the reader of " The Heart of Midlothian ;" near it is the well which deserted maidens sought.

> Saint Anton's well sall be my drink
> Since my true love's forsaken me.

Elgin.—*(See of Moray.)*

> The work of mortal hands, ·
> Cast in a mould magnificent, how stands
> The pile in stately beauty !

THE sudden descent from the surrounding barren mountainlands and tracts of rough granite into the pleasant vale of Moray offers a welcome change to the traveller. The archæologist will find a rich harvest-field in the chief town of Elgin : the Maison Dieu, the corner niches in the street which once held the image of the Blessed Virgin and an ever-burning cresset, the bishop's palace, and the tolbooth, the low-browed portal and quadrangle of some old burgher's house, with narrow lights, crowstepped and often colonnaded, reminding him of foreign streets. Some streets have arcades of stone on a level with the road, thus in a degree resembling the roads of Chester. But he will quicken his steps as he recognises

the magnificent western towers—huge, dusky, solemn—of
the ancient cathedral of the Holy Trinity, once the noblest
edifice for loveliness and majesty in Scotland, and far surpassing any church of the sister-isle : as one of its bishops
averred, it was " the beautiful gem of the country, the fair
glory of the realm, its loftiest praise in other lands."

By command of Pope Honorius the see was translated to
Elgin from Spynie on the banks of the Lossie, and on July 17,
1224, the foundation stone of the " Lantern of the North "
was laid by Andrew, Bishop of Moray. It was burned in
1270, and again, on St. Botolph's day, 1390, by Alexander, the
Wolf of Badenoch, whom the bishop had excommunicated for
sacrilege. The only punishment inflicted on this bad man
was public penance in St. John's, the Blackfriars' church, in
Perth. Elgin was plundered in 1402 by Alexander, son of the
Lord of the Isles. Bishop Barr began to rebuild the cathedral,
which was completed in 1424. It measures 282 ft. by 35 ft.,
the transept is 114 ft. long. There are two western towers,
and two large turrets flank the east end. The central tower
and spire, 198 ft. high, fell on Easter morning, 1711. Part of
the choir, a portion of the transept and chapter-house, with
the west and east fronts remain.

The architecture of the Cathedral is Early English and
Transitional Early English. The western towers, Early
English, are of four stories, 84 ft. high, and were formerly
crowned with wooden spires. The under portions are Norman.
In the first story is a lancet ; in the second a two-light window ; in the third four lancets under a round arch ; in the
uppermost is a triplet, the middle lancet alone being a light.
The great west window, 27 ft. by 19 ft., is round-headed, enclosed within a Pointed arch with four-leaved flowers in the
jambs ; it stands over a Late, shadowless but recessed, double
portal of eight quasi-shafted orders, of 22 ft. span, divided by
a single pillar. Above it is an aureole set between figures
praying. The doorway, with foliated arches, and an exquisite enrichment of flowers and foliage, is placed between two
trefoiled niches ; between these and the sill of the window are
three crocketed pediments, within which are trefoiled niches
set between quatrefoils. In the interior there is an arcade

of lancets. In the gable is a window within a depressed
arch.

The *nave*, of six bays, had five alleys, forming a double
arcade on either side: one four-light window of the 15th century, in the south aisle, has preserved its flamboyant tracery
and foliated mullions. The *choir*, of four bays, was built
1270-1390: the east window has external piers instead of
mullions to divide the lights. On the south side Bishop
Andrew was buried in 1242. The elevation of the east end
is superb. There are two grand tiers, each of five tall lancets,
splayed and enriched in the jambs with the four-leaved flower,
and filling up the whole extent of the wall. The lowermost
were foliated. In the square gable was a grand marygold.
The clerestory is composed of couplets or triplets, long and
narrow, thus occupying the place of a triforium. The pillars
are clustered. A remarkable shafted pillar, with a pyramidal
group of flowered capitals in three tiers, marks the entrance
of the sanctuary four bays from the east. The *presbytery* of
two bays, 23 ft. 7 in. long, is raised by two steps above the
level of the choir, which measures 86 ft. 4 in., and has a
Lady Chapel on the south, and a retro choir on the north,
arranged like aisles. The flanking turrets of the east end
are of seven stories, massive, octagonal, with a double arcade
below, and, above, trefoiled niches under crocketed pediments. The choir aisles terminate two bays short of the east
end to form a presbytery: the windows have geometrical
tracery. In the transept, of which the gable is lost, are two
lancets, and a Decorated door of two orders with an aureole
above it. The next story has three round-headed windows.
Communicating with the north side of the choir by a vaulted
passage is the octagonal chapter-house, Decorated, locally
called the Prentice aisle, lofty and large; with seven four-
light flamboyant windows. Each side is 15 ft. broad, the
height is 34 ft., the diameter 37 ft.; a single central pillar
clustered supported the groined roof. It has a projecting
desk with a sculptured figure on each side. The south porch
and five arched seats remain.

The bishop, P. Hepburn, was heavily fined for giving shelter
here to the excommunicated Earl of Bothwell. The Privy

Council in February, 1568, ordered the cathedrals of Elgin and Aberdeen to be unroofed, and the lead sold in Holland to pay the Regent Murray's troops. The sacrilegious plunder, happily, 'sunk off Aberdeen. High mass was sung at the altar for the last time to celebrate the victory of the Roman Catholic Earls of the north over the Presbyterians of the west. John Shanks, the sexton, 1830-1841, meritoriously cleared out the ruins, and with his own hands removed 2832 cubic feet of earth. The see has been presided over by D. Moray, founder of the Scots' College at Paris; John Winchester, envoy to England; J. Stewart and J. Hepburn, Lord Treasurers; A. Stewart, Lord Privy Seal; P. Hepburn, Secretary of State; and Alexander Jolly, who died 1838.

Arms: Az., a church arg. St. Giles pontifically vested standing in the porch; in his dexter hand a Passion cross or, in his sinister an open book arg.

Fortrose.—(*See of Ross.*)

Glorious was the design ye drew!
Yet Time itself hath built for you
A house of wisdom, far above
All ye designed, as if in love
He mellows down the stony tress
Into a solemn tenderness,
And clothes yon beauteous roof on high
With a more dread sublimity.
With quiet awe around them lingers,
Touching, as loth to harm, with soft and reverend fingers.

THE beautiful Cathedral of SS. Peter and Boniface, built of red sandstone, was an architectural gem, and remarkable for finish and the exquisite beauty of its smallest mouldings. It was of the purest and most elaborate Decorated. Little more than one roofless aisle remains; the greater part having been destroyed by Cromwell, who sent the materials to build a fort at Inverness. The church was 120 ft. long, and composed of a

west tower, choir, and nave of four bays with aisles, of which
the southern only is left; a quasi-transept formed out of the
choir-aisles; a Lady Chapel and crypt, with a chapter-house of
which the north-east end remains. The *rood turret* is still at
the junction of the south aisles of the choir and nave. The
east window had five lights, and two lancets in the gable.
The south aisle was separated from the choir by two Decorated arches: in the first is the tomb of the foundress, the
Countess of Ross, died 1300; in the second is a Perpendicular
tomb canopied with an effigy of a bishop; on the north side is
the tomb of the *Earl of Ross*; and between its foot and the
easternmost pier is a credence-table. On the south side are
windows of four lights and elaborate design, and a piscina.
This cathedral is the ancestral burial-place of the family of the
Mackenzies of Seaforth.

Arms: Arg. St. Boniface on the dexter, habited in a cope
gu., his hand across his breast; on the sinister, a bishop pontifically habited, in his sinister hand a pastoral staff.

Galloway.—*(See of Whitherne.)*

High Reformation lifts her iron rod;
But lo! with stern and threatful mien,
Fury and rancour desolate the scene;
Beneath their rage the Gothic structures nod.

THERE are only a few remains of the Cathedral of St. Ninian,
and of a priory founded by Fergus, Lord of Galloway. Sysderf,
of this see, was the only bishop left of the old succession in
1661. James Bethune, bishop in 1508, was Lord Treasurer.
The ruins, Early English, consist of a roofless choir of the
12th century, some portions of an earlier crypt, perhaps of
the 8th century, and a fine west door. There are traces of
a south-west tower and Norman details at the west end.
Within the last forty years it was used as a kirk.

On the island of Whitherne, two miles distant, is the site of
the church of St. Martin of Tours, built of stone, 412, an

unusual style, and thence called Candida Casa, the White House. It was founded by St. Ninian, himself a Briton, but a disciple of St. Columba, who was buried here, as the see of the southern Picts converted by St. Columba. The church of Whitherne, with De-hrmach, "the Field of Oaks," in Ireland, and many other monasteries in both islands, was under the rule of the abbats of the parent-house of Iona. St. Ninian's immediate successors, like the other Culdees, retained the customs of the Eastern Church; but Galloway afterwards becoming subject to the English, a succession of seven Saxon bishops of Whitherne received ordination from the Archbishops of York, and paid canonical obedience to them.

Arms: Azure, S. Ninian pontifically vested and mitred; in his dexter hand a pastoral staff, his sinister crossed upon his breast.

Glasgow.

The winds are still, or the dry church tower grass
Knows not their gentle motions as they pass.
Thou, too, aërial pile! whose pinnacles
Point from one shrine like pyramids of fire,
Obeyest in silence their sweet solemn spells,
Clothing in hues of heaven the dim and distant spire,
Around whose lessening and invisible height,
Gather among the stars the clouds of night.

GLASGOW is Glas-coed, "the dark wood:" the bell used to hang upon an oak-tree. This stupendous and magnificent Cathedral was erected in the great age of ecclesiastical architecture, and completed in the noontide of its glory and grandeur. For the most part it was built during the Lancet period; its crypt is Early English; the spire, nave, chapter-house, and transept-crypt, being either Late Decorated or Flamboyant. It is an imposing dusky fabric, stately, solemn, solid, and venerable, elevated on the brink of a ravine, gloomy,

and of peculiar character, through which flows the rivulet
Molendinar: the precinct is in the north-east quarter of the
city, in the Townhead, and at the upper end of the High
Street, from which an open space of cemetery, surrounded by
high walls, wholly sequesters it.   The choir-floor is 140 ft.
above the river.

> High o'er the lave St. Mungo rears
> His sacred fane, the pride of years;
> And stretching upward to the spheres
>   His spire, afar
> To weary travellers appears
>   A leading star.

Twice has the church been preserved from destruction; in
August, 1560, when the judicious Lord Provost dissuaded a
mob from razing it to the ground by the happily-timed sug-
gestion that it would be premature before a new kirk had
been provided; and again, in 1579, when Andrew Melville,
Principal of the University, having prevailed on the magistrates for its demolition, disgusted at his intolerant bigotry,
the incorporated trades assembled by beat of drum, and the
craftsmen and their deacons repulsed the sacrilegious fanatics
with such vigour as to terrify the magistrates, and induce them
to forbear.   Well would it have been for Scottish honour if a
similar courage had been displayed in preserving minsters as
grand as the " pride of Lanarkshire," or leaving them to the
Church which would have cherished them.

The Cathedral of St. Mungo, or Kentigern, is composed of
a nave of eight bays, north-west tower, a short transept, a
central tower and spire, a choir of five bays, Lady Chapel of
two bays, and chapter-house at the north-east end.   The
choir, Lady Chapel, and crypt are Late Early English; the
nave is Decorated, as are the chapter-house and lateral crypts.
The site was holy ground; St. Ninian, St. Kentigern, and the
pilgrim, St. Columba, had preached here.

The Glasgow folks compared the building to Penelope's web,
saying that, like St. Mungo's work, it would never be finished.
The church was erected on the site of a wooden structure
which had been burned down by Bishop Achaius in 1136; but

the new fabric having been again destroyed by fire, the foundation of another church was laid in 1181 by Bishop Jocelyn, and the crypt dedicated July 6, 1197. The spire was in progress in 1277. In 1258 Bishop William de Bondington saw the choir completed. In 1291 Edward I. gave certain oaks to Bishop Wishart to complete the steeple, but the bishop converted them into catapults for the siege of Kirkintilloch Castle. Bishop W. Lauder, 1408-25, commenced, and Bishop John Cameron, 1425-47, completed, the present spire, the chapter-house, and crypt beneath it. The north aisle was roofed by Bishop Muirhead, 1455-73. Before 1480 the nave, begun in the 14th century, and the north-west tower, were completed. Archbishop Blackadder, 1484-1508, built the rood-loft, the stairs of the great crypt, and the undercroft of the south transept. The remainder of the building was completed by Cardinal Beaton. The Cathedral has been restored by Blore.

The *west front* had a north-west tower of the latter part of the 16th century, with a short, lead-covered, and an eight-gabled spire. Two windows, round-headed and trefoiled, lighted each face of the upper story. Upon the south-west side was the stump of a similar tower,' upon which, about the same date, a *consistory court* was built. These were barbarously destroyed in 1834 by the Corporation, who left the cathedral in such a state of disgraceful neglect that the officials of the Board of Health were compelled to interfere. The west door, 17 ft. by 11 ft., is of great richness and beauty, and by half a century earlier than the nave. It is a double portal of six quasi-shafted orders with 21 ft. span, with a square head to each entrance, and the space above is filled with niches. It is divided by a single pillar, and wears a continental aspect. In the clerestory of the *nave*, Early Decorated, of the 14th century, couplets of two-light windows, with a lozenge in the head, fills each bay. In the aisles in each bay is a single three-light window, each composed of three lancets, with a trefoiled circle for tracery, and divided by chamfered buttresses. Above the corbel table in either story are grotesque gurgoyles. The proportions of the whole line of building are good, and the design appropriate to its fine situation.

In the interior, the arches of the *nave* are Pointed with deep mouldings. It is 63 ft. broad and 85 ft. high. The vaulting shafts rest upon corbels. The *triforium* in each bay is divided by clustered shafts, and consists of two trefoiled lights with a trefoil in the head. The *clerestory* has a broad wall passage, and a gallery with two noble Pointed arches in each bay. The wood roof is ribbed. The aisles retain their stone quadripartite groining. The south-easternmost windows of the triforium are of three lights, but have a curiously complicated pattern. The transept is 73 ft. long. The *choir-screen* is most elaborate; on either side of a door with a low, depressed arch are five panels, and above is an open, quatrefoiled, flamboyant parapet, with seven pairs of figures serving as corbels to support the canopied buttresses. Five stairs lead up to the pace, the sides of which have figures bearing legends under canopies. The west window was painted at Munich, 1859.

The east end of the *choir*, which has five bays, is composed of two Pointed arches, under an engaged group of four tall lancets; the two innermost being the loftiest, and filling the space which ordinarily would have been divided between the clerestory and triforium. The clerestory, of the latter part of the 13th century, is formed of triplets of equal lights, in front of them; on the interior is a screen to the wall passage of similar design. The triforium consists of double windows of two trefoiled lights with a quatrefoil in the head in each bay. The roof, of wood, 90 ft. high, is ribbed, and enriched with carved bosses. The capitals under the great arches of the tower present the earliest instance of foliation in North Britain. The Lady Chapel of two bays retains its stone vaulting, and is of great beauty and simplicity. In each transept is a five-light Decorated window, 40 ft. by 20 ft., under an aureole in the gable; below are two two-light windows like those in the nave aisles, but with an oval in the head. The south wing is called the Dripping Aisle, from a continuous dripping of water off the roof, caused by the porous nature of the stone and capillary attraction.

The *crypt* built by Bishop Joscelyn, 1181, consecrated 1197, and described by Sir Walter Scott as " low-browed, dark, and twilight," is, in reality, a second underground church, and owing to the fall in the ground is remarkably well lighted. Its architecture is matchless Early English, solid, richly, and intricately vaulted; the perspective of its aisles is varied and enchanting. It has forty-one windows, and forty-five pillars 18 ft. high, some 18 ft. in circumference: it measures 108 ft. by 72 ft.; it was long used as the Barony Kirk; in it Rob Roy appointed a meeting with Frank Osbaldistone. This crypt was cleared and opened out by Mr. Nixon in 1835. It contains the tomb of St. Mungo or Kentigern, with an effigy. In the south aisle of the choir is the only brass extant in Scotland, an oblong 3 ft. 2 in. by 6 ft., to the memory of six knights of the house of Minto, dated 1608. Edward I. in 1301, made rich offerings at St. Mungo's shrine. Stained glass and stall-work have been set up by Burns.

The central *tower* rises 30 ft. above the roof, and rests on four massive pillars, each 29 ft. in circumference. The octangular spire is of good dimensions and outline, with fine spire-lights and two rich bands. The tower has four lancets in each, the two outer being blank, under a quatrefoil parapet. The entire steeple is 225 ft. high.

The east end of the *choir* consists of four lancets, the two innermost being longer, set between two plain pilaster buttresses, with a square window under a round arch in the gable. Couplets light the four bays of the Lady Chapel above and the crypt beneath. The projection of the chapel will remind the visitor of the large eastern cross of Durham and Fountains. The two-storied chapter-house is of two bays, and is lighted with couplets in two tiers. Enthusiastic Andrew Fairservice, in "Rob Roy," thus describes the cathedral: "Ah, it's a brave kirk: nane o' your whigmaleeries and curliewurlies, and open streak-hems about it; a' solid weel-jointed mason-wark that will stand as lang as the warld, keep hands and gunpowther aff it." The total length of the church is 319 ft. It is 1090 ft. in circumference, covers an area of 26,400 ft., and contains 147 pillars and 157 windows. The devout King James IV. was honorary canon of the cathedral, and subjected Dunkeld, Dunblane, Galloway, and Argyle, to Glasgow as an archbishopric. In this church Wishart, the warlike bishop, absolved Robert Bruce after the murder of Comyn; he became blind during his imprisonment by the English. Archbishop Blackadder died a pilgrim in the Holy Land in 1508. The followers of Archbishop Gawain Douglas, regardless of the presence of the Venetian archbishop, on June, 1545, under the shadow of the holy rood, engaged in a disgraceful feud in the close with the partisans of Cardinal Beaton, the primate; and there a century later the followers of John Knox disputed for the mastery, the preacher was dragged from the pulpit, and the moderator insulted amid the crash of bells and swords, and the beat of drums. Here, in December, 1638, the General Assembly, with sword and dagger and horrible din, pronounced the abolition of Episcopacy; fifteen years later some of the members were conducted to the foot of the gallows by a sect yet fiercer than the covenanted, and warned of their fate if they dared to return. In 1650 Cromwell was compelled to sit silent during a sermon of Zachary Boyd, so insulting, that, but for his significant frown, the rash preacher would have been a head shorter under the swords of the arch-rebel's captains. Buchanan has trod these aisles, and his pupil, Andrew Melville, clamoured for their overthrow. In the chapter-house and crypt assembled the early convocations of the University, which afterwards produced Smith and Watt. In the sacristy the robes of Bruce were fashioned for his coronation, and the banner of Scotland taken down, while men cried aloud it was more righteous to die for King Robert, than to fall as Crusaders in the Holy Land. From the pulpit Leighton has uttered his seraphic eloquence; and through the nave has swept the fiery mob of Cameronians to accomplish the work of furious bigotry. Among the bishops occur John Herbert, Hugh de Roxburgh, Florence, William de Bondington, W. Wishart, and J. Bruce, Archbishop J. Beaton and Gavin Dunbar, Lord Chancellors; Cameron and W. Turnbull, Lords Privy Seal; and J. Laing, Lord Treasurer; John Lindsay, slain in action with an English squadron; and Michael Russell, died 1848.

There is a Perpendicular tower attached to the Tron (weighing beam) church. The guildry tower and some of the college buildings in the University are worthy of notice.

Arms: Arg., a tree growing out of a mount in base; surmounted by a salmon in fess, ppr., in his mouth an annulet, or; on the dexter side a bell pendent from the tree, ppr.

Jona.

There never yet came man to I,
Who did not come three times by three.

IONA, three miles long by one mile and a half in oreadth, is also called Ithona, the Isle of Waves, the Happy Island, and I-Colm-kill, "the isle of St. Columba's cell." It lies three miles southward of Staffa, and Walter Scott finely contrasts the architecture of man with the pillared cave :—

That wondrous dome,
Where, as to shame the temples decked
By skill of earthly architect,
Nature herself it seemed would raise
A minster to her Maker's praise:
Nor doth its entrance front in vain
To old Iona's holy fane,
That Nature's voice might seem to say,
" Well hast thou done, frail child of clay !
Thy humble powers that stately shrine
Tasked high and hard—but witness mine !"

The whole island is full of traditions: one part records the scene of the saint's landing; another, close to the Sound, a green eminence, the "Druids' graves," where lay the priests of an elder faith. In 563, during the reign of Eugene III., St. Columba, coming from Ireland. touched the shore which now bears his name, and P. Connal, son of Congel, King of Scots, gave him the island. His landing-place is called the " Bay of the Boat." The monks which he established were canons regular, and until 716 they observed neither the Roman Easter nor the tonsure. They were called Culdees, that is, religious recluses, Guillan De, " servants of God," and their house was entitled cuil, a cell. The abbat held jurisdiction over every member of the community, bishop or priest. Still, amid the gloomy Western Isles, the lonely cathedral is seen from Fingal's Cave, standing out, amid the wild waves and rugged barren rocks of Mull, against the western sky,—the only token of bygone civilization, the solitary record of an old world passed away,—with its crosses of stone reared up amid the stormy waters, and the scattered isles surrounded by the wildest scenery of the ocean. From that retreat the savage clans of the Highlands were taught religion : St. Aidan and Finan, the first bishops of Landisfarne, issued from its cells to convert the north of England.

"We are treading," to use the well-known words of Dr. Johnson, " that illustrious island, which was once the luminary of the Caledonian regions, whence savage clans and roving barbarians derived the benefits of knowledge and the blessings of religion. That man is little to be envied whose piety would not grow warmer among the ruins of Iona."

There is another feature of great interest, the resemblance to Irish ecclesiastical architecture presented in the cluster of graves, the crosses, and the number and diminutive size of the buildings : the round towers of Brechin and Abernethy, if transported hither, would complete the analogy.

> It was a place
> Befitting well a rigid anchorite,
> Dead to the hopes and vanities and joys
> And purposes of life.

St. Columba would not allow a cow in the island, for he said, where there was a cow there must be a woman, and where woman was, there would be mischief. St. Oran was an equally rigid celibate. The demons of the soil would suffer no church to be erected before they had been propitiated by a human sacrifice: this devoted follower consented to be buried alive, and St. Columba ordered the grave to be opened : after three days this was done, and his friend, to the horror and scandal of the assistants, sat up and professed a creed beneath Sadduceeism. Before he could propound further heresies, St. Columba commanded the earth to be heaped on him with the

utmost despatch. There is an Erse prophecy, that the sacred
isle shall escape a deluge which will precede the doom :—

> Seven years before that awful day
> When time shall be no more,
> A watery deluge shall o'ersweep
> Hibernia's mossy shore ;
> The green-clad Isla too shall sink,
> While, with the great and good,
> Columba's happy isle will rear
> Her towers above the flood.

In 797, in 801, and in 807, the heathen Northmen wasted
the island ; but after their conversion to Christianity the
Christian Norwegians seem to have respected its sanctity.
The sagas call it " Eyinhelgea " (the holy isle) — and state
that King Magnus Barfod, landing here on his first expedition to the Southern Isles and Ireland, 1047, visited
the churches, and guaranteed the peace and security of the
inhabitants. After a while, Cluniacs arrived and occupied
their church and monastery. King Alexander I. was wrecked
here, and entertained by the hermits, and in memory of his
preservation founded a religious house. Occasionally, English
marauders invaded the island, but the saint invariably avenged
their insolence. After the English conquest of Man, the Bishop
of the Isles expelled the Culdees, and made Iona his see in the
time of Edward I., with the abbat's permission. In the 16th
century, St. Mary's, Rothsay, since destroyed, was constituted
the cathedral church.

The causeway of approach is still called the main street,
and is crossed by Royal and Martyr streets. The extensive
ruins embrace the buildings known as the bishop's palace,
the chapter-house with stone seats, the abbat's lodge on the
north, and those which we proceed to describe :—

The *Cathedral of St. Mary*, built of red Mull granite, is
cruciform, with a central tower, but was made a ruin in 1561.
There is a peculiarity about the choir, which has a projecting
presbytery. On the north side was the sacristy; on the south
is an aisle divided off by two pillars, and within parted by
walls into three chantries. There are two arched cells in the
east wall of the north transept. The nave, like those of Elgin

and Paisley, was shorter than the eastern arm of the cross. Its circular pillars are Norman, as are its ornaments; but the Early English style is predominant. The tower is square, of a single story above the weather-gables of the roofs, which were of high pitch and of mica slate. The windows are square, under a square hood moulding, terminating in foliated corbels. The lights are filled on the east and west, with quatrefoils; on the north and south with a circle of flamboyant tracery of spiral mullions. The baluster-shaft may be the last relic of, perhaps, a yet earlier Norwegian temple. The angles of the tower are chamfered with a shaft between the lower string-course, and the machicolated corbel-table which runs below the plain parapet; it has the mask of a beast as a capital. On the south side there are two quatrefoils within an oblong semi-mullioned window in a corner of the face. Small trefoiled narrow windows flank the weather-gables.

The fronts of the transept and choir lack the corbel-table, which, with this exception, is continued with a flat parapet round the building. The *south transept* has a window, with three round-headed trefoiled lights and a flamboyant circle. At the angles are double buttresses with sets-off, and a moulding on their outer edges. The choir, of the 13th century, is of three bays; the pillars are circular; the arches Pointed. The aisles are in ruins; the south-east window has a plain canopy, with a simple finial and corbel heads. The clerestory consists of two narrow round-headed trefoiled windows, and in the centre a Pointed window with geometrical tracery. A *presbytery* of one bay lies to the east, lighted on the sides by a window of three round-headed trefoiled lights, with a flamboyant circle in the head, under a hood-moulding, terminating in corbel-heads. It is of the 16th century. A curious figure, spreading its arms, projects from its point, which causes the string-course of the choir to be stilted at right angles, and then continued in a line ending with a mask of a lion. In the interior the east window is of four pointed trefoiled lights, with geometrical tracery verging on flamboyant, below a square window in the steep gable. On the south side are three sedilia. The south arches are

Pointed, with plain mouldings, and rest on capitals with grotesques and figures. On the north there is a round-headed door of the early part of the 15th century, set in the blocking of one of two large arches which opened into a long and narrow *sacristy*, extending the whole length of the choir, like a north aisle. The arches are elaborately carved with network, and indented dog-tooth mouldings; on the capitals is a peculiar ornament like an Assyrian pattern. There is no triforium. The view through the arches of the dark hills and blue sea on the south is very beautiful. The aisleless nave is in ruins. The west door has deep circular hood-mouldings, and retains a benatura. The lateral buttresses resembled those of the transepts; those on the south were stunted with a steep set-off. The nave piers of granite and sandstone are rounded and plain: a corded moulding underlies capitals carved into grotesques. The triforium is composed of pointed arches with rude mouldings. Bas-reliefs of scriptural subjects adorn the capitals of the tower pillars, which are short and cylindrical, 10 ft. high and 8 ft. in circumference. The chancel screen has scriptural carvings. The high altar-slab of Skye marble was perfect in 1688, but has been since 1772 wholly destroyed: the country folks have broken it piecemeal to form talismans of success, and amulets against fire and wreck.

Among the bishops occur St. German and Plendun, to whom the cathedral of Man was dedicated; Wymund, the blind freebooter; Mark, and Bernard de Linton, Lord Chancellors; and G. Hepburn, slain at Flodden.

In the choir are the monuments of an abbat,—an effigy of purple sandstone, on the north side; of *Lachlan Mackinnon*, of Hil, died 1500; and Abbat *Kenneth Mackenzie*, died 1489, south side; and of a knight, *Macleod*, or Mial-an-Ross, an effigy of freestone, with a spear in the right hand, and a shield with a galley on the left arm; the shell is carved in memory of shell-feasts in the halls of Selma. The chapter-house retains four stalls.

The aisleless nave measures 63 ft. 7 in. by 34 ft.; the transept 70 ft. by 18 ft.; the choir is 60 ft. long, of three bays; the presbytery occupies 26 ft. 6 in. of this length; and the tower 75 ft. high. The roof of slate from Gribon fell in 1820.

There were 160 *crosses* on the island, some seven centuries old; but the bigoted Earl of Argyle hurled sixty of these symbols of our salvation, and venerable relics, into the sea at the Reformation. Presbyterian fanaticism has left only four remaining; they are named St. John's, Maclean's, St. Martin's, and John McFingon's. The last bears the name of an abbat who died in 1439; on the base is a curious representation of a galley, the device of the Norwegian kings of Man. Maclean's cross is 11 ft. high, and richly sculptured; St. Martin's, before the cathedral door, is 15 ft. high and 1½ ft. in breadth, formed of a solid block of schistose mica, and elaborately wrought with arabesques.

There are nine rows of sculptured tombstones; the third line is the kings' ridge, which marks the burial-places of one king of France, eight kings of the Sudreyjar or Southern Isles, and Irish kings of Norwegian descent; also forty-eight kings of Scotland: all her monarchs, from Kenneth III. to Macbeth, were carried hither from Corpach: some abdicated, some came as pilgrims, some as monks :—

> Round the moist marge of each cold Hebrid isle
> To that hoar pile which still its ruin shows,
> Where beneath the showery west
> The mighty kings of the three fair realms are laid,
> And foes, perhaps, together now they rest,
> No slaves revere them and no wars invade;
> Yet frequent now, at midnight's solemn hour,
> The rifted tombs their yawning cells unfold,
> And forth the monarchs stalk with sovereign power,
> In pageant robes and wreathed with sheeny gold,
> And in their twilight tombs aërial council hold.

To this place of interment, in ' Macbeth,' Shakspeare alludes :—

> *Rosse.* Where is Duncan's body?
> *Macduff.* Carried to Colmes' Hill,
> The sacred storehouse of his predecessors
> And guardian of their bones.

And again :—

> Sueno the Norway's king craves composition,
> Nor would we deign him burial of his men,
> Till he disbursed at Saint Colmes' Inch
> Ten thousand dollars to our general use.

The fourth row is that of the priors of Iona, dated 1500. A stone basin, once used for superstitious rites, closes the sixth range; in the seventh are the effigies of departed Macleans, in armour, in imitation of the Southron chivalry; a stag-hunt is represented in the eighth row.

On one side of the garth, 40 ft. by 30 ft., is the site of the Black Stone on which the ancient Highland chiefs swore to keep troth with vassals. Sanctuary was attached to the cemetery precinct.

The *Nunnery Chapel* of St. Nonad, for Augustinian canonesses, is Norman, and 120 ft. long; the nave measuring 38 ft. by 19 ft. 7 in.; the choir 20 ft. by 19 ft. 7 in. The west and south walls remain, rich in lichen, asplenium, cotyledon, and anthyllis. The west gable has a deeply-splayed round-headed lancet, below a smaller window of similar design in the gable, but separated from it by a crow-stepped round-headed moulding, which joins the capitals of the three round arches which pierce the south wall. These capitals have flowered, label, and tooth mouldings; the clerestory consists of two lancets, deeply splayed in a wall of great thickness. The choir was aisleless; the springers of the vaulting remain. The groined roof with moulded ribs rose from cylindrical corner shafts. The sedilia and drain remain. The door of the sacristy, square-headed, is still standing. The only monument remaining is that of Anne Firles, the last lady abbess, who died 1543—a black marble slab and effigy. Continuous with the aisle is a small chapel extending eastward of the choir, vaulted and ribbed, with a turret stair which led to the priests' room overhead. The windows are round-headed. The nave has a north aisle of three round arches; the pillars are round with octagonal capitals. The south-west door is Norman.

Besides four other chapels, there is also the roofless *chape of St. Oran*, of red granite, 60 ft. by 22 ft., with the saint's monument.   It is for the most part plain and unornamented, except with some grotesques; its date is, probably, the latter part of the 12th century, being earlier than the cross of St. Martin, or the church of St. Rule at Aberdeen.   The chevron moulding is, however, profusely employed.   Under the canopy of the two freestone arches of the sedilia is part of the cross of Abbat McFingon, 1489.   The choir contains the tombs of Angus M'Dinchull, who fought at Bannockburn; the " Ronald," hero of the " Lord of the Isles ;" M'Quarrie, of Ulva, in armour, in the centre, and of McLean, of Ghulin, belted with his claymore—for the Highland chiefs affected the Norman knight.   It will be observed that the Nunnery Chapel is lighter and of earlier date than Oran's chapel; the round arches being wholly without ornament, and verging on Transitional to Early English.

Arms: Az. St. Columba in a boat at sea, ppr. in chief a blazing star, or.

St. Magnus, Kirkwall.

Where restless seas
Howl round the storm-vexed Orcades;
Where erst St. Clairs held princely sway
O'er isle and islet, strait and bay;
Still nods their palace to its fall,
Thy pride and sorrow, fair Kirkwall!

AMID the ruins of the old Jarl's fortress and the broken walls of the prelate's palace, the minster yet stands entire.   The presbytery, the east bay of the choir and west door are Early English; the rest of the structure, with the exception of the tower, being Norman.   The Cathedral is cruciform, consisting of a nave of eight bays, and choir of six bays, each with aisles; a transept, each wing having two bays and eastern chapels, and a central tower.   The structure was commenced by the Norwegian Ragnvald (Reginald), Jarl of Orkney, about 1137, who built the three western bays of the choir, by the advice of his father Kol, who designed and superintended the works, and in gratitude for his conquest of the isles, and in honour of his uncle, *St. Magnus.* Bishop William I. in 1160 added the three easternmost bays of the nave. The arches of the tower and vaulting were built in the 14th century. Bishop Stewart, in the reign of James IV., added three bays at the east end of the choir, 1511; and Bishop Reid, 1540, in the time of Queen Mary, erected two bays at the west end of the nave. Stern, massive, uniform, it has all the appearance of an old Norman building; but like Roslyn Chapel, roof, walls, and pillars, which are of red sand-stone, are overgrown with byssus (or leprasia æruginosa), which wraps them with a dark velvety green. The gradual decomposition in the damp recesses of the building, has worn the sides of tombs and aisles into lines of black and grey like runic fretwork. In some places the attempt has been made to give the effect of polychrome, the stones having been purposely selected of red or soft pale yellow, or cream colour, and alternately placed in the orders of one door and in the voussoirs of anöther. The sixteen pillars in the nave are round; the mouldings of the arches are truncated angles; the three tiers of semicircular arches upon either side lend a grand effect to the interior. The choir is richer, having clustered shafts, and chevron and billet mouldings. On the south wall is a cross in a circle, which, probably, marks the place which the bishop touched with chrism at the consecration. The flamboyant wood-work of Earl Patrick deserves particular attention.

There are 103 windows; fourteen pillars in the nave, each 15 ft. in circumference, and ten in the choir; and this subdivision of a limited space, united to narrowness, height, and severity of style, gives to the building a great apparent size. The double triforia throughout the whole extent, and two tiers round the tower, render the interior labyrinthine in effect. The clerestory is composed of lancets; but the three westernmost on the south side of the choir, retain their Norman character. The *west door* is a magnificent specimen of Early English. It is of five orders, with toothed ornament and rich foliage, set under a pediment; three are double-shafted, one is moulded continuously, and the fifth is singly-shafted. The aisle doors have indented, nail-head, and pellet mouldings. The west window is of two four-light orders, the lower lights being trefoiled, and the tracery geometrical. The north transept has three tiers of round-headed windows, and a circle in the gable; the latter like those of the nave and choir is flanked by two tall turrets. The vaulting of the nave is Early English quadripartite. Its destruction was commenced by Patrick, Earl of Caithness, and his son, when in rebellion against the crown; but the exertions of Bishop Law, and the arrival of the royal troops, prevented the execution of their sacrilegious design. The east window, 36 ft. by 12 ft., is Early Decorated, with four unfoliated lights, and a marigold, 12 ft. in diameter, in the head. The presbytery, of two bays, is elevated three steps above the floor of the choir, which is of four bays, and the nave of eight. The arches of the tower are fine lofty lancets; externally on each face it has two windows, each of two trefoiled lights, transomed. The spire, which was destroyed by lightning, 1670, has been re-placed by a low pyramidal covering. There are three bells; the chimes were the gift of Bishop Maxwell in 1528. The arched vaults of the nave rest on twenty-eight pillars, of which the four that support the tower are distinguished by their size, and tasteful forms. The view over the grey slated roofs of the town, the borough, in the " Sketch " of Malcolm the poet, the bare treeless moor and hill of the suburb, and the ocean-avenues seaward, will repay the trouble of an ascent. In the choir is a white marble monument to King Hacon, who was interred here during the winter of 1263-64, until his corse was removed to Norway on the first Sunday of the following Lent. The " Maid of Norway," Margaret, daughter of King Eric, by Margaret, daughter of Alexander III. of Scotland, and as such becoming Queen of Scotland, died and was buried here in 1290, then only seven years old. Sir Walter Scott lays here the scene in the " Pirate " between Cleveland and Jack Bunce, and contrasts to their disadvantage the condition of this cathedral with those of some churches over the border. A square narrow cell is shown in the thickness of the wall; when discovered a few years since, a morsel of barley bread was found upon a rusty iron chain which hung down from the roof.

THE DIMENSIONS OF THE CATHEDRAL IN FEET.

	Length.	Breadth.	Height.
Nave	109·6	47	71
Choir	88	45	71
Transepts	89·6	35	71
Steeple	22	22	133
Extreme length	230	..	..

Among the bishops occur Douglas, mentioned in "Marmion;" Honeyman, who was shot by a poisoned bullet, designed for Archbishop Sharp; and Graham, who, when the General Assembly assailed his order, resigned, with an apology and regret that he had consented to become a bishop.

Arms: Arg., St. Magnus royally vested, crowned, and sceptred, ppr.

At the west end is a churchyard-cross, built in 1622. The *earl's palace* forms three sides of an oblong, and is of two stories in height. It faces the south front of the cathedral, and was built in the 14th century by Henry, Earl of Orkney; but great alterations, shown in Decorated corbels, doorways ornamented with tiers of pilasters, and round turrets impending at the corners, were made in grey freestone by French architects for Earl Patrick in 1660. The hall measures 60 ft. by 20 ft. The structure cost him dear, for having impressed the people to work upon his new fortalice, he incurred the charge of usurping the royal prerogative. The king's troops in consequence occupied Kirkwall, and storming the palace, the earl was imprisoned in Dumbarton Castle; his son endeavoured to recover the place, but was conquered, and sent to share his fate on the block at Edinburgh. The richly-decorated double-lighted turrets, cruciform loopholes, square mullioned and projecting windows, still give a fine effect to this noble example of a castellated palace, although now broken, roofless, and grass-grown.

The *bishop's palace*, now a ruin, on a line with the church, is Late Early English, built in the 13th century. A huge machicolated round tower, on the north-east, square

within, once formed a triangle with two other quadrangular
towers as outworks; it was built by Bishop Reid. In it King
Hacon, after the battle of Largs, died in 1263, of grief for the
loss of his army. King James V. slept in it in 1540. The
buildings, after having long served as a quarry, have been left
unmolested for many years, since a workman dropped a stone
upon the head of his fellow-labourer below.

Lismore.—(*See of Argyle*).

LIS-MORE, " the great garden," is an island nine miles long
by two in breadth. The see was separated from Dunkeld in
the 13th century. The flamboyant choir of the Cathedral
of St. Moulac remains; it was newly roofed 1749. The
church has neither aisles, nave, or transepts; apparently it
never has been completed. At the east end of the north wall
is the sharply Pointed door to the sacristy. The present
structure, an aisleless oblong, measures 60 ft. by 30 ft., internally 52 f. It is the smallest cathedral extant. The sedilia
have semicircular arches. The ancient pastoral staff of the
bishops is preserved.

　　Arms : Az. two pastoral staffs addorsed in saltire or, in chief
a mitre of the last.

St. Ninian's Cathedral, Perth.

THIS is the only cathedral church in Scotland, in which a
choral service is celebrated: the establishment consists of a
provost and three canons. The church was consecrated by
the bishop of Brechin on December 11, 1856. It will, when
complete, equal in size Brechin, Dunblane, and Dunkeld, and
be 200 ft. in length. It is at present 90 ft. long and 70 ft.
high. The structure by Butterfield will embrace an aisleless

choir of two. bays, a short aisleless transept, a nave of four bays with aisles ; two western steeples, and a sacristy on the north side; and a bell turret of wood with a spire at the intersection of the transepts and nave. The choir transept, sacristy, and one of the naves have been built. The towers will be of four stages, with double angular buttresses, three lancet-lights under straight canopies in the upper story, and crowned with broach spires, having spire-lights. The roof of the nave is of wood with simple open-work ; the piers are four-clustered ; the clerestory consists of cinquefoils within pointed arches in the nave and transept ; in the choir a cinquefoil recessed under a pointed arch ; the nave-aisle has three-light windows; the choir has four-light windows, trefoiled under a central quatrefoil and lateral trefoils. The front of the north transept has a marygold of fifteen lights. The east window is of large dimensions. The roof of the choir is coved and powdered with red flowers ; in the sanctuary it is ribbed, and diapered with quatrefoils by Crace. The choir screen, 25 ft. high, is of three arches of free-stone, supported on four columns of Peter-head granite. The organ was built by Robson ; the lectern is of brass ; the dorsal by French of Bolton ; the footpace, reached by two steps, is laid with encaustic tiles. On the south side are sedilia and a credence-table. The pulpit is of wood on a stone stem.

St. Andrew's.

Those godly men
Then swept from Scotland in a flame of zeal
Shrine, altar, image, and the massy piles
That harboured them ;
In deadly scorn of superstitious rites,
Or what their scruples construed to be such.

AT a distance towers and spires appear to rise above St. Andrew's, when seen from the sea or hills ; on a nearer approach these objects resolve themselves into pinnacles and fragments of ruin, spectral and desolate. An air of stillness and melancholy broods over the ancient city ; upon the sea even, not a single sail is to be seen : to the north is a line of sandy coast, to the south a rocky bank of no great height. The Cathedral, once equal to Melrose and Elgin, was founded by Malcolm IV., 1159. The structure, 358 ft. long, was begun by Bishop Arnold, late abbat of Kelso, in 1162, and consecrated in the presence of Robert Bruce, July 5, 1318, by Bishop Lamberton, who had crowned the Liberator of Scotland king with a fillet of gold in 1306. Great part of the nave of twelve bays, 200 ft. by 62 ft., was completed in 1279 ; the choir of five bays, 98 ft. by 33 ft. long, the transept 160 ft. long, and three bays of the nave in 1271. The transept had an eastern aisle. The presbytery was 46·7 ft. long, and occupied the place of a Lady Chapel. The presbytery, west wall of the south transept, four bays of the south aisle, and the wall of the nave west of the crossing, are Transitional Norman. The other eight bays to the west, the west door, and the chapter-house southward of the south transept, are pure Early English.

The six westernmost lights of the south nave aisle are Pointed, the remaining four are round-headed. The great west door is of five orders, with the dog-tooth moulding : above it is an arcade of eight trefoiled arches ; and over this remains only one of two beautiful three-light windows trefoiled, with three trefoiled circles in the head. The south aisle and turret

arcaded.   The east end has three round-headed windows over
the altar; above them was a similar window with trefoiled
tracery, and of three-lights under a Pointed arch.

King Henry VIII. gave orders to raze St. Andrew's, "so as
the upper stone might be the nether, and not one stick stand
by another, sparing no creature alive within the same."
Owing to one of John Knox's fiery sermons a frantic mob—

> Wi' John Calvin in their heads,
> And hammers in their hands,—and spades,

destroyed in a summer's afternoon, June 11, 1559, the
glorious cathedral, though Archbishop Hamilton, with one
hundred men, had prepared to resist them, and the Earl of
Argyle and Lord James Stuart in vain attempted to dissuade
the barbarous iconoclasts from their purpose.   The bells sank
at sea with the vessel which was designed to carry them to
Holland.

The ruins stand in a broad garth of greensward.   Towards
the sea is the fortified wall, built by Prior Hepburn, with
towers and niches of the former part of the 16th century:
from it the French gunners turned their cannon on the castle
of Cardinal Beaton.   The "golden gate" of the abbey, Early
Decorated, plain but good, stands at the west end of the
Cathedral.   One of the western turret pinnacles, with a round-
headed window and flanking turrets at the east end, 100 ft.
high, the west side of the south transept, and the south wall
of the nave with fourteen windows, remain.

The see was translated from Abernethy after the conquest
of the Picts, by Kenneth III.; and after the reign of Malcolm III., its title of Kils Rule, " St. Rule's Church," was exchanged for that of St. Andrew's.   About the year 1441,
Pope Sixtus IV., at the request of James III., constituted it
an archbishopric.   The metropolitans crowned the Scottish
kings.

Among the archbishops occur R. Malvoisin, Gamelin,
W. Wishart, G. Greenland, G. Dunbar, I. Kennedy, I. Stuart
Duke of Ross, J. Bethune, Lord Chancellors; A. Stewart,
slain at Flodden; Hamilton, hanged on a tree by the Regent
Murray, on a charge of being accessory to Darnley's murder;

Kennedy, founder of Salvador's College; Cardinal Beaton, assassinated in the castle, after the cruel death of Wishart, on February 1, 1545, by Norman Leslie; D. Behhan, Grand Chamberlain; James Sharp, barbarously murdered by a mob on Magus Moor, May 3, 1679; the learned Sage hunted like a partridge by his enemies; and the historian Spottiswoode, L. C.

The Austin *Priory of St. Rule* was founded 1114, by Bishop Robert, in memory of St. Regulus, who was wrecked here on his voyage from Achaia, 370 : an ancient church having been built here by Hergustus, king of the Picts, on his conversion. The remains arc the eastern portion of the church, 31 ft. by 25 ft. with two windows on either side; and a square central tower 108 ft. by 20 ft., wholly disproportioned to such a diminutive choir, and built by Bishop Robert, an Austin Canon of St. Oswald's, Pontefract, 1127-1144, probably to surpass the steeple of the church of the Culdees of the Rock. It somewhat resembles the towers of Monk Wearmouth and Billingham. The buildings are in a state of irretrievable decay; there are marks of three roofs of different elevation. Between the cathedral and castle is a cave with a rude altar, in which, 307, St. Regulus, monk of Achaia, found refuge when he landed with St. Andrew's relics. Many a pilgrim in after years came—

> To fair St. Andrew's bound,
> Within the ocean cave to pray,
> Where good St. Rule his holy lay,
> From midnight to the dawn of day
> Sung to the billows' sound.

There are some remains of the so-called *Black Friars' Chapel*, Decorated, with an octagonal north end, which probably was a north transept.

At St. Andrew's occurred the cruel burning of George Wishart, 1545, and of Patrick Hamilton, 1527, in the University. The College of *St. Salvador* was founded 1455, and united, 1747, with St. Leonard's, founded 1512. St. Mary's was founded 1537. The *church of St. Salvador* has a tall square tower crowned with an hexagonal spire; and a good three-light east window. The superb and symmetrical monument of Bishop James Kennedy, the founder, is of black marble, with canopied tracery of indescribable lightness, airy crocketed pinnacles, and elaborate ornament, as if the material had been malleable instead of stubborn rock; he died 1446. A silver mace is preserved here: similar but less specimens may be seen in the College of St. Andrew's, and in the universities of Aberdeen, Glasgow, and Edinburgh.

Arms: Az. a saltire arg.

THE END.

LONDON: PRINTED BY WILLIAM CLOWES AND SONS, STAMFORD STREET.

AMERICA
IN THE STEREOSCOPE.

This wonderful and extraordinary Series of Pictures is now ready; they comprehend the wildest and loveliest portions of this world-renowned Scenery.

In Leather Case, Price £7 7s. the Set.

Specimens sent (Niagara if desired) free by post, 18 stamps each.

*** As a proof of the high quality and beauty of the above, 1000 Dozen were sold on the first day of their issue.

EXPORTERS AND TRADE SUPPLIED.

Post Office Orders (crossed Union Bank of London) payable to GEORGE SWAN NOTTAGE.

"Up, Guards, and at them!"—*Duke of Wellington.*

THE

FIELD OF WATERLOO
IN THE STEREOSCOPE.

This spot, so renowned in European history, is now secured for the Stereoscope. The set of Twelve Views comprises all the chief points of this memorable field, and each picture has a most interesting description at back.

Price £1. 1s. the set of Twelve,
COLOURED.

Every Englishman should possess these graphic mementoes of the greatest battle of his countrymen, fought by a General, who, in the eloquent words of Lord Brougham, "never retreated but to eclipse the glory of his advance."

STEREOSCOPIC VIEWS OF LONDON,
ONE SHILLING EACH.

The London Stereoscopic Company,
54, Cheapside, E.C.; & 313, Oxford Street, W.

The following Catalogues issued by

EDWARD STANFORD, 6, Charing Cross, S.W.

Indicative of the character of his Stock, may be had upon application, or per Post for one Stamp.

1. Catalogue of THE ORDNANCE MAPS, published under the superintendence of LIEUT-COLONEL JAMES, R.E., Superintendent of the Ordnance Surveys.

2. Catalogue of THE GEOLOGICAL MAPS, SECTIONS, and MEMOIRS OF THE GEOLOGICAL SURVEY OF GREAT BRITAIN AND IRELAND, under the superintendence of SIR RODERICK I. MURCHISON, Director-General of the Geological Surveys of the United Kingdom.

3. Catalogue of the best GEOLOGICAL MAPS of various parts of the World.

4. GENERAL CATALOGUE of Atlases, Maps, Charts, Plans, &c., English and Foreign, including the TRIGONOMETRICAL SURVEYS of various States.

5. Catalogue of Atlases, Maps, and Plans, engraved under the superintendence of THE SOCIETY FOR THE DIFFUSION OF USEFUL KNOWLEDGE.

6. Catalogue of Charts, Plans, Views, and Sailing Directions, &c., published by order of The Lords Commissioners of THE ADMIRALTY. 178 pages royal 8vo., price 1*s*. 6*d*.

7. Catalogue of the Plans, Maps, and Drawings, issued by THE WAR DEPARTMENT, and sold by EDWARD STANFORD.

8. Catalogue of Educational Atlases and Maps, recently published by EDWARD STANFORD.

9. A List of Publications on the British Colonies and the United States, selected from the Stock of EDWARD STANFORD.

10. Johnston's List of Geographical and Educational Works, comprising Atlases, Maps, Globes, &c., sold wholesale and retail by EDWARD STANFORD.

11. Catalogue of Guide Books, Maps, Plans, Dictionaries, Conversation Books, &c., for Tourists and Travellers.

BENGOUGH, BROTHERS,

WHOLESALE AND RETAIL

Trunk & Portmanteau Manufacturers

LONDON.

CITY BRANCH, 5, CHEAPSIDE,

The Corner of St. Paul's Churchyard,

ESTABLISHED 1682.

HOLBORN BRANCH, 49, HIGH HOLBORN,

ESTABLISHED 1780.

WEST-END BRANCH & MANUFACTORY,

4, TICHBORNE STREET, PICCADILLY,

ESTABLISHED 1810.

STANFORD'S ATLASES,

DESIGNED AND ARRANGED UNDER THE SUPERINTENDENCE OF THE

Society for the Diffusion of Useful Knowledge,

Corrected to the Present Time.

THE COMPLETE ATLAS,

ANCIENT AS WELL AS MODERN.

225 Coloured Maps and Plans, and alphabetical Index to more than 25,000 Places.   In One Volume, half-russia, £9. 10s.; in Two Volumes, half-morocco, £10.

THE GENERAL ATLAS,

175 Coloured Maps, with Index. In One Volume, half-russia, £7. 7s.

THE FAMILY ATLAS,

80 Coloured Maps, with Index, half-morocco, £3. 3s.

*** The Family Atlas has been selected for general use and reference, but purchasers can form their own Atlas, with or without the Index to Places, and have it bound in their own style, on application to the Publisher.

THE CYCLOPÆDIAN ATLAS,

39 Coloured Maps, with Index. Half-bound, £1. 1s.

*** This is the Companion Atlas to the National, English, and other Cyclopædias.

ATLAS OF INDIA.

Revised by JOHN WALKER, Esq., Geographer to the Hon. E. I. Company. 26 Colored Maps, half-bound, £1s. 1s.

LONDON:

Edward Stanford, 6, Charing Cross, S. W.

STANFORD'S EDUCATIONAL ATLASES, &c.

MODERN.

The HARROW ATLAS of MODERN GEOGRA-
PHY. Thirty Maps. New Edition, enlarged, with Index.
Price 12s. 6d.

The JUNIOR HARROW ATLAS of MODERN
GEOGRAPHY. Fourteen Maps, with Index. Price 7s.

CLASSICAL.

The HARROW ATLAS of CLASSICAL GEO-
GRAPHY. Twenty-three Maps, with Index. Price 12s. 6d.

The JUNIOR HARROW ATLAS of CLASSICAL
GEOGRAPHY. Eleven Maps, with Index. Price 7s.

CLASSICAL AND MODERN.

The UNIVERSITY ATLAS of CLASSICAL and
MODERN GEOGRAPHY. Fifty-two Maps, with Indexes,
half morocco, gilt edges, £1 11s. 6d.

The SCHOOL ATLAS of CLASSICAL and
MODERN GEOGRAPHY. Twenty-five Maps, with Indexes. Price 12s. 6d.

SCHOOL GLOBES.

36 inches in Diameter.

Solid Black Frame, Iron Meridian, and Brass Quadrant, each
£12 10s.

18 inches in Diameter.

Strong Black Frame, with Brass Meridian, per pair £7 7s.
Ditto, with Iron Meridian, per pair £5.

12 inches in Diameter.

Strong Black Frame, with Brass Meridian, per pair £3 15s. 6d.
Ditto, with Iron Meridian, per pair £2 15s.

OLD GLOBES RE-COVERED WITH MODERN MAPS,
and the Brass Work cleaned, at the following prices:—

18-inch, per pair	....	£3 13	6
12-inch ,,	....	1 15	0
9-inch ,,	....	1 7	6

London: Edward Stanford, 6, Charing Cross, S.W.

KEATING'S COUGH LOZENGES.

A SAFE AND CERTAIN REMEDY FOR COUGHS, Colds, Hoarseness, and other Affections of the Throat and Chest. In Incipient Consumption, Asthma, &c., they are unfailing. Being free from every hurtful ingredient, they may be taken by the most delicate female or the youngest child.

Prepared and Sold in Boxes, 1s. 1½d. and Tins, 2s. 9d., 4s. 6d., and 10s. 6d. each, by THOMAS KEATING, Chemist, &c., 79, St. Paul's Church-yard, London. Retail by all Druggists and Patent Medicine Vendors in the World.

N.B.—Observe the words "KEATING'S COUGH LOZENGES" are engraven on the Government Stamp of each Box, without which none are genuine.

KEATING'S COD LIVER OIL,

PALE NEWFOUNDLAND—PERFECTLY PURE— nearly tasteless, and free from adulteration of any kind, having been analyzed, reported on, and recommended by Professors TAYLOR and THOMPSON, of Guy's and St. Thomas's Hospitals, who, in the words of the late DR. PEREIRA, say, that "The finest oil is that most devoid of *colour, odour,* and *flavour,*" characters this will be found to possess in a high degree. Half-pints 1s. 6d., Pints 2s. 6d., Quarts 4s. 6d., and Five-pint Bottles 10s. 6d., Imperial Measure.

KEATING'S PERSIAN INSECT POWDER.

UNRIVALLED IN EXTERMINATING MOSQUITOES, Fleas, Bugs, Flies, Beetles, Cockroaches, and every description of insect infesting animals and Poultry; protects cloths, &c., from Moths. **Only Injurious to Insect Life.** Sold in Packets, 1s., 2s. 6d., and 4s. 6d. each; free by Post, for 14 or 36 Postage Stamps.

N.B.—SEE THAT THE NAME IS ON EVERY PACKET.

Strongly recommended to Travellers on the Continent or by Steam Boat.

Thomas Keating, Chemist,
79, ST. PAUL'S CHURCH YARD, LONDON, E.C.

MAPS FOR TOURISTS,

Published by EDWARD STANFORD, 6, *Charing Cross*, *S.W.*

ENGLAND AND WALES.

ENGLAND AND WALES.—Road and Railway Tra-
velling Map, on a scale of 12 miles to an inch; size, 36 inches by 42,
fully coloured, in case. Price 8s. 6d.

ENGLAND AND WALES. — Pocket Railway Map.
Price, folded in cover, 1s.; mounted, in case, 2s.

ORDNANCE GENERAL MAP OF ENGLAND AND
WALES Scale, one mile to an inch. Price of each Division, 2s. in
sheet; mounted, in case, 4s 6d.

   ₊ Key Maps and Catalogues on application.

WALES.—Road and Railway Travelling Map of North
and South Wales. Price, folded in a cover, 1s.; mounted, in case, 2s. 6d.

ISLE OF WIGHT.—Standard Map, showing the various
Roads, and containing a list of the most remarkable places of interest.
Price, folded in cover, 1s.; mounted, in case, 2s.

CHANNEL ISLANDS.—Popular Map of Jersey, Guern-
sey, Sark, Alderney, &c., with a general Map of the Channel. Price,
folded, in cover, 1s.; mounted, in case, 2s.

SCOTLAND.

SCOTLAND.—Road and Railway Travelling Map, with
the Coach Roads, Railways, heights of Mountains, Rivers, Canals,
&c., in case, 3s. 6d.

SCOTLAND.—Pocket Railway Map. Price, folded in
cover, 1s.; mounted, in case, 2s.

EDINBURGH.—Popular Map. Price, folded in cover,
1s.; mounted in case, 2s.

ENVIRONS OF EDINBURGH.—Popular Map. Price,
folded in cover, 1s.; mounted, in case, 2s.

IRELAND.

IRELAND.—Road and Railway Travelling Map, with
the Coach Roads, Railways, Rivers, Canals, Lochs, Mountains, &c.
Price, in case, 3s. 6d.

IRELAND.—Pocket Railway Map. Price, folded in
cover, 1s.; mounted, in case, 2s.

DUBLIN.—Popular Map. Price, folded in cover, 1s.;
mounted, in case, 2s.

ENVIRONS OF DUBLIN.—Popular Map. Price,
folded in cover, 1s.; mounted, in case, 2s.

CENTRAL EUROPE.

CENTRAL EUROPE.—Davies's Map, showing all the
Railways and Stations; mounted in case, 12s.

STANFORD'S Catalogue of Maps and Books for Tourists, may be
had upon application.

Removed from 69, Strand, to 5, Charing Cross.

FOR TOURISTS & TRAVELLERS,
THE POCKET SIPHONIA,
OR WATERPROOF COAT,

Weight 12oz., price 40s; all Silk, 50s., easily folded for
the Pocket or Knapsack.

Measurement—Length, and size round Chest.

Leggings 10s. 6d. and 15s. 6d. per pair.
KNAPSACKS FOR TOURISTS, 18s. 6d.

EDMISTON & SON, Waterproofers,
5, CHARING CROSS, S.W.

Post Office Orders payable at the Charing Cross Branch.

FOREIGN OFFICE PASSPORT AGENCY.

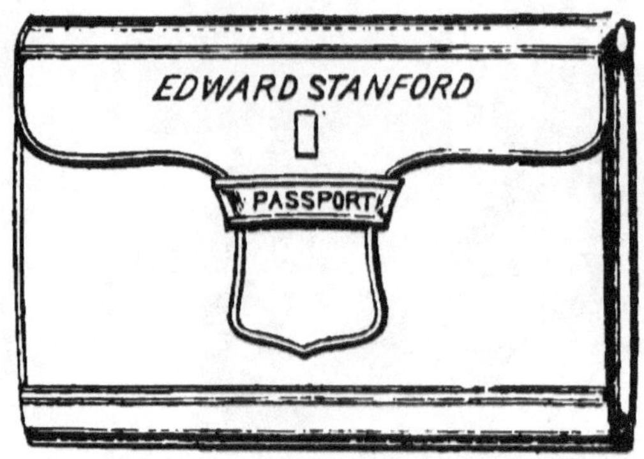

6, CHARING CROSS, LONDON, S.W.

BRITISH SUBJECTS who are preparing to visit or travel on the Continent, may be saved much trouble and expense by obtaining FOREIGN OFFICE PASSPORTS through EDWARD STANFORD'S Agency, 6, Charing Cross, London ; whose experience and long established arrrangements enable him to ensure Passports, in proper form, and duly *viséd*, without personal attendance. He mounts the Passport, which is good for Life, on Muslin or Silk, in Roan, Morocco, or Russia Case, to prevent injury or loss, as well as to lessen delay in undergoing examination abroad. Residents in the country can have Passports obtained, completed, and forwarded by post.

For further particulars, including the Forms of Application, Cost of Passport, Visas, &c., &c., see Stanford's Passport Circular, which will be forwarded per post on application.

EDWARD STANFORD has on sale at all times the best English and Foreign Maps, Hand Books, and Railway Guides, Pocket Dictionaries, and Conversation Books.

London: Edward Stanford, 6, Charing Cross, S.W

VISITORS TO LONDON

WILL FIND

MOORE'S PRIVATE HOTEL

AND

BOARDING HOUSE,

No. 30, NORFOLK STREET, STRAND,

The most central position in London,
being situated contiguous to the CITY, WEST END,
THEATRES, PRINCIPAL PLACES OF PUBLIC AMUSE-
MENTS, RAILWAYS, &c., &c.

Bed and Breakfast .. .. 3s. 6d.

APARTMENTS IN SUITE.

30, NORFOLK STREET, STRAND.

STANFORD'S SERIES OF
LARGE LIBRARY MAPS,

REPRESENTING

EUROPE, AUSTRALASIA, ASIA, AFRICA, AND AMERICA.

Constructed by ALEX. KEITH JOHNSTON, F.R.G.S., F.R.S.E.

ENGRAVED IN THE FINEST STYLE ON COPPER PLATES.
Size of each Map, 65 inches by 58.

The publication of this uniform series of Large Wall Maps, representing the Great Terrestrial Divisions of the Globe, has been undertaken in consequence of the defective state to which age and Geographical progress have reduced previous works of the same class. The best Sets of Wall Maps now in use, were chiefly engraved at the beginning of the present century; and amidst the corrections which they have undergone to meet prominent political changes or new discoveries, the bygone period of their production still remains necessarily too manifest.

The Publisher has undertaken the series now advertised, in grateful appreciation of the high patronage with which he has been favoured, and with a desire to be enabled to supply Wall Maps of the Great Terrestrial Divisions, suitable for Libraries, Offices, or Class Rooms, and creditable to the present state of Geographical Science and Art.

EUROPE.

The boundaries of all the Independent States, even the smallest, and the sub-divisions of the larger Continental States, are all distinctly shown; particular attention has been given to the delineation of the Railways, and the Lines of Submarine Telegraph are inserted. It also includes the whole of the Southern Shores of the Mediterranean.

AUSTRALASIA.

Delineating the Colonies of New South Wales, Victoria or Port Philip, South Australia, and Western Australia, divided into Counties; with the Moreton Bay and North-Eastern Districts, as well as all the discoveries towards the interior, including those of the North Australian Expedition, and of the recent explorations in the south and west. Tasmania and New Zealand are shown in their relative position to Australia, and the latter contains various improvements over former maps. New Caledonia, at present occupied by the French, New Guinea, and adjacent parts of the Asiatic Archipelago, are also included.

Each Map, price, full coloured, and mounted in a cloth case, £3; in morocco, 8vo. for Tourists, or 4to. for library table, £3 18s. 6d.; on roller, varnished, £3.; on spring roller, £6.

London:—Edward Stanford, 6, Charing Cross, S.W.

TOURISTS & TRAVELLERS,

VISITORS to the SEA SIDE, and others exposed to the scorching
rays of the Sun, and heated particles of dust, will find

ROWLANDS' KALYDOR

a most refreshing preparation for the Complexion, dispelling
the cloud of languor and relaxation, allaying all heat and
irritability, and immediately affording the pleasing sensation
attending restored elasticity and healthful state of the skin.

Freckles, Tan, Spots, Pimples, Flushes, and Discoloration,
are eradicated by its application, and give place to a healthy
clearness and purity of Complexion. In cases of sunburn, or
stings of insects, its virtues have long been acknowledged.
Price 4s. 6d. and 8s. 6d. per bottle.

The heat of the summer also induces a dryness of the hair,
and a tendency to its falling off, which may be completely
obviated by the use of

ROWLANDS' MACASSAR OIL,

A delightfully fragrant and transparent preparation for the
Hair, and as an invigorator and beautifier beyond all precedent.
The prices are 3s. 6d., 7s.; Family Bottles (equal to four small,)
10s. 6d.; and double that size, 21s.

Nor can we be too careful to preserve the Teeth from the
deleterious effects of Vegetable Acids (an immediate cause of
tooth-ache), by a systematic employment, night and morning, of

ROWLANDS' ODONTO,
OR PEARL DENTIFRICE,

White Powder, compounded of the rarest and most fragrant
exotics. It bestows on the Teeth a pearl-like Whiteness,
frees them from Tartar, and imparts to the Gums a healthy
firmness, and to the breath a grateful purity and fragrance.
Price 2s. 9d. per box.

Sold by A. Rowland & Sons, 20, Hatton Garden, London,
And by Chemists and Perfumers.

*** BEWARE OF SPURIOUS IMITATIONS!!

GEOLOGICAL MAPS FOR TOURISTS.

ENGLAND AND WALES.

MURCHISON. — GEOLOGICAL MAP OF ENGLAND AND WALES, with all the Railways, according to the most recent researches. By SIR RODERICK I. MURCHISON, D.C.L., &c., Director-General of the Geological Surveys of Great Britain and Ireland. 4th Edition. Size, 18 inches by 14; scale, 28 miles to 1 inch. Price on 1 sheet, 5s.; mounted, in case, 7s.

RAMSAY.—GEOLOGICAL MAP OF ENGLAND AND WALES. By ANDREW C. RAMSAY, F.R.S. and G.S., Local Director of the Geological Survey of Great Britain, and Professor of Geology at the Government School of Mines. Scale, 12 miles to 1 inch; size, 36 inches by 42. Price, 25s. in case; 30s. on roller.

" As regards Maps, the novice in this Country will find the guide he requires, in the beautiful Map of England and Wales, by Professor Ramsay, which contains in a condensed form the result of the labours of many men continued through half a century. It has all the latest discoveries, is excellently coloured, and of a scale just large enough to be distinct. The smaller Map, by Sir Roderick I. Murchison, is equally good in execution, but from its smaller scale, not quite so serviceable as that of Professor Ramsay."—*Quarterly Review, July*, 1859.

LONDON.

MYLNE.—GEOLOGICAL AND TOPOGRAPHICAL MAP OF LONDON AND ITS ENVIRONS. By ROBERT W. MYLNE, C.E., F.I.B.A., &c., &c. This Map comprises an area of 159 square miles, and by shaded contours indicates 10 feet altitudes above Trinity high-water mark. Sheets, price 8s. 6d.; mounted, in case. 10s. 6d.

SCOTLAND.

KNIPE.—GEOLOGICAL MAP OF SCOTLAND, including the Shetland and Orkney Isles. By J. A. KNIPE, Author of a " Geological Map of the British Isles." Price, mounted, in case, 25s.

For the best Foreign Geological Maps, see Stanford's Catalogues of the best Geological Maps of various parts of the World, to be had on application.

London: Edward Stanford, 6, Charing Cross, S.W.